Dear Rio Salado College Student:

The high cost of college textbooks has long been an issue for students across the nation.
Rio Salado College shares this concern. In an effort to control costs for our students,
Rio Salado is pleased to announce an innovative solution: the Rio Salado Textbook
Savings Program that reduces your up-front costs. Rio Salado students can now
purchase new customized textbooks for their courses for a savings up to 50%.
The result of this savings program is that the cost of a new textbook will be much
less than the cost of most used books.

Rio Salado has partnered with Pearson Custom Publishing to produce its own
streamlined versions of textbooks, starting with the Spring 2008 term–and the savings
will be passed on to you. During the next three years, most textbooks used by the
college will be revised and published under the Textbook Saving Program. In addition
to lower out-of-pocket costs, you will benefit by learning from a textbook containing
exactly the material Rio Salado's faculty have determined you need to master the course.

We know this price cut occurs just when you need it the
most–at the start of your class.

Best wishes for this and all future Rio courses!

Dr. Linda M. Thor
President

CHD 120

ETHICAL, LEGAL, AND PROFESSIONAL ISSUES IN COUNSELING

Taken from:

Ethical, Legal, and Professional Issues in Counseling,
Updated Second Edition
by Theodore P. Remley, Jr. and Barbara Herlihy

PEARSON

Custom
Publishing

Cover photograph courtesy of David Buffington/Getty Images USA, Inc.

Taken from:

Ethical, Legal, and Professional Issues in Counseling, Updated Second Edition
by Theodore P. Remley, Jr. and Barbara Herlihy
Copyright © 2007, 2005, 2001 by Pearson Education, Inc.
Published by Prentice Hall
Upper Saddle River, New Jersey 07458

This special edition published in cooperation with Pearson Custom Publishing.

All trademarks, service marks, registered trademarks, and registered service marks are the property of their respective owners and are used herein for identification purposes only.

Printed in the United States of America

10 9 8 7 6 5 4 3 2

ISBN 0-536-09138-2

2007420420

KH

Please visit our web site at *www.pearsoncustom.com*

PEARSON CUSTOM PUBLISHING
501 Boylston Street, Suite 900, Boston, MA 02116
A Pearson Education Company

To Dr. Patrick M. Flanagan, this counselor's counselor
and a true role model.

—Ted Remley

To my colleagues—far too numerous to mention—
who have questioned my assumptions, challenged my
thinking, asked me the tough questions, and in many
other ways helped me learn and grow.

—Barbara Herlihy

RESEARCH NAVIGATOR—
RESEARCH MADE SIMPLE!

www.ResearchNavigator.com

Merrill Education is pleased to introduce Research Navigator—a one-stop research solution for students that simplifies and streamlines the entire research process. At www.researchnavigator.com, students will find extensive resources to enhance their understanding of the research process so they can effectively complete research assignments. In addition, Research Navigator has three exclusive databases of credible and reliable source content to help students focus their research efforts and begin the research process.

HOW WILL RESEARCH NAVIGATOR ENHANCE YOUR COURSE?

- Extensive content helps students understand the research process, including writing, Internet research, and citing sources.
- Step-by-step tutorial guides students through the entire research process from selecting a topic to revising a rough draft.
- Research Writing in the Disciplines section details the differences in research across disciplines.
- Three exclusive databases—EBSCO's ContentSelect Academic Journal Database, *The New York Times* Search by Subject Archive, and "Best of the Web" Link Library—allow students to easily find journal articles and sources.

WHAT'S THE COST?

A subscription to Research Navigator is $7.50 but is available at no extra cost when ordered in conjunction with this textbook. To obtain free passcodes for your students, simply contact your local Merrill/Prentice Hall sales representative, and your representative will send you the Evaluating Online Resource Guide, which contains the code to access Research Navigator as well as tips on how to use Research Navigator and how to evaluate research. To preview the value of this website to your students, please go to www.educatorlearningcenter.com and use the Login Name "Research" and the password "Demo."

Preface

We think you will find it useful to know something about us, the coauthors of this text, and how we came to write this book. From 1997 to 2006, we were both professors in the counseling graduate program at the University of New Orleans. Ted Remley is an attorney with several years of legal experience and also has been a school and community college counselor. Barbara Herlihy has worked as a school counselor and a Licensed Professional Counselor in private practice, and is presently a counselor educator with a special interest in counselor ethics.

Before we became colleagues at the same institution, we worked together over a period of many years, coauthoring articles and presenting numerous workshops on law and ethics in counseling. It was through these workshops that the idea for this book was born. The counselors who attended our workshops had much in common, although they practiced in a variety of settings with diverse clientele. They shared a deep and abiding commitment to the welfare of their clients, a desire to stay current with the ethical standards of their profession, and a need to feel competent in dealing with legal issues that arose in their work. At the same time, they sometimes felt overwhelmed by the complex and conflicting demands of situations they encountered. They frequently had difficulty distinguishing between legal and ethical issues. As we worked together in our presentations to these counselors, we found that we very rarely disagreed with each other, but we did bring differing perspectives. Barbara's ethics orientation led her to focus on client welfare and to emphasize protecting the client. Ted, with his legal orientation, helped us to consider another dimension, that of protecting the counselor. We believe *both* perspectives are important.

Because both of us regularly teach graduate courses in professional orientation and ethics, we found ourselves discussing the need for a textbook written specifically for *counselors* that would address ethical, legal, and professional issues. Thus, out of our backgrounds and shared interests was conceived a textbook that is unique in that it approaches each professional issue in counseling from both an ethical perspective and a legal viewpoint. We believe you will find this integrated approach particularly helpful as you grapple with the complexities inherent in the work of the counselor.

We also believe that the best learning is active rather than passive and personalized rather than abstract. We hope that you will actively discuss and even argue the issues that are raised throughout the book and that you will work to develop your own personal stance on these issues. Typical situations and dilemmas that counseling practitioners encounter are presented in each chapter and are depicted in the CD of videotaped vignettes, available separately. We ask you to imagine that you are the counselor in each vignette and attend to what you would think, how you would feel, and what you might do in the situation. In these vignettes, as in real life, there is rarely a single right answer to the counselor's dilemma, so we hope that the vignettes will spark lively discussion.

THE PRENTICE HALL COMPANION WEBSITE:
A VIRTUAL LEARNING ENVIRONMENT

Technology is a constantly growing and changing aspect of our field that is creating a need for content and resources. To address this emerging need, Prentice Hall has developed an online learning environment for students and professors alike—Companion Websites—to support our textbooks.

In creating a Companion Website, our goal is to build on and enhance what the textbook already offers. For this reason, the content for each user-friendly website is organized by chapter and provides the professor and student with a variety of meaningful resources.
Common Companion Website features for students include:

- **Chapter Objectives**—Outline key concepts from the text.
- **Interactive Self-quizzes**—Complete with hints and automatic grading that provide immediate feedback for students. After students submit their answers for the interactive self-quizzes, the Companion Website **Results Reporter** computes a percentage grade, provides a graphic representation of how many questions were answered correctly and incorrectly, and gives a question-by-question analysis of the quiz. Students are given the option to send their quiz to up to four email addresses (professor, teaching assistant, study partner, etc.).
- **Web Destinations**—Links to www sites that relate to chapter content.

To take advantage of the many available resources, please visit the *Ethical, Legal, and Professional Issues in Counseling,* Updated Second Edition, Companion Website at

www.prenhall.com/remley

ACKNOWLEDGMENTS

The comments of the following reviewers were invaluable: Deborah Barlieb, Kutztown University; Robin Carter, California State University, Sacramento; Philip G. Cooker, University of Mississippi; Cher N. Edwards, Seattle Pacific University; Kevin A. Fall, Loyola University–New Orleans; Mary Hermann, Mississippi State University; Brandon Hunt, Pennsylvania State University; Dana Heller Levitt, Ohio University; Shoshana D. Kerewsky, University of Oregon; and Robert H. Pate, Jr., University of Virginia.

A special thank you to David Olguin, in 2003–2004 a doctoral candidate in the counselor education program at the University of New Orleans, for his assistance with research for the second edition.

Brief Contents

Contents

APPENDIXES

Note: Every effort has been made to provide accurate and current Internet information in this book. However, the Internet and information posted on it are constantly changing, so it is inevitable that some of the Internet addresses listed in this textbook will change.

Client Rights and Counselor Responsibilities

FOCUS QUESTIONS

1. When a client holds values that conflict with the counselor's values, can the counselor provide effective counseling services? Why or why not?
2. Do you believe a counselor should be able to refuse to provide counseling services to some people who request them? If so, in what circumstances?

Trust and respect are the cornerstones on which the counseling relationship is built. If clients are to do meaningful work in counseling, they need to feel safe in the relationship and to trust that the counselor is committed to safeguarding their welfare and respecting their rights. In your work as a counselor, it is fundamental that you put client welfare first and foremost. The counseling profession attaches such importance to this principle that it is the very first ethical standard in the American Counseling Association's (ACA) *Code of Ethics* (2005). Standard A.1.a. states that the "primary responsibility of counselors is to respect the dignity and to promote the welfare of clients." There are very few exceptions to this principle, and these occur only in rare circumstances when the good of others in society outweighs what might appear to be best for a particular client.

Counselors have what is known in law as *fiduciary relationships* with their clients. Although the exact meaning of *fiduciary* is debatable, it is agreed that an individual who is a fiduciary has a position of trust and confidence (Ludes & Gilbert, 1998). Clients rely on their counselor fiduciaries to act only in their best interests. The duties of fiduciaries are so strong that any transaction between a fiduciary and the recipient of services is presumed to be fraudulent and void if the fiduciary benefits from it. It will be upheld only when the fiduciary can present clear and convincing proof that the transaction is legitimate (Ludes & Gilbert). Because of the law related to fiduciaries, counselors have a significant legal burden to protect the best interests of their clients and to avoid any interactions or transactions with clients that benefit the counselors themselves.

COUNSELOR RESPONSIBILITIES

Counselors have numerous responsibilities related to safeguarding client welfare. These include honoring diversity, being aware of one's own needs and values, avoiding dependent relationships, respecting the rights of involuntary or mandated clients, using appropriate counseling techniques, managing interruptions in and termination of services, and avoiding abandonment of clients.

In our pluralistic society, honoring diversity is fundamental to counselors' efforts to promote the welfare and to respect the dignity of their clients. In this chapter and in succeeding chapters, we draw attention to diversity issues as they relate to specific topics.

COUNSELOR NEEDS AND VALUES

1-1 The Case of Lynn

Lynn has been counseling Elaine, a 30-year-old client. During this session, Elaine states that she wishes she could just walk away from her marriage, but she can't do it because it would traumatize the children. Lynn, herself a child of divorce whose father abandoned the family, further explores Elaine's fears for the children. At one point she says, "Well, yes, the statistics do show that a lot of kids lose touch with their fathers after a divorce. It would be really hard for them if that happened. It could even have repercussions well into their adult years."

- What do you think motivated Lynn to respond the way she did?
- Do you see any problem with Lynn's response?

As a counselor, it is critically important for you to be aware of your own needs, values, and life issues. If you lack self-awareness of your "unfinished business," areas of vulnerability, and defenses, there is a risk that you will inadvertently be working on your own issues in the counseling relationship, rather than on the client's issues. This problem is evident in the vignette just presented. The counselor, Lynn, is interjecting her own feelings about paternal abandonment into the session. As Corey et al. (2007) have noted, counselors who are unaware of their own issues are in a poor position to recognize the ways their personal lives are influencing their work with clients. This is particularly true when the client's problems or issues are similar to the unresolved issues of the counselor.

We are not suggesting that counselors do not have their own needs, or that it is unethical to get some of these needs met by choosing counseling as a profession. In fact, most counselors would probably say that they get a real sense of satisfaction or fulfillment from their work and from knowing that they have made a difference in the lives of others. Still, it is important for you to explore your own answers to the questions, "What do I get out of being a counselor? What needs of mine am I getting met?" Knowing your own needs system will help you identify potential areas of vulnerability and sources of therapeutic error.

To give some examples, if you have a strong need to nurture others, you may be tempted to encourage client dependency. If you have a strong need to be liked and appreciated, you may avoid confronting your clients. If you have a strong need to feel useful or prove your competence, you may want to rush in and give answers or advice. If you can recognize your potential problem areas, you will be better able to keep the best interests of your clients foremost and less likely to allow your needs to intrude into your work with clients. You will be better able to avoid actions that meet your personal needs at the expense of your clients.

Standard A.4.b. of the ACA *Code of Ethics* (2005) requires that counselors be aware of their own values, attitudes, beliefs, and behaviors and avoid imposing their values on clients. This ethical obligation is easy to state, but it can be extremely difficult—if not impossible—to uphold in practice. A counselor's values will influence the counseling process in many ways, including what goals are considered appropriate or desirable in counseling, whether and how the client will be diagnosed, and what client issues will become the focus of therapy. Even the theory from which the counselor operates can influence the counseling process in value-laden ways. Certain theories promote certain values. For instance, the Adlerian approach emphasizes the development of social interest as a benchmark of mental health, whereas the existential approach emphasizes individual freedom and responsibility. The influence of counselor values on the counseling process can be very subtle, but it can significantly affect counseling outcomes. Research has shown that the degree of congruence between the values of the counselor and those of the client can influence therapeutic outcomes and that clients tend to change in ways that are consistent with the values of their counselors.

Both the client and the counselor enter the relationship with their own set of values that they have acquired through years of experience and exposure. Value conflicts may never become a problem in counseling when the value systems of the client and counselor are similar or compatible. When the value systems of the counselor and clients differ, however, particularly around emotionally charged issues, these differences can become problematic (Barrett & McWhirter, 2002; Kiselica & Robinson, 2001; Millner & Hanks, 2002). Some issues that might cause problems include the following:

- abortion
- the right to die and assisted suicide
- beliefs and behaviors of members of cults
- beliefs and behaviors of gang members
- child or elder neglect or abuse
- genetic engineering
- interracial dating and marriage
- premarital sex or extramarital sex
- sexual identity

Value-laden issues can create problems in the counseling relationship if counselors have not clarified how their own beliefs might affect their work with clients who present with these issues. To illustrate, we discuss briefly the first two of these issues: abortion counseling and the right to die.

Abortion Counseling   In recent years, the controversies over late-term abortions and stem-cell research have generated renewed public debate between two vocal subcultures in the United States—"prochoice" advocates and "prolife" advocates. Thus, it is somewhat surprising that the counseling literature has given little mention to counselors' value conflicts and ethical decision making related to clients who are contemplating abortion (Millner & Hanks, 2002). It is vital that you clarify your own moral position and values regarding abortion before you are faced with this issue in counseling a client. If you believe that abortion poses a clear and imminent danger to the fetus and that the rights of the fetus are as important as the rights of the mother, then you might feel compelled to breach the confidentiality of a client who is planning to have an abortion.

Before you decide whether you can work with women who are considering abortion, you must answer for yourself some crucial questions. Do you believe that abortion is ever an acceptable response to an unwanted pregnancy? If so, in what circumstances? When pregnancy is endangering the mother's life or health? When pregnancy has resulted from rape or incest? When an unmarried woman does not want to marry the father or assume the responsibilities of single parenthood? When parents are living in poverty and cannot afford to raise another child?

In addition to formulating your own responses to these questions, you must know your state laws regarding abortion. Counselors can be sued for negligence under tort law if they do not act with skill, if they withhold pertinent information or provide false information, fail to refer, or make an inadequate referral (Millner & Hanks, 2002). You will not be able to offer effective counseling services to a client who is contemplating abortion if there is a danger of imposing your own values. In such cases, you must be prepared to make an appropriate referral.

The Right to Die   Another controversial issue in today's society is whether people who are terminally ill, have an incurable condition, or are in intolerable pain have the right to choose the time and means of their own deaths (Herlihy & Watson, 2004). As more members of our society live to an advanced age and as life-sustaining medical technologies continue to advance, it is likely that counselors will be called upon more frequently to work with clients who are considering hastening their own deaths. In recognition of this growing need, the ACA signed on to an *americus* brief submitted to the United States Supreme Court in 1997 in support of the role of mental health professionals in assisting individuals with their end-of-life decision making.

Counselors who work with clients facing end-of-life decisions can find explicit guidance in the 2005 ACA *Code of Ethics* regarding ethical issues they inevitably will confront. Standard A.9 (End-of-life care for terminally ill clients) describes measures that counselors should take to ensure quality of care (A.9.a.) and clarifies that counselors have the option of upholding or breaking confidentiality in these situations, depending on the circumstances (A.9.c.). Additionally, the standard acknowledges that not every counselor will feel comfortable or competent to work with terminally ill clients who wish to explore their end-of-life options (A.9.b.). If you are firmly opposed to the practice of hastening one's own death, you will need to refer any such clients to another mental health professional. If you choose to work with these clients, it is essential that you do not impose your own values, even inadvertently, about such issues as living and dying, quality of life, or religion or spirituality.

Before you decide whether you are willing to work with terminally ill clients, you will need to answer a number of questions for yourself. Under what circumstances is hastening one's own death an acceptable option to explore? When a person is terminally ill and death is imminent? When the illness is fatal but the person could live for several more years if he or she undergoes multiple, painful surgeries and agrees to take potent medications with severe side effects? When a condition is not terminal but has left a person in constant, intolerable pain? When a terminally ill person wants to hasten his death to avoid being a burden to his family? When the person already has lived well into her 90s? What if the individual is only 30 years old?

Resolving Value Conflicts

Corey et al. (2007) emphasize the important distinction between *imposing* and *exposing* one's values in counseling. Although it is unethical for counselors to impose their own values on clients, it may be helpful for counselors to disclose their values, either as part of the informed consent process at the beginning of the therapeutic relationship or when issues of conflicting values arise within the counseling process.

When issues of conflicting values arise in counseling, you might consider disclosing your values to the client, if it can be done in a manner that conveys to the client that these values may be accepted or rejected without risking the relationship (Cottone & Tarvydas, 2003). It might then be possible for differences to be discussed and new understandings to be incorporated into the working alliance. For example, a counselor who is a strong feminist might find it difficult to work with a client whose religious beliefs dictate subservience to her husband. The counselor might share her belief system with the client while framing their differences as a learning experience. Once the counselor has disclosed her values, it is hoped that she would find that she is no longer so concerned about inadvertently imposing them. It would be easier for the counselor to keep in mind that it is not her job to convert the client to feminism, but rather to assist the client in finding her own way.

Cottone and Tarvydas (2003) have pointed out that values issues that arise between counselor and client have the potential to enrich the counselor and the client, and their relationship, if they are addressed directly. When values remain unexamined and unchallenged, there is increased potential for counselors to unethically impose their values on clients.

Diversity Considerations   Values and value conflicts in the counseling relationship often can be understood within the context of differing worldviews, or ways that people see the world. An individual's worldview is influenced by culture and is the source of that person's values, beliefs, opinions, and assumptions (Pedersen et al., 2002). Worldviews affect how people think, make decisions, act, and interpret events (Sue & Sue, 1999). Values of cultures vary in how they relate to nature, time, social relations, activity, and collectivism versus individualism, among other dimensions (Hopkins, 1997). When a counselor and a client are from different cultural backgrounds, they may hold differing worldviews, which can lead to misinterpretations, misunderstandings, and conflicts (Chung & Bemak, 2002). This mismatching can, in turn, lead to clients dropping out of counseling or terminating prematurely (Sue, Fujino, Takeuchi, Hu, & Zane, 1991).

1-2 The Case of Brian

Brian is a counselor who works in an urban community agency. The agency provides reduced-fee services to some clients who cannot pay the standard fee. Three months ago, Brian began counseling with Kimberly, who is a 28-year-old single mother. Kimberly works as a maid in a local hotel and receives Aid to Families with Dependent Children (AFDC). During the weekly staffing conducted by the agency counselors, Brian presents the case of Kimberly and states that she often calls to cancel her appointments at the last minute and sometimes simply fails to show up, and when she does keep her appointments she usually arrives late. When Kimberly attends sessions, she talks at length about the problems she encounters in daily living but self-discloses very little. Brian questions whether she has a sincere commitment to counseling.

- What might be some possible explanations for Kimberly's behavior?
- What do you think of Brian's questioning the sincerity of Kimberly's commitment to counseling?

A growing body of literature suggests that counselors must develop *cultural empathy* in order to be effective in counseling clients who hold worldviews and come from cultures different from their own (Chung & Bemak, 2002; Pedersen et al., 2002; Ridley, 1995; Ridley & Lingle, 1996). Acquiring cultural empathy requires counselors not only to have fundamental empathy skills but also to learn advanced skills that will enable them to decode cultural messages (Chung & Bemak). Some of these skills or strategies include

- expressing lack of knowledge or awareness of some aspects of the client's cultural experience
- communicating an interest in learning more about the client's culture
- conveying a genuine appreciation for cultural differences
- acquiring knowledge about the historical and sociopolitical background of the client's culture
- being sensitive to the oppression, marginalization, and discrimination that clients may encounter on a daily basis
- clarifying language and other modes of communication
- incorporating culturally appropriate strategies and treatment goals into the counseling process

If Brian, the counselor in the scenario just presented, had applied cultural empathy to understand his client, Kimberly, he might have given a different explanation of her behavior. Had Brian explored with Kimberly the context of her daily life, he might have learned that she gets to the counseling agency by bus, transferring twice. Brian might have discovered that she relies on various family members to babysit for her when she comes for counseling. When the buses don't run on time or when family members fail to keep their promise to babysit, Kimberly is late for appointments or is unable to come at all.

Client Dependency

Counselors must avoid fostering dependent counseling relationships with clients. Clients have a right to expect that the counseling process will help them move toward increased autonomy and independence. In counseling, clients learn new skills for living including an increased ability to make decisions without the counselor's help.

Earlier we mentioned the possibility that some counselors might encourage client dependency on them. There are a number of ways this could happen to you if you are not alert to the potential problem. During your internship, you must complete a certain number of contact hours with clients, and you might be tempted to keep some clients in counseling longer than necessary in order to fulfill your requirement. Or, you might do so in hopes of demonstrating to your supervisors that your clients keep coming because you are being so helpful to them. After you graduate and are in practice, temptations to foster dependency might arise out of a need to feel needed, a need to nurture others, a need to feel that you are important or indispensable to your clients, or even a need for income from client fees if you are in private practice.

Sometimes it is not the counselor's needs but rather the client's needs that work to foster a dependent relationship. Some clients may attempt to maintain or even increase their dependency on the counselor. They may request more frequent sessions, have a new crisis every time the counselor suggests that they may be nearing the end of their work together, or engage in other strategies to avoid progress toward autonomy. For these clients, remaining dependent on the counselor is less risky than learning to live autonomously. Counselors must find ways to balance ongoing support for them while encouraging independence and risk taking.

The dramatic increase in the number of clients who participate in managed care health plans has had an impact on this issue. Managed care plans limit clients to a certain number of sessions and require counselors to justify any requests for additional sessions. Thus, it is much more difficult for counselors to unnecessarily prolong a counseling relationship. Nonetheless, counselors are obligated to work toward client autonomy regardless of whether the motivation for doing so comes from an external source such as managed care or from an internalized sense of responsibility to promote client welfare.

Diversity Considerations   When counselors work to uphold their ethical obligations to avoid fostering dependency and to promote client independence and autonomy, they sometimes misapply the principle of autonomy. Counselors need to keep in mind that autonomy is a highly individualistic concept (Meara, Schmidt, & Day, 1996) and that the counseling goal of achieving individual independence or autonomy may not be appropriate for clients whose choices are made in the context of family, group, or community (Herlihy & Watson, 2002). For example, Yamamoto and Chang (1987) suggested that, in counseling Asian Americans, counselors could incorporate knowledge of the family-oriented Asian culture by acknowledging and communicating cultural empathy toward the client's family and by including the family in treatment. At the same time, counselors must not lose sight of the fact that there are within-group differences and that each client is unique. Cultural misunderstandings often occur because counselors indiscriminately apply textbook norms regarding racial and ethnic groups and fail to maintain their stance as learners (Ridley, 1995).

Involuntary or Mandated Clients

Special ethical considerations exist when counselors are assigned to work with reluctant clients. In some situations, clients may attend counseling sessions because someone else has pushed them in that direction, even though they are not convinced counseling is a good idea for them. In other, more serious circumstances, clients may have been ordered to attend counseling or suffer negative consequences. Sometimes judges require individuals to attend counseling or go to jail. School principals often require students to attend counseling or face expulsion from school or other disciplinary action. There is nothing unethical about accepting clients in such circumstances.

The term *involuntary client* probably is inaccurate. A client who chooses to enter into counseling rather than accept an alternative or an unwanted consequence is, in fact, making a choice. Mandated counseling situations might appear to conflict with the ACA *Code of Ethics* (2005) Standard A.2.a., which states that clients must be offered the freedom to choose whether to enter into or remain in counseling relationships. However, mandated clients do choose counseling over other options (such as jail or school expulsion), even though the choice may be made reluctantly.

Involuntary clients usually are required to sign a waiver of their privacy rights when they begin a counseling relationship. Because they are being required to participate in counseling and would suffer some type of negative consequences if they refused, the person or entity requiring the counseling also requires some type of report regarding their participation in the counseling process.

The legal issue involved in these situations is to ensure that involuntary clients know that reports must be made and understand the types of information that will be included in the reports. The privacy waiver form that involuntary clients sign should contain as much specific information as possible. Because different individuals and entities require that various types of information be reported, the form should allow for detailed information to be added. A model agreement form for involuntary clients that includes a waiver of privacy is included in Appendix E.

An additional ACA *Code of Ethics* (2005) provision (Standard C.6.b.) addresses counseling involuntary or mandated clients. This standard says that counselors are accurate, honest, and objective in reporting their professional activities and judgments to third parties, including courts or those who receive evaluation reports. We believe that counseling and evaluation are two separate processes and that counselors who counsel individuals should refuse to evaluate them. Reporting on counseling attendance and progress toward reaching counseling goals that have been set by clients is different from evaluating clients for issues such as fitness for parenting, ability to work after an injury, or a mental condition.

Sometimes counselors do perform such evaluations, but counselors who evaluate individuals must be unbiased. If they have counseled a client in the past, they are biased and should not agree to evaluate that same person. If a counselor is evaluating a client, the counselor must make clear to the client that the purpose of their meetings is to gather information for an evaluation, not to provide counseling services. Further, clients must understand there is no confidentiality in such situations and that their counselors will report their findings to a third party.

The ACA *Code of Ethics* (2005) addresses role changes in Standard A.5.a. When counselors change from a non-forensic evaluative role to a therapeutic role, or vice versa, they must obtain the client's informed consent for the change. Counselors must be particularly sensitive to the rights of reluctant, involuntary, or mandated clients. It is essential that counselors fully disclose to such clients any privacy rights that clients are waiving as they enter into such arrangements. For example, if a judge who orders an individual to counseling requires periodic reports to a court official (such as a probation officer) on the person's attendance and progress toward counseling goals, counselors must obtain written permission from the client for such reports and must ensure that the client has a full understanding of the types of reports that will be made. Granello and Hanna (2003) suggest that counselors who provide services to individuals who are involved with the criminal legal system must develop a good understanding of the system in order to serve their clients well.

Because mandated clients may feel coerced into counseling, they may lack motivation to change. Counselors must self-monitor to ensure that they do not develop a cynicism in their work with these clients. If both the client and the counselor are just "going through the motions" in their counseling sessions, little (if any) meaningful work will be accomplished. It is the counselor's responsibility to engage the client in the counseling process, and if that cannot be accomplished, to terminate the counseling relationship.

Counseling Techniques

Another consideration in promoting client welfare is the counselor's obligation to select appropriate counseling strategies or techniques. In recent years, the mental health professions have worked to develop guides for treatment planning that match client concerns with the strategies that research has demonstrated to be the most effective in treating those concerns. Lambert and Cattani-Thompson (1996) reviewed studies on counseling effectiveness and found that some specific techniques seemed to be more efficacious with certain symptoms and disorders. They cautioned, however, that successful client outcome is determined in large part by client characteristics such as motivation, locus of control, and severity and duration of symptoms.

As a counselor, your selection of techniques will depend on a number of factors, including your theoretical orientation and your training. Corey et al. (2007) put it best when they advised that your strategies should fit your counseling style and be tailored to the specific needs of your client. Counselors must not use treatment modalities that are unsubstantiated (Standard C.6.e.), so, if you use any techniques that could be considered experimental or unusual, you should do so very cautiously. The client should be informed of any potential risks and benefits and should consent to your use of such techniques. Before attempting them, you should be sure that you are adequately trained and have a sound clinical rationale for their use. Think about how you would justify your procedures if a complaint were filed against you with a licensing board or in a court of law.

Counselors have an ethical responsibility to work jointly with clients to devise counseling plans that offer reasonable promise of success (ACA *Code of Ethics,* 2005, Standard A.1.c.). As we have mentioned, managed care organizations typically limit the number of sessions for which a client will be reimbursed and require counselors to justify any requests for additional sessions. Counselors will be more successful in making such requests when they can present empirical support for their clinical judgments. Managed care organizations demand accountability from their providers, and counselors must be able to present data that demonstrate their efficacy (Glosoff, Garcia, Herlihy, & Remley, 1999).

Diversity Considerations   Counselors who espouse traditional counseling theories and their associated techniques must be aware that these approaches have limited applicability in working with culturally diverse clients (Jencius & West, 2003). Psychodynamically oriented counselors and ego psychologists who focus on their clients' early childhood relationships with their parents and on intrapsychic conflicts may overlook a client's historic experiences with discrimination and oppression. A psychodynamic therapist's strategy of remaining relatively anonymous in order to serve as a projection screen for the client's transferences could be a poor fit for clients from cultures that value cooperative relationships or for clients who expect the helper to take an active role.

Cognitive behavior therapists are more active in implementing strategies such as direct teaching of skills and assigning homework. However, techniques such as identifying cognitive distortions or irrational self-talk fail to consider the language-bound nature of cognitions. Cognitive behavioral approaches, like psychodynamic approaches, fail to incorporate variables such as race, ethnicity, class, gender, and culture that may be salient to the client's core identity.

Humanistic counselors, particularly those with a Rogerian orientation, offer clients acceptance, unconditional positive regard, and empathy, all of which may help to transcend cultural differences and establish a therapeutic alliance. However, these approaches fail to consider that barriers to self-actualization may exist in the client's environment rather than within the self. Additionally, the nondirective stance fails to meet the needs of clients who might benefit from advocacy and assistance in navigating an oppressive culture.

Today's counselors must have repertoires of helping strategies that extend beyond those offered by traditional counseling theories (all of which were created by and reflect the worldviews of White males). They must have training in multicultural counseling theory and techniques and in working in nontraditional roles.

Interruptions and Termination

Once a counselor has accepted a client and begins providing services, there is an assumption that those services will continue on a regular basis until the client no longer needs counseling. In reality, however, counselors must sometimes interrupt counseling services for a period of time. In addition, counseling relationships are occasionally terminated by counselors before clients are prepared to discontinue counseling services. From both an ethical and a legal perspective, counselors must be careful to protect the best interests of clients when services have to be interrupted or prematurely terminated.

Interruptions in Services   There is truth in Pope and Vasquez's (1998) wry observation that both counselors and clients tend to find comfort in the fantasy that the counselor is invulnerable. The reality is, however, that counselors fall seriously ill, have accidents, or are called away by family emergencies. Counselors must plan ahead for emergency absences by developing procedures to safeguard their clients' welfare. Anticipating that unexpected events might occur, counselors should have plans in place regarding who will notify the clients, who has access to client records, and how the transfer of clients to another counselor will be handled.

Counselors are no different from other workers in that they take vacations, go out of town to attend conferences, and do other things that cause interruptions in the weekly rhythm of the therapeutic relationship. Clients sometimes have strong and even puzzling reactions to their counselor's absence, so it is important that counselors give clients adequate notice and ensure that clients know whom to contact in a crisis or emergency. The ACA *Code of Ethics* (2005) requires counselors to make appropriate arrangements for the continuation of treatment during interruptions caused by vacations, illnesses, or unexpected events (Standard A.11.a.).

Counselors who work with clients who may be at risk for harm to self or others are well advised to arrange for those clients to also be under the care of other professionals who have accepted responsibility for the well-being of the clients. Counselors should work to ensure that all clients are able to tolerate counselor absences for reasonable periods of time.

Termination   Proper termination of the counseling relationship is an important ethical consideration (Pistole, 1999; Summers, 2001) that also has serious legal consequences if done poorly. Clients should be able to expect that their counseling sessions will end when they have received what they were seeking from counseling, when they have realized the maximum benefit from the services, or when they are not likely to benefit from counseling (ACA *Code of Ethics* (2005) Standard A.11.c.). Counselors always anticipate termination as a phase or stage in the counseling relationship, and they provide pre-termination counseling or recommend other service providers when necessary (Standard A.11.c.). Counselors should raise and discuss the issue of termination with the client well in advance of the final session. This allows ample time to plan for the client's transition to functioning without the counselor and to deal with the natural and appropriate issues of separation and loss. Generally, counselors make termination decisions (Gibson & Mitchell, 2003), although it is best if the timing of the termination is mutually agreed on. However, the ultimate decision might be made independently by either the counselor or the client depending on the circumstances.

Premature Termination   In an ideal world, all counseling relationships would end smoothly by mutual agreement. In reality, however, circumstances can arise that allow the counselor to terminate the counseling relationship even against a client's wishes (Welfel, 2002). In addition to routine terminations, it is ethically permissible (Standard A.11.c.) for counselors to terminate counseling relationships in the following circumstances:

- It is clear that the client is no longer benefitting from counseling or is being harmed by continued counseling.
- Clients do not pay the fees as agreed upon.
- The counselor is in jeopardy of being harmed by the client or someone with whom the client has a relationship.

When counselors are unable to be of continued assistance to clients or decide to end the relationship over the client's objection, counselors must give adequate notice and give the client time to secure another mental health care provider (Hilliard, 1998). In addition, counselors should suggest an appropriate referral and do all they can to facilitate a smooth transition to the new mental health professional. If the client is unable to continue to pay the counselor's fee, an appropriate referral can be made to free services or to an agency that uses a sliding fee scale, if such alternatives are available. If a client refuses to accept the idea of a referral, the counselor is not obligated to provide free services. The ACA *Code of Ethics* (2005) specifies that counselors may discontinue the relationship if the client declines the referral (Standard A.11.b.). Bernstein and Hartsell (1998) have offered a checklist and form letter mental health professionals might use when notifying a client of a premature termination.

Abandonment   Ethical guidelines (ACA *Code of Ethics,* 2005, Standard A.11.a.) and legal decisions related to physicians (*Allison v. Patel*, 1993; *Manno v. McIntosh,* 1994) prohibit counselors from abandoning their clients. Once a counseling relationship has been established, the counselor cannot arbitrarily end it if the client will be put at risk as a result.

No professional is required to provide services to a client if the professional chooses not to do so. The key to ending a professional relationship with a client properly, and thus not being exposed to charges of abandonment, is to give the client adequate notice that you are ending the professional relationship and ample opportunity to locate a new counselor. It might be important, too, to discuss with the client how to locate agencies and individuals who offer counseling services. Giving notice of termination and time for the client to find a new counselor may not lead to the client taking the initiative to find a new counselor, however. If a client refuses to see another counselor after you have given notice you are withdrawing your services, it will be essential for you to document carefully and fully the notice you gave, your assistance with the referral process, and the time you gave the client to locate a new professional.

Hilliard (1998), an attorney who represents mental health professionals who are sued by their clients, has observed the events that lead individuals to sue their mental health providers. As a practical consideration, Hilliard has recommended that mental health care providers never terminate a professional relationship over a client's objection when the client is angry or when the client is in a serious crisis situation. Taking the time to address a client's distress is very important to avoid unresolved angry feelings that could lead to a lawsuit. Also, a judge or jury probably would not support a mental health professional's decision to end a relationship in the midst of a crisis (*Allison v. Patel,* 1993; *Manno v. McIntosh,* 1994). Ending a counseling relationship because insurance benefits have run out, when the client is still at risk for suicide, is very risky (Packman & Harris, 1998) for both the client and the counselor.

Of course, counselors may always refer an at-risk client to a psychiatrist or health care facility that evaluates individuals for suicide or danger to themselves or others. This referral does not always lead to a transfer of that client to another professional or termination. In many circumstances, counselors continue to provide services to a referred client in collaboration with another mental health professional. It is very important, however, when a referral of an at-risk client is made that the counselor informs all parties whether the referral is a transfer of the client to another professional, or whether the counselor will be providing services in conjunction with another professional.

To protect mental health professionals from being held accountable for abandonment of their clients, Hilliard (1998) and Macbeth, Wheeler, Sither, and Onek (1994) have developed the following guidelines for mental health professionals to use when they are terminating clients in adverse circumstances:

- Honestly discuss with the client your intention to terminate and the specific reason for your decision.
- Give the client an opportunity to make changes that would be necessary to continue the relationship.
- Give written notice to the client that the relationship will be terminated.
- Offer the client one to three termination sessions.
- Give your client up to three good referrals.
- Give your client places to contact in the event of emergencies.
- Place a summary of your interactions with the client around the termination issue in the client's file. Do not transfer that document to another individual or entity without an express written request from the client.
- Give the client plenty of time to find another mental health professional. If more time is requested, allow it.
- Transfer records to the new mental health professional promptly.

Diversity Considerations   Earlier, we referred to the ideal situation in which the counseling relationship reaches termination by mutual agreement and in a planned manner. In the real world of counselor practice, however, clients sometimes drop out of counseling without discussing their intentions with the counselor. They may cancel an appointment and fail to reschedule or simply stop coming to sessions. There are many reasons why this can happen—sometimes clients just need to "take a break" from the intense personal work involved in counseling, or they may drop out or discontinue the counseling relationship because they do not believe they are benefitting from counseling. This scenario will occur occasionally in any counselor's practice and it may be helpful to remember that no counselor is skilled enough to be able to assist every client.

It is important that you self-monitor, though, to discern whether the clients who are discontinuing counseling with you are those who are culturally different from you. If you see such a pattern, this is a signal that you must work to increase your crosscultural counseling skills.

INFORMED CONSENT

As an ethical obligation, the rationale for informed consent is simple—clients have a right to know what they are getting into when they come for counseling. Most clients are not experts in counseling, so they must trust their counselors to provide them with the information they need to make a good decision (Handelsman, 2001). Counselors believe that obtaining consent from clients before counseling begins constitutes best practice and is the proper and ethical way to proceed. In addition, there are concepts in law that require informed consent be obtained from clients before counseling relationships are initiated. Some state counseling licensing laws or regulations require that licensed counselors provide written documents to clients (e.g., La. Rev. Stat. Ann. 5 37:1101–1115), and these written documents constitute informed consent (Madden, 1998). Counselors must provide prospective clients with information that will enable them to make wise choices. This includes deciding whether to enter into a counseling relationship and, if so, choosing the mental health professional who seems best suited to their needs and the type of counseling they will receive. Providing clients with information about how the counseling process works helps demystify counseling and makes clients active partners in defining the counseling relationship.

Marczyk and Wertheimer (2001) have noted that, in the past, it was difficult for mental health professionals to provide clients with adequate information regarding treatment choices because the field of counseling and psychology was "still very much a philosophy and not a science" (p. 33). They have suggested that mental health professionals should be required to provide clients with the success rates of various forms of mental health treatment based on empirical research–based evidence, as do physicians who treat patients with conditions such as cancer. In the future, such a duty could be imposed on counselors.

Contract Law

Contract law is complex. Counselors do not need to understand the technical principles of contract law such as offer, acceptance, and consideration (Calamari, Perillo, & Bender, 1989) in order to appreciate their contractual obligations to clients, but a basic understanding of those principles can be helpful.

Generally, relationships with professionals who provide services are contractual in nature (Murphy, Speidel, & Ayres, 1997). In terms of contract law, a professional in a private practice offers services to a recipient for a fee. The professional says to the client that services will be provided that will benefit and not harm the recipient if the recipient will pay the professional the amount of money required. Once the client accepts the professional's offer of services, a legal contract is formed and all the laws of the contract govern the relationship. The process that leads up to professional services being rendered to a recipient does not look at all like a contractual process to nonlawyers. Because of the fiduciary duty owed to clients of professionals, and because clients must trust professionals to treat them appropriately, the idea of signing a contract before accepting services from a professional seems almost contradictory. If you trust someone, why would you need a contract?

Some contracts, such as real estate deals, must be in writing (Murphy et al., 1997). Contract law does not generally require, however, that contracts be in writing to be valid and enforceable. As a result, most contracts for professional services are not in writing. Although written contracts are generally not necessary under the law, many parties choose to execute them. One practical reason for reducing to writing the terms of a contract is to ensure that both parties understand exactly what they are agreeing to (i.e., the terms of the contract).

If two parties enter into a contractual arrangement, nothing goes wrong, and both are satisfied with the result, a written contract was not needed. However, written contracts allow the parties to ensure they both understand the specifics in the agreement they have reached. In addition, written contracts often anticipate changes or problems that might occur and set forth the agreement in the event such things happen. Agreements that are complex or must anticipate changes, therefore, should be in writing to protect both parties.

Informed Consent in Medicine

The process of informing recipients of professional services and obtaining their consent to receive such services is a relatively new legal concept. The requirement that health professionals obtain informed consent from their clients before rendering services began in medicine (Appelbaum, Lidz, & Meisel, 1987).

Two decades ago, it probably rarely occurred to physicians that they should explain to patients what they knew about their medical conditions. Physicians probably never thought that they should tell their patients about various treatment options or allow their patients to decide which option to choose. Perhaps consumers of medical services were once less educated or less aware of their right to receive information. In any event, the idea of informed consent for medical patients is relatively new.

As far back as 1767, a court in England determined that physicians had a responsibility to obtain consent from their patients before touching or treating them (*Slater v. Baker & Stapleton*). Originally this obligation to obtain consent was based on the basic tort principle of battery that held that members of a society have a right to personal privacy, which includes not having their bodies touched by others unless they have given permission.

It has only been in the last half-century that courts have created the requirement that patients must be educated or informed regarding their medical treatment options and consequences before they are able to give valid consent to treatment that is legally binding. The first case in the United States that took this position was *Salgo v. Leland Stanford Jr. Univ. Bd. of Trustees* (1957).

However, because there have been very few lawsuits alleging that physicians failed to obtain informed consent from patients before rendering treatment that led to harm, courts and physicians currently are unclear as to exactly what constitutes valid informed consent from patients (Appelbaum, Lidz, & Meisel, 1987). Katz (1977) has suggested that the Salgo case did nothing more than add confusion to an already vague area of the law.

The Salgo case provided the essential elements that physicians must give to patients. According to Appelbaum et al. (1987, p. 41), these elements are "disclosure of the nature of the ailment, the nature of the proposed treatment, the probability of success, and possible alternative treatments." *Canterbury v. Spence* (1972), a later case, took a different position on informed consent. It found that physicians were required to disclose information about a proposed treatment that a reasonable person, such as the patient being treated, would find necessary to make a decision to either accept or refuse treatment.

After considering the case law on informed consent, Berner (1998) has argued that there are two elements to the informed consent legal standard. These elements are professional and materiality. The *professional element* is defined as information that a reasonable physician would have provided to a patient in similar circumstances. *Materiality,* on the other hand, is defined as the amount of information the average patient would consider adequate in deciding whether to accept treatment. If Berner is correct, then courts will most likely require that physicians provide basic information to all patients *and* require that physicians ensure that the particular patient with whom they are dealing understands the information.

Although legal decisions have been rendered in the area of informed consent and a great deal has been written about the requirement in the professional literature, whether all of this activity has had an impact on the actual practice of physicians is questionable. Lidz, Meisel, Zerubavel, Sestak, and Roth (1984), in an empirical study of informed consent activities in psychiatric units of hospitals, concluded that if informed consent is being obtained from mental patients, it certainly is not occurring in hospitals.

The Health Insurance Portability and Accountability Act (HIPAA), which went into effect April 15, 2003, has had a powerful impact on informed consent practices in medicine and mental health. This federal law and its regulations are explored in detail in chapter 3. Essentially, HIPAA requires all health care providers who transmit records electronically (which most likely includes all providers) to comply with procedures to ensure consumer privacy. The requirements include explaining to health care recipients in detail their rights related to privacy and records (which essentially is the informed consent process discussed earlier). This federal law has transformed the concept of informed consent, which once was rather vague, into a concrete framework that includes disclosure of steps taken to ensure client privacy and also requires that clients sign a document that they have been informed of their rights. Figure 1-1 includes a listing of essential elements for informed consent documents to ensure that counselors and agencies meet the legal HIPAA requirements.

Informed Consent in Mental Health

At present, there have been no appellate legal cases involving the responsibility of mental health professionals to obtain informed consent from their clients. But like other legal areas in mental health, most of the precedents and rules are created first with physicians and later become verified for other mental health professionals through cases involving psychologists, counselors, and social workers. Beyond legal requirements however, we believe it is best practice to provide clients with written information about the counseling relationship before the relationship begins (Herlihy & Remley, 2001).

It is probably safe to conclude that counselors do have a legal obligation to obtain informed consent from their clients before they begin treatment with them. Further, the informed consent should include information that would be given to the client by other reasonable professionals and should be delivered in a way that the client understands. Counselors should provide information that, at a minimum, discloses the client's diagnosis, the type of treatment being proposed to address the problem, the probability of success in treating the problem, and possible alternative treatments. HIPAA requires that the informed consent of clients be verified with their signatures.

Written Disclosure Statements

Forms of model written contracts that counselors might use in various circumstances are included in Appendix E. In mental health, such contracts are commonly referred to as *disclosure statements*. These documents disclose to clients the nature of the counseling relationship they are entering into. Disclosure statements are also legal contracts. Often, they are signed by both the client and the counselor. Appendix E includes model disclosure statements for counselors who are providing counseling services to clients in a private practice and for employed counselors who are providing counseling services to clients in an agency or mental health center, respectively. The model counseling disclosure statements for private practice and agencies or mental

---

To comply with the HIPAA law, here are some areas you must include on the form your clients sign saying they have been informed about your proposed treatment and agreeing to the treatment and the arrangement with you:

✓   State that your client's personal information may be used and disclosed to complete their treatment. Also state that information may be provided to health care companies related to payment for your services.

✓   Develop a complete written description of the procedures you will follow in your office regarding keeping or disclosing personal information of clients.

✓   Tell your client that you have a more complete description of the way in which you will keep or disclose their personal information, and that the complete description is available for them to see. State that the client has a right to review the complete description prior to signing this consent form. Explain that your practices may change in the future and if they want to see any revisions, they must request to see them in writing and that you will then make them available.

✓   Tell your client that he or she may request that you restrict how the client's personal information is used or disclosed. Explain that you will consider any such requests and will notify the client whether you have agreed to them.

✓   Explain that the client has the right to revoke his or her consent in writing, except to the extent actions have already been taken by you based on prior consent.

✓   Get the client's signature and have him or her indicate the date on the form.

✓   Keep the form for at least 6 years.

Figure 1-1   HIPAA requirements for informed consent disclosure statements

health centers are similar in many ways. However, fee issues and some other aspects of the disclosure statements are quite different. Additional disclosure statements in Appendix E are for counselors who evaluate individuals, who counsel mandated or involuntary clients, and who counsel in schools.

The ACA *Code of Ethics* (2005) spells out in considerable detail, in Standard A.2.b., the elements that ethically need to be included in securing informed consent. Therefore, these elements should be included in counseling disclosure statements:

• the purposes, goals, techniques, procedures, limitations, potential risks, and benefits of proposed counseling services
• the counselor's *qualifications,* including relevant degrees held, licenses and certifications, areas of specialization, and experience
• arrangements for continuation of services if the counselor dies or becomes incapacitated
• the implications of diagnosis and the intended use of tests and reports
• fees and billing information
• confidentiality and its limitations

- clients' rights to obtain information about their records and to participate in ongoing counseling plans
- clients' rights to refuse any recommended services or modality change and be advised of the consequences of refusal

In addition to the elements addressed by the code, various writers have recommended that these additional topics be included:

- a description of the counselor's *theoretical orientation,* in lay language that the client can understand (Corey et al., 2007), or a brief statement of the counselor's *philosophy* (how the counselor sees the counseling process)
- information about *logistics* of the counseling process, such as length and frequency of sessions, procedures for making and canceling appointments, policies regarding telephone contact between sessions, how to reach the counselor or an alternative service in an emergency (Haas & Malouf, 1995)
- information about *insurance reimbursement,* including the fact that any diagnosis assigned will become part of the client's permanent health record; what information will be provided to insurance carriers and how this limits confidentiality (Welfel, 2006); and, if applicable, a description of how the *managed care* system will affect the counseling process (Corey et al., 2007; Glosoff et al., 1999)
- information about *alternatives to counseling,* such as 12-step groups or other self-help groups, books, medications, nutritional or exercise therapy, or other services (Bray, Shepherd, & Hays, 1985)
- if applicable, a statement that sessions will be *videotaped or audiotaped*, along with the information that the client's case may be discussed with a supervisor or consultant (Corey et al., 2007)
- the client's *recourse if dissatisfied with services,* including names and contact information for supervisors, and addresses and telephone numbers of licensing boards and professional organizations (Welfel)

Beyond the informed consent areas required by the ACA *Code of Ethics* (2005) and areas suggested by others, some legal concerns need to be addressed in disclosure statements. The following informed consent areas are particularly sensitive and could lead to legal problems if not handled properly. Examples of problems that could arise are included. A client might have the basis for a lawsuit against a counselor if the client believed, for some reason, that the counselor had done any of the following:

1. **Failed to include required HIPAA elements (see chap. 3).** Example: A client was not notified when she began counseling that she had the right to review her counseling records. She complained to the federal government and the counselor was asked to verify that he had informed her of these rights.
2. **Guaranteed an outcome as a result of counseling.** Example: A wife reluctantly agreed to enter marriage counseling with her husband. She believed that, by agreeing to engage in counseling, she was guaranteed that her marriage would not end. She says the counselor told her that counseling was "the only thing that would save her marriage." She felt betrayed by the counselor when, after five sessions, her husband moved out of their home and filed for divorce. She sued the counselor for breach of contract, conspiracy, and alienation of affection.

3. **Guaranteed privacy with no exceptions.** Example: A new client expresses concern to his counselor that others might find out what he tells the counselor in their sessions. To reduce the client's anxiety, the counselor explains her ethical and legal responsibilities to protect his privacy. The client believes that his counselor told him that she would never, in any circumstances, reveal to anyone else information given to her in counseling sessions. Later the counselor informs the client's wife, over his objection, that he has expressed suicidal ideas and that she believes he should be evaluated to determine whether he is at risk. He sues the counselor for breach of contract, malpractice, and intentional infliction of emotional distress.

4. **Agreed to fee arrangements different from what was intended.** Example: A counselor begins a counseling relationship with his client, charging the client his standard rate of $75 per hour. After 3 months of sessions once a week, the counselor tells his client that his fees will be increased in 1 month to $90 per hour. The client objects, saying that he feels that the new hourly rate is too high. The counselor replies that he is not willing to provide further counseling services to the client unless the client agrees to pay the new rate. The client sues the counselor for breach of contract and abandonment.

5. **Touched without implied or actual permission.** Example: In the course of a group counseling experience, a counselor asks group members who are blindfolded to allow themselves to fall backward into the arms of another group member to demonstrate the difficulty of trusting another person. A female group member reluctantly participates and is caught by a male group member. The female group member is very upset after the exercise and leaves the session visibly shaken. The female client sues the counselor for breach of contract, breach of fiduciary duty, assault, battery, and sexual assault.

6. **Misrepresented credentials.** Example: A client begins counseling sessions with a master's-level licensed counselor. The client tells his family members and friends that he is seeing a psychologist for therapy. The client makes out his checks to "Dr. ____," notes on the checks that he is paying for "psychological services," and gives the checks each week to the office receptionist, who deposits them. At the ninth session, the client calls the counselor, "Dr. ____," and she corrects him. He then says, "You are a psychologist, aren't you?" He is very upset when he realizes that she is a master's-level licensed counselor. The client sues the counselor for breach of contract and fraudulent misrepresentation.

7. **Failed to communicate the nature of counseling.** Example: A client has taken a new job in which she is required periodically to give presentations to small groups of potential clients. She is very anxious about speaking before groups and has sought counseling to overcome her anxiety. The counselor believes that her anxiety is the result of low self-esteem and focuses on positive reinforcement of the client's positive attributes. After five sessions, the client complains that she is still as anxious as she was when she began counseling. She tells the counselor that she had expected to be taught how to give presentations without being anxious and she does not understand why the counselor has not given her books to read, given her advice on how to be less anxious, or practiced speaking with her. The client sues the counselor for breach of contract and malpractice.

8. **Neglected to warn client about possible stigma.** Example: After the first session with a new client, the counselor completes an insurance form at the client's request. The counselor indicates on the form that the client has had a single episode of depression and assigns the appropriate *DSM-IV-TR* diagnosis. The counselor counsels the client for 10 sessions, terminating when the client moves to a new city hundreds of miles away. Two years later the client

contacts the counselor and complains that he has been denied a security clearance for a job he has applied for because she diagnosed him, without his knowledge or agreement, with a mental disorder. He sues the counselor for breach of contract, malpractice, and defamation.

These eight unfortunate situations illustrate the importance of ensuring that counselors and their clients have the same understanding regarding their relationship before counseling begins. All of these problems could have been avoided if the counselors had fully informed the clients regarding the counseling relationship. Since HIPAA has come into effect, all counselors must give their clients written informed consent documents to sign. However, to be effective these documents must include essential information beyond the HIPAA requirements.

1-3 The Case of Mark

Mark, a new Licensed Professional Counselor (LPC), works in a very efficient community mental health agency that utilizes the latest technology. Before he begins his first counseling session with each client, Mark types in the client's name and a personalized disclosure statement is printed out that includes all of the HIPAA, ethical, and legal requirements for such documents. Mark is counseling Maureen, a young mother, who discloses that her husband, Jake, gets angry with their infant daughter when she cries and shakes the child severely to stop her crying. Mark informs Maureen that he must report Jake's actions to the authorities as possible child abuse. Mark, being sensitive to Maureen's concerns, explains in detail what may happen as a result of the report and assures her that he will continue counseling her. Maureen complains that she never would have told Mark about Jake's actions if she had known he would make a report to authorities. Mark responds that Maureen signed the informed consent form when they began their counseling relationship, and that the form clearly stated that counselors are legally obligated to report incidents of suspected child abuse. Maureen reponds that she didn't read the document. She says she just signed it along with all those other papers for insurance. Maureen says she doesn't think she can continue her counseling relationship with Mark because she no longer trusts him.

- What could Mark have done at the outset of his counseling relationship with Maureen that might have prevented this unfortunate situation? What would have constituted *best practice* in this situation?
- How can counselors balance the need to inform new clients of the limits of confidentiality in the relationship and to establish rapport at the same time?

In the process of having clients sign counseling disclosure statements, counselors should attempt to ensure that clients know what they have read and what was in the document being signed. If questions arise later about what counselors may have said, a signed written document demonstrates the intent of the parties much more clearly than does a statement of what someone says they intended. In addition, counseling disclosure statements can be used to correct misunderstandings on the part of clients before counseling begins.

You may be thinking that a lot of information must be included in a disclosure statement and, indeed, this is true. In order for clients to give truly informed consent, they must have considerable information before deciding whether to enter into a counseling relationship. This may raise your concern that inundating prospective clients with information will overwhelm them and give the impression that the counseling relationship is nothing more than a complex, contractual business arrangement. It is difficult for counselors to achieve the delicate balance between giving clients too little information and giving them so much information that they feel overwhelmed or intimidated. Written disclosure statements allow counselors to provide detailed information. Oral exchanges between counselors and potential clients can then focus on areas the counselor wishes to emphasize or that cause particular concern for clients.

As noted earlier, every counselor should have a professional disclosure statement that can be given to clients. A complete signed disclosure statement will fulfill a counselor's legal obligation to obtain informed consent from a client. Keep in mind, though, that disclosure statements are necessary but not sufficient strategies for securing genuine informed consent. They cannot serve as a substitute for dialog with the client. We cannot rely on standard forms, no matter how well they are written, to do our work for us (Pope & Vasquez, 1998). Prospective clients are likely to have many questions, and some of these are best addressed in face-to-face conversation. Such a dialog gives clients an opportunity to clarify any information that seems confusing to them and gives counselors the opportunity to gauge the extent to which the clients comprehend the information. At the outset of the relationship, informed consent discussions present a mutual opportunity for the client and the counselor to ensure that they understand their shared journey.

Pope and Vasquez (1998) also have noted that informed consent procedures must fit the situation and setting, and be sensitive to the client's ability to understand. The ACA *Code of Ethics* (2005) affirms the obligation of counselors to communicate information in ways that are both developmentally and culturally appropriate (Standard A.2.c.). To ensure client comprehension, it may be necessary in some cases to arrange for a qualified interpreter or translator. Some clients may be presumed to lack the capacity to give informed consent. Such clients might include minors or persons who are developmentally disabled, referred, or suffering from a severe thought disorder. In these cases, counselors seek the assent of clients to services and include them in the decision-making process to the extent possible (Standard A.2.d.).

It is impossible to predict which clients will need what information and when they will need it, so it is best to be as thorough as possible in a written disclosure statement. Then later, in a face-to-face discussion, issues that arise frequently in one's practice can be emphasized and rare events can be given less attention. For example, Weinrach (1989) has suggested that the two most common problems for private practitioners concern fees and billing, and late cancellations or no-shows. Thus, it behooves counselors in private practice to be clear with their clients about methods of payment and policies regarding missed appointments.

Some counselors make it a practice to give clients not only a disclosure statement, but also a written statement of client rights and responsibilities. The NBCC has developed such a statement (see Figure 1-2) that counselors may wish to give to their clients.

From an ethical perspective, ensuring informed consent is not a one-time event. Rather, it is a recurring process that begins with the initial contact between client and counselor and continues throughout the counseling relationship. The ACA *Code of Ethics* describes informed consent as an ongoing part of the counseling process and advises counselors to document discussion of informed consent throughout the counseling relationship (Standard A.2.a.). As counseling progresses, the goals, issues, risks, and benefits often change, and clients need to have updated information so that they can continue to make sound decisions (Handelsman, 2001).

Managed care arrangements present some new considerations in informed consent. Glosoff (1998) has suggested that counselors need to expand the information they provide to clients being served by managed care systems, as compared to other clients. Clients often do not understand how their health plans affect the duration of their treatment, the implications of diagnosis, or the extent to which their insurance providers require counselors to provide them with information about treatment plans and counseling progress. Thus, Glosoff has suggested that it is incumbent on their counselors to fully understand the requirements of each client's managed care company and to discuss with the client the impact their plan will have on the length of treatment, types of treatment available, limits to confidentiality, development of treatment plans, and how diagnoses will be made and used. To be realistic, though, it would be impossible for counselors to know the details of each of the health care

Your Rights as a Consumer

- Be informed of the qualifications of your counselor: education, experience, and professional counseling certification(s) and license(s).
- Receive an explanation of services offered, your time commitments, and fee scales and billing policies prior to receipt of services.
- Be informed of the limitations of the counselor practice to special areas of expertise (e.g., career development, ethnic groups) or age group (e.g., adolescents, older adults).
- Have all that you say treated confidentially and be informed of any state laws placing limitations on confidentiality in the counseling relationship.
- Ask questions about the counseling technique and strategies and be informed of your progress.
- Participate in setting goals and evaluating progress toward meeting them.
- Be informed of how to contact the counselor in an emergency situation.
- Request referral for a second opinion at any time.
- Request copies of records and reports to be used by other counseling professionals.
- Receive a copy of the code of ethics to which your counselor adheres.
- Contact the appropriate professional organization if you have doubts or complaints relative to the counselor's conduct.
- Terminate the relationship at any time.

Your Responsibilities as a Client

- Set and keep appointments with your counselor. Let him or her know as soon as possible if you cannot keep an appointment.
- Pay your fees in accordance with the schedule you preestablished with the counselor.
- Help plan your goals.
- Follow through with agreed upon goals.
- Keep your counselor informed of your progress toward meeting your goals.
- Terminate your counseling relationship before beginning with another counselor.

What to Do If You Are Dissatisfied with the Services of a Counselor

Remember that a counselor who meets the needs of one person may be wrong for another. If you are dissatisfied with the services of your counselor:

- Express your concern directly to the counselor if possible.
- Seek the advice of the counselor's supervisor if the counselor is practicing in a setting where he or she receives direct supervision.
- Terminate the counseling relationship if the situation remains unresolved.
- Contact the appropriate state licensing board national certification organization or professional association if you believe the counselor's conduct to be unethical.

Figure 1-2   National board for certified counselors consumer rights and responsibilities

Reprinted by permission of the National Board for Certified Counselors, 3 Terrace Way, Suite D, Greensboro, NC 27403-3660.

plans of their clients. As a result, it probably would be important for counselors to stress to clients that they should investigate the terms and limits of their coverage, rather than for counselors to undertake that entire burden.

Research supports the wisdom of securing informed consent. Studies have suggested that clients want information about their prospective counselors (Braaten, Otto, & Handelsman, 1993; Hendrick, 1988); that they perceive counselors who provide informed consent information as being more expert and trustworthy (Sullivan, Martin, & Handelsman, 1993); and that clients who have received appropriate information are more likely to follow their treatment plans, to recover more quickly, to be less anxious, and to be more alert to possible negative consequences (Handler, 1990). In addition, some legal problems can be avoided by the use of disclosure statements. If allegations do arise that a counselor did not fully explain the counseling relationship to a client, a disclosure statement signed by a client often can go a long way toward vindicating an accused counselor who has done no wrong.

Diversity Considerations in Informed Consent   It is important for us to question whether the individualism inherent in our concept of informed consent is truly respectful of people of all cultures. We need to be aware that the full and truthful disclosure that counselors value may be at variance with some clients' cultural beliefs about hope and wellness, that autonomous decision making may run counter to family-centered or group-centered values, and that uncoerced choices may contradict cultural norms about obedience to the wishes of elders or spouses (Gostin, 1995). The following two case examples illustrate this point.

1-4 The Case of Henry

Joseph, a Navajo Indian who espouses the traditions of his culture, is Henry's new client. During the initial interview, Henry wants to secure Joseph's informed consent, which would include giving him information about the implications of diagnosis and the potential risks associated with counseling. Henry says, "Sometimes, clients in counseling seem to feel worse before they feel better." He adds that, based on the symptoms Joseph has described, Joseph seems to be experiencing mild depression.

- What would Henry need to know about Joseph's culture that would help him conduct informed consent procedures in a culture-sensitive way?
- Can you identify any problems with what Henry told Joseph?

In traditional Navajo culture, it is believed that language has the power to shape reality and control events. Therefore Henry, in following his standard informed consent procedures, could be *creating* a reality for Joseph that he is depressed and will feel worse before he feels better.

1-5 The Case of Loretta

Soo Jung is a 22-year-old immigrant from Korea who is brought to the counseling center by her husband. During the intake interview, she tells her counselor, Loretta, that she has been having crying spells, has lost her appetitie, and is not sleeping well. She gave birth to her first child 2 months ago. When Loretta suggests to Soo Jung that she may be experiencing postpartum depression, Soo Jung becomes upset and says, "Why are you telling me this? You need to talk to my husband."

- Why do you think Soo Jung became upset?
- How might have Loretta handled the intake interview differently, to avoid upsetting this client?

Soo Jung appears to share a family-oriented worldview that is common among people from some Asian cultures. Because the counselor did not include this client's husband in this discussion, Soo Jung may have interpreted the counselor's actions as attempting to undermine her marital relationship.

Joseph and Soo Jung illustrate the point that there are communities of clients in our pluralistic society who do not claim Euro-American values as their own. Counselors must remember to put the client's needs first. Weinrach and Thomas (1996) suggest that counselors identify, and then focus on, the frame of reference or belief and value system that is central to the client, as one way to remain sensitive to differences. Expanding our frame of reference regarding informed consent does not mean that we must abandon our commitment to client autonomy, but it does encompass respect for the cultural values that our clients bring with them to counseling.

Counselors must also be sensitive to clients' rights to informed consent when clients have been legally adjudicated as incompetent. Clients with developmental disabilities, older adults who have cognitive impairments, and persons who have been diagnosed with a psychotic or thought disorder often are judged to have diminished capacity to consent. Keep in mind that "diminished" capacity is not the same as an absence of capacity. You have an ethical obligation to discuss consent with these clients in a manner that they can understand and to obtain their assent to services even though their agreement may not be legally recognized (Handelsman, 2001).

The importance of using language that clients can understand is equally important with clients who are children, adults who are not well educated, and clients whose first language is not English. If you work with such clients, it would be wise to carefully check the readability level of your written disclosure statement. When English is a second language for clients, it would be helpful to have a copy that has been translated into the client's primary language. The overarching principle is that consent procedures, both oral and written, must be developmentally and culturally appropriate.

SUMMARY AND KEY POINTS

This chapter addresses two vitally important and interrelated ethical and legal issues in counseling: client rights and counselor responsibilities. Following are key points regarding client rights:

- Counselors are ethically responsible for putting client welfare first and foremost in their work.
- Counselors have a fiduciary relationship with their clients, which means that they have a legal obligation to protect their clients' best interests and to avoid interactions that benefit themselves.
- Respecting diversity is fundamental to protecting client welfare and promoting client dignity in our pluralistic society.
- It is vital for counselors to be aware of their own life issues, unfinished business, areas of vulnerability, and defenses, so that they will not inadvertently be working on their own issues in the counseling relationship, rather than on the client's issues.
- Counselors must be aware of their values and must not impose their own values on clients.
- Counselors must avoid fostering client dependency. They have an obligation to promote client autonomy and independence.
- When counseling involuntary or mandated clients, counselors must inform these clients of the limits of confidentiality and the nature of any reports that may be made to courts or other entities that are requiring the clients to attend counseling. Counselors must be sensitive to these clients' rights and ensure that clients understand any privacy rights they may be waiving.

- Counselors have an obligation to select appropriate counseling strategies or techniques and to make clients active partners in treatment decisions.
- Counselors must protect the best interests and welfare of clients when counseling services have to be interrupted or terminated prematurely.
- It is unethical, as well as illegal, for counselors to abandon their clients. Although there are valid reasons for a counselor to end a counseling relationship, care must be taken not to put the client at risk when doing so. Several guidelines were offered for counselors to use when they are terminating counseling relationships in adverse circumstances.

The following are key points regarding informed consent in counseling:

- As an ethical obligation, informed consent is based on the rationale that clients have a right to know what they are getting into when they come for counseling.
- Counselors should understand that counseling services are contractual in nature. Agreements should be put in writing in an informed consent document.
- The requirement that health professionals inform prospective recipients of services and obtain their consent to treatment originated in the field of medicine. More recently, it has been applied to the mental health field. A number of model disclosure statements are available to assist counselors who work in various settings with a variety of clientele.
- The requirements of the HIPAA have transformed informed consent into a legal requirement, and counselors must ensure that their procedures are in compliance with this new law.
- Informed consent in counseling involves a number of elements that are required by the code of ethics, recommended by various writers, and suggested as a means to address legal concerns.
- Counselors should be aware of at least eight areas of informed consent that, if not handled properly, could lead to legal problems.
- It can be difficult to achieve a correct balance between providing prospective clients with too little information and giving them so much information that they feel overwhelmed or intimidated. Informed consent is an ongoing process that should be conducted both orally and in written form.
- It is important for counselors to be sensitive to the fact that informed consent as traditionally conceptualized may not be respectful of people of all cultures.

2 Confidentiality and Privileged Communication

FOCUS QUESTIONS

1. Some studies have shown that clients are not very concerned about privacy or confidentiality when they seek counseling services. What do you think about such findings?
2. How would you respond if a client asked to see the notes you have taken related to his counseling sessions?
3. What do you think should happen to clients' records after they die?

Confidentiality is one of the most fundamental of all professional obligations in counseling. It is also one of the most problematic duties to manage in day-to-day practice. Consider, for instance, what you would do if you were the counselor in each of the following situations.

2-1 The Case of Elena

Elena has been seeing Pete, age 28, who came for counseling to resolve some family-of-origin issues that he believes are creating problems in his relationship with his partner, Jacob. During their last counseling session together, Pete tearfully revealed that before he met Jacob, he had a series of casual sexual encounters and that he was terrified that he might have contracted the AIDS virus through these encounters. He comes to today's session with the news that he has been fully tested and is confirmed to be HIV positive. He says he cannot tell Jacob, because he is sure Jacob will leave him if he knows.

- As Pete's counselor, is Elena obligated to keep his secret? Or do you believe she has a duty to inform Jacob of Pete's condition, even though this would involve breaching Pete's confidentiality?
- Suppose Pete tells Elena, after further discussion, that he realizes he must tell Jacob but needs some time to gather his courage. Should Elena keep his secret in this circumstance? If yes, for how long?

2-2 The Case of Nancy

Nancy, a high school counselor, has been conducting a group for freshman and sophomore girls. The focus of the group is on building self-esteem and making wise choices. During the fourth session today, the group members begin discussing boyfriends and whether to "just say no" to sex. Marlee, a 15-year-old freshman, shares that she and her boyfriend are having sexual relations and that she thinks it's okay because they are really in love. She mentions, almost in passing, that her boyfriend is 20 years old and that her parents would "kill her" if they found out about him.

- Can Marlee's counselor keep her disclosure in confidence, or must she notify Marlee's parents?
- If Nancy breaches confidentiality, what are the risks to her relationship with Marlee?
- If Nancy breaches confidentiality, what are the risks to the group process, to the trust that other group members may have come to feel toward her, and to her reputation for trustworthiness among the student population in general?
- Are these risks greater than the risks posed by keeping Marlee's relationship with her boyfriend a secret from her parents?

After pondering your responses to these scenarios, you may not be surprised to learn that counselors encounter dilemmas of confidentiality more frequently than other types of ethical challenges and find them the most difficult to resolve (Hayman & Covert, 1986). Questions surrounding confidentiality can be very complex and often involve legal as well as ethical considerations.

A useful starting place may be to clarify the distinctions among three terms—*privacy, confidentiality,* and *privileged communication.* These terms are sometimes used interchangeably by counselors, but the concepts have important differences. Both confidentiality and privileged communication arise from our societal belief that individuals have a right to privacy. *Privacy* is the broadest of the three concepts and refers to the right of persons to decide what information about themselves will be shared with or withheld from others. Confidentiality and privileged communication both apply more specifically to the professional relationship between counselors and clients. *Confidentiality* is primarily an ethical concept that refers to the counselor's obligation to respect the client's privacy and to our promise to clients that the information they reveal during counseling will be protected from disclosure without their consent. *Privileged communication* is the narrowest of the three terms and is a legal concept. Privileged communication laws protect clients from having confidential communications with their counselors disclosed in a court of law without their permission (Shuman & Weiner, 1987). For a communication to be privileged, a statute must have been enacted that grants privilege to a category of professionals and to those whom they serve.

In this chapter, we first explore confidentiality as an ethical issue and then discuss privileged communication. Later, we look at the numerous exceptions that exist, both to confidentiality and to privilege.

CONFIDENTIALITY

Origins of Confidentiality

Helping professionals assume that an assurance of confidentiality is an indispensable requirement for effective therapy and that, without this assurance, many clients would not feel safe to discuss openly the intimate and personal aspects of their lives or would not seek counseling. Actual studies, however, show only mixed support for this assumption. Some studies have supported the belief that privacy assurances are essential (McGuire, Toal, & Blau, 1985; Merluzzi & Brischetto, 1983; Miller & Thelan, 1986), whereas other studies have indicated that such assurances have little effect on encouraging disclosures (Muehleman, Pickens, & Robinson, 1985; Shuman & Weiner, 1982; Schmid, Appelbaum, Roth, & Lidz, 1983), or that limits to confidentiality matter only to some clients in some circumstances (Taube & Elwork, 1990; VandeCreek, Miars, & Herzog, 1987). Despite this lack of unequivocal evidence, confidentiality has become such an internalized norm in the counseling profession that it is rarely questioned. A brief look at some of the historical origins of the profession may be helpful in understanding how this norm developed.

Counseling represents the fusion of many diverse influences. One of these influences was the emergence of the field of psychiatry in the treatment of mental illness. Almost until the beginning of the 19th century, mental illness was viewed as mystical and demonic. These early times are associated with images of "lunatics" in chains in asylums. It was not until the 1800s that significant strides were made in the understanding of mental illness, and not until the 1960s that the deinstitutionalization of the mentally ill brought these individuals back into contact with society. Another force that bears mentioning is the emergence of psychoanalysis in the early to middle years of the 20th century. Patients of Freudian analysts were expected to work through their socially unacceptable urges, sexual fantasies, and repressed feelings and thoughts, and to do so in a society that held Victorian social mores! Our early notions about mental illness, and our impressions about the nature of personal material discussed in analysis, helped to create a social stigma. In this climate, it is understandable that the patient's need for absolute privacy was assumed and that people would want to hide any information related to their having sought and received treatment.

It was not until the middle of the 20th century that other countervailing influences emerged in the mental health field. Carl Rogers' humanistic views, other theorists who emphasized the natural developmental life stages that all individuals pass through, and the career guidance movement all helped to shift our thinking away from counseling as a service only for the mentally ill or the sexually repressed. Concurrently, as we began to discover the biological bases for some mental disorders and to find medications that could alleviate conditions formerly thought to be untreatable, the stigmatization associated with mental illness and psychotherapy began to decrease. Nonetheless, even in today's society, a notion stubbornly persists that there is something shameful about seeking the services of a mental health professional. Note, for instance, the language used by the U.S. Supreme Court in its 1996 decision in *Jaffee v. Redmond et al.* (1996, p. 8), a case we describe later:

> Because of the sensitive nature of the problems for which individuals consult psychotherapists, disclosure of confidential communications made during counseling sessions may cause *embarrassment or disgrace*. [emphasis added]

The Rationale for Confidentiality

Whatever its origin, confidentiality is universally viewed today as being essential to the counseling relationship. Clients need to know that they can trust their counselors to respect their privacy, and the counselor's confidentiality pledge is the cornerstone on which this trust is built (Herlihy & Corey, 2006). Counselors believe that an effective counseling process depends on an atmosphere of confidence and trust, in which clients are able to tell their stories freely and honestly disclose their feelings, fears, thoughts, memories, and desires.

Confidentiality is a strong moral force that helps shape the manner in which counselors relate to their clients. Bok (1983) has suggested that confidentiality is based on four premises. The first two premises relate to respect for client rights in counseling. The principle of *respect for autonomy* means that counselors honor their clients' ability to be self-determining and to make their own choices. Applied to confidentiality, it also means that counselors honor the rights of clients to decide who knows what information about them and in what circumstances. The second premise is *respect* for human relationships and for the secrets that certain types of relationships entail. In the professional relationship, the intimate context in which these secrets are shared is seen as essential to counseling. The third premise has to do with the counselor's obligation that arises from autonomy and respect. Bok contends that an additional duty is created by a *pledge of silence,* which is the offer of confidentiality extended by the counselor to the client.

Counselors are bound to this pledge both in word and in deed; when they have given their word, they are obligated to actively work to protect clients' secrets from disclosure. The final basis for confidentiality is its *utility*. The rationale here is that confidentiality in counseling relationships is useful to society, because clients would be reluctant to seek help without an assurance of privacy. Society gives up its right to certain information and accepts the risks of not knowing about some problems and dangers in society in exchange for the benefit that is gained when its members improve their mental health. Stadler (1990a) has cogently summarized the essential meaning of these four premises for counselors:

> The duties to respect autonomy, respect relationships, keep a pledge of silence, and reinforce its utility are *each* of great importance in counseling. When they are combined in support of the principles of confidentiality, they develop a powerful moral claim on counselors' actions. I believe the power of that claim makes confidentiality a compelling duty for counselors, more compelling than each of the duties taken separately. (p. 104)

Respect for autonomy is only one of the moral principles on which confidentiality rests. Another is *fidelity,* which means being faithful and keeping promises. Certainly, one of the most important promises that counselors make to clients is that they will keep the secrets shared in counseling. One perspective on fidelity is that confidentiality is based on a covenant between counselor and client (Driscoll, 1992). In ancient sacred scriptures and myths, covenants were hallmarks of a special and intimate relationship among peoples or between peoples and their gods. In the modern world, covenants are created when one person offers another person a relationship and the offer is reciprocated. Because the basic dynamic of a covenant is trust, maintaining a covenantal relationship requires a pervasive fidelity. Any breach of confidentiality violates the bond of trust between counselor and client and breaks the covenant.

Today, confidentiality is an issue not only of counselor belief systems but also of consumer rights. An equally important basis for confidentiality is that clients in counseling are involved in a deeply personal relationship and have a right to expect that what they discuss will be kept private (Corey et al., 2007). Our culture has placed increasing emphasis on the rights of service recipients, and clients are more likely to hold an expectation that their privacy will be maintained by the professionals whose help they seek. This expectation of privacy has important legal as well as ethical implications, as you will discover later in the chapter.

Counselor Practices and Confidentiality

How well do practicing counselors deal with confidentiality issues? There is some evidence to suggest that counselors feel confident of their ability to make sound ethical judgments about confidentiality issues. Gibson and Pope (1993) surveyed a large national sample of counselors regarding their beliefs about a wide range of ethical behaviors. They asked respondents to rate each behavior as ethical or unethical and then to indicate on a scale of 0 (no confidence) to 10 (highest confidence) how certain they were in making these judgments. Twenty-nine percent of the items for which the confidence rating was very high (at least 9.0) concerned confidentiality.

Counselors' confidence in their ethical judgments may be well founded. Complaints made against helping professionals for violations of confidentiality are not as common as one might expect. Various studies have shown that only 1% to 5% of complaints made to the ethics committees and state licensing boards of counselors and psychologists involve violations of confidentiality (Garcia, Glosoff, & Smith, 1994; Garcia, Salo, & Hamilton, 1995; Neukrug, Healy, & Herlihy, 1992; Pope & Vetter, 1992; Pope & Vasquez, 1998). It appears that mental health professionals take seriously their pledge to maintain their clients' confidentiality and are diligent in honoring it. Grabois (1997/1998) has reported that there are few cases in which mental health professionals have been sued for breaching confidentiality. On the other hand, she has suggested that the numbers of such cases will increase in the future because more people are seeking counseling in today's society.

Counselors should not become complacent about their confidentiality practices, because statistics regarding formal complaints may not accurately reflect the actual frequency of breaches of confidentiality. According to one study, 61.9% of psychologists reported that they had *unintentionally* violated their clients' confidentiality (Pope, Tabachnick, & Keith-Spiegel, 1987b). Clients may not have been aware of these unintentional breaches. Although it may be startling to think that the majority of practitioners may have violated their clients' confidentiality, it is somewhat understandable when we pause to consider the myriad ways that an inadvertent or careless breach could occur. A few examples illustrate this point:

New technologies present many challenges to counselors. Most counselors make some use of computers in their work and those who are not computer savvy might be unaware of the special precautions needed to keep any information stored on computers secure. Breaux (2006), in the ACA *Ethical Standards Casebook,* presents an interesting (and frightening) case study involving a counselor intern on a college campus who inadvertently allowed her roommate to gain access to the records of one of her clients at the university counseling center. The client learned that her confidentiality had been compromised and was very upset. This situation caused some serious problems for the client, the intern and her supervisor, and the counseling center director.

On a related note, counselors routinely use other modern communications devices. It is important to remember that faxes, e-mail, and cellular phones are not secure means of communication and that confidential information should not be exchanged using these systems. Answering machines present another set of pitfalls. Counselors must not play back accumulated messages within earshot of others, and if the answering machine is at home, special measures need to be taken to ensure that family members and friends do not retrieve or overhear messages from or about clients.

Counselors do not always have the luxury of having a separate entrance and exit for their clients to use. When clients who are leaving their sessions must pass through a waiting area, counselors need to take special precautions to guard their clients' privacy. We know one very conscientious counselor in private practice who routinely left 15-minute intervals between the end of one scheduled appointment and the beginning of the next, and who avoided scheduling consecutively any clients from the same part of town. Nevertheless, one day she ran late with a client, who exited into the waiting room and ran into a friend from church. Both clients appeared uncomfortable to have encountered each other in this way.

Counselors are encouraged to consult with each other regarding clients who present challenges to them, and most consultations can be managed without revealing a client's identity. However, it is important not to obtain a colleague's advice while walking through the halls of an agency or institution, at a restaurant over lunch, or in another public place. Pope and Vasquez (1998) related the story of a counselor who was consulting a colleague about a particularly "difficult" client while they were on a crowded elevator. The counselor did not mention the client's name but gave enough detail that the client, who happened to be standing only a few feet behind them in the elevator, was able to ascertain that he was the subject of the discussion and to listen with intense interest and dismay.

Clearly, it is easy for even seasoned practitioners to violate a client's privacy unintentionally. Students in counselor training programs must also take special care to maintain client confidentiality. Although it may be tempting to share with family, friends, or fellow students your excitement about what you are learning in a practicum, a practice session with a peer "client," or an experiential group, it is important to keep in mind that the ethical obligations of students are the same as those of practicing counselors (Standard F.8.a.). Your conversations must not reveal any information that could conceivably allow listeners to ascertain the identity of a client. Case notes, test protocols and interpretations, audiotapes, and videotapes of work with clients must not be left in places where they might be seen by anyone other than authorized supervisors or professors. It is a good idea to get into the habit of zealously safeguarding client confidentiality from the very beginning of your graduate studies.

Ethical Standards and Confidentiality

Confidentiality is the only specific ethical issue to which an entire section of the ACA *Code of Ethics* (2005) is devoted (see Appendix A). *Section B: Confidentiality, Privileged Communication, and Privacy* emphasizes the client's right to privacy in the counseling relationship. Exceptions and limitations to confidentiality are addressed and, because exceptions to confidentiality may be mandated by legal as well as ethical considerations, the standards are carefully written to minimize conflicts between law and ethics. This section addresses special circumstances in counseling minors, families, and groups, and offers guidelines for maintaining confidentiality when consulting or conducting research.

The Introduction to Standard B is general and states that "Counselors recognize that trust is a cornerstone of the counseling relationship." An early standard in this section states that "Counselors respect their clients' right to privacy" (Standard B.1.b.). Sometimes counselors, in their zeal to protect a client's privacy, mistakenly believe that they should maintain a client's confidentiality even when the client asks them to share information with others (Herlihy & Corey, 2006). When clients request that information be disclosed, counselors should honor these requests. If the counselor believes that releasing the information might be detrimental to the client's best interests, these concerns should be discussed with the client, but the ultimate decision belongs to the client. In many instances, client requests for disclosure are not particularly problematic for counselors, such as when clients move and later request that their records be sent to their new counselor. Other situations may cause counselors some discomfort, such as when clients ask to see their own records. It is important to realize that records are kept for the benefit of clients and that counselors are obligated to provide clients with access to their records, unless the records contain information that may be misleading or harmful to the client (Standard B.6.d.). The Health Insurance Portability and Accountability Act (HIPAA), a federal statute which is discussed at length in chapter 3, requires that clients be given access to their counseling records.

One of the reasons that confidentiality is such a difficult ethical issue is that *confidentiality is not absolute*. Although counselors should make every effort to avoid inadvertent breaches, there are other times when confidentiality *must* be breached. Counselors must inform clients at the outset that there are limitations to their confidentiality. It is important to discuss thoroughly these limitations and to identify foreseeable situations in which confidentiality must be breached (Standard B.1.d.). Prospective clients may not be aware at the time they seek your services that confidentiality is not absolute. In one survey of the general public, 69% of respondents believed that everything discussed with a professional therapist would be held strictly confidential, and 74% thought that there should be no exceptions to maintaining confidential disclosures (Miller & Thelan, 1986). Counselors may be hesitant to explain the exceptions to confidentiality to new or prospective clients, for fear that clients will feel constrained in discussing their problems. However, some researchers have found very little evidence that explaining in detail the limits of confidentiality actually inhibits client disclosures. Others have concluded that the advantages of informing clients about limits outweigh any disadvantages in terms of inhibited disclosure (Baird & Rupert, 1987; Muehleman et al., 1985).

There are numerous exceptions to confidentiality. We have identified at least 15 types of situations in which compromising a client's confidentiality might be permissible or required. Because most of these exceptions to confidentiality have both a legal and an ethical basis, we will explore them in more detail after we have discussed the legal counterpart to confidentiality—privileged communication.

PRIVILEGED COMMUNICATION

At the beginning of the chapter, we note that privacy is a broad concept that provides the underpinnings for both confidentiality and privileged communication. The right to privacy is guaranteed to all citizens by the Fourth Amendment to the U.S. Constitution, which prohibits government searches without warrants. This privacy right is not absolute, however. When the interests of society outweigh the individual's right to privacy, the privacy right is compromised in the interest of preserving a stable societal structure. The U.S. Supreme Court has never addressed the question of whether the Fourth Amendment supports the concept that some relationships are privileged because of this constitutional right to privacy. State and lower federal courts have been mixed in their results on the issue (Knapp & VandeCreek, 1987).

Basically, privileged communication means that a judge cannot order information that has been recognized by law as privileged to be revealed in court. The concept of withholding any relevant evidence is antagonistic to the entire system of justice in our country, because legal procedures demand that all evidence relevant to a case be presented to a judge or jury. The legal system also demands that the opposing side in a court case have access to the evidence before the trial takes place, through a process called *discovery*. As a counselor, you will surely want to guarantee that the information clients give you will be kept confidential. The idea that information and secrets revealed in a counseling session might someday be disclosed in court is very unsettling for counselors. However, the idea that a judge or jury might have to decide the outcome of a court case without the benefit of essential privileged information is very unsettling to judges.

A good question to ask, then, is, "Why did the idea of privileged communication emerge in our legal system in the first place?" According to Slovenko (1966), "A trial is only as good as the evidence presented to the court." Despite the strong belief that all evidence should be available to the judge or jury who will decide the outcome of a case, federal and state legislators have realized that the requirement to make available all evidence compromises many important interactions in our society. These legislators have been convinced that, without a guarantee of absolute privacy for conversations between citizens and certain professionals, it would be impossible for the professionals to provide necessary assistance to those who seek their help. As a result, legislators have passed statutes that specifically exempt certain conversations between citizens and professionals from the general rule in law that all relevant evidence will be presented in a court case. These laws are called privileged communication statutes.

Origins of Privileged Communication

According to Shuman and Weiner (1987), the first reference to courts recognizing a legal privilege between professionals and the citizens they served was in early Roman law. This privilege was based on the duty of servants (attorneys) to their masters (clients), rather than on the modern principle of a right to privacy.

Under the English common law, the foundation on which the legal system in the United States is based, there was no need for privileged communication. In early England, truth during trials was determined by various modes including "trial by oath or oath helpers, trial by ordeal, trial by battle, and trial by witnesses" (Shuman & Weiner, 1987, p. 50). Even when witnesses were used in trials, they were the jurors themselves who relied on information they had gathered as members of the community. Individuals who were not jurors who volunteered information were viewed as meddlers and could be sued for interfering with the legal process.

About 1450, English equity courts began recognizing subpoenas for nonparty witnesses, and started using them in law courts in 1562 (Wigmore, 1961). Yet, few communications were privileged under the English common law. Other than government secrets, the common law recognized as privileged only attorney–client and husband–wife relationships (Knapp & VandeCreek, 1987).

Once the English legal system allowed compelling witnesses to testify at trials, a question arose as to whether certain information obtained by professionals should be excluded from testimony for one reason or another. Wigmore (1961), the leading authority on evidence, described four requirements for a relationship to be privileged under the law:

1. The communications must originate in a *confidence* that they will not be disclosed.
2. This element of *confidentiality must be essential* to the full and satisfactory maintenance of the relation between the parties.
3. The *relationship* must be one that, in the opinion of the community, ought to be sedulously *fostered*.
4. The *injury* to the relationship that disclosure of the communications would cause must be *greater than the benefit* gained for the correct disposal of the litigation.

State and federal legislatures have used these requirements as criteria in considering whether to grant privilege to relationships between citizens and various categories of professionals. The question of which professional relationships meet these criteria and, therefore, should be accorded privilege has been a source of controversy that continues to this day. Some legal scholars have criticized all statutes that have been passed by legislatures granting privilege to relationships with professionals (Chafee, 1943; Cleary, 1984; Curd, 1938; Morgan, 1943; Wigmore, 1961). The attorney–client relationship was the first professional relationship to be recognized under the English common law, during the reign of Queen Elizabeth I. The first recorded case that recognized the attorney–client privilege was decided in 1577 (Wigmore). Currently in the United States, the attorney–client privilege is universally recognized (Rice, 1993).

Physicians, on the other hand, have been less successful at obtaining legal privilege with their patients. According to Shuman and Weiner (1987), most legal scholars agree that the concept of a physician–patient privilege fails Wigmore's test. Every jurisdiction in the United States, except South Carolina and West Virginia, now has privileged communication statutes for physician–patient interactions (Shuman & Weiner, 1987). However, many of the statutes include a multitude of exceptions, including criminal cases, worker's compensation proceedings, will contests, cases where the condition for which treatment or diagnosis was sought is raised by the patient to support a claim or defense, or cases in which the parent–child relationship is at issue.

According to Knapp and VandeCreek (1987), the clergy–communicant privilege is unique because it has its roots in the common law, but is now protected by statute. Every state except West Virginia now has a clergy–communicant privilege statute (Gumper, 1984). These statutes were passed to ensure that confessions by penitents to priests would be absolutely confidential. The clergy, in persuading legislators to pass such statutes, stressed that there was a substantial societal benefit in ensuring citizens that their confessions would never be repeated by priests or by members of the clergy outside the confessional. The clergy argued that unless citizens were absolutely convinced that their confessions would remain confidential, they would not confess their sins and this could cause serious disruption to the framework of society. They asserted that the need for privacy in the confessional far outweighed the need for all evidence to be presented in a trial. The notion of extending the clergy–communicant privilege to include counseling has been criticized by Knapp and VandeCreek. They argue that the privilege for recipients of mental health services should apply only when citizens have relationships with professionals with specialized training in counseling or psychotherapy, and that only a few specially trained pastoral counselors have such qualifications.

Once citizens had been granted privileged communication with attorneys, physicians, and clergy, a variety of other professionals, including mental health professionals, began arguing successfully for privileged communication statutes for the benefit of their clients. Remember, though, that any exception to the general rule that all evidence will be presented in court is compromised by privileged communications statutes. Each time such a statute is passed, the legislators have to be convinced that making an exception to the rule is vital to the well-being of society, and that an individual citizen's need for privacy outweighs the need for evidence in court cases.

The earlier scholars who argued for a mental health professional–client privilege (Cottle, 1956; Fisher, 1964; Guttmacher & Weihofen, 1952; Heller, 1957; Slovenko, 1960; Slovenko & Usdin, 1961) did not base their arguments on the physician–patient privilege. Instead, they contended that citizens who sought the services of mental health professionals required more privacy than patients needed with physicians (Knapp & VandeCreek, 1987). Because of physicians' status in our society, you might think that physician–patient privilege could be considered more important than mental health professional–client privilege. However, some legal scholars (Guttmacher & Weihofen, 1952; Louisell & Sinclair, 1971; Slovenko, 1960; Wigmore, 1961) have concluded that it is more important to protect the privacy of clients of mental health professionals than it is to protect the privacy of physicians' patients because of the unique nature of the psychotherapeutic relationship.

Prior to World War II, no state had a privileged communication statute for mental health professionals, although some psychiatrists were covered under physician–patient privilege statutes (Knapp & VandeCreek, 1987). State legislative bodies meet annually, changing statutes each time they meet, and sections affecting privileged communication statutes might be found in obscure places in state statute volumes. Therefore, it is impossible to give a completely accurate picture of privileged communication statutes for counselors and other mental health professionals. However, it is true that all 50 states and the District of Columbia have enacted some type of privileged communication statute for mental health professionals and their clients (*Jaffee v. Redmond,* 1996).

Statutes making relationships between mental health professionals and their clients privileged vary substantially from state to state in their language and construction. States have taken four approaches in formulating privilege laws for relationships between clients and their mental health providers (Knapp & VandeCreek, 1987). Some privilege statutes are modeled on attorney–client privilege laws. Others take the approach of the proposed, but rejected, Rule 504 of the Federal Rules of Evidence. This rule has advantages over the attorney–client privilege laws because the proposed rules specified the extent and limitations of the privilege with great precision. A third approach provides for a privilege, but allows judicial discretion in its waiver. Finally, the last group of statutes is idiosyncratic and does not follow any special pattern.

The Rationale for Privileged Communication in Counseling Relationships

Over the past few decades, counselors have been working to convince state legislators to enact privileged communication laws that protect their relationships with clients. Many of the arguments used to justify passage of these statutes were accepted and repeated by the U.S. Supreme Court (Remley, Herlihy, & Herlihy, 1997) when *Jaffee v. Redmond* (1996) was decided in favor of the existence of such a privilege under the Federal Rules of Evidence.

Counselors have argued that society benefits when individuals seek counseling to help them lead more productive lives as citizens. Mental health professionals have argued that because clients must reveal personal secrets that could be embarrassing, sensitive, or against their best interests, clients must be assured that the content of their counseling sessions will not be revealed without their permission. Society benefits when clients receive counseling that allows them to be more independent and productive, and these benefits outweigh the negative consequences of some evidence being privileged and therefore unavailable in court cases.

However, after an extensive review and analysis of empirical research studies related to confidentiality and privileged communication in the mental health professions, Shuman and Weiner (1987) concluded that although confidentiality is important in therapeutic relationships, privilege is not. Among their more interesting findings were (a) few lay persons know whether privilege exists in their states, (b) many mental health professionals indicate that clients are reassured by their disclosure or threat of disclosure of potential harm to self or others, and (c) judges do not find privilege a great impediment to finding the truth at trials. The first two findings argue against privileged communication statutes that protect relationships with mental health professionals, whereas the last one would seem to support the existence of such statutes.

Another argument used to get counselor privileged communication statutes passed is that the evidence lost to courts because of privilege statutes would never have been produced in the first place if the statutes did not exist. Clients would not go to counselors and reveal their secrets if they did not have the protection of legal privilege. As a result, society does not lose important evidence in lawsuits by granting privilege to counselor–client relationships because the evidence would never have come into existence if there were no privilege.

Psychiatrists, psychologists, and social workers have been successful in their efforts to have statutes enacted that grant privileged communication to their relationships with clients. Counselors have argued that their services are similar to those of other mental health professionals, and that they are as deserving of the protection.

Counselor–client privilege of some type existed in 44 of the 45 states that licensed counselors in 2000 (Glosoff, Herlihy, & Spence, 2000). Psychologist–client privilege statutes existed in all 50 states (Glosoff, Herlihy, Herlihy, & Spence, 1997). Privileged communication statutes vary, ranging from some that protect counselor–client relationships to the fullest extent allowed by law to others that are quite weak. (See Figure 2-1 for three examples of state privileged communication statutes.) Professional counselors in jurisdictions where there are no counselor–client privileged communication statutes, or where existing ones are weak, are continuing in their efforts to get such laws passed or strengthened.

Privileged communication statutes are not always limited to interactions between clients and licensed professional counselors. In some states, school counselors, substance abuse counselors, or other designated categories of counselors have privilege. You must investigate the statutes of the state in which you practice to determine whether your interactions with clients enjoy privilege.

If you practice in a state that does not offer statutory privilege, you should inform your clients that you will keep confidential the content of your counseling sessions with them, but that one of the exceptions would be if a judge orders you to disclose information. You must include the same exception even if you practice in a state that does include a counselor–client privileged communication statute, but it is much less likely that a judge will order disclosure in a state with such a statute.

Florida

Fla. Stat. § 90.503 (2003)

§ 90. 503. Psychotherapist-patient **privilege**

(1) For purposes of this section:

(a) A "psychotherapist" is:

1. A person authorized to practice medicine in any state or nation, or reasonably believed by the patient so to be, who is engaged in the diagnosis or treatment of a mental or emotional condition, including alcoholism and other drug addiction;

2. A person licensed or certified as a psychologist under the laws of any state or nation, who is engaged primarily in the diagnosis or treatment of a mental or emotional condition, including alcoholism and other drug addiction;

3. A person licensed or certified as a clinical social worker, marriage and family therapist, or **mental health counselor** under the laws of this state, who is engaged primarily in the diagnosis or treatment of a mental or emotional condition, including alcoholism and other drug addiction; or

4. Treatment personnel of facilities licensed by the state pursuant to chapter 394, chapter 395, or chapter 397, of facilities designated by the Department of Children and Family Services pursuant to chapter 394 as treatment facilities, or of facilities defined as community mental health centers pursuant to s. 394.907(1), who are engaged primarily in the diagnosis or treatment of a mental or emotional condition, including alcoholism and other drug addiction.

(b) A "patient" is a person who consults, or is interviewed by, a psychotherapist for purposes of diagnosis or treatment of a mental or emotional condition, including alcoholism and other drug addiction.

(c) A communication between psychotherapist and patient is "confidential" if it is not intended to be disclosed to third persons other than:

1. Those persons present to further the interest of the patient in the consultation, examination, or interview.

2. Those persons necessary for the transmission of the communication.

3. Those persons who are participating in the diagnosis and treatment under the direction of the psychotherapist.

(2) A patient has a **privilege** to refuse to disclose, and to prevent any other person from disclosing, confidential communications or records made for the purpose of diagnosis or treatment of the patient's mental or emotional condition, including alcoholism and other drug addiction, between the patient and the psychotherapist, or persons who are participating in the diagnosis or treatment under the direction of the psychotherapist. This **privilege** includes any diagnosis made, and advice given, by the psychotherapist in the course of that relationship.

Figure 2-1   Examples of counselor–client privileged communication state statutes

(3) The **privilege** may be claimed by:

    (a) The patient or the patient's attorney on the patient's behalf.

    (b) A guardian or conservator of the patient.

    (c) The personal representative of a deceased patient.

    (d) The psychotherapist, but only on behalf of the patient. The authority of a psychotherapist to claim the **privilege** is presumed in the absence of evidence to the contrary.

(4) There is no **privilege** under this section:

    (a) For communications relevant to an issue in proceedings to compel hospitalization of a patient for mental illness, if the psychotherapist in the course of diagnosis or treatment has reasonable cause to believe the patient is in need of hospitalization.

    (b) For communications made in the course of a court-ordered examination of the mental or emotional condition of the patient.

    (c) For communications relevant to an issue of the mental or emotional condition of the patient in any proceeding in which the patient relies upon the condition as an element of his or her claim or defense or, after the patient's death, in any proceeding in which any party relies upon the condition as an element of the party's claim or defense.

Idaho

STATE RULES

IDAHO RULES OF EVIDENCE

ARTICLE V. **PRIVILEGES**

I.R.E. Art. V 517 (2003)

Review Court Orders which may amend this Rule

Rule 517. Licensed counselor-client **privilege.**

(a) Definitions. As used in this rule:

    (1) Client. A "client" is a person who is rendered licensed counselor services.

    (2) Licensed counselor. A "licensed counselor" is any person licensed to be a licensed **professional counselor** or a licensed counselor in the State of Idaho pursuant to Title 54, Chapter 34, Idaho Code, or reasonably believed by the client so to be.

    (3) Confidential communication. A communication is "confidential" if not intended to be disclosed to third persons except persons present to further the interest of the client in the consultation, examination, or interview, or persons reasonably necessary for the transmission of the communication, or persons who are participating in the rendition of counseling services to the client under the direction of the licensed counselor, including members of the client's family.

Figure 2-1 *(Continued)*

(b) General rule of privilege. A client has a privilege in any civil or criminal action to which the client is a party to refuse to disclose and to prevent any other person from disclosing confidential communications made in the furtherance of the rendition of licensed counseling services to the client, among the client, the client's licensed counselor, and persons who are participating in the licensed counseling under the direction of the licensed counselor including members of the client's family.

(c) Who may claim the **privilege. The privilege** may be claimed by the client, or for the client through the client's licensed counselor, lawyer, guardian or conservator, or the personal representative of a deceased client. The authority of the licensed counselor, lawyer, guardian, conservator or personal representative to do so is presumed in the absence of evidence to the contrary.

(d) Exceptions. There is no **privilege** under this rule:

(1) Civil action. In a civil action, case or proceeding by one of the parties to the confidential communication against the other.

(2) Proceedings for guardianship, conservatorship or hospitalization. As to a communication relevant to an issue in proceedings for the appointment of a guardian or conservator for a client for mental illness or to hospitalize the client for mental illness.

(3) Child-related communications. In a criminal or civil action or proceeding as to a communication relevant to an issue concerning the physical, mental or emotional condition, of or injury to a child, or concerning the welfare of a child including, but not limited to the abuse, abandonment or neglect of a child.

(4) Licensing board proceedings. In an action, case or proceeding under Idaho Code § 54-3404.

(5) Contemplation of crime or harmful act. If the communication reveals the contemplation of a crime or harmful act.

Maine

TITLE 32. PROFESSIONS AND OCCUPATIONS

CHAPTER 119. COUNSELING PROFESSIONALS

32 M.R.S. § 13862 (2003)

§ 13862. **Privileged communication**

Except at the request or consent of the client, no person licensed under this chapter may be required to testify in any civil or criminal action, suit or proceeding at law or in equity respecting any information that the person licensed or registered may have acquired in providing counseling services or marriage and family therapy services to the client in a professional and contractual capacity if that information was necessary to enable the licensee to furnish professional counseling services to the client. When the physical or mental condition of the client

Figure 2-1   *(Continued)*

is an issue in that action, suit or proceeding or when a court in the exercise of sound discretion determines the disclosure necessary to the proper administration of justice, information communicated to or otherwise learned by that licensed or registered person in connection with the provision of counseling or marriage and family therapy services may not be privileged and disclosure may be required.

Nothing in this section may prohibit disclosure by a person licensed under this chapter of information concerning a client when that disclosure is required by law and nothing in this section may modify or affect Title 22, sections 3477 to 3479-A and 4011-A to 4015.

This section may not be construed to prevent a 3rd-party reimburser from inspecting and copying, in the ordinary course of determining eligibility for or entitlement to benefits, any and all records relating to the diagnosis, treatment or other services provided to any persons, including a minor or incompetent, for which coverage, benefit or reimbursement is claimed as long as the policy or certificate under which the claim is made provides that access to those records is permitted. This section may not be construed to prevent access to any records pursuant to any peer review or utilization review procedures applied and implemented in good faith.

34-B M.R.S. § 1207 (2003)

§ 1207. Confidentiality of information

1. GENERALLY. All orders of commitment, medical and administrative records, applications and reports, and facts contained in them, pertaining to any client shall be kept confidential and may not be disclosed by any person, except that:

A. A client, his legal guardian, if any, or, if he is a minor, his parent or legal guardian may give his informed written consent to the disclosure of information;

B. Information may be disclosed if necessary to carry out any of the statutory functions of the department, the hospitalization provisions of chapter 3, subchapter IV, the purposes of sections 3607 and 3608, the purposes of Title 22, section 3554, the purposes of United States Public Law 99-319, dealing with the investigatory function of the independent agency designated with advocacy and investigatory functions under United States Public Law 88-164, Title I, Part C or United States Public Law 99-319, or the purposes of Title 18-A, section 5-601, subsection (b), when the Department of Human Services is requested by the Department of Behavioral and Developmental Services to act as public guardian or public conservator;

B-1. Information must be disclosed to the Department of Human Services for the purpose of cooperating in an investigation or any other activity pursuant to Title 15, chapter 507, or Title 22, chapter 1071, pursuant to an agreement between the department and the Department of Human Services. The agreement, specifying the circumstances and conditions by which disclosure must be made, must be promulgated as rules by the department in accordance with the Maine Administrative Procedure Act, Title 5, chapter 375;

Figure 2-1   *(Continued)*

B-2. Information consisting of data relating to involuntarily committed patients whose care is authorized by the department must be disclosed by admitting hospitals to the Maine Health Care Finance Commission for the purpose of complying with the hospitals' obligations under Title 22, section 395;

C. Information may be disclosed if ordered by a court of record, subject to any limitation in the Maine Rules of Evidence, Rule 503;

C-1. Within 48 hours of a death reportable by the commissioner to the Chief Medical Examiner pursuant to Title 22, section 3025, subsection 1, paragraph E, the commissioner shall provide information on that death to the chairs of the joint standing committee of the Legislature having jurisdiction over health and human services matters. Within 30 days of the reportable death, the commissioner shall provide the members of the committee with a copy of the death report. Information and reports provided pursuant to this paragraph must maintain the confidentiality of the identity of all persons mentioned or referred to in the information and reports.

D. Nothing in this subsection precludes disclosure, upon proper inquiry, of information relating to the physical condition or mental status of a client to his spouse or next of kin;

E. Nothing in this subsection precludes the disclosure of biographical or medical information concerning a client to commercial or governmental insurers, or to any other corporation, association or agency from which the department or a licensee of the department may receive reimbursement for the care and treatment, education, training or support of the client, if the recipient of the information uses it for no other purpose than to determine eligibility for reimbursement and, if eligibility exists, to make reimbursement;

F. Nothing in this subsection precludes the disclosure or use of any information, including recorded or transcribed diagnostic and therapeutic interviews, concerning any client in connection with any educational or training program established between a public hospital and any college, university, hospital, psychiatric or counseling clinic or school of nursing, provided that, in the disclosure or use of the information as part of a course of instruction or training program, the client's identity remains undisclosed; and

G. Information shall be disclosed to the executive director and the members of the subcommittees on institutes and quality assurance of the Maine Commission on Mental Health for the purpose of carrying out the commission's statutory duties.

2. STATISTICAL COMPILATIONS AND RESEARCH. Confidentiality of records used for statistical compilations or research is governed as follows.

A. Persons engaged in statistical compilation or research may have access to treatment records of clients when needed for research, if:

1) The access is approved by the chief administrative officer of the mental health facility or his designee;

Figure 2-1   *(Continued)*

2) The research plan is first submitted to and approved by the chief administrative officer of the mental health facility, or his designee, where the person engaged in research or statistical compilation is to have access to communications and records; and

3) The records are not removed from the mental health facility which prepared them, except that data which do not identify clients or coded data may be removed from a mental health facility if the key to the code remains on the premises of the facility.

B. The chief administrative officer of the mental health facility and the person doing the research shall preserve the anonymity of the client and may not disseminate data which refer to the client by name, number or combination of characteristics which together could lead to his identification.

3. USE BY THE COMMISSIONER. Confidentiality of information and records used by the commissioner for administration, planning or research is governed as follows.

A. Any facility licensed by the department under section 3606 or a facility which receives funds from the department or has received or is receiving funds under the Mental Retardation Facilities and Community Mental Health Centers Construction Act of 1963, Public Law 88-164, United States Code, Title 42, Section 6001, et seq., as amended, shall send information and records to the commissioner, if requested by the commissioner pursuant to his obligation to maintain the overall responsibility for the care and treatment of the mentally ill.

B. The commissioner may collect and use the information and records for administration, planning or research, under the following conditions.

1) The use of the information is subject to subsection 1, paragraph C.

2) Data identifying particular clients by means other than case number or code shall be removed from all records and reports of information before issuance from the mental health facility which prepared the records and reports.

3) A code shall be the exclusive means of identifying clients and shall be available to the commissioner and only the commissioner.

4) The key to the code shall remain in the possession of the issuing facility and shall be available to the commissioner and only the commissioner.

5) Members of the department may not release or disseminate to any other person, agency or department of government any information which refers to a client by name, numbers, address, birth date or other characteristics or combination of characteristics which could lead to the client's identification, except as otherwise required by law.

4. PROHIBITED ACTS. Prohibited acts under this section are governed as follows.

A. A person is guilty of unlawful disclosure of information if he disseminates, releases or discloses information in violation of this section.

B. Unlawful disclosure of information is a Class D crime.

Figure 2-1   *(Continued)*

5. PERMITTED DISCLOSURE. Notwithstanding subsections 1 to 4, a licensed mental health professional providing care and treatment to an adult client may provide information authorized by this subsection to a family member or other person if the family member or other person lives with or provides direct care to the client, if without the disclosure there would be significant deterioration in the client's daily functioning and if the disclosure is in the best interest of the client.

A. Disclosure may be made only at the written request of the family member or other person living with the client.

B. Prior to the disclosure, the client must be informed in writing of the request, the name of the person requesting the information, the reason for the request and the specific information being provided. Information may not be disclosed unless the client, having received written notice of the request, consents to the disclosure. If the client does not consent to the disclosure, the person requesting the information may appeal to the department for authorization to disclose the information over the objections of the client.

C. Disclosures are limited to information regarding diagnosis, admission to or discharge from a treatment facility, the name of any medication prescribed, side effects of that medication, the likely consequences of failure of the client to take the prescribed medication, treatment plans and goals and behavioral management strategies.

D. By September 1,1994, the department shall adopt rules to implement this subsection. The rules must include, but are not limited to, an appeal process for persons who are denied access to information under paragraph B. The appeal process must determine whether the person requesting information is a person who lives with or provides direct care to a client, whether disclosure of the information is in the best interest of the client and whether denial of access to the information will result in significant deterioration in the client's daily functioning. The commissioner shall appoint an advisory committee pursuant to Title 5, section 12002, subsection 1, paragraph A to assist the department in the development of the rules. The members of the advisory committee are not entitled to reimbursement for expenses or legislative per diem. The advisory committee must include, but is not limited to, proportionate representation from each of the following:

1) Consumers nominated by the Director of the Office of Advocacy and Consumer Affairs;

2) Members of the statewide alliance for the mentally ill;

3) Mental health service providers; and

4) The protection and advocacy agency designated pursuant to Title 5, section 19502.

Figure 2-1   *(Continued)*

6. DUTY TO PROVIDE INFORMATION. Any person conducting an evaluation of a mental health client in a professional capacity, who has a clear and substantial reason to believe that the mental health client poses an imminent danger of inflicting serious physical harm on the evaluator or others, shall provide information regarding such danger or harm to any other person to whom that client's care or custody is being transferred. For purposes of this subsection, the term "evaluation" includes professionally recognized methods and procedures for the purpose of assessing and treating mental illness and includes, but is not limited to, interviews, observation, testing and assessment techniques conducted by a person licensed as a physician, psychologist, nurse, clinical social worker or clinical **professional counselor.**

Figure 2-1   *(Continued)*

Occasionally, counselors will be involved in court cases heard in federal rather than state courts. The U.S. Supreme Court ruling, *Jaffee v. Redmond et al.* (1996), has interpreted the Federal Rules of Evidence to mean that there is a licensed psychotherapist–patient privilege in some cases heard in federal courts (Remley et al., 1997). In the Jaffee case, the psychotherapist was a social worker. It seems probable, but not guaranteed, that a similar privilege would be acknowledged for licensed counselor–client relationships in future cases.

Counselors struggle with deciding the exact language to use when writing disclosure statements for clients or when informing clients orally regarding the confidentiality and privilege that might exist in the relationship. On one hand, counselors want to fully inform clients of the exceptions that exist to confidentiality and privilege, so that clients will be able to give truly informed consent to entering the counseling relationship (see chap. 1 under Informed Consent). On the other hand, counselors do not want to be so technical and detailed in describing exceptions to confidentiality and privilege that clients become confused or lose confidence in the privacy of the counseling relationship. Suggested disclosure statements regarding confidentiality and privilege are included in Appendix E.

Asserting the Privilege

A statutory privilege belongs to clients rather than to counselors. If you or your records are subpoenaed or if you are asked during a legal proceeding to disclose privileged information, it is up to your client to assert the privilege so that you will not have to disclose the information. However, sometimes the client cannot be located or is not present when counselors are asked to disclose privileged information. In these circumstances, the counselor has an obligation to assert the privilege on behalf of the client. In our opinion, counselors should secure the advice of an attorney if they are put in the position of asserting a client's privilege, because legal procedures and questions regarding privilege are quite technical.

Responding to Subpoenas

Subpoenas are legal documents that might require counselors to give a written response to a written list of questions, produce copies of records; appear for a deposition, court hearing, or trial; or appear and bring their records with them. Subpoenas are official court documents and cannot be ignored. Counselors who do not respond appropriately to subpoenas can be held in contempt of court and could be fined or jailed until they comply. Unless you deal with subpoenas on a regular basis in your work, legal advice should be obtained before responding to a subpoena.

An attorney will review a subpoena for you and will advise you in how to respond. You should inform the attorney advising you whether you believe there is a privileged communication statute that might protect the counseling relationship or records. In addition, you should tell the attorney whether you think it would violate the client's privacy for you to reveal information regarding the counseling relationship.

Attorneys might assist you in a number of ways. For example, they could ask the attorney who issued the subpoena to withdraw it, file a motion to quash the subpoena, or advise you to comply with the subpoena. After you have done your best to explain to your attorney your reasons for not wanting to comply with a subpoena, you should follow the attorney's advice. In the event you violate some legal rights of your client by complying with a subpoena, and the client wants to hold you accountable, you can in turn hold your attorney accountable for giving you inaccurate or inappropriate legal advice.

If you must appear at a deposition, hearing, or trial as a result of a subpoena, you should ask your attorney to prepare you for what to expect and advise you about how you should conduct yourself. If possible, the attorney should go with you so you could be given advice throughout the proceeding. It is especially important that you have your own legal advisor with you when you attend depositions, because a judge will not be present.

Suits for Disclosure

When counseling relationships are privileged under state or federal laws, clients have a right to expect counselors to keep information from their sessions private. With or without the privilege, counselors have a legal duty to maintain the privacy of their clients. Clients enter the counseling relationship with assurances of privacy and with very high expectations that information they disclose will not be revealed.

If a counselor discloses confidential information and the disclosure does not qualify as one of the exceptions to confidentiality and privilege, a client could sue the counselor for malpractice. The client would be required to prove the elements of a malpractice suit that are explained in chapter 4. Clients who could show that they were harmed by the counselor's disclosure might prevail in such lawsuits and collect damages from the counselor. Thus, it is crucial that you understand the exceptions to confidentiality and privileged communication and know how to apply these exceptions in your practice.

EXCEPTIONS TO CONFIDENTIALITY AND PRIVILEGED COMMUNICATION

The general rule that counselors must keep their clients' disclosures confidential is easy to understand and follow. Exceptions to this general rule, however, occur frequently in the course of counseling, and counselors must understand these exceptions and be able to apply them to real situations (Standard B.1.d.). Glosoff et al. (2000), after reviewing counselor privileged communication statutes in all states, concluded that exceptions are numerous and extremely varied. As a result, it is very important for counselors to know the content of the privileged communication statute that exists in their state (if there is one) and the specific exceptions that are included. Glosoff et al. categorized exceptions into nine areas and listed those areas from the most to the least frequently cited in state statutes:

> (a) in cases of a dispute between counselor and client; (b) when a client raises the issue of mental condition in legal proceedings; (c) when a client's condition poses a danger to self or others; (d) in cases of child abuse or neglect (in addition to mandated reporting laws); (e) when the counselor has knowledge that the client is contemplating commission of a crime; (f) during court ordered psychological evaluations; (g) for purposes of involuntary hospitalization; (h) when the counselor has knowledge that a client has been a victim of a crime; and (i) in cases of harm to vulnerable adults. (p. 455)

To facilitate understanding, we have organized the exceptions into clusters according to the purposes they serve. First, we discuss client waiver of the privilege or right to privacy and exceptions that deal with sharing information with subordinates or other professionals in order to improve the quality of services. Next, we turn to exceptions that involve protecting clients or others who may be in danger. Then we look at ways that confidentiality and privileged communication are different when working with multiple clients as opposed to individuals, and with minor clients as opposed to adults. Finally, we note some exceptions that are legally mandated.

Client Waiver of the Privilege

Confidentiality and privilege belong to clients, not to counselors. As a result, clients can waive their privacy. This occurs most often when clients explicitly ask counselors to give information regarding the counseling relationship to third parties. Usually, clients who waive the privilege have an understanding that their secrets will be revealed. In some circumstances, however, clients may unknowingly waive the privilege by their actions (Knapp & VandeCreek, 1987). For example, clients might implicitly waive the privilege by filing a lawsuit seeking damages for emotional distress caused by an accident or by filing a malpractice lawsuit against a mental health professional, as discussed later in the section on exceptions. In *Cynthia B. v. New Rochelle Hospital* (1982), the court found that the client (rather than the mental health professional) had responsibility for any embarrassment or inconvenience that resulted from the disclosure of privileged mental health information in a lawsuit she had filed.

Death of the Client

According to Cleary (1984), the common law doctrine is that privilege does not end with a person's death. Berg (2001) has argued that decisions about whether to release private information after the death of a client should be determined on a case by case basis by the professional. However, Berg's argument has not been adopted in any state statutes or case law. In some states, statutes specify how privilege is controlled after an individual dies. When there is no statutory language dealing with privilege and the death of the holder, then the common law practice of allowing a legal representative of the deceased person to assert the privilege generally is followed (Knapp & VandeCreek, 1987). An executor of an estate is not always recognized by a court as a deceased person's legal representative for the purposes of privilege (*Boling v. Superior Court,* 1980). If you believe that a deceased client's privilege must be asserted or waived, you should contact his or her family members, probate attorney, or executor to determine whether a legal representative is available to deal with the matter. The ACA *Code of Ethics* (2005) states simply that counselors must protect the confidentiality of deceased clients according to legal requirements or agency policies (Standard B.3.f.).

Sharing Information with Subordinates or Fellow Professionals

In some situations, the "umbrella" of confidentiality can be extended to cover others who assist or work with the counselor in providing services to clients. Although these situations do not involve a breach of the client's confidentiality, they do constitute exceptions to the general rule that only the counselor and client are privy to information shared in sessions. Sharing information with others in order to provide the best possible services to clients is permissible when (a) clerical or other assistants handle confidential information, (b) counselors consult with colleagues or experts, (c) counselors are working under supervision, and (d) other professionals are involved in coordinating client care.

Clerical or Other Assistants May Handle Confidential Information   It is routine business practice for many types of professionals, including physicians and attorneys as well as counselors, to have clerical assistants, employees, and other subordinates who handle confidential client information. Some state statutes that grant privilege to counselor–client relationships may also specifically extend the privilege to communications when assistants are present or when assistants see privileged information, but such specific language is rare. Knapp and VandeCreek (1987) have concluded that common law principles most likely would extend privilege to unprivileged assistants who are involved in activities that further the treatment of the client.

Counselors should be aware, however, that they are ethically responsible for any breach of confidentiality by someone who assists them. Standard B.3.a. alerts counselors to "make every effort to ensure that privacy and confidentiality of clients are maintained by subordinates, including employees, supervisees, students, clerical assistants, and volunteers." Counselors may also be held legally responsible for breaches of confidentiality by their subordinates. Under the general legal principle of *respondeat superior,* employers are held responsible for the acts of their employees. Counselors, then, can be held accountable for assistants who breach confidentiality through the doctrine of vicarious liability. It is important for counselors to impress on their employees the importance of keeping information confidential and to supervise them in such a way as to ensure they are complying with this requirement.

There are some precautions that counselors can take to help ensure that their subordinates understand both the importance of confidentiality and the procedures for maintaining it. Counselors are obligated to determine whether individuals they may hire are trustworthy. Counselors could be held accountable if they hired persons who were notorious for disregarding the privacy of others, if these persons later disclosed confidential client information. Further, we suggest that counselors take an inventory periodically of everyone who may handle confidential information about their clients. This might include answering service personnel, an office receptionist, clerical assistants, billing service staff, counselor interns or supervisees, and paraprofessionals. The counselor can conduct training sessions for these employee groups to ensure that they understand the importance of confidentiality and they know how the counselor wants them to handle confidential material. The federal HIPAA law (see chap. 3) requires that employees be trained to protect the privacy of clients.

Counselors May Consult with Colleagues or Experts   Counselors are encouraged to consult with peers or experts whenever they have questions about their ethical obligations or professional practice (Standard C.2.e.). If the questions have to do with clinical practice, counselors should seek consultation from a practitioner who has experience or expertise in the particular area of concern. If an ethical question is involved, it is a good idea to consult a fellow mental health professional who has expertise in ethics. In a particularly perplexing ethical dilemma that involves a difficult judgment call, it is wise to seek more than one opinion.

Consultation usually does not need to involve a breach of confidentiality, because most consultations can be managed without revealing the identity of the client. The ACA *Code of Ethics* (2005) gives some guidance in this respect. Standard B.8.b. states that "written and oral reports present only data germane to the purposes of the consultation, and every effort is made to protect client identity and to avoid undue invasion of privacy." Standard B.8.c cautions that, during consultations, counselors should not disclose confidential information that could lead to the identification of a client. However, because of the nature of a particular situation or because the identity of the client might be obvious, it is sometimes impossible to avoid revealing the identity of the client. In these instances, the counselor should obtain client consent, if possible, and the identity of the consultant should be revealed to the client.

Finally, counselors should choose consultants who have the appropriate expertise for the question at hand. If you have an ethical or clinical question, consult with a professional colleague. If you have a legal question, ask an attorney.

Confidential Information May Be Shared When the Counselor Is Working Under Supervision   While you are a counselor in training, your work with actual clients will be supervised by experienced professionals. During your practicum, internship, and other field experiences, university supervisors and on-site supervisors will review your counseling sessions with you and provide you with feedback about your performance. After graduation, if you are planning to obtain a credential such as a license, your initial post-master's counseling work will also be under supervision. Some day, when you are an experienced counselor yourself, you may want to provide supervision to beginning professionals, or you may need to work under supervision while you are acquiring skills in a new specialty area of practice. Supervision is likely to be a part of your experience throughout your professional career.

Supervision situations are like consultation in that information about clients is shared with other professionals who subscribe to your ethic of confidentiality. But in supervision, unlike consultation, the client's identity cannot be concealed. Supervisors may observe actual counseling sessions from behind a one-way mirror, review videotapes or audiotapes of sessions, and review your case notes and counseling records. Supervisors have the same obligations as you do; they must keep information revealed in counseling sessions that they are supervising confidential. Nonetheless, your clients have the right to know that you are working under supervision. According to Standard F.1.c., *Informed Consent and Client Rights,* you have an ethical obligation to inform your clients that their confidentiality is limited because your supervisor will have access to information about them. When you are involved in group supervision, clients have the right to know that a group of your fellow practicum students or interns may also be discussing their cases. The *Code of Ethics* also requires counselors to obtain permission from clients before they observe counseling sessions or review transcripts or videotaped recordings of sessions with their supervisors, faculty, or peers (Standard B.6.c.).

You may feel some reluctance to divulge to your clients that you are working under supervision, or to explain to them all the circumstances in which information about them might be shared. You may be concerned that clients will have less confidence in your professional abilities, or that they will feel constrained about revealing personal information. These concerns must be set aside in the interest of your clients' right to informed consent. It is best to inform your clients about the limits to confidentiality in a straightforward manner and to do so at the very outset of the counseling relationship. Clients can be told that the purpose of supervision is to help you do a better job and that the focus of the supervision will be on you and your performance, rather than on them and their problems. Sometimes clients will be unnerved by the idea of a supervisor, who is a faceless stranger to them, sitting behind the mirror. In these cases, it is a good idea to arrange for the client to meet the supervisor and have the opportunity to express concerns and ask questions directly. In our experience as supervisors, we have seen that clients typically forget their initial concerns once they become engaged in the counseling process. You may be pleasantly surprised to find that this will happen for you, too.

The relationships between counseling students who are in supervision and their clients may not be privileged. As a result, students may be forced to reveal the contents of counseling sessions if ordered to do so by a judge in a legal proceeding. If the relationship between a client and the student's supervisor would be privileged if the supervisor were providing the counseling services, then it is likely privilege will exist between the client and the counselor–supervisee as well. Usually, under the law of privilege, a privilege is extended to assistants or supervisees of professionals who have statutory privilege with their clients.

Other Professionals May Be Involved in Coordinating Client Care   In some settings, such as inpatient units in hospitals, treatment teams routinely work together in caring for patients. Although the benefits of coordinating the efforts of various professionals are obvious, as an ethical matter clients need to be told what information about them is being shared, with whom, and for what purposes (Herlihy & Corey, 2006). According to Standard B.3.b., when client care involves a continuing review by a treatment team, the client must be informed of the team's existence and composition, the information being shared, and the purposes of sharing the information.

There are numerous other situations in which you might want to share confidential client information with fellow professionals in order to ensure coordination or continuity of care. A client might be receiving psychotropic medications from a physician while seeing you for counseling. A client might be seeing you for individual counseling while being in group counseling with another counselor. Clients might move and later request that you send their records or communicate by telephone with their new counselor. In all these situations, it is ethically appropriate for you to communicate with the other professionals *when the client has given permission for you to do so*. Several standards in the ACA *Code of Ethics* (2005) address these kinds of circumstances. Standards A.3. and B.3. both speak to the need for mental health professionals to work cooperatively. When clients are receiving services from another mental health professional, the code directs counselors to obtain client consent and then to inform the other professional and develop clear agreements to avoid confusion and conflict for the client. Standard B.6.f. requires counselors to obtain written permission from clients to disclose or transfer records to legitimate third parties, and reminds counselors that they are required to work to ensure that receivers of their records are sensitive to the client's confidentiality. HIPAA requires that client permission to give information to third parties be obtained in writing, and that counselors who transfer records notify the receiving third parties that the information being transferred is confidential and should be protected.

From a legal perspective, situations in which counselors function in treatment teams or coordinate client care are similar to situations in which counselors' assistants or supervisors learn confidential information about clients. If the relationship between a counselor and a client is privileged, then it is likely that the privilege will continue to exist when confidential information is discussed in treatment teams or with other professionals when coordinating client care.

Protecting Someone Who Is in Danger

Situations sometimes arise that require counselors to breach confidentiality in order to warn or protect someone who is in danger. Certain of these situations also involve a duty to report the dangerous situation to responsible authorities. These three types of duties—to warn, to protect, and to report—constitute some of the most stressful situations you will encounter as a practicing counselor.

Because these exceptions require that you make a deliberate decision to breach a client's confidentiality, there must be a compelling justification for doing so. Winston (1991) suggests that breaching a confidence can be justified by the concept of vulnerability. A duty to protect from harm arises when someone is especially dependent on others or is in some way vulnerable to the choices and actions of others. Persons in a vulnerable position are unable to avoid risk of harm on their own and are dependent on others to intervene on their behalf. When counselors, through their confidential relations with clients, learn that a vulnerable person is at risk of harm, they have a duty to act to prevent the harm. This is a higher duty than the duty to maintain confidentiality.

Counselors Must Take Action When They Suspect Abuse or Neglect of Children or Other Persons Presumed to Have Limited Ability to Care for Themselves Counselors have both an ethical and a legal duty to protect a child or vulnerable adult if they suspect that person is being abused (Standard B.2.a.).

Counselors Must Take Action to Protect Clients Who Pose a Danger to Themselves When counselors determine that clients are suicidal, they must do something to prevent the clients from harming themselves (Standard B.2.a.). A leading cause of malpractice law suits against counselors is a charge by surviving family members that counselors were negligent and therefore committed malpractice if their clients commit suicide or harm themselves while attempting suicide. This duty to protect your clients from suicide attempts is explained and discussed in chapter 4.

Counselors Must Take Action When a Client Poses a Danger to Others When counselors believe their clients may harm someone else, the counselors must take steps to prevent harm to the person who is in danger (Standard B.2.a.). This duty, like the duty to prevent clients from harming themselves, could lead to a charge of negligence or malpractice. The duty to protect others who may be harmed is explained and discussed in chapter 4.

Counselors Must Determine Whether to Breach Confidentiality When a Client Has a Fatal, Communicable Disease and the Client's Behavior Is Putting Others at Risk This exception to confidentiality is the same as the exception to protect others if you believe your client may harm other people (Standard B.2.b.). This exception also is reviewed in chapter 4.

Counseling Multiple Clients

Unique confidentiality problems arise when working with multiple clients. Generally, when your client and one or more additional persons are in the room, confidentiality is compromised and privilege usually is waived. Although you can make your own pledge not to disclose certain information, you cannot guarantee the behavior of others such as group participants or family members. Despite the fact that others in the room might not keep a client's secrets, a counselor's responsibility is not diminished by the presence of additional persons in a counseling session.

Confidentiality Cannot Be Guaranteed in Group Counseling Confidentiality is a particularly difficult ethical issue in group counseling. Although confidentiality certainly is as important in group counseling as it is in individual counseling, it is difficult to enforce. Group counselors frequently encounter problems with maintaining confidentiality among group members who are not bound by the same professional standards. They may inadvertently breach confidentiality or yield to the temptation to discuss group experiences with family or friends. The ACA *Code of Ethics* (2005) gives some guidance for dealing with confidentiality in groups in Standard B.4.a., which states that "counselors clearly explain the importance and parameters of confidentiality for the specific group being entered." A significant portion of the ethical guidelines of the Association for Specialists in Group Work (ASGW, 1989) is devoted to confidentiality among group members. This is an especially helpful resource with which you will want to familiarize yourself.

A few states specifically provide for privilege to extend to group counseling situations, but most privileged communication statutes are silent on this issue (Knapp & VandeCreek, 1987). It is important, then, that you read the privileged communication statute in your state (if one exists for counseling relationships) to determine whether group counseling sessions are privileged. In states where group counseling situations are not mentioned, at least one court has found privilege to exist (*State v. Andring,* 1984). As a result of the Andring case, it is possible that group counseling sessions would be found by courts to be privileged even if statutes do not specify that privilege exists for group counseling clients.

Confidentiality Cannot Be Guaranteed in Couples or Family Counseling

When the focus of counseling shifts from the individual to the family system, new ethical issues arise and existing ones become more complicated (Standard B.4.b.). Counselors who provide services for couples and families encounter some unique confidentiality concerns, such as how to deal with family secrets. For example, consider the situation in the following case example.

2-3 The Case of Alexis

Bob and Carla, a husband and wife, are seeing Alexis for marriage counseling. Alexis often sees each partner in a couple alone for one or more sessions because she believes counseling progresses better that way. Bob shared during one of his individual sessions with Alexis that he is having an affair with another woman, but that Carla doesn't know it. Bob doesn't plan to tell Carla, and he insists that Alexis not tell Carla either.

- If you were Alexis, how would you respond to Bob's insistence?
- How might this situation have been avoided?

This case example points out the importance of informed consent procedures. You must make clear to both marital partners at the outset the limitations of confidentiality and how you will handle confidentiality issues (Standard B.4.b.). In an analysis of the problem of *family secrets,* Brendel and Nelson (1999) pointed out that the ethical code of the International Association of Marriage and Family Counselors (IAMFC) specifically states that information learned by counselors in individual counseling sessions may not be repeated to other family members without the client's permission. They provided guidelines for counselors on how to deal with situations that occur similar to the previously cited case example.

Counseling couples or families can also lead to very difficult legal questions regarding confidentiality and privilege. Under general legal principles, any statutory privilege that exists between a counselor and client is waived if there is a third party present when information is being disclosed. However, privilege laws in some states specifically cover relationships between counselors and married couples or between counselors and family members (Knapp & VandeCreek,

1987). In these states, it is clear that a counseling relationship will be privileged despite specific additional persons being present during the counseling session. In states without such statutes, it is unclear whether an individual who is being counseled with a spouse or other family members present could assert the privilege. Appellate court decisions are split as to whether a privilege that otherwise would exist by statute would be extended to sessions that include a married couple (*Clausen v. Clausen,* 1983; *Ellis v. Ellis,* 1971; *Sims v. State,* 1984; Virginia Court, 1979; *Wichansky v. Wichansky,* 1973; *Yaron v. Yaron,* 1975).

A very difficult dilemma for counselors is posed when one spouse demands that the counselor not reveal information related in a marital counseling session, and the other spouse demands that the counselor reveal it. Situations like this often arise when a married couple enters counseling because of marital problems and then later engage in divorce proceedings.

The spouse who does not want the contents of the counseling sessions revealed should assert the privilege through his or her attorney. Of course, a counselor never wants to reveal in court private information that was related in a counseling session (Standard B.2.c.). Counselors generally will cooperate with the spouse and attorney as arguments are made to maintain the privilege of the client who does not want the private information revealed. Counselors are quite vulnerable legally in these situations because revealing privileged information inappropriately could lead to a malpractice lawsuit. On the other hand, refusing to disclose information that is not privileged could lead to being held in contempt of court by a judge. If you find yourself in a situation like this and are unsure of your legal responsibilities, you should consult your own attorney who will advise you regarding your legal obligations and rights.

Counseling Minor or Legally Incompetent Clients

When Clients Are Minor Children or Legally Incompetent, Counselors Cannot Give the Same Assurances of Confidentiality as They Give Other Clients Minors and adults who have been adjudicated incompetent in a court of law do not have a legal right to enter into contracts. Thus, their parents or guardians control their legal rights. As a result, counselors owe legal duties to the parents or guardians of minors or incompetent adults. At the same time, counselors have ethical obligations to the clients themselves (Standard B.5.). This is a conflict between law and ethics regarding the privacy rights of minors and incompetent adults.

Court-Ordered Disclosures

Counselors Must Disclose Confidential Information When Ordered to Do So by a Court   There will be instances when counselors are called to testify in court, and their clients will ask them not to reveal information shared in counseling sessions. If the relationship is privileged, either the client or the counselor will assert the privilege. In cases where no privilege exists, counselors should ask the court not to require the disclosure and explain the potential harm that could be done to the counseling relationship (Standard B.2.c.). If the judge still requires the disclosure, only essential information should be revealed (Standard B.2.d.). Counselors who are ordered by a judge to reveal confidential information should not worry that clients may sue them for violating their privacy. Complying with a judge's order is a defense to any charge of wrongdoing (Prosser, 1971). Remember though, that a subpoena may not be valid. Confidential or privileged information should not be revealed in response to a subpoena until an attorney representing the counselor has advised that course of action. See chapter 3 for a complete discussion of subpoenas.

Legal Protections for Counselors in Disputes

Counselors May Reveal Confidential Information When It Is Necessary to Defend Themselves Against Charges Brought by Clients   When ethical or legal complaints are filed against counselors by their clients, the concepts of confidentiality or privilege could become problematic for counselors who must defend themselves. It would be odd if a client could claim that a counselor had done something wrong in a counseling relationship, and then the same client could claim that confidentiality or privilege prevented the counselor from explaining the details of the counseling relationship in presenting his or her defense. As a result, the law of privileged communication requires that clients waive their privilege when they bring complaints or malpractice lawsuits against their counselors (Knapp & VandeCreek, 1987).

Other Legal Exceptions

Clients Waive Their Privilege When They Bring Lawsuits Claiming Emotional Damage   If clients claim emotional damage in a lawsuit, then the law automatically waives their privilege associated with counseling relationships (Knapp & VandeCreek, 1987). It would be unfair to allow individuals to claim in court that they had been emotionally damaged, and then to prohibit the counselor who had treated the person for the damage from testifying. The person accused of damaging the client must be given an opportunity in a court proceeding to cross-examine the counselor regarding the nature and extent of the damage.

Nonetheless, most courts have held that suits for normal distress or physical injuries arising out of a physical trauma do not automatically waive a plaintiff's right to privilege in counseling relationships (*Ideal Publishing Corp. v. Creative Features,* 1977; *Roberts v. Superior Court,* 1973; *Tylitzki v. Triple X Service, Inc.,* 1970; *Webb v. Quincy City Lines, Inc.,* 1966). Only when individuals bringing lawsuits claim that they were emotionally damaged and that damage required them to seek mental health treatment will their therapeutic privilege be waived.

Privilege Is Generally Waived in Civil Commitment Proceedings   Privilege is usually waived by law for individuals who are being evaluated by a court to determine whether they should be involuntarily committed to a psychiatric hospital. Obviously, the contents of an evaluation conducted for the purpose of rendering an opinion to a court concerning the advisability of a commitment will not be privileged. Evaluators should carefully explain the nature of the interview to individuals who are being evaluated to ensure that the individual does not misconstrue the relationship as involving mental health treatment (Standard E.13.b.; Knapp & VandeCreek, 1987). When a mental health professional seeks a commitment of a client who initiated treatment voluntarily, privilege may also be waived by the client by law (*Commonwealth ex rel. Platt v. Platt,* 1979), although in *People v. Taylor* (1980) a Colorado court refused to waive the privilege. Individuals who are involuntarily committed do not have privileged relationships with their treating mental health professionals at a judicial review of that commitment (*State v. Hungerford,* 1978; *State v. Kupchun,* 1977). The important distinction to remember is that evaluation interviews are different from counseling interviews in terms of privilege. Evaluation interviews conducted to help determine whether a client should be committed to a residential facility are not privileged. Appendix G includes an informed consent form that may be used by counselors who conduct evaluations.

See Figure 2-2 for a listing of the exceptions to confidentiality and privileged communication that are summarized in this chapter.

Sharing information with subordinates or fellow professionals is permissible under the following circumstances:

- Clerical or other assistants handle confidential information.
- A counselor consults with colleagues or experts.
- The counselor is working under supervision.
- Other professionals are involved in coordinating client care.

Protecting someone who is in danger may require disclosure of confidential information when the following conditions exist:

- The counselor suspects abuse or neglect of children or other persons presumed to have limited ability to care for themselves.
- A client poses a danger to others.
- A client poses a danger to self (is suicidal).
- A client has a fatal, communicable disease and the client's behavior is putting others at risk.

Confidentiality is compromised when counseling multiple clients, including the following:

- Group counseling
- Counseling couples or families

There are unique confidentiality and privileged communication considerations when working with minor clients:

- Counseling minor clients

Certain exceptions are mandated by law, including the following:

- Disclosure is court ordered.
- Clients file complaints against their counselors.
- Clients claim emotional damage in a lawsuit.
- Civil commitment proceedings are initiated.

Figure 2-2   Exceptions to confidentiality and privileged communication

DIVERSITY CONSIDERATIONS IN CONFIDENTIALITY AND PRIVILEGED COMMUNICATION

Counselors must be sensitive to the cultural meanings of privacy and confidentiality (Standard B.1.a.). It is important to be aware that clients from some cultures, such as those that are collectivist in nature, may not want their confidentiality upheld in the traditional manner. In such cases, counselors might share confidential information with family members or members of the client's community, if the client so desires.

SUMMARY AND KEY POINTS

After reading this chapter, we expect that you have developed a healthy appreciation for the complexities of the ethic of confidentiality and its legal counterpart, privileged communication. We also expect that you have a clearer understanding of why counselors encounter dilemmas of confidentiality more frequently than they encounter other types of dilemmas and find them the most difficult to resolve. The considerable amount of information contained in this chapter should be helpful. These dilemmas, nevertheless, will challenge you to use your clinical judgment and your skills in ethical reasoning and in researching the current status of professional knowledge and the law. We hope we have emphasized how important it is that you do not try to go it alone when you encounter questions about confidentiality and privileged communication, but rather that you seek consultation from colleagues or an attorney. Following are some of the key points made in the chapter:

- Both confidentiality and privileged communication are based on the client's right to privacy. Confidentiality is an ethical concept, and privileged communication is a legal term.
- Although research does not clearly support the notion that assurances of privacy are essential to clients' willingness to disclose, counselors view confidentiality as a strong moral force and a fundamental ethical obligation.
- In general, counselors seem to do a very good job of protecting their clients' confidentiality. It is easy for an inadvertent breach to occur, however, and counselors need to be zealous in safeguarding client privacy.
- Privileged communication means that a judge cannot order a counselor to reveal information in court that has been recognized by law as privileged. Because privileged communication is antagonistic to the entire U.S. system of justice, courts and legislatures have been reluctant to extend privilege to relationships between mental health professionals and their clients.
- Except for cases heard in federal courts, privileged communication in counseling is determined by state statutes. It is essential that you learn your state laws regarding privileged communication in counseling relationships.
- Confidentiality and privilege both belong to the client, not to the counselor, and clients can waive their privacy.
- Confidentiality and privilege are not absolute. There are at least 15 exceptions to confidentiality and privileged communication. You must understand each exception and be able to apply exceptions to real situations you encounter in your practice.
- It is permissible to share information with subordinates and fellow professionals in order to provide the best possible services to clients.
- Stressful situations for counselors often involve decisions regarding the duties to warn, protect, or report when a client's condition poses a danger to self or others.
- Confidentiality cannot be guaranteed when counseling couples, families, groups, or minors; or adults who have been adjudicated as legally incompetent.
- Certain exceptions to confidentiality and privileged communication are legally mandated.
- When in doubt about your obligations regarding confidentiality or privileged communication, consult!

3

Records, Subpoenas, and Technology

FOCUS QUESTIONS

1. Why should counselors keep records?
2. Why is it important to carefully document events in emergency situations?
3. Why should counselors consult with an attorney if they receive a subpoena?
4. What are some of the primary benefits and problems that technology has brought to the counseling process?
5. What do you think about counselors providing professional mental health services to clients via the Internet?

Although records were mentioned in the previous chapter in relation to counselors' responsibilities regarding confidentiality and privileged communication, records are such an important (and somewhat complex) area of a counselor's practice that we are discussing them in detail in this separate chapter. Counselors typically receive little training in proper record keeping, and they tend to dislike and neglect paperwork (MacCluskie, 2001). Nonetheless, maintaining adequate records is necessary for ethical, legal, and professional reasons. Records are often subject to being subpoenaed, and counselors must be prepared to respond to legal demands for their records. Because counselors make extensive use of technology to create and transfer records, a discussion of technology is included in this chapter.

RECORDS

Records are any physical "recording" made of information related to a counselor's professional practice. When you consider the kinds of records counselors create and maintain, you probably think of the notes that counselors take concerning sessions with clients. These types of records are referred to as *clinical case notes* in this chapter. Other types that might come easily to mind are administrative records related to clients, such as appointment books, billing and payment accounts, copies of correspondence, intake forms, or other routine papers. Additional records that are often generated are audio- or videorecordings of sessions with clients. These recordings usually are used for supervision purposes, but might also be created for clients to review or by counselors for the purpose of training other counselors. Unusual records generated in counseling practices might include records of clients logging on to computerized information systems, telephone bills indicating clients' numbers called, computerized records that clients had used parking or building passes, or videorecordings of clients entering or leaving a counseling office. All the items listed here are records and the privacy of clients could be compromised if these records were not kept confidential.

Although records are a necessary part of a counselor's practice, it is important that counselors balance their need to keep documents with their obligation to provide quality counseling services to clients. Counselors who find themselves devoting inordinate or excessive amounts of time creating and maintaining records probably need to reevaluate how they are spending their professional time and energy.

In today's litigious environment, many administrators and lawyers who represent counseling agencies are requiring counselors to keep voluminous records to protect the agencies in the event a lawsuit is filed. Although counselors are wise to document actions they take when they are fulfilling an ethical or legal obligation (such as protecting an intended victim against a client's threat of harm), it is not appropriate for counselors to neglect their counseling services to clients in order to produce excessive amounts of records that are self-protective. Counselors, their administrators, and the lawyers who advise them must balance the need to protect themselves in the event of legal claims against their duty to provide quality counseling services. It is possible to keep adequate records *and* provide quality counseling services. From both a legal and an ethical standpoint, this should be the goal of counselors and counseling agencies. In this chapter, we first discuss the ethical issues and standards related to counseling records and then turn to legal requirements.

Ethical Issues and Standards Related to Records

Section B.6. of the American Counseling Association's (ACA) *Code of Ethics* (2005) includes 8 standards that specifically address counseling records. Additionally, one of the first standards in the *Code of Ethics* (Standard A.1.b.) states that counselors maintain records necessary for rendering professional services to their clients. From an ethical perspective, this is the primary purpose of keeping records—to assist you in providing clients with the best possible counseling services. Unless you have perfect recall, you will find that the clinical case notes you have recorded will help you to refresh your memory prior to sessions. They will allow you to review progress toward goals that you and the client have jointly determined, to know when and in what circumstances important decisions and actions were taken, and to maintain an overall perspective on the content and process of the entire counseling relationship.

Standard A.1.b. states that counselors maintain records required by laws, regulations, or agency or institution procedures. It is not only what is best for the client that guides the record-keeping behaviors of counselors; laws, regulations, and workplace rules also must be followed. Standard A.1.b. also requires that counseling records document client progress and services provided, and that errors in client records be corrected according to agency or institutional policies.

Keeping good records allows counselors to stay on track by documenting what kinds of treatment were undertaken and why. As Jagers (1998) has noted, counselors are by nature prone to drift in the direction of abstraction. It is helpful to us, our clients, and the therapeutic process when we work to maintain a clear conceptualization of counseling goals and our progress toward those goals. Good records can assist us in helping clients measure their change and growth. We can use our notes to reference and affirm significant turning points and successes in our clients' work.

Clinical case notes can be particularly important when a client decides to resume counseling with you after an extended break. It would be a daunting task to try to remember details of a client's life and concerns after months or even years have passed, during which so many other clients' lives and concerns have consumed your attention. If you can use your notes to refresh your recollections about former issues and events that occurred during the counseling process, you will take a significant step toward reconnecting with your returning client.

Continuity of care is a consideration when a client is referred from one mental health professional to another as well (Standard A.1.b.). Notes should be written with enough clarity that another helping professional, by learning what did and did not help the client, can provide continuation of counseling. The receiving counselor can get attuned to the meaningful aspects of a client's work if records clearly describe goals, treatment strategies, and progress that was made. If you are the receiving counselor, you will particularly appreciate these records.

Standard B.6.a. addresses the importance of keeping records in a secure location. Counselors have to take efforts to keep records in a place that is not accessible to unauthorized persons. Counselors are responsible for securing the safety and confidentiality of any counseling records they create, maintain, transfer, or destroy. This caveat includes records that are written, taped, computerized, or stored in any other medium. In the previous chapter, we discuss at some length how easy it can be for a counselor to inadvertently breach a client's confidentiality. That discussion is as pertinent to counseling records as it is to other aspects of the counseling relationship, as is evident in the case of Vanessa, presented here.

3-1 The Case of Vanessa

Vanessa is a Licensed Professional Counselor (LPC) in private practice with a group that includes three other counselors. One afternoon at 1:00, she has had a client cancellation and is using the time to work at her computer writing clinical case notes for her morning sessions. Margie, the counselor whose office is next door, pokes her head in the door and asks Vanessa for a case consultation. Vanessa and Margie go into Margie's office and close the door for privacy. Unbeknownst to Vanessa, her 2:00 client arrives early, sees that her office door is open, and goes in. The client reads the clinical case notes that Vanessa had left on her computer screen.

- What actions can counselors take to ensure that a client's records are not seen by anyone not authorized to see them?
- What steps must counselors take to preserve client privacy when they keep case notes on a computer?

Standards B.6.b. and B.6.c. address the issue of informed consent and require counselors to obtain client permission before they electronically record or observe sessions. Recording and observing sessions, common practices in supervision, are discussed in more detail later in this chapter.

Standard B.6.d. alerts us to the fact that we have an ethical obligation to provide competent clients with access to their records, unless the records contain information that might be misleading or detrimental to the clients. There is a presumption that clients have a right to see records that counselors keep related to the counseling services the clients have received. Standard B.6.d. states, "Counselors limit the access of clients to their records, or portions of their records, only when there is compelling evidence that such access would cause harm to the client." This standard also provides guidance on a trickier situation that occurs when clients have been seen in the context of group or family counseling. In situations involving multiple clients, counselors limit access to records to those parts of the records that do not include confidential information related to another client. When clients are given access to their counseling records, counselors provide them with assistance and consultation in interpreting the records (Standard B.6.a.).

Standard B.6.f. requires counselors to obtain written permission from clients to disclose or transfer records to legitimate third parties unless exceptions to confidentiality exist. Interestingly, this standard also makes counselors responsible for taking steps to ensure that receivers of counseling records are sensitive to the confidential nature of those records. It is not possible for a counselor to guarantee anyone else's behavior, including that of a fellow mental health professional who receives records. However, steps that can be taken to promote professionally appropriate transfer of records are to include a cover letter that explains the confidential nature of any transferred records, mark each page *confidential,* and include a statement on the records that the copy of the records is not to be transferred to any third party.

Standard B.6.g. provides guidelines to counselors regarding storage and disposal of counseling records after a counseling relationship has ended. Although this standard could be interpreted to infer that counselors must keep counseling records indefinitely, our suggestion is that some records be kept and others destroyed when it is clear a client will no longer receive services from a counselor. The issue of whether to keep or destroy counseling records is discussed at length in later sections of this chapter. An interesting sentence in Standard B.6.g. states, "When records are of an artistic nature, counselors obtain client (or guardian) consent with regards to handling of such records or documents." This sentence suggests that best practice would be to obtain a written understanding with clients (or guardians), at the time any item considered *artistic* is placed in a counseling record, regarding placing the item in the record and disposing of it at some later date.

Finally, Section B.6.h. imposes on counselors the duty to take *reasonable precautions* to protect their clients' privacy if counselors terminate their practice, become incapacitated, or die.

One important client privacy issue is how much information third-party payers (health insurance companies) should be allowed to demand from counselors and how much information counselors should be willing to provide them (MacCluskie, 2001). Welfel (2006) has suggested that before counselors sign a contract with a health insurance organization, they should learn the type, frequency, and extent of patient information the organization requires in order to authorize and review treatment. As an informed consent procedure, of course, this information should be thoroughly discussed with the client. Standard B.3.d. requires counselors to obtain authorization from their clients before disclosing information to third-party payers.

Legal Requirements

The ACA *Code of Ethics* (2005) provisions regarding records do not conflict with any legal requirements regarding counseling records. In fact, one ethical standard (B.6.f.) goes beyond legal requirements and indicates that written permission should be obtained from clients before records are transferred, unless specific exceptions exist. The common law in the United States does not require that counselors obtain written permission from clients to give copies of their records to third parties. However, some federal laws, state statutes, and agency policies have such written permission requirements. In addition, it is generally advisable for counselors, in order to protect themselves, to obtain written authority from clients before transferring records to third parties. If a client later denies that such permission was given or a client is not available to say whether oral permission was granted, the counselor will have a document as evidence that permission was obtained. Counselors should use the client request for records forms created by the agency in which they work. If the agency does not have a standard form, or if a counselor in private practice does not have such a form, the sample form provided in Appendix F can be used.

There is no common law principle, nor are there any general federal or state statutes that require counselors to keep clinical case notes. On the other hand, the ACA *Code of Ethics*, in Standard A.1.b., infers that ethical counselors must keep clinical case notes that document services rendered to clients and client progress. There are a number of legally related reasons why counselors do keep various types of records. For example, counselors in private practice must keep administrative records regarding their expenses and income for federal and state income tax purposes. As is discussed later, there are also some specific federal statutes that require counselors to handle records in particular ways if counselors work in settings in which these statutes apply. Additionally, lawyers always advise counselors to document carefully everything they do so they can protect themselves if their actions or judgments are later questioned in a lawsuit.

All counselors in all types of practices keep records of some kind. It is important that counselors approach their record-keeping responsibilities in both an ethical and a legal manner.

Confidentiality and Privileged Communication Requirements

All the points made in chapter 2 regarding the confidentiality and privileged communication responsibilities of counselors apply to records to the same degree they apply to oral comments regarding the privacy of clients. However, because records have physical properties, whereas *information* may not, it is important to consider carefully the responsibility of counselors to handle records appropriately.

Purposes of Records

Counseling records are created for a number of reasons (Corey et al., 1998). Some of these reasons benefit clients, whereas others benefit counselors or their employers.

In our opinion, before you write any type of note or create a record, you should carefully consider why you are taking that action. In many counseling offices or agencies, records are routinely created without giving any thought to the simple question of *why* they are being kept. It makes no sense for a counselor who is keeping clinical case notes for the sole purpose of refreshing her memory to write her notes the same way the counselor in the local hospital writes notes on a patient's chart. In a hospital, a patient's chart is read by physicians, nurses, physical therapists, counselors, and others. Each person who makes an entry on a patient's chart is writing so that other professionals will know what types of services were rendered, for the benefit of the patient. If counselors ask themselves why they are writing a note for a client record, who will read the record, and what those who read it will be looking for, there will be a better chance that the record will be appropriate for its purpose.

Overall, clinical health care records are seen as being created to benefit the person who is receiving the services. In fact, legal principles view the contents of the records about a particular client as belonging to that client, even though the paper or recording instrument belongs to someone else (*Claim of Gerkin,* 1980; *People v. Cohen,* 1979). Records can benefit clients in a number of ways.

Records are used to transfer the information one health care provider has about a client's condition to another health care provider. This efficient method of exchanging information can be very beneficial to clients.

Health care records also create a history of a client's diagnosis, treatment, and recovery. Health care providers can render better services when they have access to information regarding a client's past that is more thorough and accurate than a client's oral recall.

Clinical case notes benefit the client because they allow the counselor to summarize each interaction with the client and record plans for future sessions. The work of counselors can be more consistent, precise, and systematic when accurate and thorough notes are kept.

Counselors also keep clinical case notes for their own benefit (Schaffer, 1997). Counselors document any steps they have taken in an emergency or critical situation. Later, if counselors are accused of not having provided competent services, the records serve as evidence of their thinking and the notes document any actions taken. Without adequate documentation, there is no clear record of the course and progress of counseling (Wiger, 1999a).

Counselors keep a number of business records associated with their counseling practice for their own purposes. Counselors who work within agencies or other facilities that provide counseling services often need to document the number of persons who have been served, the categories of services rendered, and other types of information. Counselors in private practice have to keep business records to justify tax deductions they take in relation to their counseling business. Regardless of whose purpose is being served in creating records, it is the privacy of clients that dictates how records must be handled.

3-2 The Case of Paolo

Paolo has recently taken his first counseling job in the local community mental health center, after receiving his master's degree in counseling. During his first week at work, he meets with his section supervisor who goes over the records the agency keeps for each client. His supervisor shows him an intake form that is 12 pages long. The form requires the counselor to collect all types of personal information on the client including a thorough medical, health, and social history; and detailed information regarding the client's education, work background, and current job. A diagnosis and treatment plan form is given to Paolo that requires him to enter a *DSM-IV-TR* diagnosis and at least five measurable and behavioral goals for counseling. Paolo's supervisor explains that after each counseling session, Paolo must enter into the client's folder a summary of issues discussed in the session, a notation of the client's progress toward each of the counseling goals listed, and a notation of what Paolo plans to do the next counseling session. The supervisor suggests that Paolo write about three pages of notes for each client after each session. His supervisor says there are more forms to be completed after clients have their last sesssion, but they will go over those forms later. When Paolo asks his supervisor why so much information is collected on the intake form, why a diagnosis is required for each client, and why a summary of the session is needed, his supervisor replies in a patronizing tone, "This is the way all professional counseling agencies keep records. Weren't you taught record keeping in your master's degree program?"

- How should Paolo respond to his supervisior's training session?
- What kinds of records do you think would be reasonable for a community mental health agency to keep on each client?

Types of Records Kept by Counselors

Some think it is unfortunate that there is no agreed-on listing of the types of records counselors should keep or the manner in which these records should be created or maintained. According to Standard A.1.b. of the ACA *Code of Ethics* (2005), "Counselors maintain records necessary for rendering professional services to their clients and as required by laws, regulations, or agency or institutional procedures." This standard does not provide detailed information about the types of records that must be kept, which allows each counselor to determine which types of clinical case notes are needed to render professional services. The standard acknowledges that many record-keeping requirements are imposed on counselors by laws, regulations, and procedures.

It may be helpful for counselors to receive more instructions about the record-keeping responsibilities that will be a part of most of the jobs they will hold. However, it would not be wise for the profession or the ACA *Code of Ethics* to tell counselors the types of records they must keep, the contents of such records, and the ways in which those records should be created. It is best for counselors to determine the kinds of records they need based on their position, and the kinds of clinical notes they need to create in order to be effective practitioners. Keeping in mind that there will be variations depending on a counselor's style and the requirements imposed by employment settings, we offer some general guidelines regarding three types of records: administrative records, recordings, and clinical case notes.

Administrative Records   All settings that provide counseling services keep some type of administrative records. The type of agency and external pressures determine how many and what types of records are kept. When counselors accept employment in an agency, school, hospital, or other setting, they agree to conform to agency rules and procedures, which include record keeping requirements.

Administrative records are any types of records that would not be considered recordings or clinical case notes. Administrative records include appointment books, billing and payment accounts, copies of correspondence, signed informed consent documents, client permission to release information, intake forms, or other routine papers that are created as a result of providing counseling services to clients. In most businesses, records of these types are not considered confidential. Yet the very fact that someone has applied for or received counseling services is a private matter. Therefore, business records that reveal the identity of individuals who have had contact with the agency must be treated as confidential and must be protected in the same way as clinical case notes are protected.

Recordings   Clinical supervision of counseling services takes place in some form in most settings. Agencies often accept practicum or internship students who must record their sessions with clients for the purposes of clinical supervision. Mental health professionals, after they have received their graduate degrees, usually have to practice under clinical supervision for 2 to 3 years before they can become licensed themselves. In addition, many practicing counselors continue supervision throughout their careers and might record sessions for supervision purposes.

Counseling sessions could be recorded when counselors want clients to listen to or view their own behavior or interpersonal interactions during sessions. Although this therapeutic use of client session recordings is not unusual, a few cautions should be mentioned. Counselors should emphasize to their clients that these recordings would compromise their privacy if the clients did not keep them secure or erase them after using them. Counselors also should make sure clients know that until these recordings are erased or destroyed, they would be available for subpoena in some lawsuits that could arise. We suggest that counselors who give recordings of sessions to their clients for any purpose have their clients sign a form to ensure that they understand the problems that might arise and their responsibility for their own privacy protection.

There are a number of procedures that need to be followed when recordings of client sessions are created. Clients must know that recordings are being made and must agree to the process. The ACA *Code of Ethics* (Standard B.6.b.) requires that consent of clients be obtained prior to recording sessions. The consent of clients must be *informed* in that clients must understand the reason the recordings are being made and who will have access to them. It would be a violation of privacy if sessions were recorded without a client's knowledge, or if consent was given and then the recordings were used for purposes not agreed to or accessed by persons unknown to the client. The tapes, once they are created, must be kept as secure as any confidential record within the agency is kept. Once the recordings have been used, they must be erased or destroyed.

Although there is no ethical or legal requirement that the client's permission be obtained in writing, counselors often obtain written permission from clients to record counseling sessions in order to protect themselves. This self-protection would be necessary if a client later claimed that permission had never been given for the recording or that the client did not fully understand how the recording would be used. In addition, many agencies require written permission before client counseling sessions may be recorded. If such policies exist, counselors must comply. If you wish to obtain a client's permission to record a session for supervision and your agency does not have a standard form to use, a form is provided in Appendix G. Any signed form of this type obtained from a client should be placed in the client's folder and kept until the record is destroyed.

All of the cautions regarding the handling of recorded sessions apply to counselors in training as well as to seasoned counselors. The carelessness of Abby, the graduate student in the following case example, could have several repercussions.

3-3 The Case of Abby

Abby, a graduate student, is enrolled in a counseling techniques course. She has been practicing her skills with Sharon, a fellow classmate, as her client. Their practice sessions are being videotaped so that the course instructor can review Abby's performance. One day before class, Abby spends several hours in the graduate student lounge studying for an exam. When she leaves the lounge to go take her exam, she is distracted by her worries about the test and leaves behind a videotape containing a counseling session with Sharon. The tape is dated and labeled as a counseling session with Sharon. Robert, Sharon's former boyfriend who is a graduate student in the educational administration program, comes into the lounge after Abby leaves. He sees the tape and decides to look at it to see whether Sharon has been talking about their breakup. He slips it into his book bag.

- What advice would you give students or counselors who videotape or audiotape counseling sessions to help them keep the tapes secure?
- What would you do if you lost a tape like Abby did?

Our experience is that once audiotapes or videotapes of counseling sessions are made, graduate students, counselors, and supervisors tend to be somewhat lax in keeping these recordings secure. Perhaps the reason for this problem is that tapes do not look like confidential records. In any event, it is imperative that graduate students or counselors who make tapes take responsibility for delivering them to their supervisor, retrieving them once the supervisor has reviewed them, and erasing them. Clinical supervisors bear the responsibility of handling recordings appropriately during the time that tapes are in their possession. Supervisors must also return tapes to counselors after reviewing them.

We recommend that tapes of counseling sessions be labeled simply, so that the counselor and supervisor can recognize their contents, but in a manner that does not bring attention to the fact that they are confidential records. A good method of labeling the tapes is to put the counselor's name and telephone number on the tape along with the date of the counseling session. There is no need to write the client's name on the tape or to indicate that the tape contains a counseling session. Tapes labeled in this manner can be returned to the counselor if they are misplaced or lost, and those who come into contact with them will not be as likely to be tempted to listen to or view them. Also, when a new session is recorded over a previous session, the only thing on the label that will need to be changed is the date of the session.

Counselors who record counseling sessions must also ensure that tapes are erased after they have been used for supervision or for any other purposes. Most counselors record new sessions over previously recorded sessions. This method works well. If more than one tape is used for supervision tapes, it would be important to keep track of the tapes and, particularly when supervision sessions are terminated, to purposefully erase or record over them. Magnetic devices that erase the contents of audio- or videotapes are available commercially and are recommended for university and agency settings where a number of tapes are recorded and erased on a continuing basis.

Clinical Case Notes

The records that concern counselors and clients most are the clinical case notes that counselors keep regarding their sessions with clients. These notes contain detailed information about the content of counseling sessions. They often include specific details clients have told counselors, counselors' clinical impressions of clients, and generally very sensitive and personal information about clients.

A problem with clinical case notes is that counselors often think of them as being personal notes to themselves that will be seen only by their eyes in the future. However, the reality of clinical case notes is much different, and we have found that even seasoned counselors are sometimes surprised to learn how many people have a right to access their clinical case notes. Counselors must be aware of how these notes are viewed by clients, agencies, and the law.

We often have heard the suggestion that counselors simply should not take clinical case notes, so that they will not have to worry about the notes being subpoenaed or being seen at a later time by the client or any other person. This is not sound advice. In the first place, the ACA *Code of Ethics* (Standard A.1.b.) specifically states that ethical counselors do keep records. In addition, it seems to be general practice today for mental health professionals, no matter what their credentials or orientation, to routinely create and use clinical case notes in their practices. If counselors were to fail to create these notes, it is likely that they would be accused of unprofessional practice and probably would be called on to explain how they could render quality counseling services without taking clinical case notes (Anderson, 1996). Second, not having clinical case notes would not keep a counselor from having to reveal confidential information orally from memory if someone had a legal right to that information. Finally, counselors should take the clinical notes they need in order to function effectively as professionals. Counselors should not feel inhibited about creating clinical case notes just because the notes may later be seen by clients themselves or by third parties.

Assume Notes Will Be Read   Counselors never know whether others will read the clinical case notes they create. Thus, counselors should assume that notes they write will become public information at some later date. Counselors who make this assumption will be very cautious in deciding what to include in their notes. At the same time, counselors should write whatever they need to render quality counseling services to their clients.

Situations in which the clinical case notes of counselors appropriately and legally are read by others are discussed in the following sections. It is important for you to remember the following sobering information when you are writing clinical case notes:

- Your clients have a legal right to review the notes and to obtain copies of them.
- Your clients have a legal right to demand that you transfer copies of those clinical case notes to other professionals, including other mental health professionals, attorneys, physicians, and even accountants.
- Your clients can subpoena the clinical case notes when they are involved in litigation.
- Other parties can legally subpoena the clinical case notes when involved in litigation situations involving the client, sometimes over the client's objection and even when the records are privileged.

- The legal representatives of deceased clients, in most states, have the same rights to clinical case notes as the clients had when they were alive.
- Clinical case notes sometimes do become public information and get published in the media.

Appropriate Content of Clinical Case Notes   Unfortunately, very little instruction occurs in counseling graduate programs regarding the purposes and the actual creation of clinical case notes (Cottone & Tarvydas, 2003). In other professions, such as medicine, nursing, and social work, a heavy emphasis is placed on how to write health records, what information should and should not be included, and proper ways of creating such clinical notes. Most health records are passed from one professional to another, and professionals rely on each other to record information so it can be used in the care and treatment of a patient. Counseling clinical case notes, on the other hand, generally are written by a counselor for the counselor's own use. There are times, however, when these records are read by others and even when counselors offer such records to prove they acted professionally. Piazza and Baruth (1990), Mitchell (1991), and Snider (1987) have provided suggestions for keeping records. Some guidelines, based largely on those developed by the American Psychological Association (APA; 1993), are included in Appendix H. We offer some recommendations here regarding the creation of clinical case notes to assist counselors in their practices.

You should never lose sight of the purposes of clinical case notes. There are two basic reasons to keep notes: (a) to provide quality counseling services to clients and (b) to document decisions you have made and actions you have taken as a counselor. Both of these purposes are legitimate and reasonable.

It is critical that you take your notes either during sessions or immediately after. It does no good to write clinical case notes long after the counseling session occurs. The whole purpose of the notes is to record on paper what your memory will not hold. If you wait too long, you will be relying on your memory, which is what you are trying to avoid.

Your own personal style should dictate whether you take notes during a counseling session or after it is over. There are advantages and disadvantages to both approaches. Taking notes during sessions allows you to record accurate information immediately without having to rely on your memory as to what was said. Some counselors can take notes unobtrusively during sessions. Other counselors may have trouble taking notes and listening to clients at the same time. Clients could be distracted or inhibited by your note taking during sessions, if it is not done easily. Some counselors find that waiting until after the session is over is the best way for them to take clinical case notes. We suggest that you try both methods and adopt the approach that works best for you.

As we have emphasized, the first purpose for creating clinical case notes is to render quality counseling services. It would be impossible for you to see a number of clients over a relatively short period of time and remember all the information that clients revealed to you and all your thoughts regarding the clients' situations. You should take clinical case notes to remember what was said by clients, to record your own clinical impressions, and to plan future interactions with your clients.

A very important part of writing clinical case notes is to separate objective information (what was said by anyone or observed by you during the session) from your clinical impressions (hypotheses or conclusions you developed as a result of what was said or observed). Quite often, you will review notes to determine what a client actually said during a session. You must be able to separate what was actually said from what you thought about as a result of what was said. In addition, there may be times when your notes are used as evidence in a legal proceeding and being able to determine what was actually said by a client could be critical. A common format for clinical case notes is the use of "SOAP" notes, which include four separate sections:

Subjective: information reported by the client
Objective: results of the counselor's tests and other assessments administered
Assessment: the counselor's impressions generated by the data
Plans: diagnosis and treatment plan, along with any modifications to them

Another format that is similar and is also used frequently is the "DAP," which is comprised of three sections:

Data: objective description of what occurred during the session
Assessment: counselor's interpretations based on the data, in the context of the presenting problem and treatment plan
Plan: what the counselor intends to accomplish in the next session or sessions

The second purpose for keeping clinical case notes is to document decisions you have made or actions you have taken (Woody, 1988b). Such documentation would be important when you determine that a client is a danger to self or others, and take some actions to prevent harm. Documentation is also important when you consult with others regarding a client's situation. When you make decisions that clients may not like, you should also document your actions in your clinical case notes. If you decide to terminate counseling over a client's objection, instruct a client to take some action the client is reluctant to take, or impose limits to a client's interactions with you outside of sessions, it is wise to document how and why you did these things and the client's reactions.

When you document decisions or actions in your case notes, you are doing that to protect yourself in the event such decisions or actions are questioned later by anyone else (Mitchell, 1991). As a result, it is important to provide as much detailed information as possible. For example, listing the exact time a conversation took place could be vital. When you are talking to people other than your client, it is important to include the person's name, title, and contact information; date and time the conversation took place; and any other information that might be needed later. Recording exact words you used and exact words of others often can be important as well. When documenting to protect yourself, it is essential that you do so immediately after conversations take place. If you write notes hours, days, or weeks after conversations have occurred, such notes will be much less helpful to you if you are trying to prove that you made the decisions or took the actions you are claiming to have taken in your notes.

It would be impossible to write a summary of every action you take as a counselor or to make an audiotape or videotape of every counseling session. Excessive documentation can take away valuable time that might be spent providing counseling services. On the other hand, there are circumstances in which counselors should document their actions to create a record showing that they have done what they should have done.

Guidelines for documenting for self-protection are included in Figure 3-1.

Another important part of note taking is to write notes that are legible, at least to you. For notes to be useful in the future, you must be able to read and understand them. If your notes are transferred to a client or to a third party at a later date and they cannot read them, you will be called on to explain what you wrote. This can be very inconvenient for you, because it occurs in a court after you have been subpoenaed and put under oath to tell the truth. It is much better to write your notes so that others can read them than to have to interpret them later. It is definitely

1. Documentation should be undertaken in circumstances in which a counselor's actions or inaction may be later reviewed by an ethics panel, licensure board, or administrator, or within the context of a legal proceeding.

2. Some of the situations in which some level of documentation is called for include the following:

   • Someone accuses a counselor of unethical or illegal behavior.

   • A counselor reports a case of suspected child abuse.

   • A counselor determines that a client is a danger to self.

   • A counselor determines that a client is a danger to others.

   • A client who is being counseled is involved in a legal controversy that could lead to the counselor being forced to testify in court. Such controversies include counseling a child whose parents are arguing about custody in a divorce case, a husband or wife who is involved in a contentious divorce case, a couple who are contemplating a divorce, or a person who is involved in a personal injury lawsuit.

3. Documentation efforts should begin as soon as counselors determine they are in a situation in which documentation is important.

4. When documenting for self-protection, as much detail as possible should be included. Dates, exact times events occurred, and exact words spoken should be included to the degree details are remembered. Only factual information should be included. Thoughts, diagnoses, and conclusions of counselors should be avoided when documenting. If these need to be written down, they should be included in clinical case notes rather than in records kept for documentation.

5. The best documentation is created very soon after a conversation or event has occurred. Indicate the date and time anything is written. Never backdate anything that is written. In other words, do not imply or state that something was written on an earlier date than it was actually written.

6. In the event counselors realize that documentation should have been occurring sooner, they should write a summary of what has happened up to that point in time. Include as much detail as can be remembered. The date and time the summary was written should be included on the summary.

7. Maintain a documentation file that includes the originals of notes written to counselors, copies of notes written by counselors to others, copies of relevant papers counselors cannot keep for themselves, and other papers that might be relevant to the situation.

8. Records kept for documentation should be kept secure in a locked file drawer or cabinet. If counselors agree to provide copies of their files, they should never release originals of their records, only copies.

Figure 3-1   Documentation through records for self-protection

not a good idea to purposefully write notes so that they cannot be read by others or to use symbols that only you can understand. If clients or third parties try to read those notes, they often become irritated. You can be put in a difficult position, because it appears that you are not cooperating with people who have a legal right to review the notes.

Client Access to Records

It would never occur to most health care providers to have concerns about patients having access to copies of their records. Mental health care is different from physical health care in many respects. Some mental health care professionals believe it is not appropriate for patients or clients to have information about the diagnoses of mental disorders, treatment approaches being taken, or clinical impressions that have been formulated by the professional. In fact, some mental health care professionals might argue that it could be harmful to individuals who are being treated to have such information from their records.

Generally, counselors must provide access to client records to clients upon request (Standard B.6.d.). However, if there is *compelling evidence that such access would cause harm to the client,* then counselors can limit the access of clients to their records. If counselors do decide to deny client access to their counseling records, then "Counselors document the request of clients and the rationale for withholding some or all of the record in the files of clients" (B.6.d.).

The legal perspective on health care records is that they are kept for the benefit of the patient, and therefore, the patient should have access to them and must receive copies if requested (*Claim of Gerkin,* 1980; *People v. Cohen,* 1979). Further, the patient has the right to demand that one health care provider transfer the records to another health care provider. Mental health care is not seen as different from physical health care concerning patient or client records. It is important, then, for counselors to assume that clients will have access to clinical case notes created and that clients have a right to copies of those notes and have a right to request that copies of the notes be transferred to other professionals.

In the event a client requests a copy of your clinical case notes and you have any reason to think that it would be best if the client did not see your notes, there are practical steps you can take that could resolve the matter. You could explain to your client why you believe it would not be best to see your notes and your client might accept your explanation and withdraw the request. You also could suggest that it might be more helpful for the client or for the person to whom the client wants the records transferred if you were to create a summary of your notes, rather than copy the notes themselves. You might explain that the notes were written for your own clinical purposes, and that others probably would be more interested in summaries than in day-to-day notes.

If you were to refuse to show a client your clinical case notes regarding treatment or refuse to provide copies for the client or for a third party the client has designated, the client probably could take legal steps to compel you to comply with the demand. It would appear that the law would support the client's rights to the records (*Application of Striegel,* 1977).

In some circumstances, your clinical case notes may contain information about other parties involved in sessions in which the client was counseled. Such situations could arise in couples, family, or group counseling. If your clinical case notes contain information that would compromise another person's privacy if they were given to a client or to someone designated by the client, you might try to convince your client to withdraw the request or you might suggest that you provide a summary for your client. If your client insists, however, on having copies of your original records, then you should copy what you have written, eliminate references to others, and provide your client with the portions of the records that deal only with that client. When counselors provide clients with copies of their counseling records, counselors do not include confidential information related to any other clients (Standard B.6.d.).

Federal Laws Affecting Counseling Records

It would be impossible to describe every federal law or regulation that contains requirements for counseling records. The most far-reaching federal law related to mental health records is the Health Insurance Portability and Accountability Act (HIPAA). Most other federal statutes related to mental health records apply only to programs that are funded by federal tax money. Counselors who work in settings that are administered by the federal government or in agencies that receive federal funding should ask their employers whether there are any federal laws or regulations that affect the counseling records they keep as part of their jobs. Many private agencies as well as state and local government programs receive federal funding. Three federal laws affect a number of counselors—the HIPAA; the Family Educational Rights and Privacy Act of 1974 (FERPA; 20 U.S.C.A. §1232g, 1997); and the Comprehensive Alcohol Abuse and Alcoholism Prevention, Treatment and Rehabilitation Act of 1972 (42 U.S.C. §290dd-2, 1997).

Health Insurance Portability and Accountability Act

Public Law 104-191, commonly known as HIPAA, has caused a huge stir in the health care industry in the United States. According to the United States Department of Health and Human Services (HHS; 2003), the HIPAA rules strike a balance that protects the privacy of people who seek health care and still permits important uses of information.

HIPAA was enacted on August 21, 1996. The HIPAA statute required HHS to issue privacy regulations governing individually identifiable health information if Congress did not enact privacy legislation within 3 years of the passage of HIPAA. After Congress failed to act on time, HHS issued HIPAA rules, known as the *Privacy Rule,* on December 28, 2000. Final modifications to the rule were published on August 14, 2002. A full text of the rule and modifications are located at 45 CFR Part 160 and Part 164, Subparts A and E on the OCR website: http://www.hhs.gov/ocr/hipaa.

HIPAA applies only to organizations and individuals who transmit health care information in electronic form in connection with a health care transaction. As it would be very difficult to have a *paper only* mental health care practice, we recommend that all mental health organizations and professionals in private practice comply with the HIPAA requirements.

The Privacy Rule requirements went into effect April 14, 2003. All records and other individually identifiable health information held or disclosed by a covered entity in any form, whether communicated electronically, on paper, or orally, are covered by the HIPAA Privacy Rule.

Counselors must give clients a clear written explanation of how counselors use, keep, and disclose their health care information. Clients must have access to their records. A process must exist and must be in writing for clients to request amendments to their records. A written history of most disclosures must be available to clients. In addition, counselors must have available for clients to see, if they request them, a set of written privacy procedures that include who has access to protected information, how it will be used within the counseling office, and when the information would or would not be disclosed to others. Under HIPAA, clients must be given a means to make inquiries regarding their counseling records or make complaints regarding the privacy of their records.

Counselors must obtain uncoerced client consent to release information for treatment, payment, and health care operations purposes, and for nonroutine uses and most non-health-care purposes, such as releasing information to financial institutions determining mortgages and other loans or selling mailing lists to interested parties, such as life insurers.

Disclosures of treatment information without specific consumer authorization are allowed in certain circumstances including, but not limited to, quality assurance oversight activities, research, judicial and administrative hearings, limited law enforcement activities, emergency circumstances, and facility patient directories.

One provision is quite unique and could be very helpful to counselors when they provide services to clients who need a great deal of family support. If clients are first informed and given an opportunity to orally object, counselors may give health care information to family members or others assisting in the client's care. Standard B.1.a. of the ACA *Code of Ethics* cautions counselors to maintain sensitivity to cultural meanings of confidentiality, which include sharing information with family or community members of clients. In addition, Standard A.1.d. states that counselors recognize the importance of others in clients' lives and utilize them as positive resources, when appropriate. We recommend that counselors wishing to utilize this HIPAA provision indicate in their initial client agreement form the intention to communicate with family members when needed, and be sure to specifically ask clients orally whether that is acceptable to them. Under this same section in the rules, counselors may provide information to the public in the form of facility directories and to disaster relief organizations (such as the Red Cross).

When clients do give their permission to transfer their personal information regarding their counseling, only the minimum amount of information to accomplish the purpose may be transferred. As a result, it is important for counselors to have on their record release form a place for the client to specify the purpose of their request that their records be transferred. Standard B.2.d. of the ACA *Code of Ethics* states that when disclosure of confidential information is required, counselors reveal only essential information. When clients request that their records be transferred to another health care professional in conjunction with anticipated treatment from that individual, then, according to HIPAA, the full record must be transferred so the receiving professional can provide the best quality care.

Under HIPAA, each counseling office must designate a privacy officer. In a private practice, counselors themselves would also serve as the privacy officers. The privacy officer of an agency must train employees to handle confidential information appropriately, ensure procedures to protect client privacy are in place and are followed, and ensure proper forms are used by counselors and other health care personnel.

When counselors transfer records based on client written permission, they must take steps to ensure that the recipient of the records protects the privacy of the information they have received. We recommend that counselors insert statements on the records that the contents are confidential and should not be transferred to any other individuals.

What we have called *clinical case notes* are known as *psychotherapy notes* under HIPAA. Psychotherapy notes that are used only by the psychotherapist, to which no one else has access, are held to a much higher standard of protection. The rationale is that such notes are not a part of the health care record and were never intended to be shared with anyone else. In order for a client to have psychotherapy notes transferred to a third party, the client must specifically request that these notes be transferred. A general request for transfer of records is not sufficient. Clients must give their specific permission and authorization for the sensitive information contained in psychotherapy notes to be released. Health care plans cannot refuse to provide reimbursement if a client does not agree to release information covered under the psychotherapy notes provision.

Civil penalties for violations of the HIPAA rules are $100 per incident, up to $25,000 per person, per year, per standard. Criminal penalties for providers who knowingly and improperly disclose information or obtain information under false pretenses are up to $50,000 and 1 year in prison for obtaining or disclosing protected health information; up to $1,000,000 and up to 5 years in prison for obtaining protected health information under false pretenses; and up to $25,000 and up to 10 years in prison for obtaining or disclosing protected health information with the intent to sell, transfer, or use it for commercial advantage, personal gain, or malicious harm.

HIPAA is a federal law, so it applies throughout the United States and overrides state laws that are more lax. However, state laws that are stricter about protecting consumer health care privacy than HIPAA must be adhered to, if they exist.

Family Educational Rights and Privacy Act

The Family Educational Rights and Privacy Act of 1974 (FERPA), which is sometimes referred to as the "Buckley Amendment," affects all public educational institutions and any private or parochial educational institution that receives federal funding in one form or another. Almost all private and church-sponsored educational institutions receive some type of federal funding. The penalty for violating provisions of FERPA is the loss of all federal funding, which could be devastating for many educational institutions. Individuals cannot bring lawsuits under FERPA (*Tarka v. Franklin,* 1989).

Since the HIPAA rules were enacted, school personnel have wanted to know whether HIPAA requirements for health care records must be followed in educational institutions. In some cases, HIPAA applies in schools, and in other situations, it does not. Under 24 CFT 164.501, health information contained within student educational records that are subject to FERPA is exempt from the requirements of HIPAA. On the other hand, school-based health centers may be subject to HIPAA requirements if such centers are operated by HIPAA-compliant health organizations. Also, school nurses may be subject to HIPAA requirements if they engage in electronic billing. Communications between schools and health care providers may be subject to HIPAA rules as well.

FERPA legislation basically says that parents of minor students (and students who are 18 or older or who are in college) have two rights: (a) to inspect and review their education records and to challenge the contents to ensure the records are not inaccurate or misleading, and (b) to have their written authorization obtained before copies of their education records can be transferred to any third party.

After students are 18 years old or are attending a postsecondary institution, the legal rights under this legislation are vested in them. However, parents or guardians of dependent students may be given copies of the records of such students without the student's consent. *Dependent students* are defined as children or stepchildren, over half of whose support was received from the taxpayer the previous tax year (26 U.S.C.A. §152). As a result of this definition, most educational institutions give access to student records to parents who can show they claimed their child as a tax dependent the previous year.

Education records are defined in the federal legislation as records kept by educational institutions regarding students. The law specifically exempts from the right to inspect and review, any records that "are in the sole possession of the maker" [20 U.S.C.A. §1232g(a)(B)(i)]. To qualify under this exemption, counselors in schools and other educational institutions should keep their case notes separate from other records and should not let anyone else have access to those records. Treatment records "made or maintained by a physician, psychiatrist, psychologist, or other recognized professional or paraprofessional" are also exempt [20 U.S.C.A. §1232g(a)(B)(iv)]. As a result of these exemptions, clinical case notes kept by counselors in educational institutions do not have to be shown to students, parents, or guardians under FERPA requirements.

Schools are not required by FERPA to obtain written permission from parents or students to release a student's records to "other schools or school systems in which the student intends to enroll" [20 U.S.C.A. §1232g(b)(1)(b)]. Nonetheless, when copies of records of transfer students are forwarded to other schools, parents must be notified of the transfer and must be given copies of the transferred records if they desire copies.

These access exemptions to inspect and review one's records under FERPA do not in any way diminish a person's rights to counselors' records under a subpoena in relation to a lawsuit. A valid subpoena for records must be complied with in all circumstances. When an educational institution intends to release records pursuant to a subpoena, the institution must notify parents and students in advance of the release [20 U.S.C.A. §1232g(b)(2)(B); *Rios v. Read,* 1977; *Mattie T. v. Johnston,* 1976], although notification is not required if the subpoena orders that the existence of the subpoena not be disclosed [20 U.S.C.A. §1232g(b)(J)(i–ii)].

In an emergency situation, an amendment to the act has given permission to release private information without parent or student written permission. The information must be "necessary to protect the health or safety of the student or other persons" [20 U.S.C.A. §1232g(a)(1)(I)]. This provision would allow counselors to release their records on students to medical personnel or law enforcement authorities without violating FERPA, if they determined that a student was a danger to self or others.

Educational institutions may release to an alleged victim of any violence the results of any disciplinary proceeding conducted against the alleged perpetrator with respect to that specific crime [20 U.S.C.A. §1232g(b)(6)]. FERPA also allows institutions to include in education records any disciplinary action taken against students and to disclose such action to school officials in other schools [20 U.S.C.A. §1232g(h)].

There is no general common law principle that requires counselors to obtain *written* authorization from clients to transfer records to third parties. Oral permission is legally adequate, but obtaining written authorization is always recommended. Under FERPA, however, written authorization is required to transfer records.

Federally Funded Substance Abuse Programs

The federal government funds a multitude of substance abuse prevention and treatment programs. Private and public agencies apply for federal funds to operate many of these programs. Programs that receive federal funds must comply with federal laws related to substance abuse treatment.

A federal statute (42 U.S.C.A. §290dd-2) declares that records kept by any facility that is "conducted, regulated, or directly or indirectly assisted" by the federal government are confidential. Disclosure of records of individuals receiving substance abuse services (including education, prevention, training, treatment, rehabilitation, or research) is permitted only in a few circumstances. Exceptions to the nondisclosure of records requirement include the following: (a) when the person gives prior written consent, (b) medical emergencies, (c) audits or evaluations, and (d) to avert substantial risk of death or serious bodily harm if a court order is secured. Records cannot be used for criminal charges or investigations [42 U.S.C.A. §290dd-2(c)]. However, a counselor's direct observations are not a record and can be used in criminal proceedings against clients or patients (*State v. Brown,* 1985; *State v. Magnuson,* 1984).

The statute related to federal substance abuse programs does not prohibit exchange of information between the military and the Department of Veterans Affairs. The statute also permits the reporting of suspected child abuse and neglect under state laws.

Unlike FERPA, the violation of this statute or the regulations that implement it can result in criminal charges and a fine. As a result, clients may file criminal complaints against counselors in federally supported substance abuse treatment programs who violate their rights to privacy, although individuals whose confidentiality rights are violated cannot file civil lawsuits for damages (*Logan v. District of Columbia,* 1978).

Other Federal Statutes

Additional federal statutes prohibit or limit the disclosure of counseling records for the following clients who are served by federally assisted programs: (a) runaway and homeless youth (42 U.S.C.A. §5731), (b) individuals with sexually transmitted diseases [42 U.S.C.A. §247c(d)(5)], (c) voluntary clients in federal drug abuse or dependence programs [42 U.S.C.A. §260(d)], (d) older persons [42 U.S.C.A. §3026(d); 42 U.S.C. §3027(f)(1)], and (e) victims of violence against women [42 U.S.C.A. §14011(b)(5)]. On the other hand, privacy is sometimes expressly limited by statutes. A federal statute specifically denies confidentiality to individuals who are examined by a physician in civil commitment proceedings due to drug abuse (42 U.S.C.A. §3420).

Handling, Storing, and Destroying Records

Creating counseling records is an important process, but maintaining and ultimately getting rid of them are crucial matters for counselors as well. According to the ACA *Code of Ethics,* counselors must ensure that records are kept in a secure location and that access to counseling records is limited to authorized persons (Standard B.6.a.). The privacy of clients and the self-protection of counselors both have an impact on the manner in which records are handled, stored, and destroyed.

Because counseling records are so sensitive, agencies should develop written policies regarding how these records will be handled on a day-to-day basis. Agencies or practices that fall under HIPAA requirements must have written policies regarding records and must make those policies available for client review. Typically, counselors create and keep their own clinical case notes. These notes should be kept in locked drawers or cabinets. In offices with more than one person, an individual should be designated as the records manager. Generally, this person would be a clerical or administrative employee. The records manager should have the responsibility of ensuring that counseling records are kept secure, checked out and back in properly, stored safely, and finally, eliminated according to a set schedule and policy.

Everyone who handles counseling records should make sure the records are not left unattended so that unauthorized persons can read them. Care should be taken to promptly return counseling records to their proper place after they have been used.

There are no general laws that dictate how long a particular counseling record must be kept (Woody, 1988b). You should be aware, however, that some federal or state statutes require that certain types of records created for certain purposes be kept for a definite period of time. For instance, some state counselor licensure laws dictate that counselors' records be kept for a certain number of years. Attorneys who advise counseling agencies should be asked to review statutes and regulations to determine whether there are any requirements regarding records, including the length of time they must be maintained.

Many agencies have determined that they want to keep their counseling records for a set period of time. Generally, agencies also have rules and guidelines regarding how records should be handled, stored, and eliminated. Counselors should always inquire as to whether the agency in which they work has such requirements. All agency rules and regulations should be followed by counselors (Standard A.1.b.).

Counseling records often are affected by agency accreditation rules as well. Many counseling centers, hospitals, and treatment facilities are accredited by private agencies such as the Joint Commission on Accreditation of Healthcare Organizations (JCAHO), the International Association of Counseling Services (IACS), and the Commission on Accreditation of Rehabilitation Facilities (CARF). See Appendix B for contact information for these organizations. These accreditation agencies have specific requirements regarding counseling records, and many require that records be kept for a set period of time. Counselors who work in agencies that are accredited should ask about record-keeping requirements.

If there are no laws, agency rules, or accreditation standards that require records to be kept for a specific length of time, then counselors should encourage their agency to establish a written policy and to destroy counseling records on a periodic basis. There are a number of reasons for not keeping counseling records indefinitely. Practically speaking, it is expensive to keep records locked away and to keep up with logging them in and out. In addition, confidential records that exist could be compromised in some way, whereas confidential records that are destroyed cannot be seen by unauthorized persons.

It is wise to establish a record destroying policy stipulating that certain categories of records will be destroyed on a specific date each year unless one of the following applies: (a) There is reason to believe the records may be subpoenaed in a current or future lawsuit, or (b) the records contain documentation of actions taken by counselors that need to be kept longer than the usual period of time. There are no guidelines about whether individuals "believe records may be subpoenaed." Common sense should dictate this determination. If records are purposefully destroyed when someone knows or should have reasonably known that those records would be subpoenaed later, the person destroying them can be charged with a serious crime (Woody, 1988a). Records documenting actions that counselors have taken to protect themselves probably should be kept longer than counseling records normally would be kept.

Voluntarily Transferring Records

Clients often request that their counseling records be provided to another professional who is rendering services to them. In addition, professionals often request your clients' counseling records when they begin treating your current or former clients. The ACA *Code of Ethics* (B.6.f.) requires that counselors obtain written permission from clients to disclose or transfer copies of records. After clients have requested or given permission in writing that their counseling records be transferred to a third party, counselors have an obligation to comply. A form is provided in Appendix F for clients to sign when they wish to have their records transferred.

Counselors should make sure the written request of the client is followed precisely and that only records the client authorizes for transfer are actually sent. In addition, counselors should never send originals of records, only copies. Finally, records located in client files from other professionals or agencies should never be transferred to a third party. If clients want those records sent, they must contact the agency that created the records and authorize that agency to forward them.

The written and signed authorization from the client should be filed in the client's folder. In addition, a notation should be entered in the client's file that indicates which records were sent and when, the method of transfer (e.g., U.S. mail, courier service, personal delivery), to whom they were sent, and to what address.

SUBPOENAS

3-4 The Case of Paulette

Paulette, an elementary school counselor, has been counseling Billy Rosen, a third-grader whose parents are going through a contentious divorce. One afternoon after school, Paulette is working in her office when a gentleman appears at her door. He announces that he has a subpoena for her records that has been requested by Mr. Rosen's attorney. He offers to wait while she makes a copy of the records of her counseling sessions with Billy.

- How should Paulette respond to the gentleman's offer?
- What should Paulette do about the subpoena?

Subpoenas are legal documents that might require counselors to produce copies of records; appear for a deposition, court hearing, or trial; or appear and bring their records with them (Cottone & Tarvydas, 2003). Subpoenas are official court documents and cannot be ignored.

Receiving a subpoena can be an intimidating, and even frightening, experience for a counselor. Unless counselors deal with subpoenas on a routine basis in their work, there is some justification for this reaction. Dealing with a subpoena places a counselor in the legal arena—into a system that is adversarial in nature and that operates by a different set of rules than those to which counselors are accustomed. If you should receive a subpoena, the information that follows will help guide you through the process of responding to it.

In chapter 2, one of the exceptions to confidentiality and privileged communication that was noted was a court order. Court orders might be issued in hearings or trials at which judges are present and give verbal orders, or they might be issued when judges sign written orders in their official capacity. All citizens must obey court orders. The sanctions for not obeying orders issued by judges are imprisonment, fines, or both. The only alternative to obeying a court order is to appeal to a higher court. Such appeals must be filed immediately by a lawyer. Although a subpoena is a type of court order, counselors should always consult with their own attorneys before turning over records or appearing at a deposition, hearing, or trial in response to a subpoena.

Discovery in Litigation

Lawyers who are representing parties in lawsuits are members of the bar in the jurisdiction in which they are practicing. Therefore, they are considered official officers of the court. One of the privileges extended to officers of a court is to issue valid subpoenas for information related to cases they are litigating.

One of the concepts in lawsuits of any kind is that attorneys representing the parties are entitled to *discovery*. Discovery is the process whereby attorneys have the right to ask for and receive information relevant to their case before the case is tried (Swenson, 1997). The idea is that there should be no surprises during trials. Instead, each side in a lawsuit should know all the information that will be entered into evidence during the trial, before the actual trial begins.

Subpoenas are used extensively during the discovery or pretrial phase of lawsuits. Attorneys from both sides ask potential witnesses to respond in writing to written questions (interrogatories), to provide copies of records they are entitled to see, and to come to their offices for depositions. In addition, witnesses can be subpoenaed to testify at hearings before the judge presiding over the case, and finally, at the trial as well.

Validity of Subpoenas

The records of counselors might be subpoenaed or counselors themselves may be subpoenaed for their oral testimony at depositions, hearings, or trials. Also, written questions may be submitted with a demand for written answers. Counselors might also be subpoenaed to appear at a legal proceeding and instructed to bring records with them. In the event you receive a subpoena to appear at a legal proceeding, but no mention is made of records, do not take records with you unless you are instructed to do so by your own attorney. If a subpoena is issued to you by an attorney, your first step is to consult your own lawyer to determine whether the subpoena is valid and whether you must respond to it (Woody, 1988a).

An attorney will review a subpoena for you and will advise you regarding the proper manner in which to respond. Attorneys might assist you in a number of ways. For example, they could ask the attorney who issued the subpoena to withdraw it, file a motion to quash the subpoena, or advise you to comply with the subpoena.

Attorneys who are litigating cases may not issue subpoenas for records or for witnesses to testify if the attorneys know they do not have a right to the information. However, because material may be privileged without attorneys realizing it, you could receive a subpoena that is not enforceable because of privilege. Subpoenas could be unenforceable or invalid for other reasons as well. You must obtain legal advice regarding your response to any subpoena you receive. If you refuse to respond to a valid subpoena, you could be held in contempt of court and either imprisoned or fined. On the other hand, if you provide information in response to an invalid or unenforceable subpoena, you could be held legally accountable to a client or former client for any damages suffered.

When you receive a subpoena, you should take action immediately, because most subpoenas must be complied with within a fixed number of hours. Many counselors mistakenly believe that subpoenas must be personally handed to them to be valid and enforceable. In fact, if you have knowledge through any means that a subpoena has been issued to you, you should immediately take the steps listed in the following sections.

Your first step, if you are employed, should be to notify your immediate supervisor that you have received a subpoena and to request legal advice regarding your response to it. In the event your employer does not provide you with access to a lawyer, then follow the directives of your supervisor. If you are in an independent private practice, your first step should be to call your own practice attorney.

Your lawyer or supervisor should be informed if you think the information being requested might be privileged. You should also inform your attorney or supervisor if you believe testifying or producing records regarding the matter would compromise the privacy of a former or current client, even if the relationship was not privileged by law. You should feel free to openly discuss the situation with a lawyer because your relationship with the lawyer is privileged. Often it is necessary to explain to your lawyer the general concepts of counseling, the nature of your relationship to the parties involved in the lawsuit, and the details regarding clients who are involved or affected by the litigation. You should give complete information to your lawyer and answer any questions regarding the situation.

Once your attorney or supervisor understands the situation and has given you advice, follow the instructions precisely. If you have doubts or questions, discuss them with your attorney or supervisor, but ultimately you must follow the advice given to you.

Generally a subpoena received from the attorney of your client or former client will not be problematic, because the individual waives privilege, if it exists, by calling you as a witness. Nonetheless, legal advice in such situations still is needed to ensure you are proceeding properly.

Interrogatories

One of the easiest types of subpoenas to deal with is a subpoena that involves interrogatories. Included with the subpoena will be a set of written questions with a requirement that you respond to each question in writing. You must sign an oath that your answers are truthful.

If you receive a set of interrogatories and your attorney informs you that you must respond to them, you should discuss each question and your proposed answer with your attorney before you begin writing. After composing your answers, you should ask your attorney to review your answers before you submit them. Take your attorney's advice about changes or rewording of your answers.

Appearances at Proceedings

In the event you are directed by your attorney or supervisor to appear at a legal proceeding, ask that you be told what to expect. Ask your attorney or supervisor to explain in detail how such events take place. Also, request that the attorney tell you what questions you might be asked and request advice on responses you think you should make to the anticipated questions. Ask the attorney to accompany you to the proceeding if possible.

Depositions usually take place in the office of the lawyer who has issued the subpoena. Although the judge will be present at hearings and trials, the judge does not attend depositions. Generally, depositions are attended by the attorney who issued the subpoena, the attorney representing the other party involved in the lawsuit, a court reporter, and the witness being deposed.

It is important to have your own attorney present at your deposition if possible. During a hearing or trial, the judge will rule on controversies and will instruct witnesses whether to answer questions. With no judge present at depositions, you need your own attorney there to tell you how to proceed and to protect you from being pressured by the other attorneys.

Testimony Under Oath

Testimony you give at any legal proceeding will be *under oath,* which means that you will be required to swear to tell the truth. Once an oath has been administered, false statements usually are considered perjury, which is a serious crime. You might be instructed by your attorney not to answer questions at a deposition, but you should always, in all circumstances, answer questions truthfully when you do respond.

Turning Over Records

In the event your attorney or supervisor directs you to turn over your records in response to a subpoena, you should follow the advice you have been given. Sometimes attorneys who issue subpoenas will accept summaries of notes rather than case notes themselves, or other similar compromises may be needed. Your attorney will negotiate appropriately on your behalf.

You should never forward the originals of your records. Instead, make copies and deliver the copies. Sometimes records of other individuals are mixed in with records that must be turned over. In that situation, sometimes it is permissible to obliterate private information related to other parties. Again, follow the advice of your attorney in this situation.

If your records include records you have received from other professionals, such as physicians, other mental health professionals, or hospitals, do not copy and forward those records. If the attorney issuing the subpoena wants copies of those records, the individual or entity that created them will have to be subpoenaed.

The ACA *Code of Ethics* (Standard B.2.c.) states that when counselors receive subpoenas for counseling records of their clients, counselors must obtain written informed consent from their clients to release the records, or, if that is impossible, must *take steps to prohibit the disclosure or have it limited as narrowly as possible due to potential harm to the client or counseling relationship.* In our experience, clients who do not wish to have their counseling records exposed rarely agree to sign a written consent document. Usually, clients whose records have been subpoenaed, after being informed by their counselors that a subpoena exists, take appropriate legal steps through their attorneys to have the subpoena quashed. It is the duty of clients to assert their legal privilege, if one exists. In the event a client is not available to be informed that his or her counseling records have been subpoenaed, the counselor or the counselor's attorney should assert the client's privilege on behalf of the client, and should take other steps that are legally available to avoid complying with the subpoena. If the subpoena is determined to be valid, then counselors and their attorneys should do what they can to limit the disclosure of private client information.

TECHNOLOGY

Technological advances in our society have had a significant impact on the profession of counseling (Hohenshil, 2000). The various forms of technology that have been developed and are still being developed all have the same basic purpose—to facilitate the transfer of information. In this transfer process, situations are inevitably created in which sensitive or confidential information might be accessed by inappropriate persons (Welfel & Heinlen, 2001). Every form of technology discussed in this section creates records or recordings of information that, if not treated carefully, could lead to the privacy of clients being compromised.

Certainly, counselors want to maximize their effectiveness by utilizing as many forms of technology as possible (Owen & Weikel, 1999; Sampson & Bloom, 2001). The Association for Counselor Education and Supervision (ACES, 1999b) has developed a list of technology competencies graduate students in counseling should have, to assist counselor education programs in ensuring they are teaching the skills that are needed. It is also imperative that counselors educate themselves regarding the subtle ways in which their clients' privacy might be affected by the use of technology (Cottone & Tarvydas, 2003). In the 2005 ACA *Code of Ethics,* new technology and Internet standards were introduced. In the following discussion, we identify a number of areas in which technology is having an impact on the counseling process, and we provide guidelines for ensuring that the privacy of clients is protected.

Telephones

Although telephones have become such an essential means of communicating in our society that we seldom even think of them as technology, the use of telephones raises a number of significant issues for counselors. Some of the more important concerns related to telephone use and client privacy are outlined in this chapter. The following technological inventions related to telephone use are discussed as well: (a) answering machines and answering services, (b) pagers, (c) cellular telephones, and (d) facsimile machines.

Counselors must be cautious in discussing confidential or privileged information with anyone over the telephone. The ACA *Code of Ethics* (2005) addresses this need for caution, reminding counselors that they must discuss the private information of clients "only in settings in which they can reasonably ensure client privacy" (Standard B.3.c.). A second standard, B.3.e., advises counselors to "take precautions to ensure the confidentiality of information transmitted through the use of" telephones and other electronic devices. There is no way to ensure that the person with whom you are talking over the telephone is the person he or she claims to be. Also, there are many ways that telephone conversations can be monitored or intercepted without you realizing it. Even when you talk to individuals frequently and know their voices well, you still are taking a chance when you assume that you know who you are talking to or that your conversation is private. As a result of these problems, counselors are advised to be very careful when discussing confidential information over the telephone.

Counselors should follow the guidelines listed in Figure 3-2 when using the telephone. In addition, counselors have an ethical obligation to ensure that the staff members in the agency in which they work are educated regarding proper telephone use. Standard B.3.a of the ACA *Code of Ethics* (2005) states that "Counselors make every effort to ensure that privacy and confidentiality of clients are maintained by subordinates . . ." You should make sure that anyone who works for you is trained to maintain confidentiality of clients, that their actions are monitored, and corrective action is taken, if necessary.

Answering Machines, Voice Mail, and Answering Services

Many counseling offices in community mental health centers, hospitals, schools, private practices, and other settings use answering machines, voice mail, or answering services in order to conduct their business. In fact, because of the high cost of secretarial or reception services, most counseling agencies and counselors in private practice have answering machines or services. Many clients also have answering machines or answering services in their homes or at their places of employment.

Counselors must strive to protect the privacy of their clients both when receiving messages and when leaving messages for clients. Counselors who use answering machines in their offices

---

1. Never acknowledge that clients are receiving services or give out information regarding clients to unknown callers. Explain that in respect for the privacy of clients, such information is not given out unless clients first sign authorizations. Explain how authorizations from clients may be obtained.

2. Make efforts to verify that you are talking to the correct person when you receive or make calls in which confidential information will be discussed.

3. Keep in mind the possibility that your conversation is being recorded or monitored by an unauthorized person.

4. If you discuss confidential information regarding a client on the telephone, be professional and cautious throughout the conversation. Avoid becoming friendly or informal, or saying anything off the record.

5. Remember that a record will exist at the telephone company that this telephone call was made or received.

6. Do not say anything during the conversation that you would not want your client to hear or that you would not want to repeat under oath in a legal proceeding.

Figure 3-2   Guidelines for counselor telephone use

should not allow unauthorized persons to use their offices when they are not present to ensure that no one hears answering machine messages as they are being left or retrieves messages inappropriately. The audio option on answering machines should be turned to the off position when counselors are not present in their offices. In addition, counselors should not retrieve messages when people who should not hear confidential information are present in their offices.

Counselors who use voice mail or answering services must ensure that their access codes to their messages are not disclosed to unauthorized persons. It is unwise to write access codes in personal books that could be misplaced or stolen. It is also important that answering service personnel be educated regarding the confidential nature of messages taken for counselors so that they can avoid inadvertently compromising the privacy of clients.

It is common practice for counselors to make written notes as they listen to their messages from answering machines, voice mail, or answering services. Such written messages to themselves could contain confidential information and must be handled as carefully as any other confidential record.

Two important factors should be considered when using answering machines or voice mail. First, a recording is being created that will exist until it is erased or destroyed. And second, there is no way to ensure that the intended person will be the one who retrieves a message that is left. The fact that others may hear the message when answering machines or voice mail are being used requires that counselors never reveal anything that is confidential when leaving such messages. Because the fact that a person is a counseling client is itself confidential information, counselors must be very cautious when leaving messages for clients.

From a practical perspective, counselors often have to reach their clients by telephone. Appointments sometimes have to be canceled or rearranged, forms need to be signed, and other matters come up that need to be handled by telephone. It is wise for counselors who leave messages for their clients to identify themselves by name and state their message in such a manner that a third person would not hear anything that the clients would not want them to hear. Remember that clients often have others present when they retrieve their messages and that messages left at their homes could be retrieved by family members.

Telephone Pagers

Telephone pagers were very popular prior to the advent of cellular telephones. Some professionals still prefer pagers. Counselors who carry pagers must ensure that messages received from clients are kept confidential. Because pager messages can be received in public places, counselors must exercise caution in retrieving their pager messages.

Counselors who send pager messages to clients must be careful to ensure their clients' privacy, exercising the same caution they would when sending answering machine, voice mail, or secretarial service messages.

It is important for counselors to know that companies supplying pagers to individuals keep records of all calls received. It is not possible, then, to receive a pager message from a client or to send a message to a client without a record being created of the pager telephone contact.

Cellular Telephones

Cellular telephones operate just like telephones connected by wires, except that conversations are transmitted by airwaves. As a result, there may be more chance of a conversation on a cellular telephone being accidentally or purposefully intercepted by an unauthorized person.

In addition, cellular telephones are carried around wherever individuals go. As a result, persons with cellular telephones often have conversations in public places or in their automobiles. When talking to a client with a cellular telephone, it is wise to assume that the person is not in a private place.

Facsimile Machines

Facsimile (fax) machines can be a quick and convenient way for counselors to transmit client information on paper to fellow professionals, managed care organizations, and other authorized recipients. Counselors need to keep in mind, however, that they have relinquished control over the information contained in a faxed message as soon as they send it. Fax machines often are widely accessible and the intended recipient may not be available to retrieve the faxed material at the moment it is sent. These factors increase the risk of faxed messages being seen by persons who are not authorized to see the material. Welfel (2006) suggested the following strategies for protecting the privacy of faxed materials:

- Use a cover sheet that states the confidential nature of the message and specifies that it is to be read by the intended recipient only.
- Prearrange a time to send the fax so that the recipient can retrieve it immediately, and ask the recipient to confirm receipt by telephone or e-mail (this will alert the sender in case the wrong number was dialed).
- Do not send sensitive personal client information by fax.
- Train the office staff regarding how to handle faxed materials.
- Obtain a specific release from the client for fax transmissions.

Office Security

Many modern offices have security systems designed to protect the individuals who work there. These security systems can include cameras that film each person who enters the building, guards who require identification from visitors, or voice systems that require those who wish to enter to request that a door be unlocked for them. All these measures could compromise the privacy of a counseling client. Counselors who practice in environments where security measures are used should make efforts to minimize the intrusive nature of these systems. Also, clients should be informed of security measures being used that may not be readily observed.

Computer Storage

Records, once they are created in any form, are never totally secure. It is always possible for an unauthorized person to gain access to records, or for mistakes to occur that cause the privacy of records to be compromised. Just as files filled with papers can be seen by unauthorized persons, so can records kept on a computer.

Keeping counseling records on computers has become a common practice. An advantage for counselors is that, by avoiding hard copies of records, they do not have to make storage space available or worry about securing physical files and file cabinets. A disadvantage is that, in some respects, computers may not be as secure as a locked file cabinet kept in a locked room.

The preferred method of storing information in agencies and offices today is through computers. File cabinets and hard copies of documents will eventually become obsolete because computers allow incredible amounts of information to be contained on a single disk. Computers have made business environments more efficient and cost-effective.

Counselors usually think in terms of locks and keys when they consider methods of keeping confidential information secure. With so much data being stored on computers in modern counseling settings, it is important that counselors understand security problems and solutions associated with keeping information on computers (Swensen, 1997).

Access to confidential computer files is one of the first issues to consider. It is important for counselors to set up their computers so that a password must be used to access sensitive files. One of the problems with using passwords, however, is the danger that the passwords will become known to unauthorized persons. Password holders tend to be anxious about the possibility of forgetting their password. As a result, they make notes to themselves with the password on them and the notes are sometimes seen by others. Some people have even been known to post their password directly on their computer. Offices often will change passwords from time to time to help with security. But, again, this makes computer users nervous about forgetting their passwords, so they record them in a way that leads to their disclosure. Counselors who practice in offices where passwords are used for confidential computer files should be careful not to disclose the passwords to unauthorized persons and not to record the passwords in places where they might be seen by others. In addition, counselors should train office personnel about the importance of password security and alert staff members to the problems that exist in keeping passwords secure.

Printing hard copies of documents from confidential computer files can also cause problems. Printed confidential information should be filed in locked cabinets or destroyed when no longer needed.

Disposing of confidential computer files also is a problem area. Some people believe that when they delete a file in a computer, they have destroyed that information. In reality, most deleted computer files can be retrieved by computer experts. Counselors should understand that all information entered into a computer has the potential of eventually being seen by unauthorized persons, even after the information has been deleted. As in creating any type of record, counselors should assume that what they have written will someday become public information, despite their best efforts to keep the record confidential or to delete or destroy it.

Steps should be taken to prevent confidential counseling records kept on computers from being compromised. Listed in Figure 3-3 are some suggestions for counselors who use computers for their records.

Electronic Mail Communications

Electronic mail, commonly referred to as *e-mail,* is fast becoming a preferred method of communication by those individuals who have access to personal computers in their work or home environments. E-mail allows individuals to send and receive messages on their computer. These messages seem secure because a secret password must be used to send or read messages. Messages are typed, but written documents, video images, or audio messages may be attached to e-mail messages that are sent to another person.

Usually, messages are sent between individuals with periods of time passing between communications. This type of interaction resembles a letter-writing exchange. However, it is possible to send and receive messages instantly if both persons are at the computer at the same time. Instant communication by e-mail simulates a conversation.

3-5 The Case of Amahd

Amahd works as a counselor in a very busy community college mental health center. Many of the clients for whom he provides services are very adept at electronic communications. As

1. Try to avoid using a computer to which others have access. If this is not possible, store your records on a disk rather than on the computer hard drive.

2. Use passwords for accessing the files in the computer. Keep the passwords secure, limit the number of individuals who know the passwords, and change the passwords periodically.

3. Any time a confidential record is printed from the computer, ensure that it is handled as other confidential materials would be.

4. Avoid placing computers with monitors in public areas where unauthorized persons might accidentally see confidential information.

5. Limit access to computer equipment that is used to enter and retrieve confidential records.

6. Delete computer-stored records on the same basis that traditional records would be destroyed in the agency or office. Keep in mind, though, that deleted files usually can be retrieved by computer experts from a computer's hard drive even after they have been deleted.

7. When information is downloaded from a computer's hard drive to a disk, or transferred electronically, make sure that confidential material is not accidentally included.

8. Be careful in networking a computer used for confidential information. The more separate computers that can access information, the greater the chance that confidential information will be compromised.

9. Use a coding system rather than client names on disk labels so that the client identity is not obvious to anyone who might see them.

10. Regularly update virus protection software.

11. Make a backup copy of all files and keep them in a secure but separate location from the originals.

Figure 3-3   Guidelines for computerized records

a result, he encourages clients to send him e-mail messages if they need to schedule or change appointments or need to communicate with him between appointments for some reason. Amahd had intended all e-mail communications with clients to be strictly appointment or business related. Recently, however, several clients have begun to add short personal messages to their e-mail notes to him. Mark, a client he has been counseling for 3 months, has even begun to write long notes to Amahd about thoughts and feelings he has been experiencing between counseling sessions. Amahd isn't sure how to handle this situation.

• What problems could you foresee might occur if Amahd allows clients to continue sending him such notes and messages?
• What advice would you give Amahd?

A primary advantage of e-mail is that it is free once access to an e-mail system is secured through a subscription that usually involves a service fee. Many employers provide e-mail access to their employees. Other advantages to e-mail over other methods of communication are that individuals can retrieve their messages at their convenience rather than being interrupted by telephone calls, printed copies of messages can be easily created, and messages can be returned quickly and efficiently.

Disadvantages of e-mail communication, when compared to telephone conversations, are the following:

- Communication usually is one-way—it is not interactive.
- Each message is recorded in computers, often in several.
- Communication is not complete until the recipient actually accesses the messages and reads them.
- Once sent, messages cannot be retrieved.
- The quick nature of the communication can lead to sending messages that are not well conceptualized.
- Recipients may misinterpret messages and do not have the benefit of asking for clarification or of noting a person's tone of voice or inflection.
- It is easy to make errors and send messages to the wrong person or to many persons at once.
- Messages can easily be forwarded to others.
- Messages can be altered before being sent on to another person.
- The ease of using e-mail seems to encourage an informality that may not be well suited for professional communications.

The use of e-mail can be deceptive. Those who use e-mail type their message, press a button, and it disappears. Although it appears to be private between the message sender and the receiver, in reality there are a number of opportunities for e-mail messages to be intercepted or read by others.

The primary legal concern for counselors who use e-mail is that a record exists in computers for every message that is sent or received. Each message is recorded in several computers and can be retrieved. As a result, an e-mail message creates a record that is vulnerable to exposure. Although an e-mail message record is secured by the passwords of the sender and the receiver, it can be retrieved by individuals who operate the computer systems through which the message is sent. Further, the message can be forwarded easily and can be altered before being forwarded. As a result of the many ways e-mail messages can be accessed or compromised, counselors who use e-mail should be extremely cautious about disclosing confidential information to clients or other professionals through e-mail communications and should warn their clients about the possibility that e-mail messages could be compromised.

Counselors sometimes belong to e-mail communication groups. When a message is sent by an individual, it is received by all persons in the group. Counselors should understand that the increased number of individuals receiving such messages increases the possibilities of a message being sent to others or becoming public (Berge, 1994; Sampson, 1996). Also, belonging to such groups increases the possibility of mistakes in which a private message intended for an individual is sent instantly to a very large group of people.

Use of the Internet

The Internet as a Source of Information for Clients   Counselors sometimes ask clients to read or review materials relevant to the issues they are discussing in counseling. The explosion of information that is available over the World Wide Web is phenomenal. To take just one example, Dedden and James (1998) found 9,000 sites that offered career counseling and reviewed several Internet sites that they believed offered positive and helpful career resources.

Counselors who send their clients to the Internet for information must understand the nature of the materials found there (Millner & Kiser, 2002). First, sites on the Internet are not monitored for content or quality. As a result, clients must be cautioned to keep in mind that what they are reading or reviewing may not be accurate or helpful to them. In addition, sites that counselors have reviewed can be changed and may be different by the time they are viewed by clients.

Internet Counseling   The traditional process for counseling involves a counselor and one or more clients meeting face to face in a professional office. Since the Internet has come into existence, some individuals have begun offering counseling by e-mail or through fee-for-service sites. The practice of providing counseling services over the Internet is controversial. There are several advantages to this approach: (a) increased accessibility of services for those who would otherwise find it difficult to receive services, such as low-income clients, the frail elderly, individuals who are severely physically disabled, and rural or isolated individuals; (b) perceived anonymity may decrease client anxiety, thus encouraging people to ask for help and increasing the extent to which clients are willing to share intimate issues; (c) greater freedom in scheduling; and (d) the medium facilitates improved preparation by allowing better choice of written words over spoken ones (Sampson, Kolodinsky, & Greeno, 1997; Wilson, et al., 1997). Riemer-Reiss (2000) has suggested that distance counseling or *telecounseling* has the potential to supplement traditional mental health counseling services and will not replace the conventional modes of service delivery, but will become an essential component to improve the accessibility of counseling services.

On the other hand, some mental health professionals believe that WebCounseling services have multiplied faster than the evidence that they are safe or effective (Welfel, 2006). A number of concerns have been raised, including the following: (a) The possibility exists that counselors may operate from erroneous assumptions due to the absence of visual and auditory cues; (b) lack of security of communications could lead to breaches of confidentiality; (c) a relationship-building human presence between counselor and client is lacking; (d) effectiveness of counseling non-White clients may be reduced because the counselor may have difficulty attending to the high-context communication style of a population; (e) issues that are interpersonal in nature cannot be addressed effectively using this medium (Wilson et al., 1997); (f) counselors may not be able to discern when a client's condition poses a threat to self or others; (g) how counselors can determine an appropriate fee structure for WebCounseling; and (h) how clients can be protected from incompetent or unqualified cybercounselors.

Some of these potential problems may be resolved as new technologies, such as videoconferencing and encryption devices that increase the security of transmitted messages, come into wider use. Maintaining confidentiality of client records will continue to be problematic for some time, however, due to the ease with which unauthorized access can be gained and to unresolved questions regarding the number of individuals, agencies, and government entities who might make a case for having a right to access Internet databases.

The ACA *Code of Ethics* (2005) contains a number of standards related to Internet counseling. Counselors who use technology with their clients inform them of the benefits and limitations of technology, use technology only with clients for whom the use if appropriate, use face-to-face counseling when technology is inappropriate, provide access to computer applications when distance counseling services are being provided, follow laws related to their practice, and seek legal advice when they cross state or national boundaries when providing services through technology (Standards A.12.a., A.12.b., A.12.c., A.12.d., A.12.e., A.12.f.). Additionally, counselors provide extensive information to clients before engaging in technology based counseling (Standard A.12.g.).

Because Internet counseling and testing are already occurring (Sampson, 2000), some professional associations have issued guidelines to assist counselors and clients who are engaged in the activity (Jencius & Sager, 2001). These guidelines, which are included in Appendix J, include: *Ethical Standards for Internet Online Counseling* (American Counseling Association [ACA], 1999); *The Practice of Internet Counseling* (National Board for Certified Counselors [NBCC], 2001); *NCDA Guidelines for the Use of the Internet for Provision of Career Information and Planning Services* (National Career Development Association, 1997); *APA Statement on Services by Telephone, Teleconferencing, and Internet* (American Psychological Association [APA], 1997); and *ACES Guidelines for Online Instruction in Counselor Education* (Association for Counselor Education and Supervision [ACES], 1999a).

A major legal question is whether Internet counseling is permitted in states in which counselors must be licensed to practice. A further question arises as to where Internet counseling takes place—in the location of the counselor, the location of the client, or in both locations. Which laws govern the counseling process related to issues such as reporting abuse is another question. Because Internet counseling is still new, these questions will not be addressed until lawsuits are filed in which Internet counseling was used.

Counselors who consider offering counseling services through the Internet should ensure that they are not violating state laws (in the state of the counselor or of the client) that require counselors to be licensed. Counselors should also adhere to ethical guidelines when they provide counseling services in such an unconventional environment.

Listservs   Some counselors use listservs and Web-based discussion groups to communicate and exchange ideas with fellow mental health professionals. These can be a convenient means to share information on topics of mutual interest such as private practice management or dealing with third-party payers. They can also be a resource for obtaining case consultations. If you join into any of these discussions, remember that you must ensure that any client data you share are fully disguised or, if that is not possible, that you have a signed release from the client for this purpose. Keep in mind, too, that you may not know the extent to which any advice you receive is truly expert (Welfel, 2006).

Diversity Considerations in the Use of Technology

A major problem with the use of technology in counseling is that technology is not equally available or evenly distributed across cultures in the United States. Statistics published by the U.S. Department of Commerce (2002) revealed that 51% of households had a computer and 41.5% had access to the Internet. Wide gaps were evident, however, when Internet access was studied by sociorace, ethnicity, and income level:

- Whites (46%) and Asian Americans (57%) had much greater access than did African Americans (23.5%) or Hispanics (23.6%).
- Those with incomes over $75,000 (86%) had much greater access than those with incomes under $15,000 (12.7%).

Due to this *digital divide,* not all clients will have access to such services as Internet counseling or e-mail communications with their counselors. A legitimate concern is that the poor and underserved will be increasingly left behind as technology in counseling advances (Hughes, 2000). In addition, there are gender differences in the use of technology (Whitley, 1997), with males reporting higher computer self-efficacy than females. Counselors who use technologies in their work with clients should be careful not to assume that clients have access, expertise, or confidence in using computer applications.

On the positive side, technology can be of use to counselors who want to increase their multicultural counseling competence. There are numerous Web sites that offer information on various cultures and can be accessed using a search engine. It may be difficult for an individual counselor, however, to assess whether the information is valid. Counselors can also join listservs and discussion groups to gain understanding of different cultures.

Technology undoubtedly will continue to develop at a remarkably rapid pace. Challenges for the counseling profession will include ensuring equal access; addressing differences in gender, culture, and learning style inherent in technology; producing outcome research on equitable ways to utilize technology; and including a cultural lens as we continue to develop and assess the uses of technology in counseling (Jencius, 2003).

SUMMARY AND KEY POINTS

This chapter familiarizes you with the complexities of counseling records and record keeping. Subpoenas were also addressed in this chapter, because records are often subject to being subpoenaed. Finally, this chapter included a discussion of technology.

With respect to *records,* some key points made in the chapter include the following:

- Counselors keep records for two legitimate reasons: to provide the best possible quality of services to clients and for their own self-protection.
- Keeping good records can benefit clients in several significant ways. Some benefits to clients include continuity of care when client information is transferred from one mental health professional to another, or when a former client returns to counseling after an extended absence; helping clients measure and affirm their growth and change; and the creation of an accurate history of a client's diagnosis, treatment, and recovery.
- Records can also serve to protect counselors. In the event that your decisions are ever challenged, it is essential that you have documented decisions you have made and actions you have taken.
- Counselors keep three major types of records: administrative records, recordings, and clinical case notes. It is important for you to understand what is involved in keeping each of these kinds of records and that you follow sound procedures for keeping them secure and protecting the privacy of your clients.
- Many counselors are surprised to learn how many people can have access to their records. You should always make records with the assumption that they will be seen by others, including clients who have the right to access their records.
- Three important federal laws that affect counseling records are HIPAA, FERPA, and a statute related to federally funded substance abuse programs. If you work in an educational institution or in an agency that receives federal funds to provide substance abuse treatment, you will need to understand the major provisions of these laws.
- HIPAA is a recently enacted federal law that contains numerous, detailed provisions regarding client privacy, informed consent, and transfer of records. Counselors in all settings must understand how this law affects their practices.
- When you begin working with clients, you will need to have clear and consistent policies and procedures for creating, maintaining, transferring, and destroying your records. Although

your personal style and preferences may play some role, many of these policies and procedures will be dictated by your employer, laws, and accreditation standards.

The thought of receiving a *subpoena* might make you quite anxious. Subpoenas are official court documents that you cannot ignore. Unless you deal with subpoenas on a routine basis in your work, you should consult your supervisor (if you are employed) or your practice attorney (if you are in private practice) whenever you receive a subpoena. Your attorney will be an invaluable resource in helping you respond appropriately to subpoenas and deal with legal proceedings such as interrogatories, depositions, and trials. Always seek the counsel of your supervisor or attorney and follow the advice you are given.

Advances in technology have had a significant impact on the practice of counseling. Although you certainly will want to use as many forms of technology as you can to maximize your effectiveness, it is imperative that you are aware of subtle ways that the use of technology can affect your clients' privacy.

- Remember to be very cautious about discussing confidential information over the telephone.
- Messages sent and received via answering machine, voice mail, answering services, pagers, cellular phones, and facsimile machines are particularly vulnerable to unauthorized intrusions into privacy. You must keep in mind the various ways in which confidential information can be compromised when you use these means of communication.
- Although computers can help make your work more efficient and cost effective, you must be able to restrict access, secure stored information, transfer information, and dispose of files appropriately.
- E-mail communication has many advantages over telephone conversations, but there are many ways e-mail messages can be accessed or compromised. Again, you will need to have enough knowledge of how this medium works to be able to avoid inadvertent breaches of your clients' privacy.
- The Internet holds promises and pitfalls for use both as an information resource and as a counseling medium. Advances in Internet technology have outpaced the ability of mental health professionals to ensure that clients receive high-quality services.
- Some client populations may be disadvantaged by the increasing reliance of counselors on technology.

Competence and Malpractice

FOCUS QUESTIONS

1. What do you think should be done if a counselor becomes addicted to alcohol and is not counseling effectively?
2. How does a counselor determine whether a client is suicidal?
3. If a client makes a serious threat to harm another person, the law in all states except Texas requires the counselor to either warn the intended victim or inform the police of the threat. Do you think this legal requirement is good or bad? Why?

When clients come for counseling, they invest a great deal of trust and reliance in their counselors. The client's role in the therapeutic relationship, which involves dependency, self-disclosure, vulnerability, and expectations of finding relief and solutions to problems in a safe environment, underscores the counselor's obligation to provide competent services. "When clients put their trust in us as professionals, one of their most fundamental expectations is that we will be competent" (Pope & Vasquez, 1998, p. 59). Herlihy and Corey (2006) noted that the trust that clients bestow on us is "a source of power that must not be abused; clients need to be able to rely on their counselor's competence as a helper" (p. 179).

Competence in counseling is not easy to define. According to Welfel (2006), competence involves a combination of *knowledge, skill,* and *diligence.* Knowledgeable counselors have a thorough grounding in the core areas of study required to practice the profession. The core areas identified by the Council for Accreditation of Counseling and Related Educational Programs (CACREP, 2001) are professional identity, social and cultural diversity, human growth and development, career development, helping relationships, group work, assessment, and research and program evaluation. Knowledge is acquired through attaining a graduate degree in counseling and is maintained through continuing education activities.

Skilled counselors are able to select and use appropriately a range of basic interviewing techniques and therapeutic interventions. Skill building is a complex process that begins in graduate school with applied courses such as counseling techniques, group work, and practicum and internship. Skills are then honed and expanded through postdegree supervised counseling experience.

Diligence has been defined by Welfel (2006) as a consistent attentiveness to the client's needs that means putting client welfare first and foremost, above all other concerns. The first standard of the ACA *Code of Ethics* is "The primary responsibility of counselors is to respect the dignity and to promote the welfare of clients" (Standard A.1.a.). Evidence of diligent practice includes being willing to do extra reading, research, training, consultation, and follow-up to ensure that clients are served effectively.

Counselors are neither totally competent nor totally incompetent, although legal arguments during malpractice lawsuits might imply otherwise. In discussing the competency of lawyers, Cramton (1981) distinguished between "the ability to perform a task at an acceptable level" and "the reality of actually doing so in a particular situation" (p. 161). From Cramton's perspective, competency is not an abstract concept; instead, it is based on performance. Neither is competency a dichotomous concept; there is a continuum of professional expertise with gross negligence at one end and maximum effectiveness at the other extreme.

Counselors have an ethical obligation to accept employment only when "they are qualified by education, training, supervised experience, state and national professional credentials, and appropriate professional experience" for the jobs (ACA Code of Ethics, 2005, Standard C.2.c.). This standard also requires that counselors who hire other counselors employ only counselors who are qualified and competent. So, there is an ethical burden on those seeking employment to apply only for jobs they are compentent to perform, and on those who hire to employ only counselors who are competent to perform the jobs.

COMPETENCE AS AN ETHICAL AND LEGAL CONCEPT

The difference between law and ethics is that law demands a minimum level of practice from counselors, and ethics encourages counselors to approach the ideal in their level of practice. Competency is a parallel concept in that external forces require counselors to demonstrate minimum competency for professionals, whereas an internal force demands that counselors strive for ideal practice. For example, state licensure boards set the *minimum* requirements that counselors must meet to practice in that state, and counseling graduate programs require *minimum* levels of performance in order to be granted a degree. On the other hand, counselors are constantly striving to attain *maximum* knowledge and skills, and national voluntary credentialing organizations such as the National Board for Certified Counselors (NBCC) certify counselors who have distinguished themselves beyond the minimum in the field.

So, as we discuss competence in this chapter, keep in mind that competency is not an *either/or* concept. Rather, competency is a complex construct with many possible levels along a continuum.

Competency in counseling involves both ethical and legal considerations. From an ethical perspective, the moral principle that is most salient is *nonmaleficence*—Do no harm. Incompetence is often a major factor in causing harm to clients. Counselors rarely intend to harm their clients, but harm *can* occur if counselors are not knowledgeable, skillful, and capable.

The most basic ethical standard related to competence in the ACA *Code of Ethics* (2005) is that counselors "practice only within the boundaries of their competence" (Standard C.2.a.). How can a counselor determine just where these boundaries lie? It is difficult to answer this question because counseling is an exceptionally broad profession. Just as attorneys and physicians could never be competent to practice in every area within law and medicine, counselors could never be competent to offer counseling services in all areas of practice or to everyone who seeks their services. A counselor who is qualified and experienced in working with children might not be competent to work with a geriatric population. Expertise in counseling basically healthy clients who are having difficulty coping with life transitions does not qualify a counselor to work with clients who suffer from severe, clinical depression. Counselors who are very skilled at providing professional services to individuals who are seriously mentally ill may not be competent to provide developmental counseling services in an elementary school. Competence in individual counseling does not necessarily translate into competence to lead a particular type of counseling group or to counsel families.

Competence is also a legal issue, because society expects professionals to be competent and holds them to this standard through licensing boards and the courts. Legal issues relating to competence include state licensure and the law of malpractice. Counselor incompetence is the second most frequently reported area of ethical complaints (after dual relationships with clients), according to one survey of state counselor licensure boards (Neukrug, Millikin, & Walden, 2001). When a client is harmed, the counselor could be sued for malpractice and be held legally responsible in a court of law. Many lawsuits brought by plaintiffs alleging that they were harmed as clients focus on competence.

In this chapter, we first explore methods of developing and assessing competence to *enter* the counseling profession. Next we focus on ways to *maintain* competence during one's professional career. Finally, we address issues that arise when a counselor's competence is *questionable* or is called into question. These issues include malpractice, one of the most frightening of all legal issues for counselors. Considerations in counseling individuals who may be dangerous to themselves or others are discussed in this chapter because they constitute the most obvious areas of negligence and malpractice. When clients attempt or complete suicide, or perpetrate violence on others, the work of counselors often is reviewed to determine whether the counselors of these clients should have known that their clients were at risk. The issue of counselor impairment is also explored in this chapter.

COUNSELOR PREPARATION ISSUES

Competence is based on "education, training, supervised experience, state and national professional credentials, and appropriate professional experience" (ACA *Code of Ethics,* 2005, Standard C.2.a.). To be competent, counselors are also expected to "gain knowledge, personal awareness, sensitivity, and skills pertinent to working with a diverse client population" (Standard C.2.a.). Counselor preparation is obviously a basic component in developing competence to counsel; the process of becoming competent to enter professional practice begins with university counselor preparation programs.

The initial responsibility for producing competent practitioners lies with those who do the preparation—counselor educators and supervisors. They must select and admit individuals to graduate programs who are likely to succeed at developing the skills, knowledge, and characteristics needed to become effective counselors. Academic ability is one important factor. Selection criteria typically include grade-point averages and scores on standardized tests such as the Graduate Record Examination (GRE) or Miller Analogies Test (MAT). It is entirely possible, however, for a student to have strong intellectual abilities and still not possess the personal characteristics that are needed to be a "therapeutic person." Characteristics such as self-awareness, tolerance for ambiguity, and a willingness to explore one's own biases, values, and personal issues have been shown to be related to the ability to develop effective therapeutic relationships. Although these characteristics are difficult to measure, most counselor preparation programs rely on a personal interview, written essay, or other subjective criteria in selecting candidates for admission.

Once candidates have been selected and admitted into a graduate program, the next question that arises is "What does a master's degree program need to include, in order to produce competent counselors?" CACREP has developed standards for preparing counselors, and the Council on Rehabilitation Education (CORE) has set forth similar standards for rehabilitation counselors. CACREP and CORE accredit preparation programs that have undergone a rigorous review, so it can be reasonably assumed that graduates of approved programs possess certain competencies (Herlihy & Corey, 2006). It should be noted, however, that the majority of counselor preparation programs are not CACREP or CORE accredited, and that many competent counselors are educated in programs of sound quality that have not sought this accreditation. Another approach to ensuring adequacy of preparation programs is regional accreditation of universities. Regional accrediting agencies have set the minimal standard for universities in the United States. If a university is accredited by a regional accrediting agency, there is an assumption it is legitimate. The ACA *Code of Ethics* requires that "Counselors clearly state the accreditation status of their degree programs at the time the degree was earned" (Standard C.4.e.). Counselors should not explicitly state or imply that the university that granted their degree was regionally accredited if it was not at the time their degree was granted.

Although these approaches to ensuring quality of counselor preparation are both necessary and helpful, the reality remains that successful graduation from an accredited program does not guarantee competence (Kitzrow, 2002). Much depends on the individual student's motivation and ability to learn, the quality of instruction, the competencies of the faculty members, the breadth and extent of supervised experience in counseling clients that is provided by the program, and the quality of supervision received. In our own experience as counselor educators, we have found that most students who are about to graduate are keenly aware that they have only just begun to develop competence as practitioners. As a novice counselor, you need not be hobbled by a concern over your limitations and lack of experience. In most states, you will continue to be supervised closely and supported in your work as a counselor until you have been licensed for independent private practice. Nonetheless, a healthy awareness of your limitations can help you avoid exceeding your boundaries of competence in your eagerness to begin practicing your new profession.

CREDENTIALING

Credentialing is a "method of identifying individuals by occupational group" (Sweeney, 1995, p. 120). Two important types of credentialing that are found in counseling are certification, which takes various forms, and licensure. These credentials provide a tangible indicator of certain accomplishments and, as such, they have implications for assessing the competence of the credential holder.

The terms *licensure, certification,* and *registration* have many different meanings but are sometimes used interchangeably, which causes a great deal of confusion. The strict use of the terms in governmental regulation of a profession is as follows: (a) *Licensure* refers to the most rigorous form of regulation in that only those who are licensed may practice the profession in a state; (b) *certification* is the term used when a title, such as "professional counselor," can be used only by those who are certified, but anyone can practice the profession without being certified; and (c) registration is the form of governmental regulation in which members of a profession must "sign up" with the government if they practice the profession in the state, but anyone may sign the registry without a review of their credentials (Anderson & Swanson, 1994). National private organizations, such as the NBCC, offer national certification, which is a credential that is voluntary (not required by a government for practice). In addition, state departments of education require certification of school counselors employed in public school districts. In this chapter, we are using the term licensure to refer to state regulation of a profession generally, and the term certification to refer to national voluntary credentials and state department certification of school counselors.

Licensure

Licensure is the most powerful type of credentialing and is established by state law. When state legislators determine that the public's best interests are best served by creating a license to practice a particular profession, the minimum standards for practice of that profession in that state are established through a political process. State governments would rather not be involved in regulating the practice of professions. Legislators agree to license a professional group only when it can be shown that members of the public (a) do not have the ability to determine who is competent to practice within a particular profession and (b) could be harmed by incompetent practitioners. Currently, all but 2 of the 50 states and the District of Columbia license counselors (American Counseling Association [ACA], 2003; Harris, 1997).

When a state legislature passes a statute that establishes counselor licensure or passes amendments to an existing licensure statute, part of that statute specifies the minimum standards for becoming licensed to practice in that state. When counselor licensure bills or amendments are introduced, political pressures are put on politicians. Economists oppose counselor licensure, arguing that licensing of professions is self-serving, restricts entry into professions, and causes fees for services to rise unreasonably (Rottenberg, 1980). Organizations whose purpose it is to limit the role of government in citizens' lives also oppose licensure statutes. They often are joined in their opposition by other mental health professionals (including psychologists, psychiatrists, and social workers). These other professionals do not want to see counselors licensed to provide mental health services because marketplace competition will increase once counselors are officially recognized by state governments. When these groups of related mental health professionals realize that a bill or amendment is going to be passed over their objection, they often demand very high standards for licensure to keep as few individuals as possible from being licensed. All these groups put political pressure on legislators to set the minimum standards for licensure very high.

On the other side, there are pressures to set the minimum standards very low. For instance, individuals who are already practicing counseling in a state when counselor licensure statutes are being considered or amended often lobby for statutes that include very low standards so that they will not lose their status and will be entitled to licenses. The U.S. Constitution requires that individuals who were practicing counseling in a state when a licensure statute is passed be automatically licensed. This process has been referred to as *grandparenting*.

As a result of these various political pressures, states now have differing standards. According to Harris (1997) and the ACA (2003), licensing statutes for counselors range from a low of 30 required graduate credits to a high of 60 credits. In addition, the number of required post-master's-degree supervised hours range from 2,250 to 4,000. Some statutes specify a significant number of required courses; others require fewer specific courses. Most state statutes require the same courses as those required by CACREP and NBCC.

Although there is variation from state to state, all licensed counselors (except those who were grandparented) have completed at least a master's degree, have had post-master's supervised experience, and have successfully completed an examination or other form of screening. Thus, when clients select licensed professionals as their counselors, they can be assured that their counselors have demonstrated certain knowledge, skills, and abilities to the satisfaction of those professionals who evaluated them. Nonetheless, as is true of other approaches, there are limitations to what licensing can accomplish in terms of ensuring competence. Some writers have questioned whether there is evidence that licensure actually ensures general competence, protects consumers, or promotes higher standards of practice (Keith-Spiegel & Koocher, 1985; Pope & Vasquez, 1998). Hogan (1979) contended that there is no evidence that the quality of services of counselors has improved since licensing laws have been enacted, and that challenging the practices of unlicensed counselors is often aimed at attacking competition rather than eliminating incompetence. Despite Hogan's position that the licensing of mental health professionals is self-serving and has little to do with protecting the public, the licenses of mental health professionals are sometimes revoked for incompetent practice (Morris, 1984).

Corey et al. (2007) have pointed out that the possession of a license does not ensure that practitioners will competently *do* what their license permits them to do. The counselor license is a generic one. This leaves it up to licensed counselors, as individuals, to discriminate between professional titles and the professional *functions* they are competent to perform. Too, whereas licensure boards can restrict or terminate the practice of incompetent practitioners against whom they have received complaints, they are not in the business of monitoring the practices of counselors about whom they have received no complaints.

Clearly, licensing of counselors is an attempt to ensure competent practice. Government regulation of the counseling profession may have a positive influence on competency within the profession, but it falls short of accomplishing its objective of ensuring competence. In reality, the standards set for licensure are often the result of political compromises rather than of standards that have been set by the profession for minimum competency.

Certification

In addition to becoming licensed, counselors can offer evidence that supports their competence by becoming certified. Some types of certification are mandatory for practicing in certain settings and occur at the state level. For instance, public school counselors must be certified by the states in which they practice. There are also national, voluntary certifications, such as those offered by the NBCC. National Certified Counselors (NCC), like licensed counselors, have received preparation in specific content areas and clinical instruction, have had supervised counseling experience, and have passed an examination.

Specialties

In addition to generic certification as an NCC, NBCC offers specialty certifications including school, mental health, and addictions counseling (NBCC, 2003). An affiliate of NBCC offers a specialty credential in supervision (Center for Credentialing and Education [CCE], 2003). Specialty certifications are another means of establishing a counselor's competence to work with certain types of clients, in certain settings, or in specialized areas of counseling. There are also a host of other, more narrow specialty certifications offered by various groups in such areas as hypnotherapy, biofeedback, or sex therapy.

Specialty preparation is a controversial issue in counseling. Some have argued that only practitioners who have specialized preparation should be allowed to practice that specialty. Some have called for specialty *licensing* (Cottone, 1985), whereas others (Remley, 1995) strongly oppose specialty licensing. Remley has pointed out that the other major professions of medicine and law license professionals to practice their profession generally. Physicians and lawyers may practice any type of medicine or law. The only force that restrains them in limiting themselves to specialties is their own understanding that they must be competent in the professional services they render, and that no one can be competent in all areas. Specialty *accreditation* of counselor education programs is another approach that suggests that only certain counselors are qualified to practice in specified areas. This is the approach that is currently being taken (Sweeney, 1995).

There appears to be tension between proponents of two schools of thought regarding specialty preparation. Some counselors believe that establishing competence boundaries should be left up to individual professionals, who then would be accountable to licensure or certification boards if they exceeded those boundaries to the detriment of a client. Others believe that counselors should be prevented by licensure boards from practicing within specialty areas unless they have received specific preparation in the form of graduate courses or supervision. The issues of specialty preparation and specialty licensing and certification will likely be debated within the counseling profession for some time. At the present time, however, the prevailing school of thought is that counselors who have proven their minimal preparation and are licensed can decide for themselves the boundaries of their competence and may practice in areas considered specialties without holding any specialty certifications. Nonetheless, counselors have an ethical responsibility to practice in specialty areas new to them only after they have obtained appropriate education, training, and supervised experience (Standard C.2.b.). They also must take steps to ensure the competence of their work while developing skills in new specialty areas (C.2.b.).

MAINTAINING COMPETENCE

Once counselors have completed their formal education and are licensed or certified to practice, the burden of determining competence shifts away from counselor educators and supervisors and onto the counselors themselves. Counselors are autonomous professionals, responsible for monitoring their own effectiveness. The *ACA Code of Ethics* underscores this responsibility in Standard C.2.d, stating that "Counselors continually monitor their effectiveness as professionals and take steps to improve when necessary." Even when counselors are employed in agencies or institutions, they are held individually accountable for practicing in an ethical and professional manner. One of the indicators of a profession, which distinguishes it from a semiprofession or a nonprofession, is that the members of the profession practice autonomously. In return for this privilege of independence, professionals must limit themselves to practicing within the areas in which they are competent. Professionals individually determine the limits of their competence and practice accordingly.

Continuing Education

Although competence can certainly be enhanced by the skillful application on a day-to-day basis of the knowledge gained in a formal preparation program, experience alone is no guarantee against errors. Considering the constant contributions new research makes to knowledge in the field, as well as significant, ongoing changes in the environment in which counseling is practiced, we doubt that a counselor could retain even a modicum of professional competence over a 30- or 40-year career without further education. The *Code of Ethics* states that counselors recognize the need for continuing education to maintain awareness of current scientific and professional information (Standard C.2.f.), and most counselor licensure and certification boards have established continuing education requirements for maintaining one's license. As Herlihy and Corey (2006) have noted, however, there are limits to what continuing education requirements can accomplish. "It is difficult to monitor the quality of continuing education offerings or their relevance to a particular counselor's needs. The number of clock hours obtained may have little relationship to how much the counselor has actually learned and integrated into practice" (p. 180).

There are many other questions that could be raised regarding what constitutes a legitimate effort to maintain competence. For instance, is attending a seminar commensurate with teaching one? Is writing an article for a professional journal an indicator of continuing competence? What is the relative value of reading books and scholarly articles about new techniques and theories? Can counselors who regularly but informally consult with colleagues about their cases be considered to be as diligent in working to maintain competence as counselors who attend formal seminars? There may be no way to objectively assess whether a counselor has maintained competence over time. External criteria such as continuing education credits earned are not sufficient to ensure continuing competence. Perhaps more important are counselors' own efforts, as autonomous professionals operating at the aspirational level of ethics, to remain aware of their own limitations, to recognize that these limitations can increase over time, and to seek to keep skills current by both formal and informal means (Keith-Spiegel & Koocher, 1985).

PEER REVIEW

Peer review is an approach to monitoring competence that we believe can be very effective. Peer review is a system by which mental health professionals assess one another's services. Peer consultation or peer supervision groups are useful for counselors at all levels of experience and offer many benefits to counselors. They include mutual support; objective feedback in dealing with countertransference issues; information on therapeutic techniques, new research, and referral sources; and help in dealing with difficult cases, stress, and the isolation often experienced by private practitioners. Ideally, peer consultation or supervision groups would meet on a regular, scheduled basis to discuss practice challenges and ethical issues, with a flexible agenda determined by the needs of the members (Greenburg, Lewis, & Johnson, 1985). Borders (1991) has suggested that a structured peer group provides the procedure and tasks needed for participants to benefit from peer feedback and a mechanism for counselors to contribute to their own professional development as well as to that of their colleagues. Independent private practitioners are expected to seek peer supervision (Standard C.2.d.) and this is a strategy we recommend for counselors in all work settings. Remley, Benshoff, and Mowbray (1987) have developed a model for peer supervision that can be used by counseling practitioners.

Information Technologies

The cyberspace phenomenon presents counselors with a myriad of opportunities for keeping current and improving their competence as practitioners. New information technologies are developing at such a rapid pace that any attempt we might make to describe them would be obsolete almost immediately. We can, however, highlight a few key resources. The counseling profession has established a solid presence on the Internet. This offers opportunities to access virtual libraries for researching the latest information on client problems and effective counseling techniques, as well as to collaborate and consult with other professionals around the world. Many of ACA's divisions, NBCC, and CACREP have home pages on the World Wide Web, so you can communicate quickly and directly with professional groups that are working to strengthen counseling as a profession. Videoconferencing on the Internet enables you and counselors everywhere to obtain further preparation and even supervision without having to travel great distances. You can subscribe to mailing lists that allow you to share experiences, ask questions, and exchange information and ideas. See Appendix B for Web addresses of these organizations.

These new technologies present many exciting opportunities, but they also have created problems related to assuring competence of services. Some counselors have begun to provide direct counseling services over the Internet. The fact that counseling is taking place over the Internet before the profession has fully considered the ethical implications is cause for concern. The 2005

ACA *Code of Ethics* has addressed this issue, however, in Standard A.12., which has a number of provisions. As was discussed in the previous chapter, with Internet counseling there is no reliable method of regulating the services offered, of ensuring the competence of the providers, or of protecting consumers from ill-advised Internet-based services (Wilson, Jencius, & Duncan, 1997).

Making Referrals

Standard A.11.b. of the ACA *Code of Ethics* requires that counselors make appropriate referrals when they determine an inability to be of professional assistance to clients. Ethical counselors recognize that they will need to refer a client when accepting or continuing to work with that client would exceed their boundaries of competence. Sometimes it can be difficult for counselors to acknowledge that they are not competent to provide professional services to every client who might request their help. There are many sources of temptation to accept clients who might be better served by a referral. These might include a reluctance to disappoint a valued source of referrals, financial pressures to increase your client load when business has been slow, or the ego-enhancing nature of requests from clients who hold exaggerated beliefs about your talents and abilities to help them. To succumb to these kinds of temptations would not be ethical and would not be in the clients' best interest.

Another type of challenge is posed when counselors need to refer a client with whom they are already engaged in a counseling relationship. Despite the best efforts of counselors to accept only those clients whom they believe they can provide with competent services, the course of counseling is unpredictable. A client's presenting problem may be well within the counselor's scope of competence, and the counselor might in good faith begin working with that client, only to discover as therapy progresses that the client has unanticipated counseling needs. The case described in the following is an example.

4-1 The Case of Marianne

Marianne, a Licensed Professional Counselor (LPC) in private practice, began working with Ellen, a young woman who came for counseling to deal with what at first appeared to be moderate anxiety. Ellen described herself as a perfectionist and sought counseling to learn to "stop being so hard on myself." It was only after several counseling sessions that Ellen felt safe enough in the counseling relationship to reveal to Marianne that she was so fearful of becoming "fat" that she regularly engaged in self-induced vomiting after meals, abused laxatives, and exercised excessively. Marianne recognized these behaviors as symptoms of anorexia nervosa or bulimia nervosa (American Psychiatric Association, 2000), a problem area with which she had no experience.

- How should Marianne approach this situation with Ellen?
- If Marianne decides to take some workshops and do some independent reading on treatment of individuals who have eating disorders, how will she know when she is competent to provide counseling services to clients like Ellen?
- What if Marianne is able to find a suitable referral source but Ellen refuses, stating that she has complete faith in Marianne's ability to help her?
- What if Marianne practices in an isolated, rural community and a local referral resource or expert consultants or supervisors are not available?

Marianne's ethical obligation at this point is clear. She must either refer Ellen to a specialist or to another therapist who is competent to work with clients who suffer from eating disorders, or she must ensure that she provides quality counseling services to Ellen by obtaining educational experiences and consultation, or supervision from experts. This may not be as simple as it seems. Marianne must invest the effort required to meet Ellen's needs. Without the needed competence or expert assistance, Marianne cannot in good conscience continue to work with a client who may have an illness that can be life threatening. If Marianne suggests a referral, and Ellen rejects the referral, Marianne must consider Standard A.11.b. of the ACA *Code of Ethics* which states that "If clients decline the suggested referrals, counselors should discontinue the relationship."

Other situations that might raise the question of referring a client are less clear-cut. As Corey et al. (2007) have noted, even the most experienced counselors will at times seriously wonder whether they have the personal and professional abilities to work with some of their clients. Difficulty in working with some clients does not, in itself, imply incompetence. In fact, counselors who refer all clients with whom they encounter difficulties will probably have few clients. Instead, counselors can extend their boundaries of competence through reading, participating in workshops and other professional development opportunities, consulting, co-counseling with colleagues who have expertise in a needed area, and working under supervision. The key is to keep a careful balance, referring when necessary and extending your areas of competency by keeping clients in other situations. Counselors can avoid stagnation and can continue to learn and grow as professionals by taking on clients who present new concerns and issues, thus extending their scope of competence. In fact, it would be impossible to develop expertise in a new counseling specialty area without eventually accepting a client with an issue in that area. At the same time, care must be taken that clients are not harmed while the counselor is in the process of learning new skills and developing new competencies. You must make careful judgments regarding when to refer and when to keep new clients when you are preparing to provide services in a new area.

Diversity Considerations in Counseling Competence

Recognizing diversity in our society and developing intercultural counseling competence are essential to ethical practice. When you think of your own future practice, keep in mind that if you are not trained and competent to work with culturally diverse clients, you might be practicing unethically if you attempt to provide services to these clients. Counselors have an ethical obligation to actively attempt to understand the diverse cultural backgrounds of their clients and to learn how their own cultural, racial, and ethnic identities have an impact on their values and beliefs about the counseling process. The 2005 ACA *Code of Ethics* has incorporated, throughout the document, provisions requiring counselors to be culturally competent. The Introduction to Section A states, "Counselors actively attempt to understand the diverse cultural backgrounds of the clients they serve. Counselors also explore their own cultural identities and how these affect their values and beliefs about the counseling process." Every section of the code reminds counselors of their duty to be aware of cultural differences in their counseling practices.

Fortunately, the counseling profession's attention to cultural diversity has increased dramatically in recent years. There is an abundance of professional literature that can enhance counselor awareness and knowledge. The *Journal of Multicultural Counseling and Development,* the publication of the Association for Multicultural Counseling and Development (an ACA division), contains excellent cutting-edge articles. Diversity issues are addressed frequently in ACA publications that have a more general focus, as well. For example, the Spring 2003 issue of the *Journal for Counseling & Development* contained articles that provided information about counseling Arab Americans, Asian Americans, immigrant clients, and Israelis. The same issue reported results of studies on differences in how counselors perceive male and female clients and the effects of counselor ethnicity on counseling process and outcomes. A column called "Dignity, Development, and Diversity" appears regularly in the ACA newsletter, *Counseling Today*. Numerous books on multicultural counseling are now available, including several that can be purchased from the ACA bookstore at a discounted price for members.

At the same time, work remains to be done to improve counselor multicultural competence. Results of one study indicated that, whereas counselors as a group perceive themselves to be multiculturally competent, they perceive their multicultural preparation to have been less than adequate (Holcomb-McCoy & Myers, 1999). These researchers also found that differences in self-perceived multicultural competence could be explained by whether a counselor is a member of an ethnic minority group. They suggested that the experience of being a member of an ethnic minority group, and interacting daily with members of the majority group, provides in vivo multicultural education. These findings underscore the need for White counselors to seek out experiences that will allow them to interact with those who are culturally different from themselves.

Counselors who practice in rural areas face unique challenges related to practicing within the scope of their competence. Counselors who work in urban and suburban settings are able to limit their scope of practice because they typically have numerous referral resources available to them. Rural practitioners, who do not enjoy this luxury, often practice as generalists out of sheer necessity (Welfel, 2006). The geographic location of their practice places extra demands on them to increase their knowledge and skills in order to respond to the varied needs of their clientele. At the same time, they must practice diligence. They must weigh the risk of causing harm if they provide services to a client who presents problems or issues in which they are not adequately trained. It is also incumbent on rural counselors to seek out opportunities to increase their knowledge and skills through creative strategies, such as obtaining distance supervision or taking online courses via the Internet.

COUNSELOR INCOMPETENCE

Distress, Burnout, and Impairment

The counseling profession has been slow to recognize the problem of impairment among its members. Little research has been conducted on the incidence of impairment among counselors, and the ACA has not yet acted decisively to confront the issue of impairment in its members (Stadler, 2001). Counselor impairment still has not been clearly defined (Emerson & Markos, 1996). The terms *distressed, burned out,* and *impaired* have been used somewhat interchangeably in the counseling literature. However, these terms might be better viewed as ranging along a continuum from the least to most serious in relation to their impact on competent professional performance.

Counseling can be stressful work, and this stress occasionally takes its toll on practitioners. Ironically, the counseling relationship itself can be a source of stress. In other interpersonal relationships, such as friendships, there is give and take and a reciprocal meeting of needs. This balance does not exist in a counseling relationship. Counselors make a *loan of the self* to the therapeutic relationship (Squyres, 1986), receive little in return, and sometimes doubt the effectiveness of counseling. Of counselors surveyed by Farber and Heifetz (1982), 74% saw "lack of therapeutic success" as the most stressful aspect of their work, and 55% felt depleted by the nonreciprocated attentiveness, giving, and responsibility that the therapeutic relationship demands. Stress can lead to distress, and most counselors probably could be described as *distressed* at some time during their professional lives. In fact, results of one survey indicated that 82% of psychotherapists had experienced at least one episode of psychic distress (Prochaska & Norcross, 1983). Distressed counselors may experience anxious and depressed moods, somatic complaints, lowered self-esteem, and feelings of helplessness, but they are not necessarily impaired in their professional functioning. They know at some subjective level that something is wrong, and distress is usually a transitory and temporary condition.

When distress remains unalleviated, however, it can lead to *burnout,* which has been described as "physical, emotional, and mental exhaustion brought on by involvement over prolonged periods with emotionally demanding situations and people" (Pine & Aronson, 1988). Burned out counselors, exhausted and depleted, have little energy left for their clients. They tend to manifest negative attitudes toward self and work. Some writers have suggested that few counselors can expect to stay immune from burnout, and even that burnout may be nearly inevitable after 10 years in the field (Grosch & Olsen, 1994; Kottler, 1993). Burnout is not so much a state or condition as it is a process that, if not corrected, can lead to impairment.

It would be rare for a counselor to never experience a frustrating week, a difficult client, an emotional overload, or occasional symptoms of burnout, yet counselors who are functioning well can put these experiences into perspective. *Impaired counselors,* by contrast, are unable to transcend periods of stress (Stadler, 1990b). Their therapeutic skills have diminished or deteriorated to the point that they are unable to perform their responsibilities appropriately (Emerson & Markos, 1996; Guy, 1987). The medical profession has described impairment as "the inability to deliver competent patient care" (Stadler, Willing, Eberhage, & Ward, 1988, p. 258). Substituting "client" for "patient," this definition can be applied to counseling, and incompetence raises the risk that clients might be harmed. Impairment is often associated with alcohol and other drug abuse, and with the blurring of therapeutic boundaries that can lead to sexual exploitation of clients.

Why do some counselors become impaired, whereas others manage to bounce back from periods of distress or burnout? Sometimes *environmental factors* can play a key role. A counselor may experience the death of a loved one, divorce or desertion, rape, the severe physical illness of a family member, or other personal loss or trauma. These events can unbalance anyone's emotional equilibrium. If the counselor takes time off work, goes for counseling, or in some other overt way takes control and works toward a return to full functioning, this type of impairment is usually transitory and need not be a cause for ongoing concern about the counselor's competence (Emerson & Markos, 1996).

In other instances, *preexisting conditions* may put the counselor at risk. Some individuals enter the helping professions in order to work through their own unresolved problems. Personal difficulties that have led some counselors to enter the profession may be exacerbated by the practice of the profession. The practice of counseling can reactivate early experiences, open old wounds, and reawaken unresolved issues. Counselors with a history of addictions or a vulnerability to substance abuse seem to be predisposed to problems after entering the profession (Guy, 1987). Studies indicate that a significant number of impaired counselors experience alcoholism or other substance abuse problems (Deutsch, 1985; Thoreson, Nathan, Skorina, & Kilberg, 1983). Depression is also a common preexisting condition among impaired professionals; 57% of female psychologists who responded to one survey (Deutsch) reported that they had experienced more than one episode of depression. For these at-risk professionals, the connection between depression and suicide is a particular cause for concern. The death-by-suicide rate among female psychologists has been reported to be four times that of White women in general (Roeske, 1986). Glickhauf-Hughes and Mehlman (1996) contended that certain personality characteristics make counselors more vulnerable to impairment. These characteristics include parentification (a willingness to take responsibility for others), perfectionism, imposter feelings and self-doubt, and audience sensitivity (strong awareness of others' feelings and responsiveness to them).

Stressful or traumatic events in a counselor's personal or social life and preexisting conditions are not the only factors that can contribute to counselor impairment. Certain kinds of *clients* and *client problems* can promote counselor distress (Stadler, 2001). Working with suicidal clients has been shown to take an emotional toll. The high relapse rate of clients with substance abuse problems can lead to counselor discouragement and cynicism about the sincerity of clients' desires to change. Certain client characteristics such as lack of empathy for others, manipulativeness, and refusal to accept responsibility for one's behavior are often present in clients diagnosed with some personality disorders, sex offenders, and clients who abuse women or children. These characteristics can exacerbate the stress felt by counselors. Counselors who work with victims of trauma and abuse are at increased risk for developing compassion fatigue and secondary posttraumatic stress symptomology (Welfel, 2006). Having a practice that includes a large number of clients in managed care plans, with the accompanying demands for demonstrable, short-term results and often-burdensome paperwork can put counselors at greater risk for emotional exhaustion (Thompson, 1999).

The ACA *Code of Ethics* provides, in Standard C.2.g., clear guidance regarding counselors who believe they are impaired. This standard states that counselors are alert to signs of impairment resulting from their own physical, mental, or emotional problems. If they determine they are impaired, counselors must stop offering professional services to clients "when such impairment is likely to harm a client or others." Impaired counselors must seek assistance to address their problems. Further, Standard C.2.g. states that counselors assist their colleagues or supervisors in recognizing their own impairment. If counselors believe their colleagues or supervisors may be harming their clients, counselors must *intervene as appropriate*. It might be difficult for counselors to assist their colleagues and supervisors in recognizing their own impairment. At what point would you decide that a colleague or supervisor was impaired? For example, how much social drinking is too much? Or, how many absences from work indicate impairment? Once you have formulated in your mind that a colleague or supervisor is impaired, how do you go about addressing the issue with him or her? Most individuals who are impaired go through an extended period of denial and probably would reject your input. In our opinion, this part of the *Code of Ethics* may be very difficult to comply with, especially if the counselor you believe is impaired is your supervisor, who has control and authority over you. Of course, you would need to intervene in some way to prevent harm to clients, but you should be very sure that imminent harm will occur if you do not intervene and, if you do intervene, you must be prepared for a negative reaction. If you ever believe you need to confront a colleague or supervisor about your belief that he or she is impaired, this would be a good time to consult with other counselors or related professionals regarding your ethical obligations.

Ethical practice requires, first, that counselors be aware of warning signs of impairment. Some of the most common symptoms are presented in Figure 4-1.

---

(1)   Deterioration in personal relationships, including marital problems and family dysfunction

(2)   Becoming isolated and withdrawn from others

(3)   Feelings of disillusionment with the profession

(4)   Emotional distancing during counseling sessions

(5)   Alcohol and drug abuse

(6)   Changes in work habits such as increased tardiness and absenteeism

(7)   Moodiness, depression, and symptoms of anxiety

(8)   Procedural errors and sloppy record keeping

Figure 4-1   Warning signs of professional impairment

Suzanne, the counselor in the following case example, is experiencing some of these symptoms.

4-2 The Case of Suzanne

Suzanne is an LPC who went to work at a community agency when she earned her master's degree. After 5 years at the agency, Suzanne resigned and opened a private practice on her own. Now, 8 months into this venture, she finds that she isn't sleeping well at night. She tosses and turns, worrying about whether she will be able to pay the monthly bills, and trying to think of new ways to market her practice. She misses the camaraderie she enjoyed with her colleagues at the agency and feels increasingly isolated. She has lost weight recently and is starting to have episodes of gastric distress. She realizes that she needs a break from the stresses of her work. However, she feels trapped by her financial situation into taking on more clients during evening hours and on the weekends, rather than taking time for self-care activities.

- What are some indicators that Suzanne is experiencing problems that might lead to impairment?
- If Suzanne does not change her behavior, what kinds of problems might you expect her to experience?
- If you were Suzanne's friend, what options might you suggest to her to relieve her distress?

Burnout and impairment can be prevented when individual counselors monitor their own vulnerabilities and are aware of the ethical ramifications of practicing when they are unable to function effectively (Witmer & Young, 1996). Many resources and strategies are available to counselors when they recognize that they need to make changes in their lives if they are to remain competent practitioners (Kottler & Schofield, 2001). Some of these are (a) seeking counseling for themselves; (b) seeking supervision, especially of their work with clients who are difficult and tend to drain their personal resources; (c) taking a break or vacation from practice; and (d) joining a peer support group. Other self-care strategies include regular exercise, meditation, hobbies, and seeking support from family and friends.

It is crucial that you develop self-monitoring skills so that you can stay psychologically and emotionally healthy as a counselor. Because graduate school is often stressful, now is a good time to learn and practice these skills. It will be helpful for you to know the symptoms of burnout, to familiarize yourself with various wellness models, and to periodically take the time to assess how you are managing the stressors in your life.

Diversity Considerations in Prevention of Counselor Stress, Burnout, and Impairment   The results of a study conducted by Myers, Mobley, and Booth (2003) on the wellness levels of counseling graduate students bode well for the future of the profession. These investigators found that counseling students scored higher than an adult norm group on the Wellness Evaluation of Lifestyle (WEL), and that doctoral students scored even higher than entry-level students.

There is cause for concern in differences that were found along cultural variables, however. Female students scored higher than male students on the measure of Gender Identity, and non-Caucasian students scored higher than Caucasian students on the measure of Cultural Identity. The researchers suggested that these findings may reflect greater awareness of gender and cultural issues on the part of persons who belong to historically oppressed groups in our society. Still, the fact that doctoral students scored higher than entry-level students on gender and cultural identity subscales may indicate that counselor preparation programs are succeeding at developing awareness of diversity issues among their students.

MALPRACTICE

Malpractice involves professional misconduct or unreasonable lack of skill and has been defined as follows:

> Failure of one rendering professional services to exercise that degree of skill and learning commonly applied under all the circumstances in the community by the average prudent reputable member of the profession with the result of injury, loss or damage to the recipient of those services or to those entitled to rely upon them. It is any professional misconduct, unreasonable lack of skill or fidelity in professional or fiduciary duties, evil practice, or illegal or immoral conduct. (Black, 1990; p. 959)

Although malpractice includes intentional wrongdoing, the role of incompetency, or unintentional wrongdoing of the professional involved in malpractice, is clear in this definition. "Unreasonable lack of skill" and "failure to exercise . . . skill" are both indicators of incompetence that can form the basis of malpractice lawsuits against counselors. The concept of competency might be extended so that a counselor who is guilty of *professional misconduct, evil practice,* or *illegal* or *immoral conduct* also could be defined as incompetent.

Malpractice is a type of civil lawsuit that can be filed against professionals for practicing in a manner that leads to injury to a recipient of their services. Professionals have a legal obligation not to harm individuals who come to them for professional services. Although the law cannot restore people who have been injured to their former state of existence, it can require the person who harmed them to compensate them financially for their damages. If clients believe they have been harmed by their counselors, they can file a malpractice lawsuit against the counselors. Counselors who are sued must then defend themselves against the lawsuit before a judge or jury. Although there is widespread belief that juries favor plaintiffs in professional malpractice suits against health professionals, evidence from a study of physicians has demonstrated that juries' findings follow what physicians themselves consider to be negligence, and probably even favor the professionals (Vidmar, 1995).

In order for a client plaintiff to prevail in a malpractice lawsuit against a counselor, the plaintiff must prove the following elements (Prosser, Wade, & Schwartz, 1988):

- The counselor had a duty to the client to use reasonable care in providing counseling services.
- The counselor failed to conform to the required duty of care.
- The client was injured.
- There was a reasonably close causal connection between the conduct of the counselor and the resulting injury (known as *proximate cause*).
- The client suffered an actual loss or was damaged.

Proximate cause is a difficult legal concept to understand. *Actual cause* means that a person actually caused the injury of another person. *Proximate cause* has to do with whether the individual would have been injured had it not been for the action or inaction of the other person. Cohen and Mariano (1982) explained that "an intervening cause which is independent of the negligence absolves the defending negligent actor of liability" (p. 121). In other words, just because professionals are negligent does not make them responsible for an injury. It must be proven that some other intervening event did not, in fact, cause the injury. Foreseeability is important in determinations of proximate cause (Cohen & Mariano). Foreseeability has to do with whether the professional knew or should have known that the professional's actions would result in a specific outcome.

Counselors have become increasingly concerned about being sued for malpractice. Although malpractice lawsuits against mental health professionals have increased dramatically over the past decade, the total number of these lawsuits is relatively small. Hogan (1979) concluded that few malpractice lawsuits are filed against counselors because it is difficult for plaintiffs to establish an adequate case. It is not easy to prove that a counselor deviated from accepted practices and that the counselor's act or negligence caused the harm that a client suffered.

It appears that mental health professionals continue to be sued most often because of sexual relationships with their clients. However, it is likely that the next leading cause of malpractice law suits against counselors revolve around situations in which clients attempt or complete suicide (McAdams & Foster, 2000). Whether to have sex with clients is certainly under the control of a mental health professional. However, predicting whether a client will attempt suicide is scientifically impossible. Yet, counselors will be held accountable in courts if they fail to follow procedures endorsed by the profession when a client is as risk. Suicidal clients, potentially violent clients, and the duty to warn intended victims of client violence are discussed in the following sections, and guidelines for practice in these areas are offered.

Suicidal Clients

When a client threatens to commit suicide, an ethical duty arises to protect the client from harm to self. The ethical standard that applies to clients who pose a danger to others applies to suicidal clients as well: Confidentiality requirements are waived when disclosure is necessary to protect clients or others from *serious and foreseeable harm* (Standard B.2.a.). Evaluating and managing suicide risk is one of the most stressful situations that you will encounter in your work (Corey et al., 2007). You must be prepared to take measures to prevent suicide attempts (Slaby, 1999). These prevention measures begin with a thorough risk assessment and then, depending on the level of danger, might include involving the client's family or significant others, working with the client to arrange for voluntary hospitalization, or even initiating the process that leads to an involuntary commitment of the client. All of these interventions are disruptive and compromise the client's confidentiality. Ethically (Standard B.2.d.), and legally under HIPAA (United States Department of Health and Human Services, 2003), it is important to disclose only information you consider essential in order for someone else to help prevent a suicide attempt.

Similar to situations in which clients threaten harm to others, the counselor's first responsibility is to determine that a particular client is in danger of attempting suicide. There is no sure way to determine this, but experts agree that individuals who commit suicide generally give cues to those around them (Capuzzi, 1994; Capuzzi & Golden, 1988; Curran, 1987; Davis, 1983; Hafen & Frandsen, 1986; Hussain & Vandiver, 1984; Jacobs, Brewer, & Klein-Benheim, 1999; Johnson & Maile, 1987; Laux, 2002; Myer, 2001; Rogers, 2001; Rogers, Lewis, & Subich, 2002; Schwartz, 2000; Schwartz & Cohen, 2001; Stanard, 2000). In most circumstances, a counselor's determination of a client's level of risk must be based on clinical observations, not on test results. If counselors were not prepared in their graduate programs to handle crises (Allen et al., 2002), they must overcome this deficit through independent reading, workshop attendance, post-master's-degree course completion, and supervised practice.

As noted earlier, determining that a client is at risk of committing suicide leads to actions that can be exceptionally disruptive to the client's life. Just as counselors can be accused of malpractice for neglecting to take action to prevent harm when a client is determined to be suicidal, counselors also can be accused of wrongdoing if they overreact and precipitously take actions that violate a client's privacy or freedom when there is no basis for doing so (Remley, Hermann, & Huey, 2003). As a result, counselors have a legal duty to evaluate accurately a client's potential for suicide. Counselors can be held liable for overreacting and for underreacting. So, how should a determination be made as to whether a client is suicidal?

First, no matter where you work as a counselor, you are likely to provide services to individuals who might express suicidal thoughts (Hermann, 2001). Therefore, it is necessary for all counselors to know the warning signs that indicate that a particular person is at risk for committing suicide. An old legal case (*Bogust v. Iverson,* 1960) held that a college counselor was not a mental health professional and therefore had no duty to assess a client's risk of suicide. Since then, however, counselors have established themselves as mental health professionals, and the law imposes on counselors practicing in all settings the responsibility of knowing how to accurately determine a client's risk of suicide (Bursztajn, Gutheil, Hamm, & Brodsky, 1983; Drukteinis, 1985; Howell, 1988; Knuth, 1979; Perr, 1985). Courts generally have been reluctant to hold counselors accountable for harm that results from clients who attempt or complete suicide, because the act is done by the client without the counselor being a party to it. However, Lake and Tribbensee (2002), in their discussion of liability of colleges and universities for the suicides of adult students, cautioned that current legal trends suggest mental health professionals on college and university campuses may be held accountable more often in the future for adult student suicides.

There is much help available in the professional literature, including research studies and articles that provide information about warning signs of future suicidal behavior (Berman & Cohen-Sandler, 1982; Cantor, 1976; Meneese & Yutrzenka, 1990; Sudak, Ford, & Rushforth, 1984). Today's counselors must know how to make assessments of a client's risk for suicide and must be able to defend their decisions at a later time.

The law does not require that counselors always be correct in making their assessments of suicide risk, but it is legally necessary that counselors make those assessments from an informed position, and that they fulfill their professional obligations to a client in a manner comparable to what other reasonable counselors operating in a similar situation would have done. Because of this standard of care to which counselors are held, the very best action you can take if you are unsure whether a client is at risk for a suicide attempt is to consult with other mental health professionals who are similar to you (Sommers-Flanagan, Sommmers-Flanagan, & Lynch, 2001). The ACA *Code of Ethics* (Standard C.2.e.) advises counselors to consult when they have questions regarding their ethical obligations or professional practice. It also is important to look for consensus among your consultants and certainly to follow their advice in making your final decision about what to do in a particular case. Documenting your steps is essential (Boughner & Logan, 1999; Gutheil, 1999).

When you make a decision that a client is a danger to self, you must take whatever steps are necessary to prevent the harm, and your actions must be the least intrusive to accomplish that result. Again, consulting with colleagues could be very helpful. Many counselors who have determined that a client may be at risk for suicide require that the possibly suicidal client submit to an evaluation by a mental health professional who has expertise in the area of suicide as a condition for continuing to provide counseling services for that individual. For example, you might demand that your client see a psychiatrist who is on the staff at the facility where you work, if that is an option. Or you might require your client to submit to a mental evaluation at a local hospital where psychiatric services are available. Of course there are other, less intrusive, options available, such as referring the client to a primary care physician if the client is in a health plan that requires that step before gaining access to a specialist, such as a psychiatrist. But you should choose a less in-trusive option only if you are sure the client is not at imminent risk.

Because it is so difficult to decide what steps to take in a crisis situation, especially one in which a suicidal client's life may be in danger, we have provided an action plan to follow if you determine that an adult client may be at risk for suicide (see Figure 4-2). If your client is a minor, you must always notify the parents or guardians (Capuzzi, 2002). The steps we have suggested are not the only options counselors have. We are providing one possible way to manage poten-tially suicidal clients that hopefully will yield positive results.

If you work in an agency, school, hospital, or other setting, you must always follow proce-dures established by your employer. In addition, if your administrative supervisor is present, you must follow his or her directives. The following guidelines could be adopted by your agency, or you could follow these, in the absence of any agency policies or directives from superiors.

If you determine that an adult client has exhibited some behaviors that are related to suicide, but currently does not appear to be at risk for committing suicide …

1. If you believe that an adult client may be thinking about suicide or if you have observed or have information that an adult client has exhibited some behaviors that might be interpreted as suicidal, but you do not consider the situation to be an emergency, summarize in your case notes the client's behavior that supports your concern. Do not write that you believe the client may be at risk for suicide. Instead, write that although you do not believe the client may be at risk for suicide, you believe a significant person in his or her life needs to be informed of the behaviors that concern you.

2. A significant person might be your client's spouse, parent, adult child, other relative, domestic partner, dating partner, or close friend. Choose a person who lives with the client or who is in frequent contact with the client.

3. If you have consulted with colleagues, experts, or supervisors in reaching your position, document the consultations in your case notes.

4. Tell your client your concerns and, if appropriate, obtain an agreement from the client to inform a significant person in his or her life of your concerns. Tell the client to have that person contact you after being told.

5. If your client is not capable of telling the significant person, or for some other reason asking the client to inform the significant person does not seem like an appropriate course of action, explain to the client that you will be contacting a significant person to share your concern. If you are not in independent private practice, inform your supervisor of the actions you will be taking and follow any directives given.

6. Document in your case notes all conversations with your client, client's significant person, and your supervisors.

Figure 4-2   Steps to follow if you determine that your client may be at risk for suicide

If you determine that an adult client MAY BE seriously at risk for committing suicide ...

1. You are dealing with a very serious matter that requires immediate and decisive action. Make the determination that an adult client may be at risk for committing suicide only if the client has made a suicide gesture or attempt, has told you or someone else in a believable fashion that he or she plans to commit suicide, or has engaged in a pattern of behavior that the professional literature suggests is characteristic of a suicidal adult. Follow any agency policies that exist regarding managing suicidal adults. If you are not in an independent private practice, notify your supervisor of the situation and follow any directives given. If policies dictate or if your supervisor directs you to proceed differently from the steps below, follow the policies or the orders of your supervisor.

2. If you have consulted with colleagues, experts, or supervisors in reaching your position, document the consultations in your case notes.

3. Explain to your client that you will have to notify a significant person in his or her life so that the person can help.

4. Assure your client that you will continue to help and that you will disclose only the minimum information necessary to get assistance for the client. Try to calm the client, but do not minimize the seriousness of the situation. Explain what may happen in the next few hours, next few days, and long term.

5. Ensure that your client is not left alone and does not have any opportunity to harm self prior to turning the client over to the significant person.

6. Contact a significant person in your client's life and explain that you believe his or her relative, partner, or friend may be at risk for suicide. Give specific details that led to your concern. Insist that the significant person come to pick up the client immediately.

7. If a significant person cannot be found, make sure your client is under the supervision of a responsible person until a significant person is located.

8. If you cannot contact a significant person and if it is impossible to keep your adult client safe for an extended period of time, call an ambulance and have the client transported to a hospital that has psychiatric services. If you are not in an independent private practice, be sure to inform your supervisor and obtain permission and support for taking this action. If your supervisor directs you take a different course of action, do so and document in your case notes what you were told and did. Give the ambulance attendant your contact information and offer to speak with the person at the hospital who will be conducting the evaluation, if requested to do so. Continue to attempt to contact the client's significant person.

9. When you talk to the significant person, ask that person to take possession and responsibility immediately for your client.

Figure 4-2   *(Continued)*

10. When the significant person arrives, explain that you believe that your client may be at risk for suicide, give specific details that led to your concern, instruct the significant person what to do next, and ask that a document be signed that acknowledges that the significant person has been informed of your concerns, has been given directions of steps to take next, and has agreed to take responsibility for your client.

11. Also, have the client sign a form giving you permission to disclose any information you have to mental health professionals who may evaluate or treat the client in the future. If the client refuses or is not capable of signing the form, ask the family member or significant person to sign on your client's behalf.

12. Explain to the significant person that he or she must ensure that your client is not left alone, does not have any opportunities to harm self, and is taken for an evaluation as soon as possible to determine whether the client is at risk for suicide.

13. If a significant person refuses to sign the document or communicates to you in some way that he or she will not take the situation seriously, call an ambulance and follow the steps in item 8.

14. As events occur, document in detail in your case notes all the events that transpired in relation to this situation. Be sure to date each entry and indicate the time you wrote it. Make several entries if necessary, and do not delay in writing details in your case notes.

15. When your client returns to you or your agency for services, obtain written permission from your client to contact the professional who determined that your client was not at risk for suicide, or was no longer at risk for suicide.

16. Contact your client's treating physician, psychologist, or mental health provider and explain that the client has returned to you or your agency for services. Ask the treating provider to summarize his or her evaluation and treatment of the client. Inquire as to whether the provider will continue to treat the client, and if so, the details of the planned treatment. Also ask the treating provider the types of counseling services he or she would like for you to provide to the client. Do not agree to provide any counseling services that your position does not allow you to provide. Ask the provider to tell you the circumstances in which you should return the client to him or her for further evaluation or treatment.

17. As soon as possible after you have talked to the provider, document in your case notes details of your conversation. Be sure to date the entry and indicate the time you wrote it.

Figure 4-2   *(Continued)*

As you can see from Figure 4-2, it is assumed that a client you refer for an evaluation will return to you for services. Even if a client is hospitalized, the hospitalization usually is only a few days in duration. Contacting and documenting your consultation with the mental health professional who determined your client was not at risk for suicide, or was no longer at risk, are vital. You probably will counsel clients who have recently been at risk for suicide. In an interesting study, Paulson and Worth (2002) found that previously suicidal clients described these key therapeutic processes that helped them to overcome suicidal ideation and behaviors: (a) experiencing an affirming and validating relationship as a means of reconnection with others, (b) dealing with the intense emotions surrounding suicidal behavior, and (c) confronting and discarding negative patterns while establishing new, more positive behaviors.

Clients Who May Be at Risk for Harming Others

There will be situations in your counseling career when you must decide whether a particular client has the potential of harming another person, or perhaps even an individual's property. Making this decision is difficult, as there is no scientific basis for such decisions. If you do determine that a client is a danger to another person, then you must take the steps necessary to prevent harm (Gilbert, 2002; Hermann & Finn, 2002). This may include warning intended victims, whether or not their identity is known. In making these difficult decisions, it is essential to consult with other mental health professionals and to include supervisors to the extent possible.

What began as a legal requirement has now evolved into an ethical duty as well. Standard B.2.a. of the ACA *Code of Ethics* states that the counselor's confidentiality requirement "does not apply when disclosure is required to protect clients or identified others from serious and foreseeable harm." This particular exception to confidentiality has caused considerable confusion and consternation among helping professionals, not only because it involves breaching confidentiality but also because it demands that counselors be able to predict dangerousness. Human behavior is not always predictable, and counselors may find themselves caught on the horns of a dilemma, both ethically and legally, in determining whether to breach a client's confidentiality in order to prevent harm to the client or to others.

4-3 The Case of Todd

Todd is a counselor in a community mental health center. For the last 2 weeks he has been seeing a client named Bill, who is a junior in high school. Bill comes to center 1 day a week, walking from school to his sessions and then walking home afterward. This afternoon, Bill tells Todd that, after thinking about it for quite some time, he has decided to shoot the assistant principal at his school. Bill says that his father has a rifle collection in their home and he has access to the guns and to ammunition. Bill explains that he plans to wait outside the assistant principal's home until he walks out in the morning and shoot him as he walks to his car. Because Bill is so calm as he relates all of this information, Todd asks Bill if he is serious. Bill smiles, laughs, and then says, "No, I was only kidding. I would never do anything like that." Because Todd doesn't know Bill very well, he is not sure what to do next. Todd asks Bill to excuse him a minute and leaves his office to look for his supervisor. He discovers that his supervisor and all the other staff have left for the day. Todd returns to his office and finds Bill standing by a window, looking out with tears in his eyes.

- In these circumstances, what are Todd's options?
- What option would you choose if you were Todd?

Research indicates that it is impossible to predict whether a particular person is going to harm someone else; yet the law and our ethical standards require counselors to determine whether a client is dangerous. How can this legal and ethical duty be fulfilled? First, it is important to learn as much as you can about the warning signs of persons who commit violent acts against others (Daniels, 2002; Truscott & Evans, 2001). For example, it appears that the best predictor of violence is past violent behavior (Megargee, 1979; Meloy, 1987; Monahan, 1995; Mulvey & Lidz, 1995; Slovic & Monahan, 1995; Truscott, Eveans, & Mansell, 1995). But you must be careful not to profile, or assume that a category of persons are prone to violence (Bailey, 2001). Special situations, such as those involving domestic partner violence (Lawson, 2001, 2003) or violence of persons with serious mental disorders, probably require deviations from general guidelines offered in this chapter.

Once you have determined that a client is indeed dangerous and might harm another person, the law requires that you take whatever steps are necessary to prevent the harm, and further, that the steps you take be the least disruptive (Rice, 1993). You have choices that range from the least intrusive action (obtaining a promise from your client not to harm anyone else) to the most intrusive (having the client involuntarily committed to a psychiatric facility). There are numerous possibilities in between these two extremes, such as notifying the client's family members and getting one of them to take responsibility for keeping the client under control, persuading the client to be voluntarily committed to a residential facility, notifying the police, or calling the client periodically. There certainly are no right formulas for action when you determine that your client is dangerous. If at all possible, consult with other mental health professionals and use their input in making your decision.

The guidelines in Figure 4-2 regarding managing potentially suicidal clients would work equally well in managing potentially violent clients. You would just need to add the determination of whether to warn intended victims, law enforcement authorities, or both.

Duty to Warn Intended Victims   Think about how you might react if you were counseling a client who made a threat to harm someone else (Burkemper, 2002). If you were to decide that the client was only venting anger and was not likely to act on the threat, and then later the client carried out the threat, you would have acted ethically in trusting your professional judgment and in preserving confidentiality and the counseling relationship. That would be little solace, however, if someone were killed or seriously injured. Also, the question might arise before an ethics committee or in a court as to whether you could have acted, or should have acted, to avert that harm. On the other hand, if you were to decide that the danger was in fact clear and imminent and you were to issue a warning, no harm would be done to a third party. If the client did not later attempt to harm the possible victim, however, you would have erred in labeling the client dangerous and your actions probably will have destroyed the counseling relationship. You could be accused of misdiagnosis, defamation of character, or violating confidentiality (*Hopewell v. Adebimpe,* 1982). It is no wonder that counselors view these as no-win situations and might be tempted to simply avoid working with dangerous clients. Yet, it would be ethically questionable to close the doors of the counseling profession to a group of individuals who clearly need our help (Herlihy & Sheeley, 1988).

The duty to warn an identifiable or foreseeable victim of a dangerous client arose out of the landmark *Tarasoff v. Regents of University of California* (1976) court case, which established the following legal concept in California:

> … when a psychotherapist *determines,* or pursuant to the standards of his profession *should determine,* that a patient presents a serious danger or violence to others, the therapist incurs an obligation to use reasonable care to protect the foreseeable victim from such danger. (*McClarren,* 1987, p. 273)

Although the Tarasoff doctrine has not been accepted or applied in every jurisdiction in the United States, counselors have chosen to incorporate it into the ACA *Code of Ethics* and generally assume that the concept is a national legal requirement. The only jurisdiction that has specifically rejected the Tarasoff duty to warn doctrine is Texas (*Thapar v. Zezulka,* 1999). In Texas, counselors do not have a duty to warn intended victims if their clients threaten to harm another person. As a result, if a mental health professional in Texas did warn an intended victim, the professional might potentially be liable to the client who made the threat, for breach of confidentiality. Lewis (2001) has argued that the Thapar case in Texas was a wrong decision and that there should be a common-law duty to warn intended victims in Texas. However, the Thapar case currently is the law in Texas.

The facts in the Tarasoff case are important in understanding the duty that has been imposed on counselors. Prosenjit Poddar was a 26-year-old graduate student at the University of California at Berkeley. In the course of a session with his counselor, Poddar confided his intention to kill his girlfriend, Tatiana Tarasoff. His counselor was Dr. Lawrence Moore, a psychologist in the university counseling center. Because Moore believed that Poddar might be serious regarding his threat, Moore initiated proceedings to have Poddar committed for a psychiatric evaluation. Moore orally notified two campus police officers of his intentions to commit Poddar and then sent a letter to the police chief requesting assistance from the police department. The police took Poddar into custody, but released him when he promised not to contact Tarasoff. Poddar never went to see Moore again. Neither Moore nor the police notified Tarasoff of Poddar's threat. Two months later, Poddar stabbed and killed Tarasoff on the front porch of her parents' home. Tarasoff's parents sued Moore in a wrongful death action for not confining Poddar and not warning Tarasoff of the threat against her life.

Decisions subsequent to the Tarasoff case throughout the United States have interpreted the holding of the case differently. Many courts have limited its application to situations in which the victims are readily identifiable. Other courts, however, have extended the duty to all persons who are endangered by the patient's condition or threats (McClarren, 1987). In *Lipari v. Sears, Roebuck & Co.* (1980), a federal court held that a psychotherapist has a duty to warn and protect unknown victims, as well as those who are readily identifiable. This case extended a counselor's duty to those persons who are foreseeably endangered by a client's conduct.

A Washington state court, following the Lipari decision, held that a psychiatrist could possibly be held responsible for injuries sustained by a traffic accident victim. The victim was hurt when a drug-abusing patient, released by the psychiatrist, ran a red light while under the influence of drugs (*Petersen v. State,* 1983). Two California cases expanded the Tarasoff doctrine by no longer requiring that a psychotherapist be able to readily identify the patient's victim (*Hedlund v. Superior Court of Orange County,* 1983; *Jablonski v. United States,* 1983).

In a Vermont case, the supreme court held that a mental health professional has a duty to take reasonable steps to protect a third party from threats of damage to property posed by a patient (*Peck v. Counseling Service of Addison County, Inc.,* 1985). In the Peck case, the court found that a counselor could be held responsible for property damage when a client burned down a barn. The client told the counselor he intended to do so, and the counselor did not warn the owners of the barn.

Originally, the Tarasoff holding imposed a duty to warn only if the victim was specifically identifiable. Subsequent decisions have extended that duty to include warning persons who are unknown, persons who are unintentionally injured by a patient, whole classes of persons of which the victim is a member, bystanders who might be injured by a patient's negligent act, and individuals whose property a client has threatened to destroy (McClarren, 1987).

Decision making for counselors around the Tarasoff legal requirements is complex. One thing is clear, however. Because of the Tarasoff case, when you determine that a client might harm an identifiable or foreseeable person, you must directly or indirectly warn that individual of the danger, except in Texas.

Clients with AIDS or Who Are HIV-Positive The advent of AIDS has placed mental health professionals in a quandary. Do counselors have an ethical duty to warn when a client is HIV positive or AIDS confirmed and could be putting others at risk through such behaviors as unprotected sex or needle sharing? According to Standard B.2.b., *Contagious, Life-Threatening Diseases,* of the ACA *Code of Ethics*, when a counselor receives information confirming that a client has a disease commonly known to be both communicable and life threatening, the counselor may be "justified in disclosing information to identifiable third parties, if they are known to be at demonstrable and high risk of contracting the disease."

Note that, according to ethical guidelines, counselors are *justified* in disclosing, but are not necessarily *required* to disclose, information to an endangered third party. You will need to weigh a number of factors and determine your own stance regarding arguments that have been offered both for and against breaching confidentiality in working with AIDS or HIV positive clients. Due to medical advances, AIDS is no longer routinely fatal, which makes the applicability of this standard open to question. Some writers (Driscoll, 1992; Melton, 1991; Perry, 1989) have made some compelling arguments in favor of maintaining confidentiality. Breaches of confidentiality are especially countertherapeutic when working with clients who have a high level of mistrust due to discrimination against them (for instance, gay men, prostitutes, and intravenous drug users). Exposure to HIV does not carry the same level of risk as a homicidal client who threatens to use a lethal weapon; not every exposure to HIV results in harm. Individuals who have consented to unsafe sex practices or sharing needles that could be contaminated must take responsibility for their own choices. If the client's confidentiality is compromised, the client is likely to discontinue counseling, and the problems that contribute to continuation of high-risk behavior (such as fear of abandonment and loss of control) will be exacerbated.

Other writers have argued for disclosure (Cohen, 1997; Erickson, 1993; Gray & Harding, 1988), pointing out that confidentiality is not an end in itself and that the need to protect someone who may be at risk of contracting a fatal disease creates a higher duty. They suggest that, with AIDS having reached epidemic proportions, mental health professionals have an obligation to do their part to protect the health and welfare of society at large when AIDS clients are putting others at risk. These writers also argue that, although it is an injustice that clients with AIDS suffer from discrimination, the protection of others must take precedence over the possibility of discrimination.

It is crucial that you use your clinical judgment in these cases and that you evaluate each AIDS confidentiality dilemma on a case-by-case basis (Harding, Gray, & Neal, 1993; Kain, 1989). To be in compliance with the ethical standards, it is imperative that you do not act hastily to breach confidentiality. First, you should ascertain that your client really does have AIDS or actually is HIV positive, as is required by the ACA *Code of Ethics* (2005; Standard B.2.b.). Often, a consultation with the client's physician is necessary. You should obtain your client's permission for such a consultation. Because AIDS/HIV-positive status is a medical condition, in many circumstances informing the client's physician of your concern about the client endangering others will transfer to the physician the obligation of protecting others.

If you believe you must take responsibility because a physician is not available, then you must determine whether your client has already informed the partner or other third party or is intending to do so in the immediate future. It is preferable that clients make their own disclosures, so you might continue to work with the client in exploring the client's willingness to assume this responsibility, or you might involve the partner in the counseling process.

In some jurisdictions, specific statutes have been passed that address the issue of AIDS and the duty to warn. When your clients who have AIDS or who are HIV positive refuse to disclose their condition to an endangered third party and you believe that you must do so, you must be aware of any applicable state laws that might restrict or guide your reporting options. Without a doubt, keeping abreast of legal and ethical obligations related to HIV/AIDS will continue to pose real challenges for counselors as more is learned about ways to transmit, prevent, and eventually, cure the disease.

To summarize, your work with clients who are dangerous to themselves or others will be fraught with ethical and legal complexities. It is important to keep up with the literature in this area and to familiarize yourself with guidelines for practice regarding the duty to warn, such as those offered by Costa and Altekruse (1994). Whenever possible, you should consult with fellow professionals (Standard C.2.e.) if you are in doubt about whether you have a duty to warn, protect, or report in a given situation.

A Hypothetical Malpractice Case

To illustrate how a malpractice case might be considered against a counselor, we analyze a typical situation in which a counselor might be sued. Suppose that a teacher has come to Monica, a high school counselor, with a concern about Mark, an 11th-grade student. Mark has written a paper for English class in which he discusses taking his life because he is upset about his parents' recent divorce. Monica calls Mark into her office and talks with him about the paper. She asks him if he has seriously considered taking his life. After a thorough discussion with Mark, Monica determines that he is not suicidal.

That same day, after school, Mark shoots and kills himself with his father's rifle. Mark's mother, Sheila, finds out about the teacher's referral and files a malpractice lawsuit against Monica, claiming that Monica's incompetence caused her son's death. Sheila's attorney probably would name as respondents in the lawsuit Monica individually, each of her direct supervisors up through the school superintendent, the school board, and any other individuals or groups who might be responsible for Monica's actions or failure to act. If Monica had her own independent professional liability insurance policy, her insurance company would hire a lawyer who would represent Monica individually in the case. If Monica did not have her own liability insurance policy, she probably would not be able to afford to pay an attorney to represent her. She would have to rely for her defense on the school system lawyers, who ultimately represent the school system, not her. The school system would have its lawyers, or the lawyers provided by the school system's liability insurance company, file a legal response to the case. Monica's lawyer, if she had one, and the school system lawyers would work together in defending the lawsuit.

Sheila's attorney, in presenting her case in court, would first have to prove that Monica owed a duty of reasonable care in providing counseling services to Mark. This would not be difficult to prove because Monica is a counselor in the school and called Mark in for a counseling session. When a counselor accepts a person as a client, the counselor then has a duty to provide the client with professional care that meets accepted standards within the profession. Counselors have a fiduciary relationship with clients, which is a relationship that fosters the highest level of trust and confidence (Anderson, 1996). Clearly, Monica owed Mark a duty of care.

After establishing that a duty of care was owed to Mark, Sheila's attorney then would have to prove that Monica breached that duty and failed to conform to the required standard of care. Most experts would agree that counselors must assess whether a client is suicidal, even though studies have shown that it is impossible to scientifically predict suicidal behavior (Coleman & Shellow, 1992). If it is determined the client is in danger, action must be taken to prevent the impending suicide (Ahia & Martin, 1993; Austin, Moline, & Williams, 1990). The question in this situation is whether Monica was reasonable in her assessment of Mark's risk. The only way to prove that Monica made an error in her professional judgment is for Sheila's attorney to bring in one or more expert witnesses who will testify that a competent counselor would not have done what Monica did. The expert witnesses must compare the actions Monica took to the actions that a reasonable counselor with Monica's same background and preparation, practicing in the same locality, would have taken in the same set of circumstances. This is the legal standard of care to which counselors are held. Monica's attorney would arrange for a different set of experts to testify that Monica did act reasonably in this particular situation. The judge or jury would have to decide which expert witnesses to believe.

After offering evidence through expert witness testimony that Monica breached her duty of care, Sheila's attorney would have to prove that Mark was injured as a result of this breach. It would not be difficult to prove that harm occurred, because Mark killed himself.

Next, Sheila's attorney would have to prove that there was a close causal connection between what Monica did, or failed to do, and Mark's suicide. Sheila's attorney would have to prove that Sheila knew or should have known that her actions would result in Mark's death. The attorney would argue that Monica's failure to take action when Mark disclosed he intended to commit suicide was the proximate cause of Mark's death because she failed to take actions that would prevent him from committing suicide. On the opposing side, Monica's attorney would argue that a number of other intervening factors led to Mark's suicide, and that a reasonable counselor would not and could not have predicted that Mark would take his life, given the circumstances in this situation. Further, Monica's attorney would argue that even if Monica did act negligently in this situation, Mark's suicide cannot be blamed on her failure to take action. Other factors *caused* his suicide—factors such as his father leaving his gun out so that Mark had access to it, no one being at home to supervise him after school, or his distress over his parents' contentious behavior during the divorce. The judge or jury would have to decide whether Monica's failure to act to prevent Mark's suicide was the proximate cause of his death, or whether other factors caused him to take his life.

If Sheila's attorney was successful in convincing the judge or jury that Monica was responsible for Mark's death, then the damage to Sheila, expressed in financial terms, would have to be determined. If a person is damaged with a financial loss, such as a loss in the stock market or investing in a deal that has no value, then it is easy to determine how much money the person needs to be *made whole again*. However, when a person has a physical injury, or loses a loved one through death, then it is very difficult to determine how much money it would take to compensate the person for the loss. In fact, these are losses that cannot be compensated with money, but the law requires that there be a financial compensation.

Damages in this situation would be determined by expert witness testimony on Mark's life expectancy, his earning potential, and the anticipated benefit of earnings that would go to his mother, Sheila. Because the loss of a life was involved in this situation, the damages could be hundreds of thousands or several million dollars. Judges or juries have wide discretion in setting the value in these kinds of cases.

If Sheila received a judgment in her favor, the school system's professional liability insurance carrier would most likely pay the judgment. Monica's professional liability carrier might be responsible for paying a portion of the judgment, as well. Both the school's and Monica's insurance companies would pay the attorneys' fees and other costs of litigation, which could be as much as several hundred thousand dollars.

At this point, you probably are wondering how often lawsuits are based on client suicide and how often family members prevail and collect judgments. Although client suicide is not the only possible basis for a malpractice lawsuit against counselors, it is undoubtedly one of the most painful types of suits for both plaintiffs and defendants. In the following section, we review some actual cases related to client suicide.

Real Malpractice Cases

In 1960, a college counselor was sued for the wrongful death of a student who had committed suicide. The student had seen the counselor in a professional capacity (*Bogust v. Iverson*). The holding in that case was that the college counselor was not a therapist and therefore had no duty to detect or prevent a suicide of a client. Since 1960, however, the counseling profession has evolved substantially and counselors in all settings are considered mental health professionals. A similar case today would probably have a different result.

A case that is similar to *Bogust v. Iverson* and the hypothetical case of Monica was decided in Maryland in 1991. In *Eisel v. Board of Education of Montgomery County* (1991), Dorothy Jones and Deidre Morgan, school counselors at Sligo Middle School in Maryland (along with their school board, principal, and superintendent) were sued in a wrongful death action by Stephen Eisel, the father of Nicole Eisel. Nicole Eisel was a 13-year-old student at Sligo Middle School. Nicole and another 13-year-old girl consummated an apparent murder–suicide pact on November 8, 1988. The complaint filed in the lawsuit was summarized in the case report:

> The amended complaint avers that Nicole became involved in satanism, causing her to have an "obsessive interest in death and self-destruction." During the week prior to the suicide, Nicole told several friends and fellow students that she intended to kill herself. Some of these friends reported Nicole's intentions to their school counselor, Morgan, who relayed the information to Nicole's school counselor, Jones. Morgan and Jones then questioned Nicole about the statements, but Nicole denied making them. Neither Morgan nor Jones notified Nicole's parents or the school administration about Nicole's alleged statements of intent. Information in the record suggests that the other party to the suicide pact shot Nicole before shooting herself. The murder–suicide took place on a school holiday in a public park at some distance from Sligo Middle School. (pp. 449–450)

Attorneys for the school board and its employees argued that school guidance counselors had no duty to recognize or prevent an adolescent's suicide. A motion for summary judgment in favor of the school board and its employees was granted, which means that the court, without even hearing the evidence in the case, found that the counselors were not responsible. Eisel appealed to the Maryland Court of Appeals. The Court of Appeals reversed the summary judgment and required that the case go back to the trial court so that a judge or jury could determine whether the counselors would be held responsible for Nicole Eisel's death.

In coming to this decision, the Maryland Court of Appeals held that "school counselors have a duty to use reasonable means to attempt to prevent a suicide when they are on notice of a child or adolescent student's suicidal intent" (*Eisel v. Board of Education of Montgomery County*, 1991, p. 456). The decision noted that the counselors could have determined that Nicole was in danger of committing suicide even though she denied it when asked, that the school board had a policy requiring counselors to notify parents despite any confidentiality concerns, and that the school had a formal suicide prevention program in place. The decision stated, "the relationship of a school counselor and pupil is not devoid of therapeutic overtones" (p. 452). The appeals court did not decide that the two school counselors were responsible for Nicole Eisel's suicide, but it did decide that a judge or jury could determine that the facts were such that they could be held responsible.

It is almost impossible to determine how many lawsuits of a particular nature are filed in court. Many lawsuits are settled without a judgment being rendered or are determined at the trial court level and are not appealed. Only cases that are appealed are reported in case books. However, from the cases that are appealed, it appears that very few lawsuits are filed against counselors due to client suicide, and few of those filed result in judgments against the counselors. Nonetheless, counselors certainly hope to avoid experiencing the double trauma of having a client commit suicide and being named as a defendant in a lawsuit resulting from that suicide. In fact, if you practice competently, the chances are good that you will never have to respond to a malpractice lawsuit.

SUMMARY AND KEY POINTS

Counselor competence is an important concept, even though it is difficult to define from an ethical viewpoint and difficult to demonstrate in a court of law. It is best viewed as being based on performance and as existing along a continuum from gross negligence to maximum effectiveness. Some of the key points regarding competence that are made in this chapter include the following:

- The law demands a minimum level of practice from counselors, whereas ethics encourages counselors to aspire to an ideal level of practice.
- Counselors must practice within their boundaries of competence. It can be difficult to determine just where these boundaries lie.
- The development of competence begins with preparation and education, and the initial responsibility for producing competent practitioners rests with counselor educators and supervisors.
- Preparation standards established by accrediting bodies help to ensure that graduates of accredited programs possess certain competencies. Nonetheless, graduation from an accredited counselor education program does not guarantee competence.
- Licensure is a legal process that establishes minimum standards for a counselor to practice in a given state. Because licensure is a political process, counselor licensure requirements are not uniform across the states.
- It is questionable whether licensure actually accomplishes the goals of ensuring competence, protecting consumers, and promoting high standards of practice.
- Certification is another approach to attempting to ensure competence.
- Specialty preparation, licensure, and certification are controversial issues in the counseling field.
- Once counselors begin to practice, they are responsible for determining their own competence.
- Counselors are required to seek continuing education in order to maintain their competence. Peer review is an effective approach to monitoring competence.
- Many new information technologies exist and offer counselors resources for maintaining and increasing their competence.
- Counselors must know when and how to refer clients when they are not able to provide competent services to these clients.
- Counselors must exercise care while stretching their boundaries of competence to include client populations and concerns with which they have little or no experience.
- It is essential in today's society that counselors possess intercultural counseling competence.
- When counselors are experiencing distress, burnout, or impairment, they must take steps to protect clients from harm and to restore themselves to their full level of functioning.

Malpractice is the second major issue addressed in this chapter. Key points include:

- Malpractice lawsuits arise from claims of counselor incompetence. It is difficult to prove all five elements of malpractice that must be proved for a malpractice case to succeed.
- Some lawsuits have been filed against counselors for failing to prevent a client's suicide. Counselors are being held to a higher standard of care in these cases and must be able to assess a client's risk for suicide. Steps to follow in this process are included in the chapter.
- Counselors also have an obligation to take steps to prevent a client from harming others. The duty to warn and protect intended victims is extremely complex from both the ethical and the legal standpoints. Steps to follow in this process are included in the chapter.

CHAPTER

5 Boundary Issues

FOCUS QUESTIONS

1. Why do you think codes of ethics discourage counselors from having personal, social, and business relationships with clients?
2. Do you think a sexual relationship between a counselor and a former client is ever acceptable? Why or why not?
3. What would you do if you found that you felt a strong sexual attraction to one of your clients?

Perhaps no ethical and legal issue has caused more controversy among helping professionals than determining the appropriate boundaries of the therapeutic relationship. Although the term *boundary* is part of the everyday language of counseling, it has rarely been defined in the literature (Hermanson, 1997). Therefore, we define *boundaries* and the related term, *dual* or *multiple relationships,* before we explore what makes them so controversial.

A *boundary* can be conceptualized as a frame or membrane around the therapeutic dyad that defines a set of roles for the participants in the therapeutic relationship (Smith & Fitzpatrick, 1995). Viewed this way, boundaries help us understand the parameters of the relationship. Although counseling can involve a great deal of emotional intimacy, it is a professional relationship and, therefore, it has certain limits that might not apply to a personal relationship. To give just a few examples, there are limits on physical contact between counselor and client, on time and place for counseling (counseling generally takes place during regularly scheduled appointments and in a particular setting), on the amount and types of self-disclosure made by the counselor, and on the exchange of gifts. Boundaries help provide structure to the therapeutic relationship. Katherine's (1991) definition of a boundary as a "limit that promotes integrity" (p. 3) nicely captures the purpose of boundary setting. Boundaries serve to protect the welfare of clients who are in a vulnerable position in the therapeutic relationship.

Boundary issues usually have been framed in the literature as questions of dual or multiple relationships. According to Herlihy and Corey (1997), dual or multiple relationships occur when helping professionals take on two or more roles simultaneously or sequentially with a help seeker. Stated another way, dual or multiple relationships occur whenever helping professionals have another, significantly different relationship with one of their clients, students, or supervisees. Dual relationships can involve combining the role of counselor with another professional relationship (such as teacher, minister, supervisor, employer, or business partner; Smith & Smith, 2001), or combining the counselor role with a personal relationship (such as friend, relative, or lover).

Much of the early attention to boundary issues in therapeutic relationships was focused on sexual intimacies between counselor and client. Later in this chapter, we discuss in more detail the harm done to clients and the ethical and legal ramifications for counselors who become sexually involved with their clients. First, we focus on a variety of nonprofessional (other than sexual) relationship issues, exploring the complexities that make them so problematic for practitioners.

NONPROFESSIONAL INTERACTIONS OR RELATIONSHIPS WITH CLIENTS

Because the issues surrounding "dual relationships" or "multiple relationships" are so complex and controversial, and because dual relationships are not necessarily unethical per se, the 2005 ACA *Code of Ethics* does not use these terms. Instead, the code provides several standards under A.5 (Roles and Relationships with Clients). One of these standards states:

> Counselor-client nonprofessional relationships with clients, former clients, their romantic partners, or their family members should be avoided, except when the interaction is potentially beneficial to the client. (Standard A.5.c.)

Note that the code of ethics does not prohibit *all* nonprofessional relationships per se. Rather, it cautions counselors to avoid nonprofessional relationships *except when the interaction is potentially beneficial to the client.* How does one distinguish among nonprofessional relationships that might be acceptable and those that could cause harm? A beginning step is to understand the factors that create the potential for harm.

The Potential for Harm

In determining the risk of harm in a nonprofessional relationship, Kitchener and Harding (1990) suggested that counselors should consider three factors: incompatible expectations, divergent responsibilities, and the power differential. We discuss each of these in turn, using the following example:

5-1 The Case of Cora

Cora is the director of a university counseling center and Eileen is a secretary in the center's main office. Eileen has been an excellent employee for many years and Cora has come to count on her to help keep the center functioning smoothly. One day Cora comes out of her office and notices that Eileen's eyes are red and puffy and that she seems sad. When Cora expresses her concern, Eileen begins to cry. She tells Cora that she is having some personal problems and adds, "Can I just step into your office for a minute while I pull myself together?" Cora agrees to this request and they both go into Cora's office and close the door. Eileen begins to tell Cora about her personal problems. Cora listens as Eileen tells her story. After nearly an hour she suggests that Eileen might want to seek counseling. Eileen demurs, saying that she feels better now and thinks she can handle things.

Several weeks go by, during which time Eileen's work is not up to her usual high standards. She makes careless errors and forgets things. Cora calls her into her office twice to address this problem. Each time Cora spends about 30 minutes listening to Eileen's personal problems. At the end of each conversation, Eileen insists that she is "getting a grip on things." When the time comes for Cora to complete her quarterly evaluations of her counseling center staff, she gives Eileen a low rating on a number of the items on the form. When Eileen receives the evaluation, she is hurt and angry. She confronts Cora, saying, "How could you—of all people—do this to me! You know I'm a good employee but am just going through a rough time. You know what's going on in my life. I expected you to understand."

- What did Cora do in this situation that led to her problem with Eileen?
- How might Cora have avoided this problem with Eileen?

It is likely that Eileen's hurt and anger have resulted from the *incompatible expectations* she held for Cora. On the one hand, Cora has been a caring and sympathetic listener. Even though Cora did not intend to enter into a formal therapeutic relationship with Eileen, she has behaved as a counselor. Eileen has come to expect her to be understanding, accepting, and nonjudgmental while Eileen was working through her personal problems. She also expects Cora to respect her privacy and keep confidential everything she had told her. Given this set of expectations, the evaluation feels like a punishment and a betrayal. On the other hand, she has been a secretary in the center for several years and is accustomed to receiving quarterly evaluations from her supervisor. As an employee, she realizes that her work has not been up to par and in that role she would expect to receive a fair and accurate evaluation. Her expectations for Cora as a supervisor are incompatible with what she expects from Cora as a sympathetic listener and counselor.

Cora is faced with two *divergent responsibilities* in this situation. Because she has stepped into a counselor role, she needs to be accepting and supportive of Eileen, as well as patient, while Eileen works through her problems. As a supervisor, however, it is Cora's responsibility to evaluate her employees and to do so accurately. It is impossible for Cora to evaluate Eileen and be nonjudgmental at the same time.

Finally, there is a *power differential* in the relationship between Cora and Eileen. Cora is in a position of power because she is Eileen's supervisor who evaluates her work. Eileen is in a less powerful position as an employee and has made herself even more vulnerable by revealing her personal problems. It is Cora's professional responsibility to avoid misusing her power and to ensure that the more vulnerable individual in the relationship is not harmed. Certain characteristics of the therapeutic relationship place counselors in a position of power over clients. When clients come for counseling, they are in an emotionally vulnerable state. In the counseling relationship, the counselor learns much about the client's innermost thoughts and feelings, while the client learns much less about the counselor. Additionally, in most societies power is traditionally ascribed to healers (Smith & Fitzpatrick, 1995).

This unfortunate problematic situation between Cora and Eileen could have been avoided if Cora had not appeared to assume the role of counselor for Eileen. Counselors who are asked to counsel others with whom they have other relationships are put in a difficult situation, and it happens quite often. When persons with whom you have other relationships (relative, friend, employee, etc.) know that you are a counselor and ask you to counsel them, you need to be prepared to respond in both a caring and professionally appropriate manner. A good approach would be to acknowledge their distress and empathize with them. It would be good to state that you cannot function as their counselor because of your other relationship with them and offer to help them locate a good counselor. If you then proceed to listen to their situation, it is wise to remind them periodically that you are listening as a relative, friend, or supervisor rather than as a counselor.

According to Kitchener and Harding (1990), three postulates regarding the potential for harm can be derived from the risk factors. First, the greater the incompatibility of expectations in a dual role, the greater the risk of harm. Second, the greater the divergence of the responsibilities associated with dual roles, the greater the potential for divided loyalties and loss of objectivity. Third, the greater the power differential between the two parties involved in a dual relationship, the greater the potential for exploitation of the individual in the less powerful position.

Of course, counselors never *intend* to exploit their clients. Cottone (2005) has urged counselors to think in terms of detriment or harm to clients, rather than in terms of potential exploitation. He notes that the word "exploitive" implies malicious intent, whereas the term detrimental focuses on outcome regardless of intent. His point is that counselors need to be held accountable for actions they take that cause harm to clients, regardless of intent.

Considering these risk factors will help you make wise decisions when you are faced with potential dual or nonprofessional relationships. It may also be helpful for you to understand their problematic nature and how they have been debated by helping professionals.

The Problematic Nature of Dual Relationships

Herlihy and Corey (1997) identified four characteristics of dual relationships that make them so problematic. First, *potential dual relationships can be difficult to recognize.* They can evolve in subtle ways. There is no *danger sign* that marks the point at which a professional relationship crosses the line into behavior that could lead to an inappropriate relationship. It is not difficult for a counselor, or a counselor educator or supervisor, to innocently enter into a form of extraprofessional relationship. A counselor might accept a client's invitation to attend a special event that has meaning for the client. A counselor educator might find a friendship developing with a student whom the educator is mentoring. A supervisor might feel attracted to a supervisee, and think about dating the supervisee as soon as the formal supervision is completed.

When dual relationships are sequential rather than simultaneous, it can be particularly difficult to foresee potential problems. As Pope and Vasquez (1998) have pointed out, the mere fact that two roles are sequential rather than clearly concurrent "does not, in and of itself, mean that the two relationships do not constitute a dual relationship" (p. 191). Some of the questions with which conscientious professionals struggle are whether a former client can eventually become a friend, how a smooth transition can be made from a supervisory relationship to a collegial relationship once supervision is completed, and what factors need to be considered in determining whether a former therapeutic relationship can become a personal relationship of any kind.

A second complicating characteristic of dual relationships is that *their potential for harm ranges along a wide continuum from extremely harmful to benign or even beneficial,* as can be seen in the following two examples.

5-2 The Case of Gerald

Dorothy, age 23, seeks counseling from Gerald, an LPC in private practice. Her goal is to work through issues related to the sexual abuse by her stepfather that she had endured when she was a child. After 2 months of counseling, Gerald initiates a sexual relationship with Dorothy. He rationalizes his behavior by telling himself that she can benefit from having a "healthy" sexual relationship. Dorothy feels guilty, confused, and isolated by this betrayal of her trust. She wants to end the sexual relationship but has become so dependent on Gerald that she feels trapped. She begins to have thoughts of suicide.

5-3 The Case of Elizabeth

Fiona has been coming to see Elizabeth, her counselor, for nearly a year. Through counseling, Fiona has gained the self-esteem and confidence to return to college and complete the last four courses she needed in order to graduate. She asks Elizabeth to attend the graduation ceremony. She says that Elizabeth's attendance would mean a great deal to her because she credits the counseling process for making it possible for her to achieve her goal. Elizabeth agrees to attend the ceremony.

- What are differences between Gerald's motivation and Elizabeth's motivation to cross a boundary?
- What harm do you think might have resulted from Elizabeth attending Fiona's graduation ceremony?

As these examples illustrate, at one extreme are sexual dual relationships that can cause severe harm to clients. Gerald's behavior is exploitive, and he is causing harm by revictimizing his client. Near the other end of the continuum are situations in which a counselor chooses to engage in a form of dual relating in order to benefit a particular client. Elizabeth's choice to attend the graduation ceremony probably has a low risk of causing harm.

The ACA *Code of Ethics* (2005) specifically states in Standard A.5.d. that an example of a potentially beneficial interaction is "attending a formal ceremony (e.g., a wedding/commitment ceremony or graduation)." Of course, in the case of Elizabeth, Fiona would need to take the steps required in Standard A.5.d. which states: "the counselor must document in case records, prior to the interaction (when feasible), the rationale for such an interaction, the potential benefit, and anticipated consequences for the client..."

Third, *with the exception of sexual dual relationships, there is very little consensus among mental health professionals regarding the propriety of dual relationships.* Hedges (1993), presenting a psychoanalytic viewpoint, has argued that there is an essential dual relatedness in psychotherapy in that transference, countertransference, resistance, and interpretation all rest de facto on the existence of a dual relationship. Hedges urged counselors to remember that, viewed from this perspective, all beneficial aspects of counseling arise as a consequence of a dual relationship. Tomm (1993) has suggested that when counselors actively maintain interpersonal distance, they highlight the power differential and promote an objectification of the therapeutic relationship. Tomm believed that dual relating invites greater authenticity and congruence from counselors and can actually improve their professional judgments because dual relationships make it more difficult for them to hide behind the protection of a professional mask. Lazarus and Zur (2002) have taken the position that it can be extremely beneficial for counselors to engage in dual relationships with selected clients.

Other writers have taken an opposing stance. St. Germaine (1993) has reminded counselors that the potential for harm is always present in a dual relationship due to the loss of objectivity that accompanies that relationship. Bograd (1993) noted that the power differential between counselor and client makes it impossible for the client to give truly equal consent to an extraprofessional relationship. It is possible that counselors may unintentionally or unconsciously exploit or harm clients who are in a vulnerable position in the relationship. Pope and Vasquez (1998) cautioned that counselors who engage in dual relationships may rationalize their behavior in an attempt to evade their professional responsibility to find acceptable alternatives to dual relationships. Unfortunately, there has been little research conducted that explores the impact of violations of nonsexual boundaries on client improvement in counseling (Mathews & Gerrity, 2002).

Obviously, there is no consensus among professionals about this issue. You will need to give considered thought to developing your own stance toward boundary issues. As you ponder the risks and benefits of nonprofessional or dual relationships, we believe it may be helpful to keep in mind Tomm's (1993) point that it is not dual relating in itself that creates an ethical problem. Rather, it is the counselor's personal tendency to exploit clients or misuse power. Thus, simply avoiding dual relationships will not prevent exploitation. There are many ways that counselors can misuse their power and influence over clients even when they are not occupying more than one role with them.

The fourth and final characteristic that makes boundary issues so complicated is that *some dual relationships are unavoidable*. Although most of the literature regarding unavoidable dual relationships has centered on rural practice, there are a number of situations in which counselors and their clients have shared social communities. We discuss some of these situations in the following section.

Diversity Considerations

Counselors in isolated, rural communities or very small towns may find it impossible to avoid some overlap among roles (Erickson, 2001). Imagine a situation in which the local banker, beautician, auto mechanic, grocery store checkout clerk, and owner of the dry cleaners are all clients of a particular counselor who practices in a small town located a 2-hour drive from a major city. Would you expect that counselor to make a 4-hour round trip to receive all the routine services these clients provide, in order to avoid any possible overlapping of roles?

Rural and small-community practitioners face the additional problem of dealing with the effects overlapping relationships have on their own families (Schank & Skovholt, 1997). Consider the following scenario:

5-4 The Case of Paula

Marianne has been a client in counseling with Paula for several weeks. Marianne's husband and Paula's husband both serve on the advisory board for a charitable organization and the two husbands begin to develop a friendship. They decide that they would like for their wives to meet and that the two couples should go out to dinner together.

- How should Paula respond when her husband suggests this social contact?
- Do you think Marianne should tell her husband that Paula is her counselor and that she would not be comfortable in a social situation with Paula?

Similar to this case example, if the children of a client become friends with the children of the counselor, then the counselor and client will need to relate to each other as fellow parents, in addition to dealing with the effects of this added relationship on their therapeutic relationship. Without question, counselors in rural and small-town practice face dual relationship and role-overlap dilemmas more frequently than do most other practitioners.

It is important to recognize that, in addition to rural practice, there are other "small worlds" that can exist even in an urban environment. Counselors who work in the military face many of the same challenges as rural practitioners (Johnson, Ralph, & Johnson, 2005), as do those who are members of the deaf, gay, or religious communities (Glosoff, Corey, & Herlihy, 2006; Lazarus & Zur, 2002). People's political affiliations, ethnic identities, and substance dependence recovery status also can lead to dual relationships, because clients often seek counselors with similar values (Lerman & Porter, 1990).

Pastoral counselors have overlapping relationships with members of their congregations and they face some unique boundary challenges (Haug, 1999; Lynch, 2002). Syme (2003) has suggested that dual relationships are an inevitable part of pastoral practice and, thus, they have to be managed just as in other areas of counseling practice.

Some gay and lesbian counselors specialize in counseling gay and lesbian clients. These counselors might find it impossible to participate in many social or political activities in the gay community without encountering their clients. Would you expect these counselors to constrict their social lives and forgo political activities in order to avoid chance meetings with clients?

Similar issues arise in substance abuse counseling. Many substance abuse counselors are themselves in recovery. What if there is only one 12-step program in the area where a counselor practices? Would you expect that counselor to jeopardize recovery by avoiding the meetings for fear a client might be in attendance?

Kain (1997) posed some questions regarding a counselor who is HIV positive and who works with clients who are HIV positive or who are living with AIDS. What if there is only one HIV support group in the area? What if there is only one physician who specializes in treating HIV and AIDS? Would you expect this counselor to sacrifice the need for a support group or for quality medical care, in order to avoid role overlap?

Sometimes other cultural factors can create "small-world" dilemmas. For instance, imagine a counselor who immigrated from Vietnam to a city in the United States 20 years ago. He has earned his master's degree in counseling and continues to live and work in a section of the city where the population is primarily Vietnamese. Many residents of the area seek him out as a counselor, because he speaks their native language and because they believe he will be able to understand their cultural values. Many of these prospective clients are people with whom he is acquainted or are even distant relatives. Would you expect this counselor to deny his services to these clients?

Boundary Crossings Versus Boundary Violations

At this point in your reading, you have a feel for some of the complexities of nonprofessional or dual relationships. They pose many questions but very few absolute answers. You may be uncertain regarding your own stance toward some of the issues we have raised. If it is any comfort, many seasoned practitioners are also uncertain. Gibson and Pope (1993) surveyed a large national sample of counselors regarding a range of behaviors. Fully 42% of the items on their survey found to be controversial described some form of nonsexual dual relationship. At least 40% of the counselors judged nonsexual dual relationships as ethical and at least 40% judged them as unethical. Obviously, reasonable counselors disagree as to whether nonsexual dual relationships with clients are ethical.

Compounding the confusion around nonsexual dual relationships with clients is the fact that counselors may engage in some behaviors with clients from time to time that have a *potential* for creating a dual relationship but are not in themselves dual relationships. These behaviors have been described as "boundary crossings" to distinguish them from ongoing dual relationships.

Several writers (Gabbard, 1995; Gutheil & Gabbard, 1993; Simon, 1992; Smith & Fitzpatrick, 1995) have attempted to distinguish between boundary crossings and boundary violations. A boundary crossing is a departure from a commonly accepted practice that occurs to benefit a client. In a crossing, the boundary is shifted to meet the needs of a particular client at a particular moment. By contrast, a violation is a serious breach that causes harm.

An example of a boundary crossing was given earlier in the chapter in the case example involving a counselor (Elizabeth) who decided to attend her client's (Fiona's) college graduation ceremony. This counselor's behavior did not constitute an ongoing dual relationship and, arguably, it had the potential to enhance the therapeutic relationship. You should be aware, though, that not all counselors would agree with Elizabeth's decision. When Borys (1988) surveyed a large sample of mental health professionals regarding their beliefs about the ethics of certain boundary-crossing and dual relationship behaviors, she found very little agreement about most of the behaviors. We have adapted some of the survey items described in a later article (Borys & Pope, 1989) into a questionnaire (see Figure 5-1). We encourage you to complete the questionnaire, and then discuss your responses with fellow class members or with colleagues. Think about the rationale you would offer for your responses, should a class member or colleague challenge your decisions.

One factor that the survey does not address, and that probably will influence your decisions regarding whether you are willing to engage in occasional boundary crossings in your practice, is that each client is unique. Some clients have generally clear interpersonal boundaries, and an

For each item below, place an X in the box that best represents your opinion.

How ethical is it for a counselor to:	Never Ethical	Rarely Ethical	Sometimes Ethical	Usually Ethical	Always Ethical
1. Barter with a client for goods or services?					
2. Invite a client to a personal party or social event?					
3. Provide counseling to a friend who is in crisis?					
4. Accept a gift from a client if the gift is worth less than $10?					
5. Accept a gift from a client if the gift is worth more than $50?					
6. Accept a client's invitation to a special event?					
7. Go out for coffee with a client after a counseling session?					
8. Become friends with a client after termination of the counseling relationship?					
9. Give a home phone number to a client?					
10. Share personal experiences as a member of a self-help group when a client is in attendance?					
11. Occasionally hire a client to babysit?					

Figure 5-1   Boundary issues survey of opinion

occasional crossing during your relationship with them may have no further repercussions. Other clients present a real challenge to maintaining therapeutic boundaries. Clients with borderline personality traits or disorder, for example, are often adept manipulators who will try to draw their counselors into a "special" relationship (Gutheil, 1989; Simon, 1989). You will want to be very firm and consistent in maintaining the therapeutic frame with them.

In general, from an ethical standpoint, occasional boundary crossings probably can be justified when there is benefit to the client and very little risk of harm. Counselors must take care, however, not to let these crossings become routine. As Herlihy and Corey (1997) have noted:

> Interpersonal boundaries are not static and may be redefined over time as counselors and clients work closely together. Nonetheless, even seemingly innocent behaviors … can, if they become part of a pattern of blurring the professional boundaries, lead to dual relationship entanglements with a real potential for harm. (p. 9)

As small, well-intended boundary crossings become more frequent in a therapeutic relationship or in a counselor's practice in general, it has been suggested (Gutheil & Gabbard, 1993; Pope, Sonne, & Holroyd, 1993; Sonne, 1994) that the "slippery slope phenomenon" may come into effect. That is, the gradual erosion of the boundaries of the professional relationship can take counselors down an insidious path toward serious ethical violations.

As we discuss next, reasoning about boundary crossings from a legal perspective leads to similar conclusions.

The Legal Perspective on Boundary Crossings

Counselors who are accused of wrongdoing for any reason may have their peers investigate complaints against them, or may even have to defend themselves in an ethics hearing or criminal court. Once you have been accused of having done something wrong, it is too late to undo any small indiscretions from your past. Often in the area of boundary issues, counselors will think, "Well, maybe just this one time it will be all right to ask my client to babysit for my daughter," or "This client is particularly mature, so I'm sure we can have lunch together after our session today."

Unfortunately, these small and seemingly insignificant boundary crossings can be the very evidence that causes an ethics panel, judge, or jury to find against you when you have been accused of having done something wrong. When people judging you consider the small boundary crossings that you have committed, they may come to the conclusion that you are incapable of understanding your profession's prohibition against engaging in multiple relationships that are harmful to clients. Whether you have been falsely accused or even have been accused of something you wish you had not done, it is best if you have very few boundary crossings in your past.

Specific Boundary Issues

In this section of the chapter, we explore some specific issues that are associated with nonsexual dual relationships and boundaries. These issues include bartering, social and business relationships with clients, accepting gifts from clients, the limits of counselor self-disclosure, and touching or hugging a client.

Bartering   Bartering with a client for goods or services is not prohibited by the ethical standards of the counseling profession, although it is discouraged as a routine practice. There is no consensus among counseling practitioners as to whether they consider bartering to be ethical. In Gibson and Pope's (1993) survey, 53% rated accepting services and 63% rated accepting goods in lieu of payment as ethical. Counselors who enter into bartering arrangements with clients usually are motivated by a desire to provide services to clients whose financial resources are limited and who could not afford counseling without some sort of alternative arrangement for payment. This intention is admirable and you may find yourself tempted to enter into bartering agreements with clients from time to time in your professional career. However, you should be aware of the problems that are inherent in this practice.

One form of bartering involves the exchange of services. For example, a client might be a self-employed interior decorator who is having difficulty paying for continued counseling because his business has been slack lately. His counselor's office suite needs new paint and wallpaper, so they agree to exchange counseling services for redecorating services. It is possible that an arrangement like this could work smoothly, but there are a number of potential pitfalls. For one thing, most services that clients can offer do not have monetary value equal to an hour of counseling (Kitchener & Harding, 1990). Unless clients can devote considerable time each week to holding up their end of the agreement, they are likely to fall further and further behind in the amount owed. They can become trapped in a kind of indentured servitude and come to feel resentful.

In addition to the question of quantity of bartered services, the issue of quality of services provided can be problematic. To take the example of the decorator, what if the counselor thinks the client is doing a sloppy and inferior job of painting and wallpapering the office suite? What if the redecorating work is excellent, but the decorator is not satisfied with the counseling services? Feelings of resentment that build up in the counselor or in the client are bound to have a negative effect on the counseling relationship.

Another form of bartering involves the exchange of goods for counseling services. For example, a client who is an artist might wish to pay for counseling services by giving the counselor an oil painting. The issues of quality that arise in bartering of services apply to this type of bartering as well. In addition, the issue of how many hours of counseling are equivalent to the value of the painting needs to be addressed. What criteria should be used to make such a determination?

In the ACA *Code of Ethics* (2005), a blanket prohibition against bartering is not made. Instead, the code offers guidelines for counselors to help them determine whether a potential bartering arrangement might be acceptable. The code states that counselors may participate in bartering only if three criteria are met: The relationship is not exploitive or harmful and does not place the counselor in an unfair advantage, if the client requests it, and if such arrangements are an accepted practice among professionals in the community (Standard A.10.d.).

Diversity Considerations in Bartering   If you establish your practice in a rural community, you may find that bartering is common among local physicians and other professionals. In such a setting, it would be acceptable for you to engage in bartering if your clients initiate the request and if you believe you and the client can work out fair and equitable terms of agreement. We believe it would also be wise for you to consider other alternatives to bartering with clients who cannot pay your full fee. Some of these alternatives might include using a sliding scale fee or providing a set amount of pro bono services.

Social Relationships with Clients   Individuals who choose to become professional counselors do not cease to be members of their communities, nor are they expected to forgo their social lives in order to avoid all nonprofessional contacts with clients (Glosoff, 1997). As we noted earlier, some social contact with clients is difficult to avoid for counselors who share "small worlds" with their clients. Even when extraprofessional contacts with clients can be avoided with relative ease, however, counselors can find it tempting to develop social relationships and even friendships with their clients.

As Glosoff (1997) has noted, individuals ordinarily look to work as one setting where they can gratify certain psychological and social needs. For many people, their work environment is a place to meet others with whom they can socialize and form friendships. Choosing to become a counselor can limit these opportunities. Almost all counselors will have some clients who are likable and who would make nice friends, but a friendship and a therapeutic relationship cannot exist simultaneously. The therapeutic relationship is like a friendship in that it involves emotional intimacy, but it is different in a significant way. In a therapeutic relationship, the intimacy is one way. Friendships are coequal relationships in which personal disclosures, support, challenge, and other interpersonal dynamics are reciprocal. For a counselor to seek a friendship with a client would be to look for reciprocity in a relationship that is not, by its nature, reciprocal (Hill, 1990).

When counselors blend the roles of friend and counselor, they create a conflict of interest that compromises the objectivity needed for sound professional judgment (Pope & Vasquez, 1998). As professionals, counselors place the interests of their clients foremost, but the dual relationship creates a second set of interests—those of the counselor. For example, a counselor may be reluctant to confront a client who is also a friend, out of fear of jeopardizing the friendship.

Short of an ongoing friendship, there are many possibilities for more limited types of social contact with clients, and a counselor's stance toward these contacts may depend on several factors. The counselor's theoretical orientation might make a difference. Borys (1988) suggested that a psychodynamically oriented counselor might be quite strict about out-of-the-office social contacts with clients, because psychodynamic theory stresses the importance of *maintaining the frame of counseling* and attention to transference and countertransference issues. In contrast, relationship-oriented counselors or those who espouse systems theory might be more willing to interact with clients outside the therapeutic setting. Another factor may be the nature of the social function. Of the respondents in Borys' study, only 33% thought it was never or only rarely ethical to accept a client's invitation to a special occasion, whereas 92% disapproved of inviting a client to a personal party.

Although there has been much debate in the literature, our opinion is that counselors have an ethical obligation to keep their professional and personal or social lives as separate as they reasonably can. Counselors should not get their social needs or personal needs for friendship met through interactions with their clients.

Counselors and clients do, however, meet each other in social contexts without prior planning on either person's part. Therefore, it is essential that counselors discuss with their clients how they might be affected by encountering the counselor outside the office and how these chance meetings should be handled.

A closely related issue that has also been debated in the literature is the question of post-termination friendships with clients. Counselors are often aware of clients' attributes that would make them desirable friends. Clients, for their part, may hope to continue the intimacy they felt and the caring attention they received during the therapeutic relationship. The code of ethics offers no guidance regarding post-termination friendships with clients, and there is no consensus among helping professionals regarding the advisability of such relationships.

Several risks in postcounseling friendships have been identified. Vasquez (1991) noted that many clients consider reentering counseling with their counselors, and that if a friendship develops this option is closed. Other writers have argued that therapeutic gains are jeopardized when a friendship follows a therapeutic relationship, because a post-termination friendship may disrupt a healthy resolution of transference issues (Gelso & Carter, 1985; Kitchener, 1992). The power differential that existed during the therapeutic relationship is not automatically negated when the counseling is terminated. As Salisbury and Kinnier (1996) have noted, "Unreciprocated knowledge of a former client's most sensitive weaknesses and most intimate secrets can render a client particularly vulnerable" (p. 495) in a friendship with a former counselor.

Despite these risks, there is some evidence that most counselors find the development of friendships with former clients to be ethically acceptable. Fully 70% of counselors surveyed by Salisbury and Kinnier (1996) believed that a postcounseling friendship with a client could be acceptable. Approximately one third of them actually had engaged in this behavior. The fact that a substantial number of counselors condone or engage in a practice does not necessarily indicate that the practice is ethical, however. You should avoid a tendency to reflexively accept "prevalence" arguments as a justification for dual relationship behaviors (Pope & Vasquez, 1998).

There are a number of factors that you should consider before pursuing a friendship with a former client. These include the time that has passed since termination, transference and countertransference issues, the length and nature of the counseling, the client's issues and diagnosis, the circumstances of the termination, the client's freedom of choice, whether any exploitation might have occurred in the professional relationship, the client's ego strength and mental health, the possibility of reactivation of counseling, and whether any harm to the client's welfare can be foreseen (Akamatsu, 1988; Kitchener, 1992; Salisbury & Kinnier, 1996). It would be difficult to demonstrate that none of these factors were at play if a counselor were challenged by a licensing board or in court. As a general rule, we believe counselors would be wise to avoid developing friendships with both current and former clients.

Diversity Considerations in Social Relationships   Cautions against counseling friends or close acquaintances may present difficulties for counselors of color (Herlihy & Watson, 2003). The concern about dual relationships is not widely shared in the African American community, where helpers typically play multiple roles (Parham, 1997). Having a shared primary language with a counselor can be pivotal in the choices of some clients. For instance, there may be only one Spanish-speaking Latino counselor in an elementary school, and that counselor may know and socialize with the families of the Latino students. These students may seek out this counselor precisely because of this connection and because of the counselor's fluency in the language they speak at home.

Business or Financial Relationships with Clients   Business and financial relationships with clients have received little focused attention in the literature, perhaps because the issues are much the same as those raised by personal and social dual relationships. For instance, counselors who work in rural settings may be more likely to have business-related encounters with clients. Schank and Skovholt (1997) described a situation in which a counselor took his car to a shop to be serviced. He thought the bill was rather high for the services performed, but was reluctant to question the charges when he realized that one of his clients had done the work. Of course, such unintended encounters can happen in urban and suburban practice. A counselor might have an electrical or plumbing problem at home, and have a client who is employed by the electric company or plumbing contractor show up to do the work. These occurrences, although awkward, might be resolved through an open discussion during the next counseling session.

Anderson and Kitchener (1996) asked counselors to describe critical incidents involving postcounseling relationships with clients. Business or financial relationships were second only to personal or friendship relationships in the frequency with which they were related. Their respondents identified two types of situations that could apply equally to relationships with current clients. The first involved the counselor paying for a client's expertise or assistance. Examples might include hiring a client or former client to perform clerical work or to cater a party at the counselor's home. The second involved a counselor and client joining areas of expertise to produce income, such as going into business together. It appears that counselors regard going into business with a current client as unethical; only 9% of respondents in Gibson and Pope's (1993) survey rated this behavior as ethical. When the question was one of going into business with a former client, however, the percentage who rated it as ethical rose to 46%.

Other types of dual relating that involve financial considerations occur when a counselor patronizes a client's place of business, or when a counselor sells goods (such as a relaxation tape or a book) to a client. In the former situation, the client could feel pressured to give the counselor a discount or some kind of special services. In the second instance, the client might feel coerced to buy the counselor's product. Only 16% of the counselors who participated in Gibson and Pope's (1993) study rated selling goods to a client as ethical.

Although the practice of entering into business or financial relationships with clients needs further study, our own recommendation is that counselors should avoid entering into these relationships with current or former clients. Whenever a counselor is making a monetary profit from a secondary relationship with a client, that counselor's self-interest is clearly involved.

Accepting Gifts from Clients   When clients offer gifts to their counselors—even small, token gifts—it can make counselors feel uncomfortable. They may be torn between wanting to decline the gift in order to keep the relationship within proper boundaries, yet wanting to accept the gift so that the client will not feel hurt or rejected. The best way to minimize such conflicts is to have a general policy that you do not accept gifts from clients and to include a statement to that effect in your informed consent document. This procedure will not solve completely all potential problems, however. Clients may vary in how they interpret the idea of a gift, or they may forget or choose to ignore that you have a policy. For your part, you probably will not want to interpret your own policy too rigidly. It is difficult to imagine an elementary school counselor refusing to accept a child client's offering of a handmade Valentine, for instance.

The 2005 ACA *Code of Ethics* has a standard on accepting gifts from clients. Standard 10.e. states, "Counselors understand the challenges of accepting gifts from clients and recognize that in some cultures, small gifts are a token of respect and showing gratitude. When determining whether or not to accept a gift from clients, counselors take into account the therapeutic relationship, the monetary value of the gift, a client's motivation for giving the gift, and the counselor's motivation for wanting or declining the gift."

It is certainly possible that a client may offer you a gift at some point. It is wise for you to think through how you plan to handle this event. The *Code of Ethics* suggests some criteria you might use in determining whether to accept or refuse a gift.

The monetary value of the gift is one obvious consideration. When you responded to the Boundary Issues Survey, did you answer the fourth item differently from how you answered the fifth? If so, a gift's monetary value played some part in your decision-making process. Apparently, many mental health professionals would reason similarly. When Borys (1988) asked these same two questions in her survey, only 16% of her respondents answered that they believed it was "never" or "only rarely" ethical to accept a gift worth less than $10, but the percentage jumped to 82% when the gift was worth more than $50.

It may be useful to consider the client's motivation for offering the gift. A client might offer a small gift as a way of expressing appreciation. This seems different from a gift that the counselor perceives to be a form of manipulation or an attempt to buy loyalty or friendship. Sometimes a client's need to offer gifts can become a useful therapeutic tool. For example, we know of a client who came to each of her first three sessions bringing a small home-baked item such as a brownie or a loaf of banana bread, saying that she had just finished baking and thought the counselor might like to sample the result. She was an excellent baker, and the counselor accepted the first two offerings with pleasure. When the client came to the third session with a treat, the counselor used this as an entree to exploring the client's motivations. Through this exploration, the client became aware of her need to "make herself welcome" everywhere she went because she believed that she could not possibly be valued just for herself. This became a very productive session.

It may be equally useful to consider the counselor's motivation for wanting to accept or decline the gift. For example, assume that your client has an extra ticket to a championship sports event and asks you to go along. You are a great sports fan and have been unable to get a ticket to the game. If you find yourself tempted to accept the ticket, keep in mind that you have a fiduciary relationship with your client (see chap. 1) and that you must not benefit from the relationship. It would also be useful to think about the implicit messages you would be sending to the client, who may think it is now acceptable to call you at home or invite you to future social functions. What if you are not really a sports fan but find yourself thinking that going to the game would be more enjoyable than sitting home alone? In this case, consider your obligation to avoid using clients to meet your own social needs. When you are determining whether to accept a gift from a client, your reasoning must be based on consideration for the client's welfare.

Related to the issue of motivation is the nature or stage of the therapeutic relationship. A client might bring a small gift to a mutually agreed-on termination session as a way of saying "thank you" to the counselor. Accepting such a gift might not be problematic. By contrast, accepting a gift during the early stages of counseling before a stable therapeutic relationship has been established could set in motion a blurring of boundaries that could become problematic down the road.

Diversity Considerations in Accepting Gifts   Cultural factors need to be considered, because gift giving has different meanings in different cultures. For instance, giving gifts is a common practice in many Asian communities as a means of showing gratitude and respect (Sue & Zane, 1987). Counselors responding from a European American perspective might politely refuse an offered gift without realizing the great insult and cultural meaning of their refusal for the client (Sue, 1997). Counselors need to take care that their own discomfort at being presented with a gift does not overshadow their sensitivity to what the gift means to the client.

Self-Disclosure   The extent to which counselors engage in self-disclosure depends in large measure on their theoretical orientation and on their skill and comfort in using this technique. Psychodynamically oriented counselors, whose tradition includes Freud's belief that the counselor should remain anonymous, are not likely to engage in much self-disclosure. Counselors who view the therapeutic relationship as coequal, such as feminist counselors and existential counselors, place more value on self-disclosure. As a technique, counselor self-disclosure can be a powerful intervention that can strengthen the therapeutic alliance. It is important that you learn the skill of self-disclosure and be able to articulate your rationale for using it in the counseling process. It is equally important that you understand self-disclosure as an ethical issue.

Counselor self-disclosures that are ethically appropriate are done for the client's benefit within the context of the therapeutic process (Smith & Fitzpatrick, 1995). Self-disclosures are considered unethical when they are used to meet the counselor's own needs for intimacy or understanding. Counselors in independent private practice may be particularly vulnerable to using self-disclosure as a way to counter feelings of isolation (Glosoff, 1997). Self-disclosure, used improperly or excessively, can lead to a role reversal in which the client becomes the emotional caretaker of the counselor. Topics that are not considered appropriate for counselors to disclose are details of current stressors, personal fantasies or dreams, and their social or financial circumstances (Borys, 1988; Gutheil & Gabbard, 1993; Simon, 1991).

Self-disclosure has become an area of increasing ethical concern as more research has demonstrated that when treatment boundaries become blurred, they usually erode gradually over time. Inappropriate counselor self-disclosure, more than any other kind of boundary violation, is likely to precede counselor–client sexual intimacy (Simon, 1991).

Guidelines for distinguishing appropriate from inappropriate self-disclosure may seem fairly clear as you read about them, but judging what may benefit the client can be very difficult in practice (Smith & Fitzpatrick, 1995). Self-disclosure is a complex issue. You will need to think about whether to self-disclose, and how and when, in working with each of your clients. When you choose to self-disclose, your primary reason must be that you believe the disclosure will benefit the client. It is also important that you take cultural factors into consideration in your decision making.

Diversity Considerations in Self-Disclosure   In some Asian cultures, self-disclosing to strangers (counselors) is considered a violation of familial and cultural values. Some Asian clients believe that personal matters are best discussed with intimate acquaintances or friends (Sue, 1997). Counselor self-disclosure might facilitate the establishment of the close personal relationship that these clients need in order to feel comfortable in sharing their concerns.

Studies have shown mixed results in determining the effects of counselor self-disclosure in counseling African American clients. However, a recent study provided some empirical support for greater counselor self-disclosure when working with African American clients, regardless of whether the counselor is African American or Caucasian (Cashwell, Shcherbakova, & Cashwell, 2003).

Physical Contact with Clients   The boundary question of whether counselors should touch or hug their clients is not easy to resolve. For certain clients, at certain times, a reassuring touch or a gentle hug can be facilitative. Yet, counselors who engage in these behaviors risk having their gestures misinterpreted as sexual advances or as violations of the client's personal space.

Smith and Fitzpatrick (1995) have noted that the issue of therapeutic touch has an interesting history. When *talk therapy* first began in the Freudian era, physical contact with clients was prohibited because of its presumed negative effect on transference and countertransference. Later, in the 1960s and 1970s, touching became an accepted practice within the human potential movement. One study (Holroyd & Brodsky, 1977) found that 30% of humanistic counselors, as compared to only 6% of psychodynamic counselors, believed that touching could be beneficial to clients. A decade later Pope, Tabachnick, and Keith-Spiegel (1987b) investigated the beliefs of mental health professionals regarding three types of physical contact. Their respondents believed that the most unethical type was kissing a client (with 85% stating that is was never or only rarely ethical), followed by hugging (with 44% disapproval), and finally by handshakes, which were deemed ethical by 94%.

In today's litigious climate, it appears to us that the pendulum of opinion has swung back nearly to its starting point. Generally, counselors are now trained to be cautious about making physical contact. They are often advised to hug a client only when the client requests it or, at the very least, when the counselor first secures the client's permission. Certainly, professional liability insurance carriers have become concerned that clients might bring suit against their counselors for even well-meaning instances of physical contact. Some applications for malpractice insurance directly ask the question, "Do you ever touch a client beyond a routine handshake?" Counselors who answer "yes" must attach an explanation and run the risk of being deemed a risky applicant and having their application for insurance rejected.

Diversity Considerations in Touching Clients   When you begin to practice as a counselor, you will need to determine your own stance toward physical contact with your clients. There are many factors that might be considered, such as the age of the client. Routinely hugging elementary school children is probably more acceptable than giving frequent hugs to adult clients. However, counselors who hug clients who are of the opposite sex run the risk of a sexual impropriety complaint if people report having seen them hugging their young clients. With teens and adults, you will want to assess the likelihood that the client may sexualize or misinterpret your touch. The client's diagnosis and history may also be relevant. For instance, hugging or touching a client who has been sexually abused generally is contraindicated.

Cultures vary widely with respect to the acceptability of touch. For example, people from some European countries routinely kiss each other on both cheeks as a way of greeting, and these clients might think you are cold and distant if you avoid physical contact with them.

The bottom line regarding the issue of therapeutic touch is that it is a matter of professional judgment. There are no definitive guidelines to be found in codes of ethics or in the body of literature. In making your own determination about whether to touch a client, you will want to be clear about your motivations for doing so. You must be able to demonstrate that touching has served the client's needs and not your own.

The Legal Perspective on Business, Social, or Romantic Relationships with Clients

O'Laughlin (2001) made an interesting argument that legal prohibitions on dual relationships violate a number of provisions of the United States Constitution. He argued that by prohibiting clients from entering into business, social, or romantic relationships with their counselors, state laws have violated the First Amendment, the due process right of intimate association, and the right of business association embodied in the Privileges or Immunities clause of the Fourteenth Amendment. O'Laughlin suggested that by mixing law and ethics, state lawmakers have violated constitutional rights of citizens. Although we believe O'Laughlin's position is interesting, it probably is not legally correct. If it were, counselors accused of violating dual relationships prohibitions with clients would prevail in their defenses by arguing that the prohibitions are unconstitutional.

Ethical Decision Making

Cultural factors are often important variables in ethical decision making regarding therapeutic boundaries. In this chapter, we have noted that bartering, gift giving, self-disclosure, and therapeutic touch are viewed differently in various cultures. Multiculturally sensitive counselors know that for many minority clients, the idea of seeking traditional counseling is foreign, and that these clients are often more comfortable turning to social support systems within their own community. They may be more likely to put their trust in healers who are a part of their culture such as shamans, folk healers, acupuncturists, or cueranderos(as). Counselors who work with ethnic minority clients need to be flexible and willing to take on different roles, such as advocate, change agent, advisor, and facilitator of indigenous support systems if they are to effectively assist these clients. They need to balance their understanding of and adherence to their codes of ethics with their understanding of and sensitivity to the values and worldviews of minority clients.

Herlihy and Corey (1997) offered a decision-making model to assist counselors who are faced with potential dual or multiple relationships. In their model, the first step is to determine whether the potential dual relationship is avoidable or unavoidable. If it would be possible to avoid entering into the dual relationship, an important next step is to have a full and open discussion with the client, exploring the possible problems and benefits. Third, counselors must judge whether the benefits outweigh the risks or whether the reverse is true. They need to consider the factors that create a potential for harm, including differences in the client's expectations of the counselor in the two roles, the counselor's divergent responsibilities in the two roles, and the power differential in their relationship.

If the counselor believes that the risk of harm to the client is greater than the potential benefits, the counselor should decline to enter the dual relationship and refer if needed. An explanation should be given so the client understands the rationale for not proceeding with the problematic part of the dual relationship.

If the counselor believes that the potential benefits to the client are great and the risk of harm is small, or if the potential dual relationship cannot be avoided, then the dual relationship can be initiated and the following safeguards put in place:

- Secure the client's informed consent to proceed with the dual relationship. The counselor and client should discuss the potential problems and reach an understanding regarding how they want to handle these problems if they arise.
- Seek consultation. Because one of the most intransigent problems in managing dual relationships is the counselor's loss of objectivity, it is important for the counselor to seek ongoing consultation for help in monitoring the relationship and the risk for harm.
- Engage in ongoing discussion with the client. As we discussed in chapter 1, informed consent is not a one-time matter. The counselor can involve the client in a mutual, ongoing monitoring of the relationship and can discuss any potential problems that they might foresee and attempt to resolve any problems that do arise.
- Document and self-monitor. Although we have heard of instances in which counselors were advised to keep any mention of a dual relationship out of their case notes, we think this is unwise. If a dual relationship ever became an issue in a complaint proceeding before a licensure board or in a court of law, behavior that appears as if the counselor is trying to hide something will not be seen favorably by the parties adjudicating the complaint. It is much better for counselors to be able to demonstrate that they were aware of dualities, that they considered the risks and benefits for the client, and that they took steps to protect the client.
- Obtain supervision. If the risks in a dual relationship seem high, if the relationship is particularly complex, or if the counselor is concerned about the ability to assess the situation objectively, seeking consultation may not be sufficient. In these instances, counselors are wise to engage a fellow mental health professional in ongoing supervision of their work throughout the dual relationship.

In concluding this section of the chapter, we want to emphasize that boundary issues and dual relationships pose some complex and difficult questions. Counselors will struggle with boundary setting throughout their professional careers. There are few certainties regarding this issue. In the absence of absolute answers, counselors must think carefully about the consequences of their decisions, have a clear rationale for any boundary crossings, be open to discussing the issues with their clients who are equally affected by any decisions, and consult with colleagues.

SEXUAL DUAL RELATIONSHIPS

The prohibition against sexual intimacies with help seekers is one of the oldest ethical mandates in the health care professions, predating even the Hippocratic oath. Nonetheless, ethics codes of mental health professions made no mention of this behavior until research began to demonstrate its prevalence and the harm done to clients (Pope & Vasquez, 1998). Although the problem of sexual relationships between counselors and their clients has existed for many decades, it remained unacknowledged in the professional literature through the 1970s. Counselor–client sexual intimacy was the "problem with no name" (Davidson, 1977) because helping professionals were reluctant to confront the issue. The reluctance was so pervasive that Pope (1988) concluded that helping professionals had engaged in "massive denial" (p. 222) of the problem. It was through the pioneering work of a few researchers, such as Gartrell and her colleagues (1987) in psychiatry, and Pope (1986, 1988) in psychology and counseling, that helping professionals were made aware that such violations were occurring, and in startling numbers.

Although the limitations of self-report data make it difficult to gauge how commonly counselor–client sexual intimacies actually occur, various studies indicate that approximately 7% of male counselors and 1.6% of female counselors reported sexual relationships with their current or former clients (Akamatsu, 1988; Borys, 1988; Holroyd & Brodsky, 1977; Pope & Bouhoutsos, 1986; Pope et al., 1993; Pope, Tabachnick, & Keith-Speigel, 1987a; Salisbury & Kinnier, 1996; Thoreson, Shaughnessy, & Frazier, 1995; Thoreson, Shaughnessy, Heppner, & Cook, 1993). It is safe to state that these estimates are probably conservative. When Pope (1986) surveyed patients rather than counselors, as many as 20% of them reported having had sexual contact with their counselors. One hopeful note among these statistics was provided by Anderson and Kitchener (1996). They reviewed studies that had been conducted since 1977 and concluded that the frequency of sexual contact between counselors and current clients is decreasing.

The Offending Mental Health Professional

Mental health professionals who engage in sex with their clients have not been well studied, but the male counselor or female client dyad clearly dominates. It appears that most offenders are repeat offenders. Holroyd and Brodsky (1977) found that 80% of psychologists who reported sexual contact also reported that they had been sexually intimate with more than one client. Pope and Bouhoutsos (1986) described several typical scenarios and rationalizations used by offending counselors:

- In a reversal of roles, the wants and needs of the counselor become the focus of the treatment.
- The counselor claims that sexual intimacy with the client is a valid treatment for sexual or other problems.
- The counselor fails to treat the emotional closeness that develops in counseling with professional attention and respect, claiming that the dual relationship "just got out of hand."
- The counselor exploits the client's desire for nonerotic physical contact (e.g., a need to be held).
- The counselor fails to acknowledge that the therapeutic relationship continues between sessions and outside the office.
- The counselor creates and exploits an extreme dependence on the part of the client.
- The counselor uses drugs as part of the seduction.
- The counselor uses threat or intimidation.

Although offending counselors do not fit a single profile, the portrait that emerges from the scant literature is one of a professionally isolated, male counselor who is experiencing distress or crisis in his personal life (Simon, 1987; Smith & Fitzpatrick, 1995). He shares many characteristics with other impaired professionals, including professional burnout and a pattern of attempting to meet his own personal needs though his clients. Not all offenders will fit this description, however. Golden (in Schafer, 1990) and Schoener and Gonsiorek (1988) described a wide range of professionals who become sexually involved with their clients. At one end of the range are those who are naive and uninformed about ethical standards. At the other extreme are professionals who suffer from sociopathic, narcissistic, or borderline personality disorders and the attendant inability to appreciate the impact of their behavior on others.

It is natural to feel compassion for those naive offenders who feel remorse for their behavior, but it is important to remember that ignorance is never a valid excuse, nor is blaming the client for being "seductive." It is always the responsibility of the helping professional to ensure that sexual intimacies do not occur.

Harm to Clients

We believe that sexual relationships with counselors are extremely detrimental and sometimes even devastating to clients. The harm is deep, lasting, and occasionally permanent. At least 90% of clients who have been sexually involved with a counselor are damaged by the relationship, according to their subsequent counselors (Bouhoutsos, Holroyd, Lerman, Forer, & Greenberg, 1983).

Pope (1988) suggested that clients are likely to suffer from *therapist–patient sex syndrome,* with reactions similar to those of victims of rape, spouse battering, incest, and posttraumatic stress disorder. He described a range of associated symptoms. Clients often experience a deep *ambivalence* toward the offending counselor. They are trapped between extreme dependency on and fear of separation from the counselor and a longing to escape from his power and influence. Like many victims of incest and battering, clients vacillate between wanting to flee from the abuser and wanting to cling to and protect him.

Clients often suffer from feelings of *guilt,* believing that they are to blame for the relationship. They may think that they did something to invite the counselor's behavior. Although they may be deeply angry at the counselor, their rage remains suppressed due to the counselor's continuing power, their feelings of ambivalence, and their sense of guilt. This guilt and rage, when turned inward, leads to an *increased risk of suicide.*

Because the offending counselor insists that the client keep their sexual relationship secret, clients feel *isolated,* alone, and cut off from the normal world of human experience. Not surprisingly, many victims manifest a profound *confusion* about their sexuality and about appropriate roles and interpersonal boundaries. When roles are reversed and the client becomes the counselor's emotional caretaker, the client does not know where safe and appropriate boundaries lie.

Counseling involves a high degree of trust, and violation of that trust can have lifelong consequences. Clients' *impaired ability to trust* often prevents them from seeking help from other counselors and may impair their ability to form other close relationships.

Finally, many clients display symptoms similar to those experienced by victims of posttraumatic stress disorder. These symptoms include difficulties with attention and concentration, reexperiencing of overwhelming emotional reactions when they become involved with a sexual partner, and nightmares and flashbacks.

The harm to clients caused by sexual intimacies with their counselors is now well recognized. The ethical standards of all mental health providers' professional organizations, including the ACA *Code of Ethics* (2005), prohibit sexual relationships with clients. There are no credible voices in the profession arguing that sexual relationships with clients should be allowed.

The ACA *Code of Ethics* prohibits counselors from having sexual or romantic relationships with current clients, their romantic partners, or their family members (Standard A.5.a.). Romantic or sexual relationships with *former* clients (and their romantic partners or family members) are prohibited for at least 5 years following the last professional contact (Standard A.5.b.).

Typically, codes of ethics for mental health professionals prohibit sexual relationships with former clients for a minimum of 2 years. The ACA *Code of Ethics* (2005) has extended the sexual relationship prohibitions as described above. However, it is doubtful a court of law would do the same. Ethical standards reach for the ideal and legal standards define the minimally acceptable behavior society will tolerate from a professional counselor. A board of ethics might find a counselor in violation of the ethical code for having had a harmful romantic relationship with a former client's sister-in-law four years after the counseling relationship ended, but it is doubtful that a judge would find that the counselor had committed malpractice for the same behavior.

Legal Consequences for Offending Counselors

Civil Law Suits   The impropriety of sexual intimacies with clients is universally recognized. As a result, clients who sue counselors for having been sexually involved with them have an excellent chance of winning their lawsuits, if the allegations are true. These lawsuits are civil, which means that one citizen has to sue another for action to be taken against a person who does something wrong.

For example, clients who were sexually victimized by their counselors and who are ashamed, uneducated, or lacking in self-confidence might choose not to file formal complaints or file civil lawsuits against their perpetrators. When that happens, counselors who violate our ethical standards and violate the rights of their clients are never held accountable. In fact, many believe that the lack of accountability often encourages offending counselors to sexually violate other clients. When some counselors observe that others are getting away with having sexual relationships with clients, they may be inclined to do so as well.

Counselors who engage in sexual relationships with their clients may be sued on a number of grounds. Jorgenson (1995) has listed the following causes of action that victimized clients might allege in their lawsuits: malpractice, negligent infliction of emotional distress, battery, intentional infliction of emotional distress, fraudulent misrepresentation, breach of contract, breach of warranty, and spouse loss of consortium (love, companionship, and services). As discussed in chapter 4, one of the elements a client must prove in a malpractice suit is that a counselor behaved in a manner that breached the standard of care expected or required of counselors.

To encourage clients who are victimized by their mental health professionals to sue, some state legislatures have now passed laws that automatically make it negligence for certain categories of mental health professionals to have sexual relationships with their clients (e.g., Cal. Civ. Code sec. 43.93, West, 1993; Ill. Ann. State. Ch. 70, secs. 801–802, Smith-Hurd, 1992; Minn. Stat. Ann. Sec. 148A, West, 1993; Texas Senate Bill 210, engrossed May 22, 1993; Wis. Stat. Ann. Sec. 895. 70(2), West, 1992). Those who sue must still prove they were harmed as a result of the sexual relationships, but harm can be emotional and financial as well as physical.

Some of these statutes have unusual and forceful components. For example, the Wisconsin statute (Wis. Stat. Ann. sec. 895.70(5), West, 1992) forbids accused mental health professionals from settling their cases without public disclosure. In other words, mental health professionals (or their professional liability insurance companies) who are sued by their clients for having engaged in sex with them cannot agree to an out-of-court settlement that is never reported to the public.

Criminalization of Sex with Clients   Our society has become so convinced that counselor–client sexual relationships are wrong that some states have now passed statutes that make it a crime for mental health professionals to engage in sex with their clients. Losing a civil lawsuit for having sex with a client can be distressing for counselors, but going to jail for the same thing is a much more dramatic result.

Between 1983 and 1992, 13 states enacted legislation that criminalized sexual relationships between mental health professionals and their clients. Kane (1995) reported that the following states had passed such statutes at the time the review was conducted: California, Colorado, Connecticut, Florida, Georgia, Iowa, Maine, Michigan, Minnesota, New Mexico, North Dakota, South Dakota, and Wisconsin. Each state statute varies in language, but the following professionals have been included in some of the laws: psychotherapists, counselors, marriage and family counselors, clergy, social workers, psychiatrists, and psychologists.

Some of these criminal statutes take unusually tough positions with mental health professionals. For example, the Colorado statute (Colo. Rev. Stat. secs. 12-43-708 [b&c], 1988) permits prosecutors to file injunctions that will put a mental health professional out of business even before the individual has been found guilty, if it can be proven that the professional presents a risk to clients by continuing to practice.

Roberts-Henry (1995), in giving a history of the passage of the Colorado statute, reported that the law was passed in 1988 over a great deal of objection from mental health professionals. Proponents had to compromise and exclude clergy from the bill before it could be passed. Roberts-Henry summarized the law as stating, in essence, that "any psychotherapist who perpetrates sexual penetration or intrusion on a client commits a felony" (p. 340). The law does not allow accused mental health professionals to use consent of the client as a defense.

Although Kane (1995) concluded that the laws criminalizing sexual relationships between mental health professionals and their clients have had a deterrent effect, it appears that they do not totally solve the problem. In Colorado, 8 years after the law had been passed, Roberts-Henry (1995) reported that victims were still treated poorly during the investigation process, and that many prosecutors were unwilling to proceed with cases because they did not understand abuse generally.

Postcounseling Sexual Relationships

Ethical standards of the various mental health professions are divided on the issue of whether it is *ever* ethical for professionals to have sexual relationships with former clients. Social workers are forbidden from ever having a sexual relationship with an individual after a professional relationship has been established (National Association of Social Workers, 1997). However, counselors (American Counseling Association, 2005) and psychologists (American Psychological Association [APA], 2002) have determined that after a set period of time following termination, sexual relationships may be permissible with former clients. APA has set 2 years after termination as an acceptable period before a sexual relationship with a former client might be acceptable, while ACA has set 5 years. The APA and ACA codes should not be interpreted as blanket permission. Counselors who consider entering into romantic or sexual relationships with former clients, even after several years have passed, still have an ethical responsibility to ensure that no harm is done. Not only do all the risk factors for post-termination friendships apply to post-termination sexual relationships, but because of the severity of potential harm, it is even more important to put safeguards in place. The ACA code states that before counselors engage in sexual or romantic interactions or relationships with clients, their romantic partners, or client family members, even after 5 years, counselors must "demonstrate forethought and document (in written form) whether the interactions or relationship can be viewed as exploitive in some way and/or whether there is still potential to harm the former client" (Standard A. 5.b.)

Just as professional associations disagree about whether sexual relationships are acceptable after a waiting period, scholars are also divided on the issue. Although Friedman and Boumil (1995) have struggled with the arguments for and against the idea, Simon (1998) has recommended never having a sexual relationship with a former client. Apparently there is no consensus among counseling practitioners, either. In two studies that surveyed ACA members, 63.5% of male counselors believed sexual contact with former clients was unethical (Thoreson, et al., 1993), and 45% of female counselors believed that this behavior was harmful and constituted misconduct (Thoreson, Shaughnessy, & Frazier, 1995). As Herlihy and Corey (1997) noted, whether sexual relationships with former clients are ever acceptable probably will be a subject of continuing debate for some time to come. In our opinion, sexual relationships with former clients are not appropriate under any circumstances. The risk of harm is far too high; according to one study, 80% of clients who had begun sexual relationships with mental health professionals after counseling ended were found to have been harmed (Pope & Vetter, 1991).

Sexual Attraction to Clients

Although the ACA *Code of Ethics* (2005) explicitly forbids sexual relationships with clients, it does not address more subtle ways that sexuality can become part of a counseling relationship. It is not at all unlikely that, at some point in your professional career, you will find that you are sexually attracted to a client. When this happens, it is natural to react with feelings of guilt or self-doubt. Sexual attraction to a client is not aberrant or unusual, however. Research indicates that 70% to 95% of mental health professionals have experienced attraction to at least one client (Bernsen, Tabachnick, & Pope, 1994; Pope, Keith-Spiegel, & Tabachnick, 1986). It is important to remember that *feeling* a sexual attraction to a client is not unethical. What is unethical is to *act* on that attraction.

When you feel a sexual attraction to a client, you have an ethical responsibility to acknowledge and deal with it appropriately. Some useful strategies include consulting with colleagues, carefully considering issues of client welfare, seeking supervision, and self-monitoring to ascertain whether you are feeling particularly needy or vulnerable. If your own needs and issues seem to be causing you to act in ways that are uncharacteristic of you, you will be wise to seek counseling for yourself to resolve those issues.

Counseling Clients Who Have Been Abused by Previous Counselors

In your practice, you should be prepared to counsel clients who report that they have been sexually exploited by a previous counselor. Welfel (2006), after reviewing prevalence studies, concluded that between 22% and 65% of mental health professionals have encountered such clients.

Counselors who provide services to individuals who have been sexually abused by mental health professionals are put in awkward positions. Most counselors feel obligated to take some action to bring attention to the wrongdoing of a fellow mental health professional. These counselors are afraid if they do not take some action, more clients may be abused.

We caution you though, if you are ever put in this situation, to be respectful of your client's wishes in the matter. Clients must be willing not only to allege that a mental health professional has abused them, but they must also testify at formal hearings, will probably be cross-examined in a hostile and accusing manner, and must deal with the emotional strain of the process.

Your role, as a counselor, is to assist your client in meeting the counseling goals the two of you establish together. If the client decides to proceed against the perpetrator in some manner, you can be very helpful in assisting the client deal with a very difficult situation.

It most likely will do no good for you to file an ethics complaint against another mental health professional if the victim refuses to participate. You would be violating your client's privacy if you disclose the client's identity without his or her permission. In addition, most licensure boards, criminal prosecutors, or certification groups will not proceed in a case without a witness who was a victim.

Your role as a counselor is not to push your client toward accusing the mental health professional. You must guard against *intrusive advocacy* in your zeal to ensure that the wrong is redressed (Pope et al., 1993; Wohlberg, 1999). Rather, your job is to provide appropriate counseling services, to avoid imposing your own values, and to assist clients in meeting their personal goals.

It is important to be aware that clients who have been sexually exploited by a previous mental health professional tend to be especially vulnerable to revictimization when their counseling needs are not recognized and addressed. Counseling these clients requires sensitivity and expertise. If you undertake a counseling relationship with such a client, you should read the literature on the topic, get qualified supervision, and be prepared to have strong emotional reactions to the client's disclosures (Welfel, 2006).

To avoid becoming inappropriately involved if a client is trying to decide whether to accuse a former mental health professional of inappropriate sexual activity, you might consider referring the client to an advocacy group. There are many such groups that assist clients in making the initial decisions and then support them once the process begins. Biele and Barnhill (1995) and Schoener (1989) have listed such advocacy groups in their publications.

SUMMARY AND KEY POINTS

Therapeutic boundaries and dual relationships are among the most controversial of all ethical issues. A boundary can be conceptualized as a frame around the therapeutic relationship that defines the participants' roles in that relationship. Counselors enter into dual relationships whenever they take on two or more roles, simultaneously or sequentially, with their clients.

Codes of ethics discourage nonprofessional or dual relationships but do not prohibit them completely. The only type of dual relationship that is absolutely forbidden is sexual intimacy with a current client or the client's romantic partner or family members, or with a former client, the client's romantic partner or family members for at least 5 years. There are a number of factors that counselors must consider when they are contemplating entering into a nonsexual dual relationship, to determine the potential for harm to the client.

Most counselors occasionally engage in boundary crossings, which are departures from usual practice that are made to benefit a particular client at a particular time. For instance, a counselor would not routinely meet all clients at out-of-the-office functions but might choose to attend a client's graduation or other special occasion. From a legal perspective, counselors who develop a pattern of frequent boundary crossings are at risk.

Several specific boundary issues were discussed in this chapter. These included bartering, social and business relationships with clients, post-termination friendships, accepting gifts from clients, counselor self-disclosure, and physical contact with clients. Throughout the discussion of these issues, multicultural considerations were highlighted. Guidelines for ethical decision making completed the first section of the chapter. Key points with respect to nonsexual dual relationships are as follows:

- Codes of ethics caution counselors to avoid those dual relationships that could impair professional judgment or increase the risk of harm to the client.
- Factors that should be considered in assessing the risk of harm are incompatible expectations on the part of the client, divergent responsibilities on the part of the counselor, and the power differential between the two parties.
- Potential dual relationships can evolve in subtle ways and can be difficult to recognize.
- Dual relationships can be relatively benign but can also be extremely harmful to clients.
- With the exception of sexual dual relationships, there is very little consensus among counselors regarding the propriety of various types of dual relationships.
- Some dual relationships are unavoidable, particularly when counselors practice in rural communities or other types of "small worlds."
- There are a number of counselor behaviors that do not by themselves constitute dual relationships but have the potential to create dual relationships. These behaviors can be termed *boundary crossings*.

- From both an ethical and a legal perspective, counselors are well advised to avoid developing a pattern of frequent boundary crossings with clients.
- Although bartering with a client for goods or services is fraught with potential problems, it is ethically permissible when the client requests it, when exploitation can be avoided, and when bartering is a common practice among professionals in the community.
- Although counselors may be tempted to develop social relationships or even friendships with current or former clients, counselors should not get their own social needs met through their interactions with clients.
- Business or financial relationships with clients should be avoided.
- Although counselors should be cautious about accepting gifts from their clients, there may be instances when accepting a gift is appropriate. There are a number of factors that counselors should consider when deciding whether to accept or refuse a gift from a client.
- Appropriate self-disclosure on the part of counselors is therapeutic, but when it is used inappropriately or excessively it can create a role reversal in which the client becomes the counselor's emotional caretaker.
- The issue of physical contact with clients is difficult to resolve and, again, there are many factors to consider. Today's legal climate tends to discourage counselors from the practice of therapeutic touch.
- Multicultural factors are often important variables in ethical decision making regarding nonprofessional or dual relationships and professional boundaries.
- An ethical decision-making model is available to assist counselors in deciding what actions to take when faced with a potential dual relationship.

The second section of the chapter focused on sexual dual relationships. Sexual intimacies with clients are probably the most harmful of all types of dual relationships. Although estimates of the prevalence of sexual relationships between counselors and their clients seem to vary, it is clear that male counselors are more frequent offenders than are female counselors. Pope has described the harm to clients as a "counselor–patient sex syndrome" that is similar to posttraumatic stress disorder. Legal consequences for offending counselors can be severe. They can be prosecuted in civil court and, in some states, in criminal court as well. Although there is universal agreement among mental health professionals that sexual intimacies with current clients are unethical, the question of posttermination sexual relationships is the subject of some debate. Counselors who provide services to clients who have been sexually abused by their former counselors face some difficult decisions. They must keep in mind that their role is to assist these clients in meeting goals that are chosen by the clients themselves.

Appendix A

ACA Code of Ethics

PREAMBLE

The American Counseling Association is an educational, scientific, and professional organization whose members work in a variety of settings and serve in multiple capacities. ACA members are dedicated to the enhancement of human development throughout the life span. Association members recognize diversity and embrace a cross-cultural approach in support of the worth, dignity, potential, and uniqueness of people within their social and cultural contexts.

Professional values are an important way of living out an ethical commitment. Values inform principles. Inherently held values that guide our behaviors or exceed prescribed behaviors are deeply ingrained in the counselor and developed out of personal dedication, rather than the mandatory requirement of an external organization.

ACA CODE OF ETHICS PURPOSE

The *ACA Code of Ethics* serves five main purposes:

1. The *Code* enables the association to clarify to current and future members, and to those served by members, the nature of the ethical responsibilities held in common by its members.
2. The *Code* helps support the mission of the association.
3. The *Code* establishes principles that define ethical behavior and best practices of association members.
4. The *Code* serves as an ethical guide designed to assist members in constructing a professional course of action that best serves those utilizing counseling services and best promotes the values of the counseling profession.
5. The *Code* serves as the basis for processing of ethical complaints and inquiries initiated against members of the association.

The *ACA Code of Ethics* contains eight main sections that address the following areas:

Section A: The Counseling Relationship
Section B: Confidentiality, Privileged Communication, and Privacy
Section C: Professional Responsibility
Section D: Relationships With Other Professionals
Section E: Evaluation, Assessment, and Interpretation
Section F: Supervision, Training, and Teaching
Section G: Research and Publication
Section H: Resolving Ethical Issues

Each section of the *ACA Code of Ethics* begins with an Introduction. The introductions to each section discuss what counselors should aspire to with regard to ethical behavior and responsibility. The Introduction helps set the tone for that particular section and provides a starting point that invites reflection on the ethical mandates contained in each part of the *ACA Code of Ethics*.

When counselors are faced with ethical dilemmas that are difficult to resolve, they are expected to engage in a carefully considered ethical decision-making process. Reasonable differences of opinion can and do exist among counselors with respect to the ways in which values, ethical principles, and ethical standards would be applied when they conflict. While there is no specific ethical decision-making model that is most effective, counselors are expected to be familiar with a credible model of decision making that can bear public scrutiny and its application.

Through a chosen ethical decision-making process and evaluation of the context of the situation, counselors are empowered to make decisions that help expand the capacity of people to grow and develop.

A brief glossary is given to provide readers with a concise description of some of the terms used in the *ACA Code of Ethics*.

SECTION A: THE COUNSELING RELATIONSHIP

Introduction

Counselors encourage client growth and development in ways that foster the interest and welfare of clients and promote formation of healthy relationships. Counselors actively attempt to understand the diverse cultural backgrounds of the clients they serve. Counselors also explore their own cultural identities and how these affect their values and beliefs about the counseling process.

Reprinted by permission of the American Counseling Association, 5999 Stevenson Avenue, Alexandria, VA 22304.

Counselors are encouraged to contribute to society by devoting a portion of their professional activity to services for which there is little or no financial return (pro bono publico).

A.1. Welfare of Those Served by Counselors
A.1.a. Primary Responsibility
The primary responsibility of counselors is to respect the dignity and to promote the welfare of clients.

A.1.b. Records
Counselors maintain records necessary for rendering professional services to their clients and as required by laws, regulations, or agency or institution procedures. Counselors include sufficient and timely documentation in their client records to facilitate the delivery and continuity of needed services. Counselors take reasonable steps to ensure that documentation in records accurately reflects client progress and services provided. If errors are made in client records, counselors take steps to properly note the correction of such errors according to agency or institutional policies. *(See A.12.g.7., B.6., B.6.g., G.2.j.)*

A.1.c. Counseling Plans
Counselors and their clients work jointly in devising integrated counseling plans that offer reasonable promise of success and are consistent with abilities and circumstances of clients. Counselors and clients regularly review counseling plans to assess their continued viability and effectiveness, respecting the freedom of choice of clients. *(See A.2.a., A.2.d., A.12.g.)*

A.1.d. Support Network Involvement
Counselors recognize that support networks hold various meanings in the lives of clients and consider enlisting the support, understanding, and involvement of others (e.g., religious/spiritual/community leaders, family members, friends) as positive resources, when appropriate, with client consent.

A.1.e. Employment Needs
Counselors work with their clients considering employment in jobs that are consistent with the overall abilities, vocational limitations, physical restrictions, general temperament, interest and aptitude patterns, social skills, education, general qualifications, and other relevant characteristics and needs of clients. When appropriate, counselors appropriately trained in career development will assist in the placement of clients in positions that are consistent with the interest, culture, and the welfare of clients, employers, and/or the public.

A.2. Informed Consent in the Counseling Relationship
(See A.12.g., B.5., B.6.b., E.3., E.13.b., F.1.c., G.2.a.)
A.2.a. Informed Consent
Clients have the freedom to choose whether to enter into or remain in a counseling relationship and need adequate information about the counseling process and the counselor. Counselors have an obligation to review in writing and verbally with clients the rights and responsibilities of both the counselor and the client. Informed consent is an ongoing part of the counseling process, and counselors appropriately document discussions of informed consent throughout the counseling relationship.

A.2.b. Types of Information Needed
Counselors explicitly explain to clients the nature of all services provided. They inform clients about issues such as, but not limited to, the following: the purposes, goals, techniques, procedures, limitations, potential risks, and benefits of services; the counselor's qualifications, credentials, and relevant experience; continuation of services upon the incapacitation or death of a counselor; and other pertinent information. Counselors take steps to ensure that clients understand the implications of diagnosis, the intended use of tests and reports, fees, and billing arrangements. Clients have the right to confidentiality and to be provided with an explanation of its limitations (including how supervisors and/or treatment team professionals are involved); to obtain clear information about their records; to participate in the ongoing counseling plans; and to refuse any services or modality change and to be advised of the consequences of such refusal.

A.2.c. Developmental and Cultural Sensitivity
Counselors communicate information in ways that are both developmentally and culturally appropriate. Counselors use clear and understandable language when discussing issues related to informed consent. When clients have difficulty understanding the language used by counselors, they provide necessary services (e.g., arranging for a qualified interpreter or translator) to ensure comprehension by clients. In collaboration with clients, counselors consider cultural implications of informed consent procedures and, where possible, counselors adjust their practices accordingly.

A.2.d. Inability to Give Consent
When counseling minors or persons unable to give voluntary consent, counselors seek the assent of clients to services, and include them in decision making as appropriate. Counselors recognize the need to balance the ethical rights of clients to make choices, their capacity to give consent or assent to receive services, and parental or familial legal rights and responsibilities to protect these clients and make decisions on their behalf.

A.3. Clients Served by Others
When counselors learn that their clients are in a professional relationship with another mental health professional, they request release from clients to inform the other professionals and

strive to establish positive and collaborative professional relationships.

A.4. Avoiding Harm and Imposing Values

A.4.a. Avoiding Harm

Counselors act to avoid harming their clients, trainees, and research participants and to minimize or to remedy unavoidable or unanticipated harm.

A.4.b. Personal Values

Counselors are aware of their own values, attitudes, beliefs, and behaviors and avoid imposing values that are inconsistent with counseling goals. Counselors respect the diversity of clients, trainees, and research participants.

A.5. Roles and Relationships with Clients
(See F.3., F.10., G.3.)

A.5.a. Current Clients

Sexual or romantic counselor–client interactions or relationships with current clients, their romantic partners, or their family members are prohibited.

A.5.b. Former Clients

Sexual or romantic counselor–client interactions or relationships with former clients, their romantic partners, or their family members are prohibited for a period of 5 years following the last professional contact. Counselors, before engaging in sexual or romantic interactions or relationships with clients, their romantic partners, or client family members after 5 years following the last professional contact, demonstrate forethought and document (in written form) whether the interactions or relationship can be viewed as exploitive in some way and/or whether there is still potential to harm the former client; in cases of potential exploitation and/or harm, the counselor avoids entering such an interaction or relationship.

A.5.c. Nonprofessional Interactions or Relationships (Other Than Sexual or Romantic Interactions or Relationships)

Counselor–client nonprofessional relationships with clients, former clients, their romantic partners, or their family members should be avoided, except when the interaction is potentially beneficial to the client. *(See A.5.d.)*

A.5.d. Potentially Beneficial Interactions

When a counselor–client nonprofessional interaction with a client or former client may be potentially beneficial to the client or former client, the counselor must document in case records, prior to the interaction (when feasible), the rationale for such an interaction, the potential benefit, and anticipated consequences for the client or former client and other individuals significantly involved with the client or former client. Such interactions should be initiated with appropriate client consent. Where unintentional harm occurs to the client or former client, or to an individual significantly involved with the client or former client, due to the nonprofessional interaction, the counselor must show evidence of an attempt to remedy such harm. Examples of potentially beneficial interactions include, but are not limited to, attending a formal ceremony (e.g., a wedding/ commitment ceremony or graduation); purchasing a service or product provided by a client or former client (excepting unrestricted bartering); hospital visits to an ill family member; mutual membership in a professional association, organization, or community. *(See A.5.c.)*

A.5.e. Role Changes in the Professional Relationship

When a counselor changes a role from the original or most recent contracted relationship, he or she obtains informed consent from the client and explains the right of the client to refuse services related to the change. Examples of role changes include

1. changing from individual to relationship or family counseling, or vice versa;
2. changing from a nonforensic evaluative role to a therapeutic role, or vice versa;
3. changing from a counselor to a researcher role (i.e., enlisting clients as research participants), or vice versa; and
4. changing from a counselor to a mediator role, or vice versa.

Clients must be fully informed of any anticipated consequences (e.g., financial, legal, personal, or therapeutic) of counselor role changes.

A.6. Roles and Relationships at Individual, Group, Institutional, and Societal Levels

A.6.a. Advocacy

When appropriate, counselors advocate at individual, group, institutional, and societal levels to examine potential barriers and obstacles that inhibit access and/or the growth and development of clients.

A.6.b. Confidentiality and Advocacy

Counselors obtain client consent prior to engaging in advocacy efforts on behalf of an identifiable client to improve the provision of services and to work toward removal of systemic barriers or obstacles that inhibit client access, growth, and development.

A.7. Multiple Clients

When a counselor agrees to provide counseling services to two or more persons who have a relationship, the counselor clarifies at the outset which person or persons are clients and the nature of the relationships the counselor will have with each involved person. If it becomes apparent that the counselor may be called upon to perform potentially conflicting roles, the counselor will clarify, adjust, or withdraw from roles appropriately. *(See A.8.a., B.4.)*

A.8. Group Work
(See B.4.a.)
A.8.a. Screening

Counselors screen prospective group counseling/therapy participants. To the extent possible, counselors select members whose needs and goals are compatible with goals of the group, who will not impede the group process, and whose well-being will not be jeopardized by the group experience.

A.8.b. Protecting Clients

In a group setting, counselors take reasonable precautions to protect clients from physical, emotional, or psychological trauma.

A.9. End-of-Life Care for Terminally Ill Clients
A.9.a. Quality of Care

Counselors strive to take measures that enable clients

1. to obtain high quality end-of-life care for their physical, emotional, social, and spiritual needs;
2. to exercise the highest degree of self-determination possible;
3. to be given every opportunity possible to engage in informed decision making regarding their end-of-life care; and
4. to receive complete and adequate assessment regarding their ability to make competent, rational decisions on their own behalf from a mental health professional who is experienced in end-of-life care practice.

A.9.b. Counselor Competence, Choice, and Referral

Recognizing the personal, moral, and competence issues related to end-of-life decisions, counselors may choose to work or not work with terminally ill clients who wish to explore their end-of-life options. Counselors provide appropriate referral information to ensure that clients receive the necessary help.

A.9.c. Confidentiality

Counselors who provide services to terminally ill individuals who are considering hastening their own deaths have the option of breaking or not breaking confidentiality, depending on applicable laws and the specific circumstances of the situation and after seeking consultation or supervision from appropriate professional and legal parties. *(See B.5.c., B.7.c.)*

A.10. Fees and Bartering
A.10.a. Accepting Fees From Agency Clients

Counselors refuse a private fee or other remuneration for rendering services to persons who are entitled to such services through the counselor's employing agency or institution. The policies of a particular agency may make explicit provisions for agency clients to receive counseling services from members of its staff in private practice. In such instances, the clients must be informed of other options open to them should they seek private counseling services.

A.10.b. Establishing Fees

In establishing fees for professional counseling services, counselors consider the financial status of clients and locality. In the event that the established fee structure is inappropriate for a client, counselors assist clients in attempting to find comparable services of acceptable cost.

A.10.c. Nonpayment of Fees

If counselors intend to use collection agencies or take legal measures to collect fees from clients who do not pay for services as agreed upon, they first inform clients of intended actions and offer clients the opportunity to make payment.

A.10.d. Bartering

Counselors may barter only if the relationship is not exploitive or harmful and does not place the counselor in an unfair advantage, if the client requests it, and if such arrangements are an accepted practice among professionals in the community. Counselors consider the cultural implications of bartering and discuss relevant concerns with clients and document such agreements in a clear written contract.

A.10.e. Receiving Gifts

Counselors understand the challenges of accepting gifts from clients and recognize that in some cultures, small gifts are a token of respect and showing gratitude. When determining whether or not to accept a gift from clients, counselors take into account the therapeutic relationship, the monetary value of the gift, a client's motivation for giving the gift, and the counselor's motivation for wanting or declining the gift.

A.11. Termination and Referral
A.11.a. Abandonment Prohibited

Counselors do not abandon or neglect clients in counseling. Counselors assist in making appropriate arrangements for the continuation of treatment, when necessary, during interruptions such as vacations, illness, and following termination.

A.11.b. Inability to Assist Clients

If counselors determine an inability to be of professional assistance to clients, they avoid entering or continuing counseling relationships. Counselors are knowledgeable about culturally and clinically appropriate referral resources and suggest these alternatives. If clients decline the suggested referrals, counselors should discontinue the relationship.

A.11.c. Appropriate Termination

Counselors terminate a counseling relationship when it becomes reasonably apparent that the client no longer needs assistance, is not likely to benefit, or is being harmed by continued counseling. Counselors may terminate counseling when in jeopardy of harm by the client, or another person with whom the client has a relationship, or when clients do not pay fees as agreed upon. Counselors provide pretermination counseling and recommend other service providers when necessary.

A.11.d. Appropriate Transfer of Services

When counselors transfer or refer clients to other practitioners, they ensure that appropriate clinical and administrative processes are completed and open communication is maintained with both clients and practitioners.

A.12. Technology Applications

A.12.a. Benefits and Limitations

Counselors inform clients of the benefits and limitations of using information technology applications in the counseling process and in business/billing procedures. Such technologies include but are not limited to computer hardware and software, telephones, the World Wide Web, the Internet, online assessment instruments and other communication devices.

A.12.b. Technology-Assisted Services

When providing technology-assisted distance counseling services, counselors determine that clients are intellectually, emotionally, and physically capable of using the application and that the application is appropriate for the needs of clients.

A.12.c. Inappropriate Services

When technology-assisted distance counseling services are deemed inappropriate by the counselor or client, counselors consider delivering services face to face.

A.12.d. Access

Counselors provide reasonable access to computer applications when providing technology-assisted distance counseling services.

A.12.e. Laws and Statutes

Counselors ensure that the use of technology does not violate the laws of any local, state, national, or international entity and observe all relevant statutes.

A.12.f. Assistance

Counselors seek business, legal, and technical assistance when using technology applications, particularly when the use of such applications crosses state or national boundaries.

A.12.g. Technology and Informed Consent

As part of the process of establishing informed consent, counselors do the following:

1. Address issues related to the difficulty of maintaining the confidentiality of electronically transmitted communications.
2. Inform clients of all colleagues, supervisors, and employees, such as Informational Technology (IT) administrators, who might have authorized or unauthorized access to electronic transmissions.
3. Urge clients to be aware of all authorized or unauthorized users including family members and fellow employees who have access to any technology clients may use in the counseling process.
4. Inform clients of pertinent legal rights and limitations governing the practice of a profession over state lines or international boundaries.
5. Use encrypted Web sites and e-mail communications to help ensure confidentiality when possible.
6. When the use of encryption is not possible, counselors notify clients of this fact and limit electronic transmissions to general communications that are not client specific.
7. Inform clients if and for how long archival storage of transaction records are maintained.
8. Discuss the possibility of technology failure and alternate methods of service delivery.
9. Inform clients of emergency procedures, such as calling 911 or a local crisis hotline, when the counselor is not available.
10. Discuss time zone differences, local customs, and cultural or language differences that might impact service delivery.
11. Inform clients when technology-assisted distance counseling services are not covered by insurance. *(See A.2.)*

A.12.h. Sites on the World Wide Web

Counselors maintaining sites on the World Wide Web (the Internet) do the following:

1. Regularly check that electronic links are working and professionally appropriate.
2. Establish ways clients can contact the counselor in case of technology failure.
3. Provide electronic links to relevant state licensure and professional certification boards to protect consumer rights and facilitate addressing ethical concerns.
4. Establish a method for verifying client identity.
5. Obtain the written consent of the legal guardian or other authorized legal representative prior to

rendering services in the event the client is a minor child, an adult who is legally incompetent, or an adult incapable of giving informed consent.

6. Strive to provide a site that is accessible to persons with disabilities.
7. Strive to provide translation capabilities for clients who have a different primary language while also addressing the imperfect nature of such translations.
8. Assist clients in determining the validity and reliability of information found on the World Wide Web and other technology applications.

SECTION B: CONFIDENTIALITY, PRIVILEGED COMMUNICATION, AND PRIVACY

Introduction

Counselors recognize that trust is a cornerstone of the counseling relationship. Counselors aspire to earn the trust of clients by creating an ongoing partnership, establishing and upholding appropriate boundaries, and maintaining confidentiality. Counselors communicate the parameters of confidentiality in a culturally competent manner.

B.1. Respecting Client Rights

B.1.a. Multicultural/Diversity Considerations

Counselors maintain awareness and sensitivity regarding cultural meanings of confidentiality and privacy. Counselors respect differing views toward disclosure of information. Counselors hold ongoing discussions with clients as to how, when, and with whom information is to be shared.

B.1.b. Respect for Privacy

Counselors respect client rights to privacy. Counselors solicit private information from clients only when it is beneficial to the counseling process.

B.1.c. Respect for Confidentiality

Counselors do not share confidential information without client consent or without sound legal or ethical justification.

B.1.d. Explanation of Limitations

At initiation and throughout the counseling process, counselors inform clients of the limitations of confidentiality and seek to identify foreseeable situations in which confidentiality must be breached. *(See A.2.b.)*

B.2. Exceptions

B.2.a. Danger and Legal Requirements

The general requirement that counselors keep information confidential does not apply when disclosure is required to protect clients or identified others from serious and foreseeable harm or when legal requirements demand that confidential information must be revealed. Counselors consult with other professionals when in doubt as to the validity of an exception. Additional considerations apply when addressing end-of-life issues. *(See A.9.c.)*

B.2.b. Contagious, Life-Threatening Diseases

When clients disclose that they have a disease commonly known to be both communicable and life threatening, counselors may be justified in disclosing information to identifiable third parties, if they are known to be at demonstrable and high risk of contracting the disease. Prior to making a disclosure, counselors confirm that there is such a diagnosis and assess the intent of clients to inform the third parties about their disease or to engage in any behaviors that may be harmful to an identifiable third party.

B.2.c. Court-Ordered Disclosure

When subpoenaed to release confidential or privileged information without a client's permission, counselors obtain written, informed consent from the client or take steps to prohibit the disclosure or have it limited as narrowly as possible due to potential harm to the client or counseling relationship.

B.2.d. Minimal Disclosure

To the extent possible, clients are informed before confidential information is disclosed and are involved in the disclosure decision-making process. When circumstances require the disclosure of confidential information, only essential information is revealed.

B.3. Information Shared with Others

B.3.a. Subordinates

Counselors make every effort to ensure that privacy and confidentiality of clients are maintained by subordinates, including employees, supervisees, students, clerical assistants, and volunteers. *(See F.1.c.)*

B.3.b. Treatment Teams

When client treatment involves a continued review or participation by a treatment team, the client will be informed of the team's existence and composition, information being shared, and the purposes of sharing such information.

B.3.c. Confidential Settings

Counselors discuss confidential information only in settings in which they can reasonably ensure client privacy.

B.3.d. Third-Party Payers

Counselors disclose information to third-party payers only when clients have authorized such disclosure.

B.3.e. Transmitting Confidential Information

Counselors take precautions to ensure the confidentiality of information transmitted through the use of computers, electronic mail, facsimile machines, telephones, voicemail, answering machines, and other electronic or computer technology. *(See A.12.g.)*

B.3.f. Deceased Clients

Counselors protect the confidentiality of deceased clients, consistent with legal requirements and agency or setting policies.

B.4. Groups and Families

B.4.a. Group Work

In group work, counselors clearly explain the importance and parameters of confidentiality for the specific group being entered.

B.4.b. Couples and Family Counseling

In couples and family counseling, counselors clearly define who is considered "the client" and discuss expectations and limitations of confidentiality. Counselors seek agreement and document in writing such agreement among all involved parties having capacity to give consent concerning each individual's right to confidentiality and any obligation to preserve the confidentiality of information known.

B.5. Clients Lacking Capacity to Give Informed Consent

B.5.a. Responsibility to Clients

When counseling minor clients or adult clients who lack the capacity to give voluntary, informed consent, counselors protect the confidentiality of information received in the counseling relationship as specified by federal and state laws, written policies, and applicable ethical standards.

B.5.b. Responsibility to Parents and Legal Guardians

Counselors inform parents and legal guardians about the role of counselors and the confidential nature of the counseling relationship. Counselors are sensitive to the cultural diversity of families and respect the inherent rights and responsibilities of parents/guardians over the welfare of their children/charges according to law. Counselors work to establish, as appropriate, collaborative relationships with parents/guardians to best serve clients.

B.5.c. Release of Confidential Information

When counseling minor clients or adult clients who lack the capacity to give voluntary consent to release confidential information, counselors seek permission from an appropriate third party to disclose information. In such instances, counselors inform clients consistent with their level of understanding and take culturally appropriate measures to safeguard client confidentiality.

B.6. Records

B.6.a. Confidentiality of Records

Counselors ensure that records are kept in a secure location and that only authorized persons have access to records.

B.6.b. Permission to Record

Counselors obtain permission from clients prior to recording sessions through electronic or other means.

B.6.c. Permission to Observe

Counselors obtain permission from clients prior to observing counseling sessions, reviewing session transcripts, or viewing recordings of sessions with supervisors, faculty, peers, or others within the training environment.

B.6.d. Client Access

Counselors provide reasonable access to records and copies of records when requested by competent clients. Counselors limit the access of clients to their records, or portions of their records, only when there is compelling evidence that such access would cause harm to the client. Counselors document the request of clients and the rationale for withholding some or all of the record in the files of clients. In situations involving multiple clients, counselors provide individual clients with only those parts of records that related directly to them and do not include confidential information related to any other client.

B.6.e. Assistance with Records

When clients request access to their records, counselors provide assistance and consultation in interpreting counseling records.

B.6.f. Disclosure or Transfer

Unless exceptions to confidentiality exist, counselors obtain written permission from clients to disclose or transfer records to legitimate third parties. Steps are taken to ensure that receivers of counseling records are sensitive to their confidential nature. *(See A.3., E.4.)*

B.6.g. Storage and Disposal After Termination

Counselors store records following termination of services to ensure reasonable future access, maintain records in accordance with state and federal statutes governing records, and dispose of client records and other sensitive materials in a manner that protects client confidentiality. When records are of an artistic nature, counselors obtain client (or guardian) consent with regards to handling of such records or documents. *(See A.1.b.)*

B.6.h. Reasonable Precautions

Counselors take reasonable precautions to protect client confidentiality in the event of the counselor's termination of practice, incapacity, or death. *(See C.2.h.)*

B.7. Research and Training

B.7.a. Institutional Approval

When institutional approval is required, counselors provide accurate information about their research proposals and obtain approval prior to conducting their research. They conduct research in accordance with the approved research protocol.

B.7.b. Adherence to Guidelines

Counselors are responsible for understanding and adhering to state, federal, agency, or institutional policies or applicable guidelines regarding confidentiality in their research practices.

B.7.c. Confidentiality of Information Obtained in Research

Violations of participant privacy and confidentiality are risks of participation in research involving human participants. Investigators maintain all research records in a secure manner. They explain to participants the risks of violations of privacy and confidentiality and disclose to participants any limits of confidentiality that reasonably can be expected. Regardless of the degree to which confidentiality will be maintained, investigators must disclose to participants any limits of confidentiality that reasonably can be expected. (See G.2.e.)

B.7.d. Disclosure of Research Information

Counselors do not disclose confidential information that reasonably could lead to the identification of a research participant unless they have obtained the prior consent of the person. Use of data derived from counseling relationships for purposes of training, research, or publication is confined to content that is disguised to ensure the anonymity of the individuals involved. (See G.2.a., G.2.d.)

B.7.e. Agreement for Identification

Identification of clients, students, or supervisees in a presentation or publication is permissible only when they have reviewed the material and agreed to its presentation or publication. (See G.4.d.)

B.8. Consultation

B.8.a. Agreements

When acting as consultants, counselors seek agreements among all parties involved concerning each individual's rights to confidentiality, the obligation of each individual to preserve confidential information, and the limits of confidentiality of information shared by others.

B.8.b. Respect for Privacy

Information obtained in a consulting relationship is discussed for professional purposes only with persons directly involved with the case. Written and oral reports present only data germane to the purposes of the consultation, and every effort is made to protect client identity and to avoid undue invasion of privacy.

B.8.c. Disclosure of Confidential Information

When consulting with colleagues, counselors do not disclose confidential information that reasonably could lead to the identification of a client or other person or organization with whom they have a confidential relationship unless they have obtained the prior consent of the person or organization or the disclosure cannot be avoided. They disclose information only to the extent necessary to achieve the purposes of the consultation. (See D.2.d.)

SECTION C: PROFESSIONAL RESPONSIBILITY

Introduction

Counselors aspire to open, honest, and accurate communication in dealing with the public and other professionals. They practice in a non-discriminatory manner within the boundaries of professional and personal competence and have a responsibility to abide by the *ACA Code of Ethics*. Counselors actively participate in local, state, and national associations that foster the development and improvement of counseling. Counselors advocate to promote change at the individual, group, institutional, and societal levels that improve the quality of life for individuals and groups and remove potential barriers to the provision or access of appropriate services being offered. Counselors have a responsibility to the public to engage in counseling practices that are based on rigorous research methodologies. In addition, counselors engage in self-care activities to maintain and promote their emotional, physical, mental, and spiritual well-being to best meet their professional responsibilities.

C.1. Knowledge of Standards

Counselors have a responsibility to read, understand, and follow the *ACA Code of Ethics* and adhere to applicable laws and regulations.

C.2. Professional Competence

C.2.a. Boundaries of Competence

Counselors practice only within the boundaries of their competence, based on their education, training, supervised experience, state and national professional credentials, and appropriate professional experience. Counselors gain knowledge, personal awareness, sensitivity, and skills pertinent to working with a diverse client population. (See A.9.b., C.4.e., E.2., F.2.,F.11.b.)

C.2.b. New Specialty Areas of Practice

Counselors practice in specialty areas new to them only after appropriate education, training, and supervised experience. While developing skills in new specialty areas, counselors take steps to ensure the competence of their work and to protect others from possible harm. (See F.6.f.)

C.2.c. Qualified for Employment

Counselors accept employment only for positions for which they are qualified by education, training, supervised experience, state and national professional credentials, and appropriate professional experience. Counselors hire for professional counseling positions only individuals who are qualified and competent for those positions.

C.2.d. Monitor Effectiveness

Counselors continually monitor their effectiveness as professionals and take steps to improve when necessary. Counselors in private practice take reasonable steps to seek peer supervision as needed to evaluate their efficacy as counselors.

C.2.e. Consultation on Ethical Obligations

Counselors take reasonable steps to consult with other counselors or related professionals when they have questions regarding their ethical obligations or professional practice.

C.2.f. Continuing Education

Counselors recognize the need for continuing education to acquire and maintain a reasonable level of awareness of current scientific and professional information in their fields of activity. They take steps to maintain competence in the skills they use, are open to new procedures, and keep current with the diverse populations and specific populations with whom they work.

C.2.g. Impairment

Counselors are alert to the signs of impairment from their own physical, mental, or emotional problems and refrain from offering or providing professional services when such impairment is likely to harm a client or others. They seek assistance for problems that reach the level of professional impairment, and, if necessary, they limit, suspend, or terminate their professional responsibilities until such time it is determined that they may safely resume their work. Counselors assist colleagues or supervisors in recognizing their own professional impairment and provide consultation and assistance when warranted with colleagues or supervisors showing signs of impairment and intervene as appropriate to prevent imminent harm to clients. *(See A.11.b., F.8.b.)*

C.2.h. Counselor Incapacitation or Termination of Practice

When counselors leave a practice, they follow a prepared plan for transfer of clients and files. Counselors prepare and disseminate to an identified colleague or "records custodian" a plan for the transfer of clients and files in the case of their incapacitation, death, or termination of practice.

C.3. Advertising and Soliciting Clients

C.3.a. Accurate Advertising

When advertising or otherwise representing their services to the public, counselors identify their credentials in an accurate manner that is not false, misleading, deceptive, or fraudulent.

C.3.b. Testimonials

Counselors who use testimonials do not solicit them from current clients nor former clients nor any other persons who may be vulnerable to undue influence.

C.3.c. Statements by Others

Counselors make reasonable efforts to ensure that statements made by others about them or the profession of counseling are accurate.

C.3.d. Recruiting Through Employment

Counselors do not use their places of employment or institutional affiliation to recruit or gain clients, supervisees, or consultees for their private practices.

C.3.e. Products and Training Advertisements

Counselors who develop products related to their profession or conduct workshops or training events ensure that the advertisements concerning these products or events are accurate and disclose adequate information for consumers to make informed choices. *(See C.6.d.)*

C.3.f. Promoting to Those Served

Counselors do not use counseling, teaching, training, or supervisory relationships to promote their products or training events in a manner that is deceptive or would exert undue influence on individuals who may be vulnerable. However, coun-selor educators may adopt textbooks they have authored for instructional purposes.

C.4. Professional Qualifications

C.4.a. Accurate Representation

Counselors claim or imply only professional qualifications actually completed and correct any known misrepresentations of their qualifications by others. Counselors truthfully represent the qualifications of their professional colleagues. Counselors clearly distinguish between paid and volunteer work experience and accurately describe their continuing education and specialized training. *(See C.2.a.)*

C.4.b. Credentials

Counselors claim only licenses or certifications that are current and in good standing.

C.4.c. Educational Degrees

Counselors clearly differentiate between earned and honorary degrees.

C.4.d. Implying Doctoral-Level Competence

Counselors clearly state their highest earned degree in counseling or closely related field. Counselors do not imply doctoral-level competence when only possessing a master's degree in counseling or a related field by referring to themselves as "Dr." in a counseling context when their doctorate is not in counseling or related field.

C.4.e. Program Accreditation Status

Counselors clearly state the accreditation status of their degree programs at the time the degree was earned.

C.4.f. Professional Membership

Counselors clearly differentiate between current, active memberships and former memberships in associations. Members of the American Counseling Association must clearly differentiate between professional membership, which implies the possession of at least a master's degree in counseling, and regular membership, which is open to individuals whose interests and activities are consistent with those of ACA but are not qualified for professional membership.

C.5. Nondiscrimination

Counselors do not condone or engage in discrimination based on age, culture, disability, ethnicity, race, religion/spirituality, gender, gender identity, sexual orientation, marital status/partnership, language preference, socioeconomic status, or any basis proscribed by law. Counselors do not discriminate against clients, students, employees, supervisees, or research participants in a manner that has a negative impact on these persons.

C.6. Public Responsibility

C.6.a. Sexual Harassment

Counselors do not engage in or condone sexual harassment. Sexual harassment is defined as sexual solicitation, physical advances, or verbal or nonverbal conduct that is sexual in nature, that occurs in connection with professional activities or roles, and that either

1. is unwelcome, is offensive, or creates a hostile workplace or learning environment, and counselors know or are told this; or
2. is sufficiently severe or intense to be perceived as harassment to a reasonable person in the context in which the behavior occurred.

Sexual harassment can consist of a single intense or severe act or multiple persistent or pervasive acts.

C.6.b. Reports to Third Parties

Counselors are accurate, honest, and objective in reporting their professional activities and judgments to appropriate third parties, including courts, health insurance companies, those who are the recipients of evaluation reports, and others. (See B.3., E.4.)

C.6.c. Media Presentations

When counselors provide advice or comment by means of public lectures, demonstrations, radio or television programs, prerecorded tapes, technology-based applications, printed articles, mailed material, or other media, they take reasonable precautions to ensure that

1. the statements are based on appropriate professional counseling literature and practice,
2. the statements are otherwise consistent with the *ACA Code of Ethics,* and
3. the recipients of the information are not encouraged to infer that a professional counseling relationship has been established.

C.6.d. Exploitation of Others

Counselors do not exploit others in their professional relationships. (See C.3.e.)

C.6.e. Scientific Bases for Treatment Modalities

Counselors use techniques/procedures/modalities that are grounded in theory and/or have an empirical or scientific foundation. Counselors who do not must define the techniques/procedures as "unproven" or "developing" and explain the potential risks and ethical considerations of using such techniques/procedures and take steps to protect clients from possible harm. (See A.4.a., E.5.c., E.5.d.)

C.7. Responsibility to Other Professionals

C.7.a. Personal Public Statements

When making personal statements in a public context, counselors clarify that they are speaking from their personal perspectives and that they are not speaking on behalf of all counselors or the profession.

SECTION D: RELATIONSHIPS WITH OTHER PROFESSIONALS

Introduction

Professional counselors recognize that the quality of their interactions with colleagues can influence the quality of services provided to clients. They work to become knowledgeable about colleagues within and outside the field of counseling. Counselors develop positive working relationships and systems of communication with colleagues to enhance services to clients.

D.1. Relationships With Colleagues, Employers, and Employees

D.1.a. Different Approaches

Counselors are respectful of approaches to counseling services that differ from their own. Counselors are respectful of traditions and practices of other professional groups with which they work.

D.1.b. Forming Relationships

Counselors work to develop and strengthen interdisciplinary relations with colleagues from other disciplines to best serve clients.

D.1.c. Interdisciplinary Teamwork

Counselors who are members of interdisciplinary teams delivering multifaceted services to clients, keep the focus on how to best serve the clients. They participate in and contribute to decisions that affect the well-being of clients by drawing on the perspectives, values, and experiences of the counseling profession and those of colleagues from other disciplines. *(See A.1.a.)*

D.1.d. Confidentiality

When counselors are required by law, institutional policy, or extraordinary circumstances to serve in more than one role in judicial or administrative proceedings, they clarify role expectations and the parameters of confidentiality with their colleagues. *(See B.1.c., B.1.d., B.2.c., B.2.d., B.3.b.)*

D.1.e. Establishing Professional and Ethical Obligations

Counselors who are members of interdisciplinary teams clarify professional and ethical obligations of the team as a whole and of its individual members. When a team decision raises ethical concerns, counselors first attempt to resolve the concern within the team. If they cannot reach resolution among team members, counselors pursue other avenues to address their concerns consistent with client well-being.

D.1.f. Personnel Selection and Assignment

Counselors select competent staff and assign responsibilities compatible with their skills and experiences.

D.1.g. Employer Policies

The acceptance of employment in an agency or institution implies that counselors are in agreement with its general policies and principles. Counselors strive to reach agreement with employers as to acceptable standards of conduct that allow for changes in institutional policy conducive to the growth and development of clients.

D.1.h. Negative Conditions

Counselors alert their employers of inappropriate policies and practices. They attempt to effect changes in such policies or procedures through constructive action within the organization. When such policies are potentially disruptive or damaging to clients or may limit the effectiveness of services provided and change cannot be effected, counselors take appropriate further action. Such action may include referral to appropriate certification, accreditation, or state licensure organizations, or voluntary termination of employment.

D.1.i. Protection from Punitive Action

Counselors take care not to harass or dismiss an employee who has acted in a responsible and ethical manner to expose inappropriate employer policies or practices.

D.2. Consultation

D.2.a. Consultant Competency

Counselors take reasonable steps to ensure that they have the appropriate resources and competencies when providing consultation services. Counselors provide appropriate referral resources when requested or needed. *(See C.2.a.)*

D.2.b. Understanding Consultees

When providing consultation, counselors attempt to develop with their consultees a clear understanding of problem definition, goals for change, and predicted consequences of interventions selected.

D.2.c. Consultant Goals

The consulting relationship is one in which consultee adaptability and growth toward self-direction are consistently encouraged and cultivated.

D.2.d. Informed Consent in Consultation

When providing consultation, counselors have an obligation to review, in writing and verbally, the rights and responsibilities of both counselors and consultees. Counselors use clear and understandable language to inform all parties involved about the purpose of the services to be provided, relevant costs, potential risks and benefits, and the limits of confidentiality. Working in conjunction with the consultee, counselors attempt to develop a clear definition of the problem, goals for change, and predicted consequences of interventions that are culturally responsive and appropriate to the needs of consultees. *(See A.2.a., A.2.b.)*

SECTION E: EVALUATION, ASSESSMENT, AND INTERPRETATION

Introduction

Counselors use assessment instruments as one component of the counseling process, taking into account the client personal and cultural context. Counselors promote the well-being of individual clients or groups of clients by developing and using appropriate educational, psychological, and career assessment instruments.

E.1. General

E.1.a. Assessment

The primary purpose of educational, psychological, and career assessment is to provide measurements that are valid and reliable in either comparative or absolute terms. These include, but are not limited to, measurements of ability, personality, interest, intelligence, achievement, and performance. Counselors recognize the need to interpret the statements in this section as applying to both quantitative and qualitative assessments.

E.1.b. Client Welfare

Counselors do not misuse assessment results and interpretations, and they take reasonable steps to prevent others from misusing the information these techniques provide. They respect the client's right to know the results, the interpretations made, and the bases for counselors' conclusions and recommendations.

E.2. Competence to Use and Interpret Assessment Instruments

E.2.a. Limits of Competence

Counselors utilize only those testing and assessment services for which they have been trained and are competent. Counselors using technology assisted test interpretations are trained in the construct being measured and the specific instrument being used prior to using its technology based application. Counselors take reasonable measures to ensure the proper use of psychological and career assessment techniques by persons under their supervision. *(See A.12.)*

E.2.b. Appropriate Use

Counselors are responsible for the appropriate application, scoring, interpretation, and use of assessment instruments relevant to the needs of the client, whether they score and interpret such assessments themselves or use technology or other services.

E.2.c. Decisions Based on Results

Counselors responsible for decisions involving individuals or policies that are based on assessment results have a thorough understanding of educational, psychological, and career measurement, including validation criteria, assessment research, and guidelines for assessment development and use.

E.3. Informed Consent in Assessment

E.3.a. Explanation to Clients

Prior to assessment, counselors explain the nature and purposes of assessment and the specific use of results by potential recipients. The explanation will be given in the language of the client (or other legally authorized person on behalf of the client), unless an explicit exception has been agreed upon in advance. Counselors consider the client's personal or cultural context, the level of the client's understanding of the results, and the impact of the results on the client. *(See A.2., A.12.g., F.1.c.)*

E.3.b. Recipients of Results

Counselors consider the examinee's welfare, explicit understandings, and prior agreements in determining who receives the assessment results. Counselors include accurate and appropriate interpretations with any release of individual or group assessment results. *(See B.2.c., B.5.)*

E.4. Release of Data to Qualified Professionals

Counselors release assessment data in which the client is identified only with the consent of the client or the client's legal representative. Such data are released only to persons recognized by counselors as qualified to interpret the data. *(See B.1., B.3., B.6.b.)*

E.5. Diagnosis of Mental Disorders

E.5.a. Proper Diagnosis

Counselors take special care to provide proper diagnosis of mental disorders. Assessment techniques (including personal interview) used to determine client care (e.g., locus of treatment, type of treatment, or recommended follow-up) are carefully selected and appropriately used.

E.5.b. Cultural Sensitivity

Counselors recognize that culture affects the manner in which clients' problems are defined. Clients' socioeconomic and cultural experiences are considered when diagnosing mental disorders. *(See A.2.c.)*

E.5.c. Historical and Social Prejudices in the Diagnosis of Pathology

Counselors recognize historical and social prejudices in the misdiagnosis and pathologizing of certain individuals and groups and the role of mental health professionals in perpetuating these prejudices through diagnosis and treatment.

E.5.d. Refraining from Diagnosis

Counselors may refrain from making and/or reporting a diagnosis if they believe it would cause harm to the client or others.

E.6. Instrument Selection

E.6.a. Appropriateness of Instruments

Counselors carefully consider the validity, reliability, psychometric limitations, and appropriateness of instruments when selecting assessments.

E.6.b. Referral Information

If a client is referred to a third party for assessment, the counselor provides specific referral questions and sufficient objective data about the client to ensure that appropriate assessment instruments are utilized. *(See A.9.b., B.3.)*

E.6.c. Culturally Diverse Populations

Counselors are cautious when selecting assessments for culturally diverse populations to avoid the use of instruments that lack appropriate psychometric properties for the client population. *(See A.2.c., E.5.b.)*

E.7. Conditions of Assessment Administration
(See A.12.b., A.12.d.)
E.7.a. Administration Conditions

Counselors administer assessments under the same conditions that were established in their standardization. When assessments are not administered under standard conditions, as may be necessary to accommodate clients with disabilities, or when unusual behavior or irregularities occur during the administration, those conditions are noted in interpretation, and the results may be designated as invalid or of questionable validity.

E.7.b. Technological Administration

Counselors ensure that administration programs function properly and provide clients with accurate results when technological or other electronic methods are used for assessment administration.

E.7.c. Unsupervised Assessments

Unless the assessment instrument is designed, intended, and validated for self-administration and/or scoring, counselors do not permit inadequately supervised use.

E.7.d. Disclosure of Favorable Conditions

Prior to administration of assessments, conditions that produce most favorable assessment results are made known to the examinee.

E.8. Multicultural Issues/Diversity in Assessment

Counselors use with caution assessment techniques that were normed on populations other than that of the client. Counselors recognize the effects of age, color, culture, disability, ethnic group, gender, race, language preference, religion, spirituality, sexual orientation, and socioeconomic status on test administration and interpretation, and place test results in proper perspective with other relevant factors. *(See A.2.c., E.5.b.)*

E.9. Scoring and Interpretation of Assessments
E.9.a. Reporting

In reporting assessment results, counselors indicate reservations that exist regarding validity or reliability due to circumstances of the assessment or the inappropriateness of the norms for the person tested.

E.9.b. Research Instruments

Counselors exercise caution when interpreting the results of research instruments not having sufficient technical data to support respondent results. The specific purposes for the use of such instruments are stated explicitly to the examinee.

E.9.c. Assessment Services

Counselors who provide assessment scoring and interpretation services to support the assessment process confirm the validity of such interpretations. They accurately describe the purpose, norms, validity, reliability, and applications of the procedures and any special qualifications applicable to their use. The public offering of an automated test interpretations service is considered a professional-to-professional consultation. The formal responsibility of the consultant is to the consultee, but the ultimate and overriding responsibility is to the client. *(See D.2.)*

E.10. Assessment Security

Counselors maintain the integrity and security of tests and other assessment techniques consistent with legal and contractual obligations. Counselors do not appropriate, reproduce, or parts thereof without acknowledgment and permission from the publisher.

E.11. Obsolete Assessments and Outdated Results

Counselors do not use data or results from assessments that are obsolete or outdated for the current purpose. Counselors make every effort to prevent the misuse of obsolete measures and assessment data by others.

E.12. Assessment Construction

Counselors use established scientific procedures, relevant standards, and current professional knowledge for assessment design in the development, publication, and utilization of educational and psychological assessment techniques.

E.13. Forensic Evaluation: Evaluation for Legal Proceedings
E.13.a. Primary Obligations

When providing forensic evaluations, the primary obligation of counselors is to produce objective findings that can be substantiated based on information and techniques appropriate to the evaluation, which may include examination of the individual and/or review of records. Counselors are entitled to form professional opinions based on their professional knowledge and expertise that can be supported by the data gathered in evaluations. Counselors will define the limits of their reports or testimony, especially when an examination of the individual has not been conducted.

E.13.b. Consent for Evaluation

Individuals being evaluated are informed in writing that the relationship is for the purposes of an evaluation and is not counseling in nature, and entities or individuals who will receive the evaluation report are identified. Written consent to be evaluated is obtained from those being evaluated unless a court orders evaluations to be conducted without the written consent of individuals being evaluated. When children or vulnerable adults are being evaluated, informed written consent is obtained from a parent or guardian.

E.13.c. Client Evaluation Prohibited

Counselors do not evaluate individuals for forensic purposes they currently counsel or individuals they have counseled in the past. Counselors do not accept as counseling clients individuals they are evaluating or individuals they have evaluated in the past for forensic purposes.

E.13.d. Avoid Potentially Harmful Relationships

Counselors who provide forensic evaluations avoid potentially harmful professional or personal relationships with family members, romantic partners, and close friends of individuals they are evaluating or have evaluated in the past.

SECTION F: SUPERVISION, TRAINING, AND TEACHING

Introduction

Counselors aspire to foster meaningful and respectful professional relationships and to maintain appropriate boundaries with supervisees and students. Counselors have theoretical and pedagogical foundations for their work and aim to be fair, accurate, and honest in their assessments of counselors-in-training.

F.1. Counselor Supervision and Client Welfare

F.1.a. Client Welfare

A primary obligation of counseling supervisors is to monitor the services provided by other counselors or counselors-in-training. Counseling supervisors monitor client welfare and supervisee clinical performance and professional development. To fulfill these obligations, supervisors meet regularly with supervisees to review case notes, samples of clinical work, or live observations. Supervisees have a responsibility to understand and follow the *ACA Code of Ethics*.

F.1.b. Counselor Credentials

Counseling supervisors work to ensure that clients are aware of the qualifications of the supervisees who render services to the clients. *(See A.2.b.)*.

F.1.c. Informed Consent and Client Rights

Supervisors make supervisees aware of client rights including the protection of client privacy and confidentiality in the counseling relationship. Supervisees provide clients with professional disclosure information and inform them of how the supervision process influences the limits of confidentiality. Supervisees make clients aware of who will have access to records of the counseling relationship and how these records will be used. *(See A.2.b., B.1.d.)*

F.2. Counselor Supervision Competence

F.2.a. Supervisor Preparation

Prior to offering clinical supervision services, counselors are trained in supervision methods and techniques. Counselors who offer clinical supervision services regularly pursue continuing education activities including both counseling and supervision topics and skills. *(See C.2.a., C.2.f.)*

F.2.b. Multicultural Issues/Diversity in Supervision

Counseling supervisors are aware of and address the role of multiculturalism/diversity in the supervisory relationship.

F.3. Supervisory Relationships

F.3.a. Relationship Boundaries With Supervisees

Counseling supervisors clearly define and maintain ethical professional, personal, and social relationships with their supervisees. Counseling supervisors avoid nonprofessional relationships with current supervisees. If supervisors must assume other professional roles (e.g., clinical and administrative supervisor, instructor) with supervisees, they work to minimize potential conflicts and explain to supervisees the expectations and responsibilities associated with each role. They do not engage in any form of nonprofessional interaction that may compromise the supervisory relationship.

F.3.b. Sexual Relationships

Sexual or romantic interactions or relationships with current supervisees are prohibited.

F.3.c. Sexual Harassment

Counseling supervisors do not condone or subject supervisees to sexual harassment. *(See C.6.a.)*

F.3.d. Close Relatives and Friends

Counseling supervisors avoid accepting close relatives, romantic partners, or friends as supervisees.

F.3.e. Potentially Beneficial Relationships

Counseling supervisors are aware of the power differential in their relationships with supervisees. If they believe nonprofessional relationships with a supervisee may be potentially beneficial to the supervisee, they take precautions similar to those taken by counselors when working with clients. Examples of potentially beneficial interactions or relationships include attending a formal ceremony; hospital visits; providing support during a stressful event; or mutual membership in a professional association, organization, or community. Counseling supervisors engage in open discussions with supervisees when they consider entering into relationships with them outside of their roles as clinical and/or administrative supervisors. Before engaging in nonprofessional relationships, supervisors discuss with supervisees and document the rationale for such interactions, potential benefits or drawbacks, and anticipated consequences for the supervisee. Supervisors clarify the specific nature and limitations of the additional role(s) they will have with the supervisee.

F.4. Supervisor Responsibilities
F.4.a. Informed Consent for Supervision
Supervisors are responsible for incorporating into their supervision the principles of informed consent and participation. Supervisors inform supervisees of the policies and procedures to which they are to adhere and the mechanisms for due process appeal of individual supervisory actions.

F.4.b. Emergencies and Absences
Supervisors establish and communicate to supervisees procedures for contacting them or, in their absence, alternative on-call supervisors to assist in handling crises.

F.4.c. Standards for Supervisees
Supervisors make their supervisees aware of professional and ethical standards and legal responsibilities. Supervisors of postdegree counselors encourage these counselors to adhere to professional standards of practice. (See C.1.)

F.4.d. Termination of the Supervisory Relationship
Supervisors or supervisees have the right to terminate the supervisory relationship with adequate notice. Reasons for withdrawal are provided to the other party. When cultural, clinical, or professional issues are crucial to the viability of the supervisory relationship, both parties make efforts to resolve differences. When termination is warranted, supervisors make appropriate referrals to possible alternative supervisors.

F.5. Counseling Supervision Evaluation, Remediation, and Endorsement
F.5.a. Evaluation
Supervisors document and provide supervisees with ongoing performance appraisal and evaluation feedback and schedule periodic formal evaluative sessions throughout the supervisory relationship.

F.5.b. Limitations
Through ongoing evaluation and appraisal, supervisors are aware of the limitations of supervisees that might impede performance. Supervisors assist supervisees in securing remedial assistance when needed. They recommend dismissal from training programs, applied counseling settings, or state or voluntary professional credentialing processes when those supervisees are unable to provide competent professional services. Supervisors seek consultation and document their decisions to dismiss or refer supervisees for assistance. They ensure that supervisees are aware of options available to them to address such decisions. (See C.2.g.)

F.5.c. Counseling for Supervisees
If supervisees request counseling, supervisors provide them with acceptable referrals. Counselors do not provide counseling services to supervisees. Supervisors address interpersonal competencies in terms of the impact of these issues on clients, the supervisory relationship, and professional functioning. (See F.3.a.)

F.5.d. Endorsement
Supervisors endorse supervisees for certification, licensure, employment, or completion of an academic or training program only when they believe supervisees are qualified for the endorsement. Regardless of qualifications, supervisors do not endorse supervisees whom they believe to be impaired in any way that would interfere with the performance of the duties associated with the endorsement.

F.6. Responsibilities of Counselor Educators
F.6.a. Counselor Educators
Counselor educators who are responsible for developing, implementing, and supervising educational programs are skilled as teachers and practitioners. They are knowledgeable regarding the ethical, legal, and regulatory aspects of the profession, are skilled in applying that knowledge, and make students and supervisees aware of their responsibilities. Counselor educators conduct counselor education and training programs in an ethical manner and serve as role models for professional behavior. (See C.1., C.2.a., C.2.c.)

F.6.b. Infusing Multicultural Issues/Diversity
Counselor educators infuse material related to multicultluralism/diversity into all courses and workshops for the development of professional counselors.

F.6.c. Integration of Study and Practice
Counselor educators establish education and training programs that integrate academic study and supervised practice.

F.6.d. Teaching Ethics
Counselor educators make students and supervisees aware of the ethical responsibilities and standards of the profession and the ethical responsibilities of students to the profession. Counselor educators infuse ethical considerations throughout the curriculum. (See C.1.)

F.6.e. Peer Relationships
Counselor educators make every effort to ensure that the rights of peers are not compromised when students or supervisees lead counseling groups or provide clinical supervision. Counselor educators take steps to ensure that students and supervisees understand they have the same ethical obligations as counselor educators, trainers, and supervisors.

F.6.f. Innovative Theories and Techniques
When counselor educators teach counseling techniques/procedures that are innovative, without an empirical foundation, or without a well-grounded theoretical foundation, they define the counseling techniques/procedures as "unproven" or "developing" and explain to students the potential risks and ethical considerations of using such techniques/procedures.

ACA CODE OF ETHICS   155

F.6.g. Field Placements

Counselor educators develop clear policies within their training programs regarding field placement and other clinical experiences. Counselor educators provide clearly stated roles and responsibilities for the student or supervisee, the site supervisor, and the program supervisor. They confirm that site supervisors are qualified to provide supervision and inform site supervisors of their professional and ethical responsibilities in this role.

F.6.h. Professional Disclosure

Before initiating counseling services, counselors-in-training disclose their status as students and explain how this status affects the limits of confidentiality. Counselor educators ensure that the clients at field placements are aware of the services rendered and the qualifications of the students and supervisees rendering those services. Students and supervisees obtain client permission before they use any information concerning the counseling relationship in the training process. *(See A.2.b.)*

F.7. Student Welfare
F.7.a. Orientation

Counselor educators recognize that orientation is a developmental process that continues throughout the educational and clinical training of students. Counseling faculty provide prospective students with information about the counselor education program's expectations:

1. the type and level of skill and knowledge acquisition required for successful completion of the training;
2. program training goals, objectives, and mission, and subject matter to be covered;
3. bases for evaluation;
4. training components that encourage self-growth or self-disclosure as part of the training process;
5. the type of supervision settings and requirements of the sites for required clinical field experiences;
6. student and supervisee evaluation and dismissal policies and procedures; and
7. up-to-date employment prospects for graduates.

F.7.b. Self-Growth Experiences

Counselor education programs delineate requirements for self-disclosure or self-growth experiences in their admission and program materials. Counselor educators use professional judgment when designing training experiences they conduct that require student and supervisee self- growth or self-disclosure. Students and supervisees are made aware of the ramifications their self-disclosure may have when counselors whose primary role as teacher, trainer, or supervisor requires acting on ethical obligations to the profession. Evaluative components of experiential training experiences explicitly delineate predetermined academic standards that are separate and do not depend on the student's level of self- disclosure. Counselor educators may require trainees to seek professional help to address any personal concerns that may be affecting their competency.

F.8. Student Responsibilities
F.8.a. Standards for Students

Counselors-in-training have a responsibility to understand and follow the *ACA Code of Ethics* and adhere to applicable laws, regulatory policies, and rules and policies governing professional staff behavior at the agency or placement setting. Students have the same obligation to clients as those required of professional counselors. *(See C.1., H.1.)*

F.8.b. Impairment

Counselors-in-training refrain from offering or providing counseling services when their physical, mental, or emotional problems are likely to harm a client or others. They are alert to the signs of impairment, seek assistance for problems, and notify their program supervisors when they are aware that they are unable to effectively provide services. In addition, they seek appropriate professional services for themselves to remediate the problems that are interfering with their ability to provide services to others. *(See A.1., C.2.d., C.2.g.)*

F.9. Evaluation and Remediation of Students
F.9.a. Evaluation

Counselors clearly state to students, prior to and throughout the training program, the levels of competency expected, appraisal methods, and timing of evaluations for both didactic and clinical competencies. Counselor educators provide students with ongoing performance appraisal and evaluation feedback throughout the training program.

F.9.b. Limitations

Counselor educators, throughout ongoing evaluation and appraisal, are aware of and address the inability of some students to achieve counseling competencies that might impede performance. Counselor educators

1. assist students in securing remedial assistance when needed,
2. seek professional consultation and document their decision to dismiss or refer students for assistance, and
3. ensure that students have recourse in a timely manner to address decisions to require them to seek assistance or to dismiss them and provide students with due process according to institutional policies and procedures. *(See C.2.g.)*

F.9.c. Counseling for Students

If students request counseling or if counseling services are required as part of a remediation process, counselor educators provide acceptable referrals.

F. 10. Roles and Relationships Between Counselor Educators and Students
F.10.a. Sexual or Romantic Relationships

Sexual or romantic interactions or relationships with current students are prohibited.

F.10.b. Sexual Harassment

Counselor educators do not condone or subject students to sexual harassment. *(See C.6.a.)*

F.10.c. Relationships With Former Students

Counselor educators are aware of the power differential in the relationship between faculty and students. Faculty members foster open discussions with former students when considering engaging in a social, sexual, or other intimate relationship. Faculty members discuss with the former student how their former relationship may affect the change in relationship.

F.10.d. Nonprofessional Relationships

Counselor educators avoid nonprofessional or ongoing professional relationships with students in which there is a risk of potential harm to the student or that may compromise the training experience or grades assigned. In addition, counselor educators do not accept any form of professional services, fees, commissions, reimbursement, or remuneration from a site for student or supervisee placement.

F.10.e. Counseling Services

Counselor educators do not serve as counselors to current students unless this is a brief role associated with a training experience.

F.10.f. Potentially Beneficial Relationships

Counselor educators are aware of the power differential in the relationship between faculty and students. If they believe a nonprofessional relationship with a student may be potentially beneficial to the student, they take precautions similar to those taken by counselors when working with clients. Examples of potentially beneficial interactions or relationships include, but are not limited to, attending a formal ceremony; hospital visits; providing support during a stressful event; or mutual membership in a professional association, organization, or community. Counselor educators engage in open discussions with students when they consider entering into relationships with students outside of their roles as teachers and supervisors. They discuss with students the rationale for such interactions, the potential benefits and drawbacks, and the anticipated consequences for the student. Educators clarify the specific nature and limitations of the additional role(s) they will have with the student prior to engaging in a nonprofessional relationship. Nonprofessional relationships with students should be time-limited and initiated with student consent.

F.11. Multicultural/Diversity Competence in Counselor Education and Training Programs

F.11.a. Faculty Diversity

Counselor educators are committed to recruiting and retaining a diverse faculty.

F.11.b. Student Diversity

Counselor educators actively attempt to recruit and retain a diverse student body. Counselor educators demonstrate commitment to multicultural/diversity competence by recognizing and valuing diverse cultures and types of abilities students bring to the training experience. Counselor educators provide appropriate accommodations that enhance and support diverse student well-being and academic performance.

F.11.c. Multicultural/Diversity Competence

Counselor educators actively infuse multicultural/diversity competency in their training and supervision practices. They actively train students to gain awareness, knowledge, and skills in the competencies of multicultural practice. Counselor educators include case examples, role-plays, discussion questions, and other classroom activities that promote and represent various cultural perspectives.

SECTION G: Research and Publication
Introduction

Counselors who conduct research are encouraged to contribute to the knowledge base of the profession and promote a clearer understanding of the conditions that lead to a healthy and more just society. Counselors support efforts of researchers by participating fully and willingly whenever possible. Counselors minimize bias and respect diversity in designing and implementing research programs.

G.1. Research Responsibilities

G.1.a. Use of Human Research Participants

Counselors plan, design, conduct, and report research in a manner that is consistent with pertinent ethical principles, federal and state laws, host institutional regulations, and scientific standards governing research with human research participants.

G.1.b. Deviation from Standard Practice

Counselors seek consultation and observe stringent safeguards to protect the rights of research participants when a research problem suggests a deviation from standard or acceptable practices.

G.1.c. Independent Researchers

When independent researchers do not have access to an Institutional Review Board (IRB), they should consult with researchers who are familiar with IRB procedures to provide appropriate safeguards.

G.1.d. Precautions to Avoid Injury

Counselors who conduct research with human participants are responsible for the welfare of participants throughout the research process and should take reasonable precautions to avoid causing injurious psychological, emotional, physical, or social effects to participants.

G.1.e. Principal Researcher Responsibility

The ultimate responsibility for ethical research practice lies with the principal researcher. All others involved in the research activities share ethical obligations and responsibility for their own actions.

G.1.f. Minimal Interference

Counselors take reasonable precautions to avoid causing disruptions in the lives of research participants that could be caused by their involvement in research.

G.1.g. Multicultural/Diversity Considerations in Research

When appropriate to research goals, counselors are sensitive to incorporating research procedures that take into account cultural considerations. They seek consultation when appropriate.

G.2. Rights of Research Participants

(See A.2, A.7.)

G.2.a. Informed Consent in Research

Individuals have the right to consent to become research participants. In seeking consent, counselors use language that

1. accurately explains the purpose and procedures to be followed,
2. identifies any procedures that are experimental or relatively untried,
3. describes any attendant discomforts and risks,
4. describes any benefits or changes in individuals or organizations that might be reasonably expected,
5. discloses appropriate alternative procedures that would be advantageous for participants,
6. offers to answer any inquiries concerning the procedures,
7. describes any limitations on confidentiality,
8. describes the format and potential target audiences for the dissemination of research findings, and
9. instructs participants that they are free to withdraw their consent and to discontinue participation in the project at any time without penalty.

G.2.b. Deception

Counselors do not conduct research involving deception unless alternative procedures are not feasible and the prospective value of the research justifies the deception. If such deception has the potential to cause physical or emotional harm to research participants, the research is not conducted, regardless of prospective value. When the methodological requirements of a study necessitate concealment or deception, the investigator explains the reasons for this action as soon as possible during the debriefing.

G.2.c. Student/Supervisee Participation

Researchers who involve students or supervisees in research make clear to them that the decision regarding whether or not to participate in research activities does not affect one's academic standing or supervisory relationship. Students or supervisees who choose not to participate in educational research are provided with an appropriate alternative to fulfill their academic or clinical requirements.

G.2.d. Client Participation

Counselors conducting research involving clients make clear in the informed consent process that clients are free to choose whether or not to participate in research activities. Counselors take necessary precautions to protect clients from adverse consequences of declining or withdrawing from participation.

G.2.e. Confidentiality of Information

Information obtained about research participants during the course of an investigation is confidential. When the possibility exists that others may obtain access to such information, ethical research practice requires that the possibility, together with the plans for protecting confidentiality, be explained to participants as a part of the procedure for obtaining informed consent.

G.2.f. Persons Not Capable of Giving Informed Consent

When a person is not capable of giving informed consent, counselors provide an appropriate explanation to, obtain agreement for participation from, and obtain the appropriate consent of a legally authorized person.

G.2.g. Commitments to Participants

Counselors take reasonable measures to honor all commitments to research participants. *(See A.2.c.)*

G.2.h. Explanations After Data Collection

After data are collected, counselors provide participants with full clarification of the nature of the study to remove any misconceptions participants might have regarding the research. Where scientific or human values justify delaying or withholding information, counselors take reasonable measures to avoid causing harm.

G.2.i. Informing Sponsors

Counselors inform sponsors, institutions, and publication channels regarding research procedures and outcomes. Counselors ensure that appropriate bodies and authorities are given pertinent information and acknowledgement.

G.2.j. Disposal of Research Documents and Records

Within a reasonable period of time following the completion of a research project or study, counselors take steps to destroy records or documents (audio, video, digital, and written) containing confidential data or information that identifies research participants. When records are of an artistic nature, researchers obtain participant consent with regard to handling of such records or documents. *(See B.4.a, B.4.g.)*

G.3. Relationships with Research Participants (When Research Involves Intensive or Extended Interactions)

G.3.a. Nonprofessional Relationships

Nonprofessional relationships with research participants should be avoided.

G.3.b. Relationships With Research Participants

Sexual or romantic counselor–research participant interactions or relationships with current research participants are prohibited.

G.3.c. Sexual Harassment and Research Participants

Researchers do not condone or subject research participants to sexual harassment.

G.3.d. Potentially Beneficial Interactions

When a nonprofessional interaction between the researcher and the research participant may be potentially beneficial, the researcher must document, prior to the interaction (when feasible), the rationale for such an interaction, the potential benefit, and anticipated consequences for the research participant. Such interactions should be initiated with appropriate consent of the research participant. Where unintentional harm occurs to the research participant due to the nonprofessional interaction, the researcher must show evidence of an attempt to remedy such harm.

G.4. Reporting Results

G.4.a. Accurate Results

Counselors plan, conduct, and report research accurately. They provide thorough discussions of the limitations of their data and alternative hypotheses. Counselors do not engage in misleading or fraudulent research, distort data, misrepresent data, or deliberately bias their results. They explicitly mention all variables and conditions known to the investigator that may have affected the outcome of a study or the interpretation of data. They describe the extent to which results are applicable for diverse populations.

G.4.b. Obligation to Report Unfavorable Results

Counselors report the results of any research of professional value. Results that reflect unfavorably on institutions, programs, services, prevailing opinions, or vested interests are not withheld.

G.4.c. Reporting Errors

If counselors discover significant errors in their published research, they take reasonable steps to correct such errors in a correction erratum, or through other appropriate publication means.

G.4.d. Identity of Participants

Counselors who supply data, aid in the research of another person, report research results, or make original data available take due care to disguise the identity of respective participants in the absence of specific authorization from the participants to do otherwise. In situations where participants self-identify their involvement in research studies, researchers take active steps to ensure that data is adapted/changed to protect the identity and welfare of all parties and that discussion of results does not cause harm to participants.

G.4.e. Replication Studies

Counselors are obligated to make available sufficient original research data to qualified professionals who may wish to replicate the study.

G.5. Publication

G.5.a. Recognizing Contributions

When conducting and reporting research, counselors are familiar with and give recognition to previous work on the topic, observe copyright laws, and give full credit to those to whom credit is due.

G.5.b. Plagiarism

Counselors do not plagiarize, that is, they do not present another person's work as their own work.

G.5.c. Review/Republication of Data or Ideas

Counselors fully acknowledge and make editorial reviewers aware of prior publication of ideas or data where such ideas or data are submitted for review or publication.

G.5.d. Contributors

Counselors give credit through joint authorship, acknowledgment, footnote statements, or other appropriate means to those who have contributed significantly to research or concept development in accordance with such contributions. The principal contributor is listed first and minor technical or professional contributions are acknowledged in notes or introductory statements.

G.5.e. Agreement of Contributors

Counselors who conduct joint research with colleagues or students/supervisees establish agreements in advance regarding allocation of tasks, publication credit, and types of acknowledgement that will be received.

G.5.f. Student Research

For articles that are substantially based on students course papers, projects, dissertations or theses, and on which students have been the primary contributors, they are listed as principal authors.

G.5.g. Duplicate Submission

Counselors submit manuscripts for consideration to only one journal at a time. Manuscripts that are published in whole or in substantial part in another journal or published work are not submitted for publication without acknowledgment and permission from the previous publication.

G.5.h. Professional Review

Counselors who review material submitted for publication, research, or other scholarly purposes respect the confidentiality and proprietary rights of those who submitted it. Counselors use care to make publication decisions based on valid and defensible standards. Counselors review article submissions in a timely manner and based on their scope and competency in research methodologies. Counselors who serve as reviewers at the request of editors or publishers make every effort to only review materials that are within their scope of competency and use care to avoid personal biases.

SECTION H: RESOLVING ETHICAL ISSUES

Introduction

Counselors behave in a legal, ethical, and moral manner in the conduct of their professional work. They are aware that client protection and trust in the profession depend on a high level of professional conduct. They hold other counselors to the same standards and are willing to take appropriate action to ensure that these standards are upheld.

Counselors strive to resolve ethical dilemmas with direct and open communication among all parties involved and seek consultation with colleagues and supervisors when necessary. Counselors incorporate ethical practice into their daily professional work. They engage in ongoing professional development regarding current topics in ethical and legal issues in counseling.

H.1. Standards and the Law

(See F.9.a.)

H.1.a. Knowledge

Counselors understand the *ACA Code of Ethics* and other applicable ethics codes from other professional organizations or from certification and licensure bodies of which they are members. Lack of knowledge or misunderstanding of an ethical responsibility is not a defense against a charge of unethical conduct.

H.1.b. Conflicts Between Ethics and Laws

If ethical responsibilities conflict with law, regulations, or other governing legal authority, counselors make known their commitment to the *ACA Code of Ethics* and take steps to resolve the conflict. If the conflict cannot be resolved by such means, counselors may adhere to the requirements of law, regulations, or other governing legal authority.

H.2. Suspected Violations

H.2.a. Ethical Behavior Expected

Counselors expect colleagues to adhere to the *ACA Code of Ethics.* When counselors possess knowledge that raises doubts as to whether another counselor is acting in an ethical manner, they take appropriate action. *(See H.2.b., H.2.c.)*

H.2.b. Informal Resolution

When counselors have reason to believe that another counselor is violating or has violated an ethical standard, they attempt first to resolve the issue informally with the other counselor if feasible, provided such action does not violate confidentiality rights that may be involved.

H.2.c. Reporting Ethical Violations

If an apparent violation has substantially harmed, or is likely to substantially harm a person or organization and is not appropriate for informal resolution or is not resolved properly, counselors take further action appropriate to the situation. Such action might include referral to state or national committees on professional ethics, voluntary national certification bodies, state licensing boards, or to the appropriate institutional authorities. This standard does not apply when an intervention would violate confidentiality rights or when counselors have been retained to review the work of another counselor whose professional conduct is in question.

H.2.d. Consultation

When uncertain as to whether a particular situation or course of action may be in violation of the *ACA Code of Ethics,* counselors consult with other counselors who are knowledgeable about ethics and the *ACA Code of Ethics,* with colleagues, or with appropriate authorities

H.2.e. Organizational Conflicts

If the demands of an organization with which counselors are affiliated pose a conflict with the *ACA Code of Ethics,* counselors specify the nature of such conflicts and express to their supervisors or other responsible officials their commitment to the *ACA Code of Ethics.* When possible, counselors work toward change within the organization to allow full adherence to the *ACA Code of Ethics.* In doing so, they address any confidentiality issues.

H.2.f. Unwarranted Complaints

Counselors do not initiate, participate in, or encourage the filing of ethics complaints that are made with reckless disregard or willful ignorance of facts that would disprove the allegation.

H.2.g. Unfair Discrimination Against Complainants and Respondents

Counselors do not deny persons employment, advancement, admission to academic or other programs, tenure, or promotion based solely upon their having made or their being the subject of an ethics complaint. This does not preclude taking action based upon the outcome of such proceedings or considering other appropriate information.

H.3. Cooperation with Ethics Committees

Counselors assist in the process of enforcing the *ACA Code of Ethics*. Counselors cooperate with investigations, proceedings, and requirements of the ACA Ethics Committee or ethics committees of other duly constituted associations or boards having jurisdiction over those charged with a violation. Counselors are familiar with the *ACA Policy and Procedures for Processing Complains of Ethical Violations* and use it as a reference for assisting in the enforcement of the *ACA Code of Ethics*.

Appendix B

Contact Information

Counseling Professional Associations

American Counseling Association
5999 Stevenson Avenue
Alexandria, VA 22304-3300
800/442-2648
Fax 800/473-2329
membership@counseling.org (e-mail)
www.counseling.org (Web page)

All divisions of the American Counseling Association may be contacted at this address.

National Certifying Boards for Counselors

National Board for Certified Counselors (NBCC)
3 Terrace Way, Suite D
Greensboro, NC 27403-3660
336/547-0607
Fax 336/547-0017
nbcc@nbcc.org (e-mail)
www.nbcc.org (Web page)

NBCC offers the National Certified Counselor (NCC) credential.

Those who hold the NCC may also earn the following specialized credentials:

- Certified Clinical Mental Health Counselor (CCMHC)
- National Certified School Counselor (NCSC)
- Master Addictions Counselor (MAC)
- NBCC Approved Clinical Supervisor (ACS)

Commission on Rehabilitation Counselor Certification (CRCC)
1835 Rohlwing Road, Suite E
Rolling Meadows, IL 60008
847/394-2104
Fax 847/394-2108
www.crccertification.com (Web page)

CRCC offers the Certified Rehabilitation Counselor (CRC) credential.

CRCC also offers the following specialized credentials:

- Master Addictions Counselor (MAC)
- Clinical Supervisor (CS)

Agencies That Accredit Counseling Facilities

Commission on Accreditation of Rehabilitation Facilities (CARF)
4891 E. Grant Road
Tucson, AZ 85712
520/325-1044
Fax 520/318-1129

International Association of Counseling Services (IACS)
101 S. Whiting Street, Suite 211
Alexandria, VA 22304
703/823-9840
Fax 703/823-9843

Joint Commission on Accreditation of Healthcare Organizations (JCAHO)
I Renaissance Boulevard
Oakbrook Terrace, IL 60181
630/792-5000

Appendix C

American Counseling Association Cross-Cultural Competencies

The following information first appeared in 1992, when it was published simultaneously in ACA's Journal of Counseling and Development and in the Journal of the Association for Multicultural Counseling and Development (AMCD). Since that time, the multicultural competencies outlined in the article have become an important part of the counseling literature and a central aspect of all counselors' work.

For more information about multicultural counseling, we suggest that you make frequent visits to AMCD's Web site that is located at **www.amcd-aca.org.**

In April 1991, the Association for Multicultural Counseling and Development (AMCD) approved a document outlining the need and rationale for a multicultural perspective in counseling. The work of the Professional Standards committee went much further in proposing 31 multicultural counseling competencies and strongly encouraged the American Counseling Association (then known as the American Association for Counseling and Development [AACD]) and the counseling profession to adopt these competencies in accreditation criteria. The hope was to have the competencies eventually become a standard for curriculum reform and training of helping professionals.

CROSS-CULTURAL COMPETENCIES AND OBJECTIVES

I. **Counselor Awareness of Own Cultural Values and Biases**

   A. Attitudes and Beliefs
   1. Culturally skilled counselors have moved from being culturally unaware to being aware and sensitive to their own cultural heritage and to valuing and respecting differences.
   2. Culturally skilled counselors are aware of how their own cultural backgrounds and experiences and attitudes, values, and biases influence psychological processes.
   3. Culturally skilled counselors are able to recognize the limits of their competencies and expertise.

   4. Culturally skilled counselors are comfortable with differences that exist between themselves and clients in terms of race, ethnicity, culture, and beliefs.

   B. Knowledge
   1. Culturally skilled counselors have specific knowledge about their own racial and cultural heritage and how it personally and professionally affects their definitions of normality–abnormality and the process of counseling.
   2. Culturally skilled counselors possess knowledge and understanding about how oppression, racism, discrimination, and stereotyping affects them personally and in their work. This allows them to acknowledge their own racist attitudes, beliefs, and feelings. Although this standard applies to all groups, for White counselors it may mean that they understand how they may have directly or indirectly benefited from individual, institutional, and cultural racism (White identity development models).
   3. Culturally skilled counselors possess knowledge about their social impact on others. They are knowledgeable about communication style differences, how their style may clash or foster the counseling process with minority clients, and how to anticipate the impact it may have on others.

   C. Skills
   1. Culturally skilled counselors seek out educational, consultative, and training experience to improve their understanding and effectiveness in working with culturally different populations. Being able to recognize the limits of their competencies, they (a) seek consultation, (b) seek further training or education, (c) refer out to more qualified individuals or resources, or (d) engage in a combination of these.
   2. Culturally skilled counselors are constantly seeking to understand themselves as racial and cultural beings and are actively seeking a nonracist identity.

II. Counselor Awareness of Client's Worldview

A. Attitudes and Beliefs

1. Culturally skilled counselors are aware of their negative emotional reactions toward other racial and ethnic groups that may prove detrimental to their clients in counseling. They are willing to contrast their own beliefs and attitudes with those of their culturally different clients in a nonjudgmental fashion.

2. Culturally skilled counselors are aware of their stereotypes and preconceived notions that they may hold toward other racial and ethnic minority groups.

B. Knowledge

1. Culturally skilled counselors possess specific knowledge and information about the particular group they are working with. They are aware of the life experiences, cultural heritage, and historical background of their culturally different clients. This particular competency is strongly linked to the minority identity development models available in the literature.

2. Culturally skilled counselors understand how race, culture, ethnicity, and so forth may affect personality formation, vocational choices, manifestation of psychological disorders, help-seeking behavior, and the appropriateness or inappropriateness of counseling approaches.

3. Culturally skilled counselors understand and have knowledge about sociopolitical influences that impinge upon the life of racial and ethnic minorities. Immigration issues, poverty, racism, stereotyping, and powerlessness all leave major scars that may influence the counseling process.

C. Skills

1. Culturally skilled counselors should familiarize themselves with relevant research and the latest findings regarding mental health and mental disorders of various ethnic and racial groups. They should actively seek out educational experiences that foster their knowledge, understanding, and cross-cultural skills.

2. Culturally skilled counselors become actively involved with minority individuals outside of the counseling setting (community events, social and political functions, celebrations, friendships, neighborhood groups, and so forth) so that their perspective of minorities is more than an academic or helping exercise.

III. Culturally Appropriate Intervention Strategies

A. Attitudes and Beliefs

1. Culturally skilled counselors respect clients' religious and/or spiritual beliefs and values, including attributions and taboos, because they affect worldview, psychosocial functioning, and expressions of distress.

2. Culturally skilled counselors respect indigenous helping practices and respect minority community intrinsic help-giving networks.

3. Culturally skilled counselors value bilingualism and do not view another language as an impediment to counseling (monolingualism may be the culprit).

B. Knowledge

1. Culturally skilled counselors have a clear and explicit knowledge and understanding of the generic characteristics of counseling and therapy (culture bound, class bound, and monolingual) and how they may clash with the cultural values of various minority groups.

2. Culturally skilled counselors are aware of institutional barriers that prevent minorities from using mental health services.

3. Culturally skilled counselors have knowledge of the potential bias in assessment instruments and use procedures and interpret findings keeping in mind the cultural and linguistic characteristics of the clients.

4. Culturally skilled counselors have knowledge of minority family structures, hierarchies, values, and beliefs. They are knowledgeable about the community characteristics and the resources in the community as well as the family.

5. Culturally skilled counselors should be aware of relevant discriminatory practices at the social and community level that may be affecting the psychological welfare of the population being served.

C. Skills

1. Culturally skilled counselors are able to engage in a variety of verbal and nonverbal helping responses. They are able to *send* and *receive* both *verbal* and *non-verbal* messages *accurately* and *appropriately*. They are not tied down to only one method or approach to helping but recognize that helping styles and approaches may be culture bound. When they sense that their helping style is limited and potentially inappropriate, they can anticipate and ameliorate its negative impact.

2. Culturally skilled counselors are able to exercise institutional intervention skills on behalf of their clients. They can help clients determine whether a problem stems from racism or bias in others (the concept of health paranoia) so that clients do not inappropriately personalize problems.

3. Culturally skilled counselors are not averse to seeking consultation with traditional healers and

religious and spiritual leaders and practitioners in the treatment of culturally different clients when appropriate.

4. Culturally skilled counselors take responsibility for interacting in the language requested by the client and, if not feasible, make appropriate referral. A serious problem arises when the linguistic skills of a counselor do not match the language of the client. This being the case, counselors should (a) seek a translator with cultural knowledge and appropriate professional background and (b) refer to a knowledgeable and competent bilingual counselor.

5. Culturally skilled counselors have training and expertise in the use of traditional assessment and testing instruments. They not only understand the technical aspects of the instruments but are also aware of the cultural limitations. This allows them to use test instruments for the welfare of the diverse clients.

6. Culturally skilled counselors should attend to as well as work to eliminate biases, prejudices, and discriminatory practices. They should be cognizant of sociopolitical contexts in conducting evaluation and providing interventions and should develop sensitivity to issues of oppression, sexism, elitism, and racism.

7. Culturally skilled counselors take responsibility in educating their clients to the processes of psychological intervention, such as goals, expectations, legal rights, and the counselor's orientation.

Appendix D

Association for Specialists in Group Work

PRINCIPLES FOR DIVERSITY-COMPETENT GROUP WORKERS

Approved by the Executive Board, August 1, 1998. Prepared by Lynn Haley-Banez, Sherlon Brown, and Bogusia Molina. Consultants: Michael D'Andrea, Patricia Arrendondo, Niloufer Merchant, and Sandra Wathen

PREAMBLE

The Association for Specialists in Group Work (ASGW) is committed to understanding how issues of diversity affect all aspects of group work. This includes but is not limited to: training diversity-competent group workers; conducting research that will add to the literature on group work with diverse populations; understanding how diversity affects group process and dynamics; and assisting group facilitators in various settings to increase their awareness, knowledge, and skills as they relate to facilitating groups with diverse memberships.

As an organization, ASGW has endorsed this document with the recognition that issues of diversity affect group process and dynamics, group facilitation, training, and research. As an organization, we recognize that racism, classism, sexism, heterosexism, ableism, and so forth, affect everyone. As individual members of this organization, it is our personal responsibility to address these issues through awareness, knowledge, and skills. As members of ASGW, we need to increase our awareness of our own biases, values, and beliefs and how they impact the groups we run. We need to increase our awareness of our group members' biases, values, and beliefs and how they also impact and influence group process and dynamics. Finally, we need to increase our knowledge in facilitating, with confidence, competence, and integrity, groups that are diverse on many dimensions.

DEFINITIONS

For the purposes of this document, it is important that the language used is understood. Terms such as "dominant," "nondominant," and "target" persons and/or populations are used to define a person or groups of persons who historically, in the United States, do not have equal access to power, money, certain privileges (such as access to mental health services because of financial constraints, or the legal right to marry, in the case of a gay or lesbian couple), and/or the ability to influence

or initiate social policy because of unequal representation in government and politics. These terms are not used to denote a lack of numbers in terms of representation in the overall U.S. population. Nor are these terms used to continue to perpetuate the very biases and forms of oppression, both overt and covert, that this document attempts to address.

For the purposes of this document, the term "disabilities" refers to differences in physical, mental, emotional, and learning abilities and styles among people. It is not meant as a term to define a person, such as a learning disabled person, but rather in the context of a person with a learning disability.

Given the history and current cultural, social, and political context in which this document is written, the authors of this document are limited to the language of this era. With this in mind, we have attempted to construct a "living document" that can and will change as the sociopolitical and cultural context changes.

THE PRINCIPLES

I. Awareness of Self
A. Attitudes and Beliefs

Diversity-competent group workers demonstrate movement from being unaware to being increasingly aware and sensitive to their own race, ethnic and cultural heritage, gender, socioeconomic status (SES), sexual orientation, abilities, and religion and spiritual beliefs, and to valuing and respecting differences.

Diversity-competent group workers demonstrate increased awareness of how their own race, ethnicity, culture, gender, SES, sexual orientation, abilities, and religion and spiritual beliefs are impacted by their own experiences and histories, which in turn influence group process and dynamics.

Diversity-competent group workers can recognize the limits of their competencies and expertise with regard to working with group members who are different from them in terms of race, ethnicity, culture (including language), SES, gender, sexual orientation, abilities, religion, and spirituality and their beliefs, values, and biases. (For further clarification on limitations, expertise, and type of group work, refer to the training standards and best practice guidelines, Association for Specialists in Group Work, 1998; and the ethical guidelines, American Counseling Association, 1995.)

Diversity-competent group workers demonstrate comfort, tolerance, and sensitivity with differences that exist between themselves and group members in terms of race, ethnicity, culture, SES, gender, sexual orientation, abilities, religion, and spirituality and their beliefs, values, and biases.

B. Knowledge

Diversity-competent group workers can identify specific knowledge about their own race, ethnicity, SES, gender, sexual orientation, abilities, religion, and spirituality, and how they personally and professionally affect their definitions of "normality" and the group process.

Diversity-skilled group workers demonstrate knowledge and understanding regarding how oppression in any form-such as, racism, classism, sexism, heterosexism, ableism, discrimination, and stereotyping-affects them personally and professionally.

Diversity-skilled group workers demonstrate knowledge about their social impact on others. They are knowledgeable about communication style differences, how their style may inhibit or foster the group process with members who are different from themselves along the different dimensions of diversity, and how to anticipate the impact they may have on others.

C. Skills

Diversity-competent group workers seek out educational, consultative, and training experiences to improve their understanding and effectiveness in working with group members who self-identify as Indigenous Peoples, African Americans, Asian Americans, Hispanics, Latinos/Latinas, gays, lesbians, bisexuals, or transgendered persons and persons with physical, mental/emotional, and/or learning disabilities, particularly with regard to race and ethnicity. Within this context, group workers are able to recognize the limits of their competencies and: (a) seek consultation, (b) seek further training or education, (c) refer members to more qualified group workers, or (d) engage in a combination of these.

Group workers who exhibit diversity competence are constantly seeking to understand themselves within their multiple identities (apparent and unapparent differences), for example, gay, Latina, Christian, working class and female, and are constantly and actively striving to unlearn

the various behaviors and processes they covertly and overtly communicate that perpetuate oppression, particularly racism.

II. Group Worker's Awareness of Group Member's Worldview
A. Attitudes and Beliefs

Diversity-skilled group workers exhibit awareness of any possible negative emotional reactions toward Indigenous Peoples, African Americans, Asian Americans, Hispanics, Latinos/Latinas, gays, lesbians, bisexuals, or transgendered persons and persons with physical, mental/emotional, and/or learning disabilities that they may hold. They are willing to contrast in a nonjudgmental manner their own beliefs and attitudes with those of Indigenous Peoples, African Americans, Asian Americans, Hispanics, Latinos/Latinas, gays, lesbians, bisexuals, or transgendered persons and persons with physical, mental/emotional, and/or learning disabilities who are group members.

Diversity-competent group workers demonstrate awareness of their stereotypes and preconceived notions that they may hold toward Indigenous Peoples, African Americans, Asian Americans, Hispanics, Latinos/Latinas, gays, lesbians, bisexuals, or transgendered persons and persons with physical, mental/emotional, and/or learning disabilities.

B. Knowledge

Diversity-skilled group workers possess specific knowledge and information about Indigenous Peoples, African Americans, Asian Americans, Hispanics, Latinos/Latinas, gays, lesbians, bisexuals, and transgendered people and group members who have mental/emotional, physical, and/or learning disabilities with whom they are working. They are aware of the life experiences, cultural heritage, and sociopolitical background of Indigenous Peoples, African Americans, Asian Americans, Hispanics, Latinos/Latinas, gays, lesbians, bisexuals, or transgendered persons and group members with physical, mental/emotional, and/or learning disabilities. This particular knowledge-based competency is strongly linked to the various racial/minority and sexual identity development models available in the literature (Atkinson, Morten, & Sue, 1993; Cass, 1979; Cross, 1995; D'Augelli & Patterson, 1995; Helms, 1992).

Diversity-competent group workers exhibit an understanding of how race, ethnicity, culture, gender, sexual identity, different abilities, SES, and other immutable personal characteristics may affect personality formation, vocational choices, manifestation of psychological disorders, physical "dis-ease" or somatic symptoms, help-seeking behavior(s), and the appropriateness or inappropriateness of the various types of and theoretical approaches to group work.

Group workers who demonstrate competency in diversity in groups understand and have the knowledge about sociopolitical influences that impinge upon the lives of Indigenous Peoples, African Americans, Asian Americans, Hispanics, Latinos/Latinas, gays, lesbians, bisexuals, or transgendered persons and persons with physical, mental/emotional, and/or learning disabilities. Immigration issues, poverty, racism, oppression, stereotyping, and/or powerlessness adversely impacts many of these individuals and therefore impacts group process or dynamics.

C. Skills

Diversity-skilled group workers familiarize themselves with relevant research and the latest findings regarding mental health issues of Indigenous Peoples, African Americans, Asian Americans, Hispanics, Latinos/Latinas, gays, lesbians, bisexuals, or transgendered persons and persons with physical, mental/emotional, and/or learning disabilities. They actively seek out educational experiences that foster their knowledge and understanding of skills for facilitating groups across differences.

Diversity-competent group workers become actively involved with Indigenous Peoples, African Americans, Asian Americans, Hispanics, Latinos/Latinas, gays, lesbians, bisexuals, or transgendered persons and persons with physical, mental/emotional, and/or learning disabilities outside of their group work/counseling setting (community events, social and political functions, celebrations, friendships, neighborhood groups, etc.) so that their perspective of minorities is more than academic or experienced through a third party.

III. Diversity-Appropriate Intervention Strategies
A. Attitudes and Beliefs

Diversity-competent group workers respect clients' religious and/or spiritual beliefs and values, because they affect worldview, psychosocial functioning, and expressions of distress.

Diversity-competent group workers respect indigenous helping practices and respect Indigenous Peoples, African Americans, Asian Americans, Hispanics, Latinos/Latinas, gays, lesbians, bisexuals, or transgendered persons and persons with physical, mental/emotional, and/or learning disabilities and can identify and utilize community intrinsic help-giving networks.

Diversity-competent group workers value bilingualism and sign language and do not view another language as an impediment to group work.

B. Knowledge

Diversity-competent group workers demonstrate a clear and explicit knowledge and understanding of generic characteristics of group work and theory and how they may clash with the beliefs, values, and traditions of Indigenous Peoples, African Americans, Asian Americans,

Hispanics, Latinos/Latinas, gays, lesbians, bisexuals, or transgendered persons and persons with physical, mental/emotional, and/or learning disabilities.

Diversity-competent group workers exhibit an awareness of institutional barriers that prevent Indigenous Peoples, African Americans, Asian Americans, Hispanics, Latinos/Latinas, gays, lesbians, bisexuals, or transgendered members and members with physical, mental/emotional, and/or learning disabilities from actively participating in or using various types of groups, that is, task groups, psychoeducational groups, counseling groups, and psychotherapy groups or the settings in which the services are offered.

Diversity-competent group workers demonstrate knowledge of the potential bias in assessment instruments and use procedures and interpret findings, or actively participate in various types of evaluations of group outcome or success, keeping in mind the linguistic, cultural, and other self-identified characteristics of the group member.

Diversity-competent group workers exhibit knowledge of the family structures, hierarchies, values, and beliefs of Indigenous Peoples, African Americans, Asian Americans, Hispanics, Latinos/Latinas, gays, lesbians, bisexuals, or transgendered persons and persons with physical, mental/emotional, and/or learning disabilities. They are knowledgeable about the community characteristics and the resources in the community as well as about the family.

Diversity-competent group workers demonstrate an awareness of relevant discriminatory practices at the social and community level that may be affecting the psychological welfare of persons and access to services of the population being served.

C. Skills

Diversity-competent group workers are able to engage in a variety of verbal and nonverbal group-facilitating functions, dependent upon the type of group (task, counseling, psychoeducational, psychotherapy), and the multiple, self-identified status of various group members (such as Indigenous Peoples, African Americans, Asian Americans, Hispanics, Latinos/Latinas, gays, lesbians, bisexuals, or transgendered persons and persons with physical, mental/emotional, and/or learning disabilities). They demonstrate the ability to send and receive both verbal and nonverbal messages accurately, appropriately, and across/between the differences represented in the group. They are not tied down to one method or approach to group facilitation and recognize that helping styles and approaches may be culture-bound. When they sense that their group facilitation style is limited and potentially inappropriate, they can anticipate and ameliorate its negative impact by drawing upon other culturally relevant skill sets.

Diversity-competent group workers have the ability to exercise institutional intervention skills on behalf of their group members. They can help a member determine whether a "problem" with the institution stems from the oppression of Indigenous Peoples, African Americans, Asian Americans, Hispanics, Latinos/Latinas, gays, lesbians, bisexuals, or transgendered persons and persons with physical, mental/emotional, and/or learning disabilities, such as in the case of developing or having a "healthy" paranoia, so that group members do not inappropriately personalize problems.

Diversity-competent group workers do not exhibit a reluctance to seek consultation with traditional healers and religious and spiritual healers and practitioners in the treatment of members who are self-identified Indigenous Peoples, African Americans, Asian Americans, Hispanics, Latinos/Latinas, gays, lesbians, bisexuals, and transgendered persons and/or group members with mental/emotional, physical, and/or learning disabilities when appropriate.

Diversity-competent group workers take responsibility for interacting in the language requested by the group member(s) and, if not feasible, make an appropriate referral. A serious problem arises when the linguistic skills of a group worker and a group member or members, including sign language, do not match. The same problem occurs when the linguistic skills of one member or several members do not match. This being the case, the group worker, should (a) seek a translator with cultural knowledge and appropriate professional background, and (b) refer to a knowledgeable, competent bilingual group worker or a group worker competent or certified in sign language. In some cases, it may be necessary to have a group for group members of similar languages or to refer the group member for individual counseling.

Diversity-competent group workers are trained and have expertise in the use of traditional assessment and testing instruments related to group work, such as in screening potential members, and they also are aware of the cultural bias/limitations of these tools and processes. This allows them to use the tools for the welfare of diverse group members following culturally appropriate procedures.

Diversity-competent group workers attend to as well as work to eliminate biases, prejudices, oppression, and discriminatory practices. They are cognizant of how sociopolitical contexts may affect evaluation and provision of group work and should develop sensitivity to issues of oppression, racism, sexism, heterosexism, classism, and so forth.

Diversity-competent group workers take responsibility in educating their group members to the processes of group work, such as goals, expectations, legal rights, sound ethical practice, and the group worker's theoretical orientation with regard to facilitating groups with diverse membership.

CONCLUSION

This document is the "starting point" for group workers as we become increasingly aware, knowledgeable, and skillful in facilitating groups whose memberships represent the diversity of our society. It is not intended to be a "how to" document. It is written as a call to action and/or a guideline and represents ASGW's commitment to moving forward with an agenda for addressing and understanding the needs of the populations we serve. As a "living document," the Association for Specialists in Group Work acknowledges the changing world in which we live and work and therefore recognizes that this is the first step in working with diverse group members with competence, compassion, respect, and integrity. As our awareness, knowledge, and skills develop, so too will this document evolve. As our knowledge as a profession grows in this area and as the sociopolitical context in which this document was written, changes, new editions of these Principles for Diversity-Competent Group Workers will arise. The operationalization of this document (article in process) will begin to define appropriate group leadership skills and interventions as well as make recommendations for research in understanding how diversity in group membership affects group process and dynamics.

References

American Counseling Association. (1995). *Code of ethics and standards*. Alexandria, VA: Author.

Association for Multicultural Counseling and Development. (1996). *Multicultural competencies*. Alexandria, VA: American Counseling Association.

Association for Specialists in Group Work (1991). Professional standards for training of group workers. *Together, 20*, 9–14.

Association for Specialists in Group Work (1998). Best practice guidelines. *Journal for Specialists in Group Work, 23*, 237–244.

Atkinson, D. R., Morten, G., & Sue, D. W. (Eds.). (1993). *Counseling American minorities* (4th ed.). Madison, WI: Brown & Benchmark.

Cass, V. C. (1979). Homosexual identity formation: A theoretical model. *Journal of Homosexuality, 4*, 219–236.

Cross, W .E. (1995). The psychology of Nigrescence: Revising the cross model. In J. G. Ponterotto, J. M. Casas, L. A. Suzuki, & C. M. Alexander (Eds.), *Handbook of multicultural counseling* (pp. 93–122). Thousand Oaks, CA: Sage.

D'Augelli, A. R., & Patterson, C. J. (Eds.). (1995). *Lesbian, gay and bisexual identities over the lifespan*. New York: Oxford University Press.

Helms, J. E. (1992). *A race is a nice thing to have*. Topeka, KS: Context Communications.

Appendix E

Counseling Disclosure and Agreement Forms

CLIENT INFORMATION AND AGREEMENT FOR COUNSELORS IN PRIVATE PRACTICE
_____, M. Ed., NCC
Licensed Professional Counselor (LPC)

I am pleased you have chosen me as your counselor. This document is designed to inform you about my background and to insure that you understand our professional relationship.

I am licensed as a Professional Counselor by the _____ Board of Examiners for Licensed Professional Counselors. Only licensed mental health professionals may provide counseling services in this state. In addition, I am certified by the National Board of Certified Counselors, a private certifying agency that recognizes counselors who have distinguished themselves through meeting the board's standards for education, knowledge, and experience.

I hold a Master's (M.Ed.) degree in counseling from the University of _____. The graduate program I completed is accredited by the Council on Accreditation of Counseling and Related Education Programs (CACREP).

I have been a counselor since _____. I provide services for clients in my private practice who I believe have the capacity to resolve their own problems with my assistance. A counseling relationship between a Professional Counselor and client is a professional relationship in which the Professional Counselor assists the client in exploring and resolving difficult life issues. I believe that as people become more accepting of themselves, they are more capable of finding happiness and contentment in their lives. Self-awareness and self-acceptance are goals that sometimes take a long time to achieve. While some clients may need only a few counseling sessions to feel complete, others may require months or even years of counseling. Clients are in complete control and may end our counseling relationship at any point and I will be supportive of that decision. If counseling is successful, clients should feel that they are able to face life's challenges in the future without my support or intervention.

My counseling services are limited to the scheduled sessions we have together. In the event you feel your mental health requires emergency attention or if you have an emotional crisis, you should report to the emergency room of a local hospital and request mental health services.

Although our sessions will be very intimate, it is important for you to realize that we have a professional, rather than a personal, relationship. Our contact will be limited to the paid session you have with me. Please do not invite me to social gatherings, offer gifts, or ask me to relate to you in any way outside our counseling sessions. You will be best served if our relationship stays strictly professional and if our sessions concentrate exclusively on your concerns. You will learn a great deal about me as we work together during your counseling experience. However, it is important for you to remember that you are experiencing me only in my professional role.

My counseling practice is limited to adolescents and adults and includes career, personal, couples, marriage, and group counseling. I also am available for divorce mediation.

I will keep confidential anything you say to me with the following general exceptions: you direct me to tell someone else, I determine you are a danger to yourself or others, or I am ordered by a court to disclose information.

In the event you are dissatisfied with my services for any reason, please let me know. If I am not able to resolve your concerns, you may report you complaints to the State of _____ Licensed Professional Counselors Board of Examiners, (address, telephone number). I hold license # _____.

In return for a fee of $ _____ per session, I agree to provide counseling services for you. Session are 50 minutes in duration. It is impossible to guarantee any specific results regarding your counseling goals. However, I assure you that my services will be rendered in a professional manner consistent with accepted ethical standards.

The fee for each session will be due and must be paid at the conclusion of each session. Cash or personal checks are acceptable forms for payment. I will provide you with a monthly receipt for all fees paid.

In the event you will not be able to keep an appointment, you must notify me 24 hours in advance. If I do not receive such advance notice, you will be responsible for paying for the session you missed.

If you are a member of a HMO, PPO, or some type of managed health care plan, I can tell you if I am an authorized provider of services under that plan. If I am an authorized provider, services will be provided to you under the terms of that plan's contract. Fees will be billed and collected according to the requirements of that plan. If I am not an authorized provider, you may still receive services from me for a fee, but your plan will not reimburse you for the cost of any of my services. Plans often will reimburse for only a limited number of visits per year. If you exceed that limit, you may still receive services from me, but your plan will not reimburse you for the cost of services that exceed their maximum number of visits.

If you wish to seek reimbursement for my services from your health insurance company, I will be happy to complete any necessary forms related to your reimbursement provided by you or the insurance company. Since you will be paying each sessions for my services, any later reimbursement from the insurance company should be sent directly to you. Please do not assign any payments to me.

Most health insurance companies will reimburse clients for my counseling services, but some will not. Those that do reimburse usually require that a standard amount be paid by you before reimbursement is allowed and usually only a percentage of my fee is reimbursable. You should contact a company representative to determine whether your insurance company will reimburse you and the schedule of reimbursement that is used.

Health insurance companies usually require that I diagnose your mental condition and indicate that you have an illness before they will agree to reimburse you. In the event a diagnosis is required, I will inform you of the diagnosis I plan to render before I submit it to health insurance company.

If you have any questions, feel free to ask. Please sign and date both copies of this form. You keep one and give the other copy to me.

_____
Your Signature

_____
Your Client's Signature

_____
Date

_____
Date

**CLIENT INFORMATION AND AGREEMENT FOR
COUNSELORS EMPLOYED IN AN AGENCY**

_____ Community Mental Health Center
address
city, state, zip
telephone number
_____, M.Ed., NCC
Licensed Professional Counselor (LPC)

_____ Community Mental Health Center will be providing counseling services to you and I have been assigned as your counselor. This document is designed to inform you about the services provided by this agency and my background.

_____ Community Mental Health Center offers a variety of services which include the following: _____. All residents of _____ County are eligible for services.

I am licensed as a Professional Counselor by the _____ Board of Examiners for Licensed Professional Counselors. In addition, I am certified by the National Board of Certified Counselors, a private certifying agency that recognizes counselors who have distinguished themselves through meeting the board's standards for education, knowledge, and experience.

I hold a Master's (M.Ed.) degree in counseling from the University of _____. The graduate program I completed is accredited by the Council on Accreditation of Counseling and Related Educational Programs (CACREP).

I have been a counselor since _____. A counseling relationship between a Professional Counselor and client is a professional relationship in which the Professional Counselor assists the client in exploring and resolving difficult life issues. I believe that as people become more accepting of themselves, they are capable of finding happiness and contentment in their lives. Self-awareness and self-acceptance are goals that sometimes take a long time to achieve. While some clients may need only a few counseling sessions to feel complete, others may require months or even years of counseling. Clients are in complete control and may end our counseling relationship at any point and I will be supportive of that decision. If counseling is successful, clients should feel that they are able to face life's challenges in the future without my support or intervention. My counseling services are limited to the scheduled sessions we have together. In the event you feel your mental health requires emergency attention or if you have an emotional crisis, you should report to the emergency room of a local hospital and request mental health services.

Although our sessions will be very intimate, it is important for you to realize that we have a professional, rather than a personal, relationship. Our contact will be limited to the paid session you have with me. Please do not invite me to social gatherings, offer gifts, or ask me to relate to you in any way outside our counseling sessions. You will be best served if our relationship stays strictly professional and if our sessions concentrate exclusively on your concerns. You will learn a great deal about me as we work together during your counseling experience However, it is important for you to remember that your are experiencing me only in my professional role. My counseling practice is limited to adolescents and adults and includes career, personal, couples, marriage, and group counseling. I also am available for divorce mediation.

I will keep confidential anything you say to me with the following general exceptions: you direct me to tell someone else, I determine you are a danger to yourself or others, or I am ordered by a court to disclose information.

In the event you are dissatisfied with my services for any reason, please let me know. If I am not able to resolve your concerns, you may report your complaints to _____, my supervisor here at the _____ Community Mental Health Center.

The general fee for services at _____ Community Mental Health Center is $75 per session. However, if you apply for a reduction in fees for services based on your family's income, you may be eligible for a reduction in fees. If you are granted a reduction in fees, United Way, a local charitable organization pays the portion of the fees that you cannot afford. Based on your application for a reduction in fees for services, your fees have been established at $ _____ per session.

Sessions are 50 minutes in duration. It is impossible to guarantee any specific results regarding your counseling goals. However, I assure you that my services will be rendered in a professional manner consistent with accepted ethical standards.

The fee for each session will be due and must be paid at the conclusion of each session. Cash or personal checks are acceptable forms for payment. I will provide you with a monthly receipt for all fees paid. In the event you will not be able to keep an appointment, you must notify me 24 hours in advance. If I do not receive such advance notice, you will be responsible for paying for the session you missed. If you are a member of a HMO, PPO, or some type of managed health care plan, I can tell you if this agency is an authorized provider of services under that plan. If this agency is an authorized provider, services will be provided to you under the terms of that plan's contract. Fees will be billed and collected according to the requirements of that plan. If this agency is not an authorized provider, you may still receive services from me for a fee, but your plan will not reimburse you for the cost of any of my services. Plans often will reimburse for only a limited number of visits per year. If you exceed that limit, you may still receive services from me, but your plan will not reimburse you for the cost of services that exceed their maximum number of visits.

If you have any questions, feel free to ask. Please sign and date both copies of this form. You keep one and give the other copy to me.

_____

Your Signature

_____

Date

_____

Your Client's Signature

_____

Date

CLIENT INFORMATION AND AGREEMENT FOR
COUNSELORS WHO EVALUATE INDIVIDUALS

The purpose of our relationship is for me to gather information from you and to evaluate you so that I will be able to render an opinion regarding the best custody situation for your minor child. This process will work best if you are cooperative in providing me with the information I need and if we maintain a professional relationship throughout the evaluation.

Nothing that we discuss will be confidential. I will be required to give a written opinion to the judge who appointed me to your case. I may use any information in that report that you give to me during the duration of our relationship. In addition, I may be required to testify under oath at legal proceedings regarding interactions we have had and opinions I have rendered.

I guarantee you that I will be fair and unbiased in rendering my opinions in this case. The best interest of your child will guide my decisions.

In the event you feel I am acting in an unfair or biased manner, please have your attorney notify the judge who is presiding in this case and request that the judge determine whether my actions have been unprofessional.

Although I am a Licensed Professional Counselor in this state, I am not serving as your counselor. In the event you feel a need for counseling, I will be happy to refer you to agencies or individuals who might be able to assist you.

If you have any questions, feel free to ask. Please sign and date both copies of this form. You keep one and give the other copy to me.

_____

Your Signature

_____

Date

_____

Your Client's Signature
Being Evaluated

_____

Date

**CLIENT INFORMATION AND AGREEMENT FOR
COUNSELORS EMPLOYED IN AN AGENCY WHO
ARE COUNSELING INVOLUNTARY CLIENTS**
_____ Community Mental Health Center
address
city, state, zip
telephone number
_____, M.Ed., NCC
Licensed Professional Counselor (LPC)

_____ Community Mental Health Center will be providing counseling services to you and I have been assigned as your counselor. This document is designed to inform you about the services provided by this agency and my background.

_____ Community Mental Health Center offers a variety of services which included the following: _____. All residents of _____ County are eligible for services.

You have been required to obtain counseling sessions from this agency by the judge who is handling your criminal case. As your counselor, I will be required to report to your probation officer whether you attended counseling sessions, whether you paid for services received, and whether I believe that you are benefitting from our counseling sessions. As a result, you must understand that anything you say to me in counseling may be transmitted to your probation officer and that I may be required to testify regarding the contents of our sessions at court proceeding regarding your case.

I am licensed as a Professional Counselor by the _____ Board of Examiners for Licensed Professional Counselors. In addition, I am certified by the National Board of Certified Counselors, a private certifying agency that recognizes counselors who have distinguished themselves through meeting the board's standards for education, knowledge, and experience.

I hold a Master's (M.Ed.) degree in counseling from the University of _____. The graduate program I completed is accredited by the Council on Accreditation of Counseling and Related Educational Programs (CACREP).

I have been a counselor since _____. A counseling relationship between a Professional Counselor and client is a professional relationship in which the Professional Counselor assists the client in exploring and resolving difficult life issues. I believe that as people become more accepting of themselves, they are more capable of finding happiness and contentment in their lives. Self-awareness and self-acceptance are goals that sometimes take a long time to achieve. While some clients may need only a few counseling sessions to feel complete, others may require months or even years of counseling. If counseling is successful, clients should feel that they are able to face life's challenges in the future without my support or intervention.

My counseling services are limited to the scheduled sessions we have together. In the event you feel your mental health requires emergency attention or if you have an emotional crisis, you should report to the emergency room of a local hospital and request mental health services.

Although our sessions will be very intimate, it is important for you to realize that we have a professional, rather than a personal, relationship. Our contact will be limited to the paid session you have with me. Please do not invite me to social gatherings, offer gifts, or ask me to relate to you in any way outside our counseling sessions. You will be best served if our relationship stays strictly professional and if our sessions concentrate exclusively on your concerns. You will learn a great deal about me as we work together during your counseling experience. However, it is important for you to remember that you are experiencing me only in my professional role.

My counseling practice is limited to adolescents and adults and includes career, personal, couples, marriage, and group counseling. I also am available for divorce mediation.

In the event you are dissatisfied with my services for any reason, please let me know. If I am not able to resolve your concerns, you may report your complaints to _____, my supervisor here at the _____ Community Mental Health Center.

The general fee for services at _____ Community Mental Health Center is $75 per session. However, if you apply for a reduction in fees for services based on your family's income, you may be eligible for a reduction in fees. If you are granted a reduction in fees, United Way, a local charitable organization pays the portion of the fees that you cannot afford. Based on your application for a reduction of fees for services, your fees have been established at $_____ per session.

Sessions are 50 minutes in duration. It is impossible to guarantee any specific results regarding your counseling goals. However, I assure you that my services will be rendered in a professional manner consistent with accepted ethical standards.

The fee for each session will be due and must be paid at the conclusion of each session. Cash or personal checks are acceptable forms for payment. I will provide you with a monthly receipt for all fees paid.

In the event you will not be able to keep an appointment, you must notify me 24 hours in advance. If I do not receive such advance notice, you will be responsible for paying for the session you missed.

If you are a member of a HMO, PPO, or some type of managed health care plan, I can tell you if this agency is an authorized provider of services under that plan. If this agency is an authorized provider, services will be provided to you under the terms of that plan's contract. Fees will be billed and collected according to the requirements of that plan. If this agency is not an authorized provider, you may still receive services from me for a fee, but your plan will not reimburse you for the cost of any of my services. Plans often will reimburse for only a limited number of visits per year. If you exceed that limit, you may still receive services from me, but your plan will not reimburse you for the cost of services that exceed their maximum number of visits.

_____ Community Mental Health Agency does not participate in any type of health insurance reimbursement. If you have a health insurance policy that allows reimburses you for mental health services, it is suggested that you seek a provider who is qualified to render those services to you. If you receive services from me at this agency, you will be responsible for the fees for all services received.

If you have any questions, feel free to ask. Please sign and date both copies of this form. You keep one and give the other copy to me.

_____   _____
Your Signature   Your Client's Signature

_____   _____
Date   Date

CLIENT INFORMATION AND AGREEMENT FOR COUNSELORS
EMPLOYED IN A SCHOOL

Include a statement similar to the one below in a letter to parents at the beginning of the year, orientation materials, etc. The statement could be easily modified to be addressed to students themselves and included in a student handbook.

"I'm Your Child's School Counselor"

The counseling program at _____ school is designed to assist your child make the most of his or her educational experiences. As your child's counselor, I am concerned about his or her emotional well-being, academic progress, and personal and social development.

I have a master's degree in school counseling from the University of _____. My graduate program is accredited by the American Counseling Association's Council for the Accreditation of Counseling and Related Educational Program (CACREP), the nationally recognized accrediting agency for counseling graduate programs. I am a National Certified Counselor (NCC), National Certified School Counselor (NCSC), and a Licensed Professional Counselor (LPC) in _____. In addition, I am certified as a school counselor by the state of _____. Before beginning my duties as a counselor at _____ school, I held the following positions: _____. I currently serve as President of the _____ School Counselor Association.

The following specific activities are offered by the counseling program:
1. Periodic classroom lessons related to positive personal growth and development.
2.
3.
etc.

Reasons that I might contact parents regarding their child include, but are not limited to, the following:
1. Assistance is needed from parents in specific areas to help their children achieve success in school.
2.
etc.

Unfortunately, I am not able to provide the following services to your child or to parents:
1. Testifying in court in child-custody matters.
2. Providing intensive long-term counseling services when they are needed by a child.
3.
etc.

Your child will be participating in the school counseling program on a regular basis. In the event you have questions about the counseling program, please call me at _____. I sincerely look forward to working with you in the coming year to help your child have a successful experience in our school.

Appendix F

Client Request Form to Transfer Records

[This form was constructed to meet HIPAA requirements. In the event an agency or practice is not subject to HIPAA requirements, such a form could be simpler.]

I, _____ (fill in name of client), hereby request that copies of my counseling records as described below be transferred to the following individual or institution:

Name and address to where records should be transferred

Only copies of records will be sent that are necessary to fulfill the purpose you are requesting this transfer. With that in mind, what is the purpose for requesting that copies of your records be sent?

Generally, notes made by your counselor after each session (known as *psychotherapy notes*) are not transferred. Would you like for copes of these psychotherapy notes to be sent also?
_____ Yes
_____ No

Generally, copies of your records are sent one time only as soon as possible, and you would have to complete and sign a form again for additional requests. If you would like to alter this general procedure in any way, please indicate below your preferences:

To the best of your knowledge, when did you begin and end counseling services at this agency?
_____ Date Counseling Services Began
_____ Date Counseling Services Ended

_____   _____
Client Signature   Date

Appendix G

**CLIENT PERMISSION FORM TO RECORD
COUNSELING SESSION FOR
SUPERVISION PURPOSES**

I, _____ [fill in name of client], hereby give my permission for my counselor, _____ [fill in your name] to audiotape/vidoetape [one or the other] our counseling session _____ [fill in date, or if over a period of time, fill in inclusive dates].

    I understand that the purpose of this recording is for the clinical supervision of my counselor's work. I understand that only my client's clinical supervisor, _____ [fill in name of supervisor], will review the tape and that the tape will be erased after the supervisor has reviewed it.

_____   _____
Client's Signature   Date

Appendix H

Guidelines for Counseling Case Notes*

1. Write any case notes that assist you in being a more effective counseling practitioner. Do not hesitate to keep case notes if they help you be a better counselor.
2. There is no general legal duty to keep case notes but, because maintaining case notes is a standard procedure in the counseling profession, it could be considered unusual if a counselor did not have case notes for a particular case.
3. Always assume any note you write will someday be read in open court with you and your client present, along with newspaper, radio, and television reporters.
4. Separate your notes into at least two distinct sections: objective and subjective.
5. In the objective section, record precisely what the client said, what you said, and what you observed. Do not draw any conclusions or enter any speculations at this point. You might entitle this section "Observations."
6. In the subjective section, record any thoughts that you will need for the future; impressions of the client, speculations about the reasons for the client's problems, reminders to yourself of your present thoughts, or plans for the next session would all be acceptable. You might entitle this section "Impressions."
7. Keep case notes in locked file drawers and ensure that only clerical assistants and you have access to your notes. If notes are kept in a computer, be sure they are not accessible to others.
8. There is no general legal principle regarding the length of time you need to keep case notes once they are recorded. However, there are federal statutes that cover certain federally-funded projects, hospital and counseling center accreditation standards, and particular agency procedures that require that case notes be kept for certain periods of time. Of course, such statutes, standards, and procedures should be followed if they apply to your case.
9. Regularly destroy your case notes. When you destroy them, be sure no identifying information remains. It is best to shred, burn, or in some other manner, totally destroy the records.
10. Because there are no requirements in work settings regarding the length of time for retention, keep case notes as long as you think you might need them. However, you should destroy case notes on a systematic basis. For example, some counselors destroy case notes of terminated clients six months after termination, one year after termination, or three years after termination. It is a good idea to destroy notes only one or two days each year, for example on every December 31st.
11. When destroying your case notes, do not include those notes in which you have documented steps you have taken to protect yourself in the event you are accused of wrongdoing. Keep these case notes for longer periods of time, perhaps indefinitely.
12. Never, under any circumstances, destroy case notes after you receive a subpoena or if you think you might be receiving a subpoena in the future. Such acts could be interpreted as obstruction of justice and you could be held in contempt of court.

*Composed by T. Remley.

Appendix I

Examples of Mandatory Child Abuse Reporting Statutes

LOUISIANA

LSA-R.S. 14:403 (2000)

C. (1) Any person, including licensed physicians, interns or residents, nurses, hospital staff members, teachers, social workers, coroners, and others persons or agencies having responsibility for the care of children, having cause to believe that a child's physical or mental health or welfare has been or may be further adversely affected abuse or neglect or that abuse or neglect was contributing factor in a child's death shall report. . .

D. (1) Reports reflecting the reporter's belief that a child has been abused or neglect or that abuse or neglect was a contributing factor in a child's death shall be made to the parish child welfare unit or the parish agency responsible for the protection of juveniles and, if necessary, to a local or state law enforcement agency. These reports need not name the persons suspected of the alleged abuse or neglect . . .

(2) All reports shall contain the name and address of the child, the name and address of the person responsible for the care of the child, if available, and any other pertinent information.

(4) An oral report shall be made immediately upon learning of the abuse or neglect . . . and a written report shall follow within five days to the same agency or department.

TEXAS

V.T.C.A., Family Code § 261.101 (1999)

(a) A person having cause to believe that a child's physical or mental health or welfare has been adversely affected by abuse or neglect by any person shall immediately make a report . . .

(b) If a professional has cause to believe that a child has been abused or neglect or may be abused or neglected or that a child is a victim of an offense under Section 21.11, Penal Code the professional shall make a report not later than the 48th hour after the hour the professional first suspects that the child has been or may be abused or neglected or is a victim of an offense under Section 21.11, Penal Code. A professional may not delegate to or rely on another person to make the report . . .

(c) The requirement to report under this section applies without exception to an individual whose personal communications may otherwise be privileged, including an attorney, a member of the clergy, a medical practitioner, a social worker, a mental health professional, and an employee of a clinic or health care facility that provides reproductive services.

WISCONSIN

W.S.A. 48.981 (1999)

(2) Persons required to report. A physician, coroner, medical examiner, nurse, dentist, chiropractor, optometrist, acupuncturist, other medical or mental health professional, social worker, marriage and family therapist, professional counselor, public assistance worker, . . . having reasonable cause to suspect that a child seen in the course of professional duties has been abused or neglected or having reason to believe that a child seen in the course of professional duties has been threatened with abuse or neglect and that abuse or neglect of the child will occur shall, . . . report as provided in sub. (3). Any other person, including an attorney, having reason to suspect that a child has been abused or neglected or reason to believe that a child has been threatened with abuse or neglect and that abuse or neglect of the child will occur may make such a report. Any person, including an attorney having reason to suspect that an unborn child has been abused or reason to believe that an unborn child is as substantial risk of abuse may report as provided in sub. (3). No person making a report under this subsection may be discharged from employment for so doing.

(3) Reports; investigation. (a) Referral of report. A person required to report under sub. (2) shall immediately inform, by telephone or personally, the county department or, in a country having a population of 500,000 or more, the department or a licensed child welfare agency under contract with the department or the sheriff or city, village or town police department of the facts and circumstances contributing to a suspicion of child abuse, or neglect or of unborn child abuse or to a belief that abuse or neglect will occur . . .

Appendix J-1

American Counseling Association: Standards for the Internet

APPROVED BY THE ACA GOVERNING COUNCIL, OCTOBER 1999

These guidelines establish appropriate standards for the use of electronic communications over the Internet to provide on-line counseling services, and should be used only in conjunction with the latest ACA Code of Ethics & Standards of Practice.

CONFIDENTIALITY

a. Privacy Information.

Professional counselors ensure that clients are provided sufficient information to adequately address and explain the limitations of (i) computer technology in the counseling process in general and (ii) the difficulties of ensuring complete client confidentiality of information transmitted through electronic communications over the Internet through on-line counseling. (See A.12.a., B.1.a., B.1.g.)

1. SECURED SITES: To mitigate the risk of potential breaches of confidentiality, professional counselors provide one-on-one on-line counseling only through "secure" Web sites or e-mail communications applications which use appropriate encryption technology designed to protect the transmission of confidential information from access by unauthorized third parties.

2. NON-SECURED SITES: To mitigate the risk of potential breaches of confidentiality, professional counselors provide only general information from "non-secure" Web sites or e-mail communications applications.

3. GENERAL INFORMATION: Professional counselors may provide general information from either "secure" or "non-secure" Web sites, or through e-mail communications. General information includes non-client-specific, topical information on matters of general interest to the professional counselor's clients as a whole, third-party resource and referral information, addresses and phone numbers, and the like. Additionally, professional counselors using either "secure" or "non-secure" Web sites may provide "hot links" to third-party Web sites such as licensure boards, certification bodies, and other resource information providers. Professional counselors investigate and continually update the content, accuracy and appropriateness for the client of material contained in any "hot links" to third-party Web sites.

4. LIMITS OF CONFIDENTIALITY: Professional counselors inform clients of the limitations of confidentiality and identify foreseeable situations in which confidentiality must be breached in light of the law in both the state in which the client is located and the state in which the professional counselor is licensed.

b. Informational Notices.

1. SECURITY OF PROFESSIONAL COUNSELOR'S SITE: Professional counselors provide a readily visible notice that (i) information transmitted over a Web site or e-mail server may not be secure; (ii) whether or not the professional counselor's site is secure; (iii) whether the information transmitted between the professional counselor and the client during on-line counseling will be encrypted; and (iv) whether the client will need special software to access and transmit confidential information and, if so, whether the professional counselor provides the software as part of the on-line counseling services. The notice should be viewable from all Web site and e-mail locations from which the client may send information. (See B.1.g.)

2. PROFESSIONAL COUNSELOR IDENTIFICATION: Professional counselors provide a readily visible notice advising clients of the identities of all professional counselor(s) who will have access to the information transmitted by the client and, in the event that more than

Reprinted by permission of the American Counseling Association, 5999 Stevenson Avenue, Alexandria, VA 22304.

one professional counselor has access to the Web site or e-mail system, the manner, if any, in which the client may direct information to a particular professional counselor. Professional counselors inform clients if any or all of the sessions are supervised. Clients are also informed if and how the supervisor preserves session transcripts. Professional counselors provide background information on all professional counselor(s) and supervisor(s) with access to the on-line communications, including education, licensing and certification, and practice area information. (See B.l.g.)

3. CLIENT IDENTIFICATION: Professional counselors identify clients, verify identities of clients, and obtain alternative methods of contacting clients in emergency situations.

c. Client Waiver.
Professional counselors require clients to execute client waiver agreements stating that the client (i) acknowledges the limitations inherent in ensuring client confidentiality of information transmitted through on-line counseling and (ii) agrees to waive the client's privilege of confidentiality with respect to any confidential information transmitted through on-line counseling that may be accessed by any third party without authorization of the client and despite the reasonable efforts of the professional counselor to arrange a secure on-line environment. Professional counselors refer clients to more traditional methods of counseling and do not provide on-line counseling services if the client is unable or unwilling to consent to the client waiver. (See B.1.b.)

d. Records of Electronic Communications.
Professional counselors maintain appropriate procedures for ensuring the safety and confidentiality of client information acquired through electronic communications, including but not limited to encryption software; proprietary on-site file servers with fire walls; saving on-line or e-mail communications to the hard drive or file server computer systems; creating regular tape or diskette back-up copies; creating hard-copies of all electronic communications; and the like. Clients are informed about the length of time for, and method of, preserving session transcripts. Professional counselors warn clients of the possibility or frequency of technology failures and time delays in transmitting and receiving information. (See B.4.a., B.4.b.)

e. Electronic Transfer of Client Information.
Professional counselors electronically transfer client confidential information to authorized third-party recipients only when (i) both the professional counselor and the authorized recipient have "secure" transfer and acceptance communication capabilities, (ii) the recipient is able to effectively protect the confidentiality of the client confidential information to be transferred; and (iii) the informed written consent of the client, acknowledging the limits of confidentiality, has been obtained. (See B.4.e., B.6.a., B.6.b.)

ESTABLISHING THE ON-LINE COUNSELING RELTIONSHIP

a. The Appropriateness of On-Line Counseling.
Professional counselors develop an appropriate in-take procedure for potential clients to determine whether on-line counseling is appropriate for the needs of the client. Professional counselors warn potential clients that on-line counseling services may not be appropriate in certain situations and, to the extent possible, informs the client of specific limitations, potential risks, and/or potential benefits relevant to the client's anticipated use of on-line counseling services. Professional counselors ensure that clients are intellectually, emotionally, and physically capable of using the on-line counseling services, and of understanding the potential risks and/or limitations of such services. (See A.3.a., A.3.b.)

b. Counseling Plans.
Professional counselors develop individual on-line counseling plans that are consistent with both the client's individual circumstances and the limitations of on-line counseling. Professional counselors shall specifically take into account the limitations, if any, on the use of any or all of the following in on-line counseling: initial client appraisal, diagnosis, and assessment methods employed by the professional counselor. Professional counselors who determine that on-line counseling is inappropriate for the client should avoid entering into or immediately terminate the on-line counseling relationship and encourage the client to continue the counseling relationship through an appropriate alternative method of counseling. (See A.11.b., A.11.c.)

c. Continuing Coverage.
Professional counselors provide clients with a schedule of times during which the on-line counseling services will be available, including reasonable anticipated response times, and provide clients with an alternate means of contacting the professional counselor at other times, including in the event of emergencies. Professional counselors obtain from, and provide clients with, alternative means of communication, such as telephone numbers or pager numbers, for back-up purposes in the event the on-line counseling service is unavailable for any reason. Professional counselors provide clients with the name of at least one other professional counselor who will be able to respond to the client in the event the professional counselor is unable to do so for any extended period of time. (See A.11.a.)

d. Boundaries of Competence.

Professional counselors provide on-line counseling services only in practice areas within their expertise and do not provide on-line counseling services to clients located in states in which professional counselors are not licensed. (See C.2.a., C.2.b.)

e. Minor or Incompetent Clients.

Professional counselors must verify that clients are above the age of minority, are competent to enter into the counseling relationship with a professional counselor, and are able to give informed consent. In the event clients are minor children, incompetent, or incapable of giving informed consent, professional counselors must obtain the written consent of the legal guardian or other authorized legal representative of the client prior to commencing on-line counseling services to the client.

LEGAL CONSIDERATIONS

Professional counselors confirm that their liability insurance provides coverage for on-line counseling services, and that the provision of such services is not prohibited by or otherwise violate any applicable (i) state or local statutes, rules, regulations, or ordinances; (ii) codes of professional membership organizations and certifying boards; and/or (iii) codes of state licensing boards.

Professional counselors seek appropriate legal and technical assistance in the development and implementation of their on-line counseling services.

Appendix J-2

National Board for Certified Counselors Standards for the Ethical Practice of WebCounseling

The relative newness of the use of the Internet for service and product delivery leaves authors of standards at a loss when beginning to create ethical practices on the Internet. This document, like all codes of conduct, will change as information and circumstances not yet foreseen evolve. However, each version of this code of ethics is the current best standard of conduct passed by the NBCC Board of Directors. As with any code, and especially with a code such as this, created for an evolving field of work, NBCC and CCE welcome comments and ideas for further discussion and inclusion. Further, the development of these WebCounseling standards has been guided by the following principles:

These standards are intended to address practices which are unique to WebCounseling and WebCounselors,

These standards are not to duplicate non-Internet-based standards adopted in other codes of ethics,

Recognizing that significant new technology emerges continuously, these standards should be reviewed frequently,

WebCounseling ethics cases should be reviewed in light of delivery systems existing at the moment rather than at the time the standards were adopted.

WebCounselors who are not National Certified Counselors may indicate at their WebSite their adherence to these standards, but may not publish these standards in their entirety without written permission of the National Board for Certified Counselors.

The Practice of WebCounseling shall be defined as "the practice of professional counseling and information delivery that occurs when client(s) and counselor are in separate or remote locations and utilize electronic means to communicate over the Internet."

In addition to following the NBCC Code of Ethics pertaining to the practice of professional counseling, WebCounselors shall:

1. Review pertinent legal and ethical codes for possible violations emanating from the practice of WebCounseling and supervision.

Last modified: September 30, 1999.

Liability insurance policies should also be reviewed to determine if the practice of WebCounseling is a covered activity. Local, state, provincial, and national statutes as well as the codes of professional membership organizations, professional certifying bodies and state or provincial licensing boards need to be reviewed. Also, as no definitive answers are known to questions pertaining to whether WebCounseling takes place in the WebCounselor's location or the WebClient's location, WebCounselors should consider carefully local customs regarding age of consent and child abuse reporting.

2. Inform WebClients of encryption methods being used to help insure the security of client/counselor/supervisor communications.

Encryption methods should be used whenever possible. If encryption is not made available to clients, clients must be informed of the potential hazards of unsecured communication on the Internet. Hazards may include authorized or unauthorized monitoring of transmissions and/or records of WebCounseling sessions.

3. Inform clients if, how and how long session data are being preserved.

Session data may include WebCounselor/WebClient e-mail, test results, audio/video session recordings, session notes, and counselor/supervisor communications. The likelihood of electronic sessions being preserved is greater because of the ease and decreased costs involved in recording. Thus, its potential use in supervision, research and legal proceedings increases.

4. In situations where it is difficult to verify the identity of WebCounselor of WebClient, take steps to address impostor concerns, such as by using code words, numbers, or graphics.

5. When parent/guardian consent is required to provide WebCounseling to minors, verify the identity of the consenting person.

6. Follow appropriate procedures regarding the release of information for sharing WebClient information with other electronic sources.

Beacause of the relative ease with which e-mail messages can be forwarded to formal and casual referral sources,

WebCounselors must work to insure the confidentiality of the WebCounseling relationship.

7. Carefully consider the extent of self disclosure presented to the WebClient and provide rationale for WebCounselor's level of disclosure.

WebCounselors may wish to ensure that, minimally, the WebClient has the same data available about his/her service provider as would be available if the counseling were to take place face to face (i.e., possibly ethnicity, gender, etc.). Compelling reasons for limiting disclosure should be presented.

WebCounselors will remember to protect themselves from unscrupulous users of the Internet by limiting potentially harmful disclosure about self and family.

8. Provide links to websites of all appropriate certification bodies and licensure boards to facilitate consumer protection.

9. Contact NBCC/CEE or the WebClient's state or provincial licensing board to obtain the name of at least one Counselor-On-Call within the WebClient's geographical region.

WebCounselors who have contacted an individual to determine his or her willingness to serve as a Counselor-On-Call (either in person, over the phone or via e-mail) should also ensure that the WebClient is provided with Local crisis intervention hotline numbers, 911 and similar numbers in the event that the Counselor-On-Call is unavailable.

10. Discuss with their WebClients procedures for contacting the WebCounselor-On-Call when he or she is off-line.

This means explaining exactly how often e-mail messages are to be checked by the WebCounselor.

11. Mention at their websites those presenting problems they believe to be inappropriate for WebCounseling.

While no conclusive research has been conducted to date, those topics might include: sexual abuse as a primary issue, violent relationships, eating disorders, and psychiatric disorders that involve distortions of reality.

12. Explain to clients the possibility of technology failure. The WebCounselor

- gives instructions to WebClients about calling if problems arise,
- discusses the appropriateness of the client calling collect when the call might be originating from around the world,
- mentions differences in time zones,
- talks about dealing with response delays in sending and receiving e-mail messages

13. Explain to clients how to cope with potential misunderstandings arising from the lack of visual cues from WebCounselor or WebClient.

For example, suggesting the other person simply say, "Because I couldn't see your face or hear your tone of voice in your e-mail message, I'm not sure how to interpret that last message."

Reprinted by permission of the National Board for Certified Counselors, 3 Terrace Way, Suite D, Greensboro, NC 27403-3660.

Appendix J-3

APA Statement on Services by Telephone, Teleconferencing, and Internet

A statement by the Ethics Committee of the American Psychological Association

The American Psychological Association's Ethics Committee issued the following statement on November 5, 1997, based on its 1995 statement on the same topic.

The Ethics Committee can only address the relevance of and enforce the "Ethical Principles of Psychologists and Code of Conduct" and cannot say whether there may be other APA Guidelines that might provide guidance. The Ethics Code is not specific with regard to telephone therapy or teleconferencing or any electronically provided services as such and has no rules prohibiting such services. Complaints regarding such matters would be addressed on a case by case basis.

Delivery of services by such media as telephone, teleconferencing and internet is a rapidly evolving area. This will be the subject of APA task forces and will be considered in future revision of the Ethics Code. Until such time as a more definitive judgment is available, the Ethics Committee recommends that psychologists follow Standard 1.04c, Boundaries of Competence, which indicates that "In those emerging areas in which generally recognized standards for preparatory training do not yet exist, psychologists nevertheless take reasonable steps to ensure the competence of their work and to protect patients, clients, students, research participants, and others from harm." Other relevant standards include Assessment (Standards 2.01–2.10), Therapy (4.01–4.09, especially 4.01 Structuring the Relationship and 4.02 Informed Consent to Therapy), and Confidentiality (5.01–5.11). Within the General Standards section, standards with particular relevance are 1.03, Professional and Scientific Relationship; 1.04 (a, b, and c), Boundaries of Competence; 1.06, Basis for Scientific and Professional Judgments; 1.07a, Describing the Nature and Results of Psychological Services; 1.14, Avoiding Harm; and 1.25, Fees and Financial Arrangements. Standards under Advertising, particularly 3.01–3.03 are also relevant.

Psychologists considering such services must review the characteristics of the services, the service delivery method, and the provisions for confidentiality. Psychologists must then consider the relevant ethical standards and other requirements, such as licensure board rules.

*This policy statement was issued in regard to the 1992 Ethics Code. The 2003 Ethics Code now supersedes the 1992 version, so this statement is considered inactive.

Appendix J-4

NCDA Guidelines for the Use of the Internet for Provision of Career Information and Planning Services

Approved by the NCDA Board of Directors, October 1997

Developed by members of the NCDA Ethics Committee:
Dr. David Caulum, Don Doerr, Dr. Pat Howland, Dr. Spencer Niles,
Dr. Ray Palmer, Dr. Richard Pyle (Chair), Dr. David Reile, Dr. James Sampson, and Dr. Don Schutt

- Introduction
- Guidelines for Use of the Internet for Delivery of Career Counseling and Career Planning Services
- Professional and Ethical Guidelines Related to the Use of the Internet for Job Posting and Searching
- Unacceptable Counselor Behavior on the Internet
- Need for Research and Review

INTRODUCTION

Based on readily-available capabilities at the time of this writing, the Internet could be used in four ways for the purpose of providing career counseling and/or career planning services to clients. These are:

1. To deliver information about occupations, including their descriptions, employment outlook, skills requirements, estimated salary, etc. through text, still images, graphics, and/or video. In this event, the standards for information development and presentation are the same as those for print materials and audiovisual materials as stated in NCDA's documents on these matters.
2. To provide online searches of occupational databases for the purpose of identifying feasible occupational alternatives. In this event, the standards developed by NCDA and the Association of Computer-based Systems for Career Information (ACSCI) apply.
3. To deliver interactive career counseling and career planning services. This use assumes that clients, either as individuals or as part of a group, have intentionally placed themselves in direct communication with a professional career counselor. Standards for use of the Internet for these purposes are addressed in this document.
4. To provide searches through large databases of job openings for the purpose of identifying those that the user may

pursue. Guidelines for this application are included in this document.

GUIDELINES FOR USE OF THE INTERNET FOR DELIVERY OF CAREER COUNSELING AND CAREER PLANNING SERVICES

"Career planning services" are differentiated from "career counseling" services. Career planning services include an active provision of information designed to help a client with a specific need, such as review of a resumé; assistance in networking strategies; identification of occupations based on interests, skills, or prior work experience; support in the job-seeking process; and assessment by means of online inventories of interest, abilities, and/or work-related values. Although "Career Counseling" may include the provision of the above services, the use of the term implies a deeper level of involvement with the client, based on the establishment of a professional counseling relationship and the potential for dealing with career development concerns well beyond those included in career planning.

Multiple means of online provision of career planning or career counseling services currently exist, the most common of which are e-mail, newsgroups, bulletin boards, chat rooms, and websites offering a wide variety of services. Telephone or audiovisual linkages supported by the Internet exist in their infancy, and will likely grow in potential as the technology improves and the costs decline.

1. **Qualifications of Developer or Provider**
   Websites and other services designed to assist clients with career planning should be developed with content input from professional career counselors. The service should clearly state the qualifications and credentials of the developers not only in the content area of professional

career counseling, but also in the development of interactive online services.

2. Access and Understanding of Environment

The counselor has an obligation to be aware of free public access points to the Internet within the member's community, so that a lack of financial resources does not create a significant barrier to clients accessing counseling services or information, assessment or instructional resources over the internet.

The counselor has an obligation to be as aware as possible of local conditions, cultures, and events that may impact the client.

3. Content of Career Counseling and Planning Services on the Internet

The content of a website or other service offering career information or planning services should be reviewed for the appropriateness of content offered in this medium. Some kinds of content have been extensively tested for online delivery due to the long existence of computer-based career information and guidance systems. This includes searching of databases by relevant search variables; display of occupational information; development of a resumé; assessment of interests, abilities, and work-related values and linkage of these to occupational titles; instruction about occupational classification systems; relationship of school majors to occupational choices; and the completion of forms such as a financial needs assessment questionnaire or a job application.

When a website offers a service which has not previously been extensively tested (such as computer-based career guidance and information systems), this service should be carefully scrutinized to determine whether it lends itself to the Internet. The website should clearly state the kinds of client concerns that the counselor judges to be inappropriate for counseling over the Internet, or beyond the skills of the counselor.

4. Appropriateness of Client for Receipt of Services via the Internet

The counselor has an ethical and professional responsibility to assure that the client who is requesting service can profit from it in this mode. Appropriate screening includes the following:

a. A clear statement by clients of their career planning or career counseling needs.

b. An analysis by the counselor of whether meeting those needs via Internet exchange is appropriate **and** of whether this particular client can benefit from counseling services provided in this mode. A judgment about the latter should be made by means of a telephone or videophone teleconference designed to specify the client's expectations, how the client has sought to meet these through other modes, and whether or not the client appears to be able to process information through an Internet medium.

5. Appropriate Support to the Client

The counselor who is providing services to a client via the Internet has ethical responsibility for the following:

a. Periodic monitoring of the client's progress via telephone or videophone teleconference.

b. Identification by the counselor of a qualified career counselor in the client's geographic area should referral become necessary. If this is not possible, the web counselor using traditional referral sources to identify an appropriate practitioner, should assist the client in the selection of a counselor.

c. Appropriate discussion with the client about referral to face-to-face service should the counselor determine that little or no progress is being made toward the client's goals.

6. Clarity of Contract with the Client

The counselor should define several items in writing to the client in a document that can be downloaded from the Internet or faxed to the client. This document should include at least the following items:

a. The counselor's credentials in the field.

b. The agreed-upon goals of the career counseling or career planning Internet interchange.

c. The agreed-upon cost of the services and how this will be billed.

d. Where and how clients can report any counselor behavior which they consider to be unethical.

e. Statement about the degree of security of the Internet and confidentiality of data transmitted on the Internet and about any special conditions related to the client's personal information (such as potential transmission of client records to a supervisor for quality-control purposes, or the collection of data for research purposes).

f. A statement of the nature of client information electronically stored by the counselor, including the length of time that data will be maintained before being destroyed.

g. A statement about the need for privacy when the client is communicating with the counselor, e.g., that client communication with the counselor is not limited by having others observe or hear interactions between the counselor and client.

h. If the service includes career, educational, or employment information, the counselor is responsible for making the client aware of the typical circumstances where individuals need counseling support in order to effectively use the information.

7. Inclusion of Linkages to Other Websites

If a career information or counseling website includes links to other websites, the professional who creates this linkage is responsible for assuring that the services to which his or hers are linked also meet these guidelines.

8. Use of Assessment

If the career planning or career counseling service is to include online inventories or tests and their interpretation, the following conditions should apply:

a. The assessments must have been tested in computer delivery mode to assure that their psychometric properties are the same in this mode of delivery as in print form; or the client must be informed that they have not yet been tested in this same mode of delivery.

b. The counselor must abide by the same ethical guidelines as if he or she were administering and interpreting these same inventories or tests in face-to-face mode and/or in print form.

c. Every effort must be exerted to protect the confidentiality of the user's results.

d. If there is any evidence that the client does not understand the results, as evidenced by e-mail or telephone interchanges, the counselor must refer the client to a qualified career counselor in his or her geographic area.

e. The assessments must have been validated for self-help use if no counseling support is provided, or that appropriate counseling intervention is provided before and after completion of the assessment resource if the resource has not been validated for self-help use.

PROFESSIONAL AND ETHICAL GUIDELINES RELATED TO THE USE OF THE INTERNET FOR JOB POSTING AND SEARCHING

1. The posting must represent a valid job opening for which those searching on the Internet have an opportunity to apply.

2. Job postings must be removed from the Internet database within 48 hours of the time that the announced position is filled.

3. Names, addresses, resumés, and other information that may be gained about individuals should not be used for any purposes other than provision of further information about job openings.

UNACCEPTABLE COUNSELOR BEHAVIORS ON THE INTERNET

1. Use of a false e-mail identity when interacting with clients and/or other professionals. When acting in a professional capacity on the Internet, a counselor has a duty to identify him/herself honestly.

2. Accepting a client who will not identify him/herself and be willing to arrange for phone conversation as well as on-line interchange.

3. "Sharking" or monitoring chat rooms and bulletin board services, and offering career planning and related services when no request has been made for services. This includes sending out mass unsolicited e-mails. Counselors may advertise their services but must do so observing proper "netiquette" and standards of professional conduct.

NEED FOR RESEARCH AND REVIEW

Since the use of the Internet is new for the delivery of career planning and counseling services, it is mandatory that the career counseling profession gain experience with this medium and evaluate its effectiveness through targeted research. The capabilities of Internet delivery of services will expand rapidly as the use of sound and video becomes more feasible. These early guidelines will need constant monitoring and revision as research data become available and additional capabilities become cost-feasible.

NCDA opposes discrimination against
any individual on the basis of race,
ethnicity, gender, sexual orientation,
age, mental/physical disability, or creed.

*Revised by the NCDA Board of Directors,
April 1994.*

© 2003 National Career Development Association
c/o Creative Management Alliance
10820 East 45th Street
Suite 210
Tulsa, OK 74146
tel: (918) 663-7060
fax: (918) 663-7058
toll-free: (866) 367-6232

Appendix J-5

ACES Guidelines for Online Instruction in Counselor Education*

ACES Technology Interest Network (1999)

COURSE QUALITY:

1. **The course must offer, at a minimum, an equivalent educational opportunity to that provided in a traditional course. This should include equality in the domains of information, skill building, and course evaluation.**

   Discussion: Distance learning offerings should be held accountable to the same standards for quality as traditional courses. Objectives which cannot be maintained at the same level, and which cannot be reasonably modified or replaced with equivalent objectives, should be delivered in a traditional format.

2. **Specific course content must be amenable to effective delivery in the manner proposed.**

   Discussion: Some courses may readily lend themselves to many distance learning formats. Other courses may lend themselves to only a limited range of formats, while some may not be appropriate for distance delivery. In deciding when and how to deliver instruction outside of a traditional framework, faculty should focus on specific objectives, and determine the best manner in which to meet each group of learning objectives.

3. **Reasonable efforts must be taken by the institution to ensure that the student has been responsible for course work submitted.**

   Discussion: Some arrangement needs to be made to attempt to ensure that the registered student has completed the required course work. This does not necessarily mean that every course will require some direct meeting, but at some point a direct meeting where the identity of the student can be verified, and a thorough evaluation of all distance courses and student learning can be completed should be included. One alternative may be to use proctored exams which can be administered at distance sites.

4. **Distance learning courses must provide an opportunity for the students to be actively engaged in a learning process beyond simply reviewing text-based material, if the parallel traditional course provides opportunities beyond the review of text-based materials.**

   Discussion: Current learning theory suggests that appropriate education of adults involves opportunities to process information, formulate solutions to real world problems, and apply abstract theoretical models to specific settings and situations. Traditional classrooms provide opportunity for student interaction, social construction of knowledge and human contact that cannot be replicated simply by reviewing text materials. Distance learning offerings need to carefully consider how to replicate these experiences to provide a broad range of learning opportunity.

5. **Distance learning courses should not be limited to a recreation of a traditional face-to-face course but should be specifically designed to take advantage of educational opportunities provided by the medium used to deliver the course.**

   Discussion: To provide the most effective educational opportunities available, instructors must fully utilize the tools available to them, and build upon the strength of each tool utilized. Advanced technology offers the opportunity to develop new approaches to learning that take full advantage of the technology to move beyond what has been done in the past.

6. **The differential impact on student learning which is likely to occur to those students taught in a distance fashion must be considered, and any potential problems must be guarded against or steps for redemption provided.**

   Discussion: It is unclear at the current time if distance education approaches are equal in all respects to more traditional instructional settings. In some cases, students may gain more, while in others they may gain less. To ensure appropriate educational standards, a range of potential outcomes should be assessed including skills, knowledge, attitudes, personal development, and professional orientation. Distance courses should meet the needs of students in each domain, or steps must be taken to ensure that student's needs in those domains not met through distance education are met in an alternative format.

7. **In those cases where distance classes provide for a meeting opportunity for students, the meeting environment should be one that is supportive of and conducive to the educational process.**
   Discussion: Not all physical environments meet the needs for educational meetings. If groups of students are meeting in a face-to-face setting, the physical space provided must be adequately designed and equipped to meet the specific needs of the learning group.

8. **As in all courses at the University level, issues of equity and diversity should be addressed and promoted in a distance environment.**
   Discussion: A variety of variables influence individual students' communication styles, learning needs, and behavioral patterns. Approaches to distance education may not meet the needs of all students, and the instructor and institution involved have a responsibility to monitor student behavior, learning, and communication to ensure that individual needs are met, and individual differences are recognized as strengths and, as appropriate, built upon.

COURSE CONTENT/OBJECTIVES:

9. **Distance based classes should be designed to meet a specific need.**
   Discussion: Distance education opportunities should be judiciously and wisely chosen to meet a specific set of needs. The availability of technology does not dictate its use anymore than the availability of medication suggests it is the best response to all clients. By focusing on specific needs and working to meet these, institutions can ensure that distance offerings are beneficial.

10. **Because counseling courses often involve the exchange of sensitive information about clients and students, security precautions need to be implemented and enforced that ensure appropriate protection of this information.**
    Discussion: Client and Student confidentiality will be maintained via methods such as, but not limited to, data encryption, pseudonym use, password protection on various access levels to the Internet and other communication programs, and a method of security for the verification of postal delivery of sensitive information.

11. **If the objectives for a specific distance class are different than those for an on-campus class, then appropriate steps must be taken to ensure that every distance student receives appropriate redemption to meet all objectives.**
    Discussion: Programs which provide opportunities for students to learn at a distance must ensure that the educational opportunities provided for all students are equivalent. In some cases, certain objectives may not be appropriately addressed through some distance modalities. In those cases, equivalent opportunities may be provided through alternative formats to ensure student success.

12. **Appropriate procedures for evaluation of student learning must be implemented.**

INSTRUCTIONAL SUPPORT:

13. **Students must have access to equivalent educational supports including library resources, tutorial assistance, and access to the course instructor.**
    Discussion: The University experience expands beyond the walls of the individual classroom, and the information provided in a text. A variety of support materials, ancillary contacts and personal relationships are successfully combined in a well balanced academic environment. Care must be taken to move beyond simply providing class lectures or reading material on-line to incorporating the entirety of the academic experience that the student otherwise would have in a traditional setting.

14. **Students must be provided with the opportunity to receive complete training in the technology prior to being required to use the technology and should be provided with ongoing support throughout the educational experience.**
    Discussion: Just as faculty cannot be expected to maintain currency in all aspects of technology, neither can students. Clear expectations should be established prior to enrollment in a course about the student's competencies in relation to the use of specific technology. If students who are enrolled do not meet these competencies, than it is the responsibility of the institution to provide training and support to help students in those areas where skills and knowledge are lacking. If during the period of time that a student is receiving instruction the interface, technological demands, or other aspects of technology change, the institution must take reasonable steps to ensure that students are trained/retrained to adequately handle these changes. Institutions have a responsibility to provide adequate support services that can be readily accessed to resolve student difficulties that result from a lack of knowledge or skills, changes in software or equipment, software or equipment malfunction, or other circumstances over which the institution has control or responsibility

15. **Financial resources must be available to meet the needs of the distance learning activities.**
    Discussion: Institutions should be aware prior to undertaking distance based educational offerings that standard

methods of calculating the institution's financial commitment and needs may not be applicable to new modalities. In all cases, institutions must, in advance, make the necessary financial commitment to ensure that student needs are met

16. **Students must be provided with adequate access to faculty in a timely fashion.**

    Discussion: This may occur through the use of specific electronic media as long as students have been provided the opportunity for appropriate training.

17. **The specific purpose and outcomes of a distance delivery method is to be explained prior to the beginning of the course and included in the syllabus.**

    Discussion: For most students, distance learning opportunities will be new. Prior to agreeing to participate in this environment, students must have adequate information about the course, procedures, and expectations to make an informed decision about the appropriateness of this modality in meeting their own learning goals.

18. **Appropriate policies must be developed and disseminated concerning expectations for student attendance, time commitments, and other faculty expectations for performance.**

19. **Courses need to reflect sound pedagogy, and where appropriate, opportunities for student interaction and collaboration on specific course materials must be provided.**

20. **Support resources, such as books, videos, computer software, must be made available to students in a manner that is reasonable for those students who have enrolled in an on-line or distance class.**

    Discussion: If services are anticipated to be provided to students at a long distance from the main campus, than reasonable steps must be taken to provide those students with access to support materials at distance sites—or the students must be fully informed in advance that they will not have access and that there will be portions of the learning opportunity that they will not be able to participate in.

FACULTY QUALIFICATIONS:

21. **Faculty instructing distance education courses should be of equivalent experience and eligible for academic rank in the same manner as their on-site counterparts.**

    Discussion: Faculty involved in distance learning opportunities need to be fully involved in all aspects of the academic program, just as they would be if they were involved in more traditional offerings. While some distinctions in qualifications may be appropriate in terms of knowledge of technology or other specialty areas, the breadth and degree of training and experience should be as extensive as any other faculty member.

22. **Faculty must be fully trained in all aspects of the technology that is used to deliver the course, and continuous ongoing support must be provided by the educational institution.**

    Discussion: The faculty member delivering instruction needs to have the requisite skills necessary to successfully implement the effective use of whatever teaching tools are used in the delivery of material. However, faculty outside of computer oriented disciplines cannot be expected to stay current in the rapidly evolving field of computers and related technology. Therefore, institutions that use advanced technology as a delivery tool must be prepared to provide the support necessary to ensure that these tools are used appropriately. This must include support in the design, delivery, student access, and updating of on-line or computer based materials.

23. **In those cases where appropriate, qualified mentors or discussion leaders are required, the same standards must exist for determining quality and ability of these support personnel as would be used in a traditional setting.**

24. **Faculty assignment to distance education courses must reflect the actual faculty involvement, including adequate time and resources for faculty training, course preparation, and technology adaptation.**

    Discussion: Faculty who undertake to teach classes at a distance are substantially increasing their responsibilities in ways that many institutions are unprepared to understand and acknowledge. Institutions are responsible to monitor faculty behavior and involvement, to assist faculty in transitioning to new modalities of teaching, and to adequately compensate faculty for the additional time necessary to succeed in this new arena.

INSTRUCTOR/COURSE EVALUATION:

25. **Course/instructor evaluations for distance classes must be implemented to be commensurate with procedures used for evaluation of classes taught through traditional methods. Students participating in distance classes must be given the opportunity to provide course/instructor evaluations anonymously (e.g., by returning evaluations via the U.S. Postal Service).**

TECHNOLOGICAL STANDARDS:

26. **Technological problems will occur that will require appropriate back-up and/or face-to-face technologies.**

    Discussion: These back-up technologies should be designed to maintain the integrity of the course in a manner that provides as little disruption to student learning as possible. If student learning is disrupted or a student cannot compete a course due to technological issues that are the responsibility of the educational institution, then the institution is responsible for providing the student with alternative means that will meet their specific needs in relation to the original learning contract.

GRIEVANCE PROCEDURES:

27. Procedures to address grievances of the student must be implemented.

ACES TECHNOLOGY INTEREST NETWORK MEMBERS**

Thomas H. Hohenshil - Chair
Annette Albrecht
Ed Butler
Robert J. Chapman

Scott Christie
Harry Daniels
David Delmonico
Gary Goodnough
Grafton Eliason
Hildy Getz
Cary Houseman
Keith Iris
Marty Jencius
Wayne Lanning
David Lundberg
Dolores Jenerson Madden
Jane Myers
Theresa M. O'Halloran
Patrick B Romine
Russ Sabella
Robert J. Slencak II
Holly Stadler
Michael Tyler
Larry Tyson

*Endorsed by ACES Executive Council, May, 1999.
**Special appreciation is extended to Harry Daniels, Scott Christie, and Michael Tyler for their leadership in the development of these Guidelines.
Reprinted by permission of the Association for Counselor Education and Supervision, 5999 Stevenson Avenue, Alexandria, VA 22304.
http://www.acesonline.net/onlineguidelines.htm

Appendix K

Clinical Supervision Model Agreement*

I, Theodore P. Remley, Jr., agree to provide supervision for you for the purposes of becoming a Licensed Professional Counselor in the state of Louisiana.

I am licensed by the state of Louisiana as a Professional Counselor. I am also licensed as a Professional Counselor in Virginia and Mississippi. I hold M.Ed., Ed.S., and Ph.D. degrees in counseling from the University of Florida. I am a National Certified Counselor (NCC). In the past, I have served as a high school counselor, community college counselor, university career counselor, counselor educator, community mental health center counselor, and counselor in private practice. My areas of counseling expertise include personal and social adjustment, relationship issues, career decision-making, work adjustment, divorce mediation, anger management, and serious mental illnesses.

It is your responsibility to obtain the degree necessary, meet the specific course content requirements, and complete the required practicum and internship necessary to register our supervision with the Louisiana Licensed Professional Counselors Board of Examiners (LPC Board) so that you may obtain the status of Intern. You must complete the LPC Board "Registration of Supervision" form and include all attachments. I will complete the section of the form for the supervisor, will provide you with a copy of my "Declaration of Practice and Procedures," and will sign where necessary. You must then submit the form to the LPC Board for approval.

The supervision I provide for you will be individual supervision. You will meet with me one hour each week during the time you are completing your required 3,000 hours of supervised experience as a counselor intern. The hourly fee for my services is $_____, which has been set according to a fee schedule based on the income of you and your spouse or partner. This fee schedule will be reviewed annually and adjusted as appropriate. Fees are payable by check before each supervision session begins. In the event you must reschedule a session for some reason, you must notify me 24 hours in advance. If such notice is not received, you must pay the full fee for the missed session plus the fee for the current session prior to the next scheduled session. If you miss a session for circumstances beyond your control and were unable to contact me prior to missing the session, no fee will be charged.

Once our supervision relationship has been approved and you have been granted Intern status, our supervisory relationship will begin. Our professional relationship will be limited to the formal scheduled hours we have agreed to for your supervision. In the event situations occur in your role as counselor in which you need direction and advice, you should consult your immediate supervisor at the site where you are providing counseling services and follow his or her direction. My regular hourly fee for supervision must be paid by you for any telephone or face-to-face consultation requested by you outside our regularly scheduled supervision sessions.

*NOTE: This agreement was developed specifically to provide supervision to counselors preparing to be licensed as Professional Counselors in Louisiana. It should be modified to reflect the specific purpose and circumstances of supervision relationships.

My philosophy of supervision is that my role as your clinical supervisor is to assist you in practicing counseling in the most effective manner possible, given your choice of counseling theories, approaches, and interventions. I will review your work and give you my impressions of your strengths and weakness and will assist you in improving your skills as a counselor. In addition, I will evaluate your work on a continuing basis.

It is your responsibility to notify your administrative supervisor at the site or sites where you are collecting your hours of experience that you are receiving clinical supervision from me. You should explain the nature of our supervisory relationship. If your administrative supervisor wishes to consult with me regarding your work, ask him or her to contact me.

In order for me to supervise you, you must be able to audiotape or videotape one counseling session each week. You must follow any requirements your site or sites may impose regarding these tapes. At each meeting we have, you will provide me with a new tape. During the time the tape is in my possession, I shall ensure no one else has access to it. I will keep information revealed in the tape confidential. I will review the tape before our next meeting and will return the tape to you at that next meeting. It will then be your responsibility to erase or destroy the tape that has been reviewed.

During the time I am serving as your clinical supervisor, I will make every effort to review with you cases that you choose to bring to my attention for consultation. In addition, I will review the tapes you provide to me of counseling session. My duty to you is to provide you with professional clinical supervision. However, I will not be responsible for your day-to-day activities as a counseling intern. Your administrative supervisor or supervisors at your site or sites will be responsible for your ongoing counseling activities.

Because I must evaluate your professional performance as a counselor intern, we will not have a personal friendship during the time I am serving as your supervisor. While we may have a congenial and collegial professional relationship and may attend social functions together, we should not include each other in social interactions one of us has initiated. Please do not offer me gifts or invite me to your home or nonprofessional social events you are hosting during the time I am serving as your clinical supervisor.

You must complete a total of 3,000 hours of supervised experience. When you have completed the first 1,000 hours, I will provide you with a written evaluation of your progress and performance, including my determination of whether you are progressing satisfactorily toward your goal of becoming a Licensed Professional Counselor. I will provide you with another written evaluation at the end of the second 1,000 hours. At the end of your total 3,000 hours of supervised experience, I will verify the supervision I have provided to you to the LPC Board and will either recommend or not recommend you for licensure as a Professional Counselor.

I agree to provide clinical supervision to you of your counseling responsibilities in a professional manner to the extent described within this agreement. Our relationship is limited to the terms and conditions set forth herein. Either of us, with a two-week written notice to the other, may cancel this agreement for any reason. In the event the agreement is canceled by either of us, you agree to notify the LPC Board immediately.

By signing below, I am agreeing to provide you with clinical supervision according to the terms of this agreement, and you are agreeing to pay my fee and comply with the terms of this agreement as well.

Theodore P. Remley, Jr.	Date	Supervisee's Signature	Date

Appendix L

Ethical Guidelines for Counseling Supervisors

ASSOCIATION FOR COUNSELOR EDUCATION AND SUPERVISION

Adopted by ACES Executive Counsel and Delegate Assembly March, 1993

PREAMBLE:

The Association for Counselor Education and Supervision (ACES) is composed of people engaged in the professional preparation of counselors and people responsible for the on-going supervision of counselors. ACES is a founding division of the American Counseling Association (ACA) and as such adheres to ACA's current ethical standards and to general codes of competence adopted throughout the mental health community.

ACES believes that counselor educators and counseling supervisors in universities and in applied counseling settings, including the range of education and mental health delivery systems, carry responsibilities unique to their job roles. Such responsibilities may include administrative supervision, clinical supervision, or both. Administrative supervision refers to those supervisory activities which increase the efficiency of the delivery of counseling services; whereas, clinical supervision includes the supportive and educative activities of the supervisor designed to improve the application of counseling theory and technique directly to clients.

Counselor educators and counseling supervisors encounter situations which challenge the help given by general ethical standards of the profession at large. These situations require more specific guidelines that provide appropriate guidance in everyday practice.

The Ethical Guidelines for Counseling Supervisors are intended to assist professionals by helping them:

1. Observe ethical and legal protection of clients' and supervisee's rights;
2. Meet the training and professional development needs of supervisees in ways consistent with clients' welfare and programmatic requirements; and
3. Establish policies, procedures, and standards for implementing programs.

The specification of ethical guidelines enables ACES members to focus on and to clarify the ethical nature of responsibilities held in common. Such guidelines should be reviewed formally every five years, or more often if needed, to meet the needs of ACES members for guidance.

The Ethical Guidelines for Counselor Educators and Counseling Supervisors are meant to help ACES members in conducting supervision. ACES is not currently in a position to hear complaints about alleged non-compliance with these guidelines. Any complaints about the ethical behavior of any ACA member should be measured against the ACA Ethical Standards and a complaint lodged with ACA in accordance with its procedures for doing so.

One overriding assumption underlying this document is that supervision should be ongoing throughout a counselor's career and not stop when a particular level of education, certification, or membership in a professional organization is attained.

DEFINITIONS OF TERMS:

Applied Counseling Settings—Public or private organizations of counselors such as community mental health centers, hospitals, schools, and group or individual private practice settings.

Supervisees—Counselors-in-training in university programs at any level who working with clients in applied settings as part of their university training program, and counselors who have completed their formal education and are employed in an applied counseling setting.

Supervisors—Counselors who have been designated within their university or agency to directly oversee the professional clinical work of counselors. Supervisors also may be persons who offer supervision to counselors seeking state licensure and so provide supervision outside of the administrative aegis of an applied counseling setting.

1. Client Welfare and Rights

1.01 The Primary obligation of supervisors is to train counselors so that they respect the integrity and promote the welfare of their clients. Supervisors should have supervisees inform clients that they are being supervised and that observation and/or recordings of the session may be reviewed by the supervisor.

1.02 Supervisors who are licensed counselors and are conducting supervision to aid a supervisee to become licensed should instruct the supervisee not to communicate or in any way convey to the supervisee's clients or to other parties that the supervisee is himself/herself licensed.

1.03 Supervisors should make supervisees aware of clients' rights, including protecting clients' right to privacy and confidentiality in the counseling relationship and the information resulting from it. Clients also should be informed that their right to privacy and confidentiality will not be violated by the supervisory relationship.

1.04 Records of the counseling relationship, including interview notes, test data, correspondence, the electronic storage of these documents, and audio and videotape recordings, are considered to be confidential professional information. Supervisors should see that these materials are used in counseling, research, and training and supervision of counselors with the full knowledge of the clients and that permission to use these materials is granted by the applied counseling setting offering service to the client. This professional information is to be used for full protection of the client. Written consent from the client (or legal guardian, if a minor) should be secured prior to the use of such information for instructional, supervisory, and/or research purposes. Policies of the applied counseling setting regarding client records also should be followed.

1.05 Supervisors shall adhere to current professional and legal guidelines when conducting research with human participants such as Section D-1 of the ACA Ethical Standards.

1.06 Counseling supervisors are responsible for making every effort to monitor both the professional actions, and failures to take action, of their supervisees.

2. Supervisory Role

Inherent and integral to the role of supervisor are responsibilities for:

a. Monitoring client welfare;

b. encouraging compliance with relevant legal, ethical, and professional standards for clinical practice;

c. monitoring clinical performance and professional development of supervisees; and

d. evaluating and certifying current performance and potential of supervisees for academic, screening, selection, placement, employment, and credentialing purposes.

2.01 Supervisors should have had training in supervision prior to initiating their role as supervisors.

2.02 Supervisors should pursue professional and personal continuing education activities such as advanced courses, seminars, and professional conferences on a regular and ongoing basis. These activities should include both counseling and supervision topics and skills.

2.03 Supervisors should make their supervisees aware of professional and ethical standards and legal responsibilities of the counseling profession.

2.04 Supervisors of post-degree counselors who are seeking state licensure should encourage these counselors to adhere to the standards for practice established by the state licensure board of the state in which they practice.

2.05 Procedures for contacting the supervisor, or an alternative supervisor, to assist in handling crisis situations should be established and communicated to supervisees.

2.06 Actual work samples via audio and/or video tape or live observation in addition to case notes should be reviewed by the supervisor as a regular part of the ongoing supervisory process.

2.07 Supervisors of counselors should meeting regularly in face-to-face sessions with their supervisees.

2.08 Supervisors should provide supervisees with ongoing feedback on their performance. This feedback should take a variety of forms, both formal and informal, and should include verbal and written evaluations. It should be formative during the supervisory experience and summative at the conclusion of the experience.

2.09 Supervisors who have multiple roles (e.g., teacher, clinical supervisor, administrative supervisor, etc.) with supervisees should minimize potential conflicts. Where possible, the roles should be divided among several supervisors. Where this is not possible, careful explanation should be conveyed to the supervisee as to the expectations and responsibilities associated with each supervisory role.

2.10 Supervisors should not participate in any form of sexual contact with supervisees. Supervisors should not engage in any form of social contact or interaction which would compromise the supervisor-supervisee relationship. Dual relationships with supervisees that might impair the supervisor's objectivity and professional judgment should be avoided and/or the supervisory relationship terminated.

2.11 Supervisors should not establish a psychotherapeutic relationship as a substitute for supervision. Personal issues should be addressed in supervision only in terms of the impact of these issues on clients and on professional functioning.

2.12 Supervisors, through ongoing supervisee assessment and evaluation, should be aware of any personal or professional limitations of supervisees which are likely to impede future professional performance. Supervisors have the responsibility of recommending remedial assistance to the supervisee and of screening from the training program, applied counseling setting, or state licensure those supervisees who are unable to provide competent professional services. These recommendations should be clearly and professionally explained in writing to the supervisees who are so evaluated.

2.13 Supervisors should not endorse a supervisee for certification, licensure, completion of an academic training program, or continued employment if the supervisor believes the supervisee is impaired in any way that would interfere with the performance of counseling duties. The presence of any such impairment should begin a process of feedback and remediation wherever possible so that the supervisee understands the nature of the impairment and has the opportunity to remedy the problem and continue with his/her professional development.

2.14 Supervisors should incorporate the principles of informed consent and participation; clarity of requirements, expectations, roles and rules; and due process and appeal into the establishment of policies and procedures of their institutions, program, courses, and individual supervisory relationships. Mechanisms for due process appeal of individual supervisory actions should be established and made available to all supervisees.

3. Program Administration Role

3.01 Supervisors should ensure that the programs conducted and experiences provided are in keeping with current guidelines and standards of ACA and its divisions.

3.02 Supervisors should teach courses and/or supervise clinical work only in areas where they are fully competent and experienced.

3.03 To achieve the highest quality of training and supervision, supervisors should be active participants in peer review and peer supervision procedures.

3.04 Supervisors should provide experiences that integrate theoretical knowledge and practical application. Supervisors also should provide opportunities in which supervisees are able to apply the knowledge they have learned and understand the rationale for the skills they have acquired. The knowledge and skills conveyed should reflect current practice, research findings, and available resources.

3.05 Professional competencies, specific courses, and/or required experiences expected of supervisees should be communicated to them in writing prior to admission to the training program or placement/employment by the applied counseling setting, and, in case of continued employment, in a timely manner.

3.06 Supervisors should accept only those persons as supervisees who meet identified entry level requirements for admission to a program of counselor training or for placement in an applied counseling setting. In the case of private supervision in search of state licensure, supervisees should have completed all necessary prerequisites as determined by the state licensure board.

3.07 Supervisors should inform supervisees of the goals, policies, theoretical orientations toward counseling, training, and supervision model or approach on which the supervision is based.

3.08 Supervisees should be encouraged and assisted to define their own theoretical orientation toward counseling, to establish supervision goals for themselves, and to monitor and evaluate their progress toward meeting these goals.

3.09 Supervisors should assess supervisees' skills and experience in order to establish standards for competent professional behavior. Supervisors should restrict supervisees' activities to those that are commensurate with their current level of skills and experiences.

3.10 Supervisors should obtain practicum and fieldwork sites that meet minimum standards for preparing student to become effective counselors. No practicum or fieldwork setting should be approved unless it truly replicates a counseling work setting.

3.11 Practicum and fieldwork classes would be limited in size according to established professional standards to ensure that each student has ample opportunity for individual supervision and feedback. Supervisors in applied counseling settings should have a limited number of supervisees.

3.12 Supervisors in university settings should establish and communicate specific policies and procedures regarding field placement of students. The respective roles of the student counselor, the university supervisor, and the field supervisor should be clearly differentiated in areas such as evaluation, requirements, and confidentiality.

3.13 Supervisors in training programs should communicate regularly with supervisors in agencies used as practicum and/or fieldwork sites regarding current professional practices, expectations of students, and preferred models and modalities of supervision.

3.14 Supervisors at the university should establish clear lines of communication among themselves, the field supervisors, and the students/supervisees.

3.15 Supervisors should establish and communicate to supervisees and to field supervisors specific procedures regarding consultation, performance review, and evaluation of supervisees.

3.16 Evaluations of supervisee performance in universities and in applied counseling settings should be available to supervisees in ways consistent with the Family Rights and Privacy Act and the Buckley Amendment.

3.17 Forms of training that focus primarily on self understanding and problem resolution (e.g., personal growth groups or individual counseling) should be voluntary. Those who conduct these forms of training should not serve simultaneously as supervisors of the supervisees involved in the training.

3.18 A supervisor may recommend participation in activities such as personal growth groups or personal counseling when it has been determined that a supervisee has deficits in the areas of self understanding and problem resolution which impede his/her professional functioning. The supervisors should not be the direct provider of these activities for the supervisee.

3.19 When a training program conducts a personal growth or counseling experience involving relatively intimate self disclosure, care should be taken to eliminate or minimize potential role conflicts for faculty and/or agency supervisors who may conduct these experiences and who also serve as teachers, group leaders, and clinical directors.

3.20 Supervisors should use the following prioritized sequence in resolving conflicts among the needs of the client, the needs of the supervisee, and the needs of the program or agency. Insofar as the client much be protected, it should be understood that client welfare is usually subsumed in federal and state laws such that these statutes should be the first point of reference. Where laws and ethical standards are not present or are unclear, the good judgment of the supervisor should be guided by the following list.
   a. Relevant legal and ethical standards (e.g., duty to warn, state child abuse laws, etc.);
   b. Client welfare;
   c. Supervisee welfare;
   d. Supervisor welfare; and
   e. Program and/or agency service and administrative needs.

Reprinted by permission of the Association for Counselor Education and Supervision, 5999 Stevenson Avenue, Alexandria, VA 22304.

References

Abbott, A. (1988). *The system of professions: An essay on the division of expert labor.* Chicago: University of Chicago Press.

Abraham, S. C. (1978). *The public accounting profession: Problems and prospects.* Lexington, MA: Lexington Books.

Adarand Constructors, Inc. v. Pena, 515 U.S. 200, 115 S.Ct. 2097, 132 L.Ed.2d 158 (1995).

Administration on Aging. (1998). Aging into the 21st century. Retrieved July 3, 2003, from http://www.aoa.dhhs.gov/aoa/stats/aging21/

Age Discrimination in Employment Act of 1967, 29 U.S.C. §621 *et seq.* (1999)

Age Discrimination in Employment Act of 1975, 42 U.S.C. §§1601 *et seq.* (1999)

Ahia, C. E., & Martin, D. (1993). *The danger-to-self-or-others exception to confidentiality.* Alexandria, VA: American Counseling Association.

Akamatsu, T. J. (1988). Intimate relationships with former clients: National survey of attitudes and behavior among practitioners. *Professional Psychology: Research and Practice, 199,* 454–458.

Alberty, S. C. (1989). *Advising small business.* Deerfield, IL: Callaghan & Company.

Allen, M., Burt, K., Bryan, E., Carter, D., Orsi, R., & Durkan, L. (2002). School counselors' preparation for and participation in crisis intervention. *Professional School Counseling, 6,* 96–102.

Allison v. Patel, 211 Ga. App. 376, 438 S.E.2d 920 (1993).

American Association for Marriage and Family Therapists. (1991). *Code of ethics.* Washington, DC: Author.

American Association of State Counseling Boards. (2005). Retrieved November 3, 2005, from http://www.aascb.org/lpcchart

American Bar Association. (1999). Legal malpractice claims in the 1990s. [On-line] Available at http://www.kvi-calbar.com/abaclaimdata.html. Washington, DC: Author.

American Counseling Association. (1995). *Code of ethics and standards of practice.* Alexandria, VA: Author.

American Counseling Association. (1998). *Early warning, timely response: A guide to safe schools.* Alexandria, VA: Author.

American Educational Research Association. (1999). *Standards for educational and psychological testing.* Washington, DC: Author.

American Psychiatric Association. (2000). *Diagnostic and statistical manual of mental disorders* (4th ed., text revision). Washington, DC: Author.

American Psychological Association. (1982). *Ethical principles in the conduct of research with human participants.* Washington, DC: Author.

American Psychological Association. (1993). Record keeping guidelines. *American Psychologist 48,* 984–986.

American Psychological Association. (2002). *Ethical principles of psychologists and code of conduct.* Washington, DC: Author.

Anastasi, A. (1988). *Psychological testing* (6th ed.). New York: Macmillan.

Anderson, B. S. (1996). *The counselor and the law* (4th ed.). Alexandria, VA: American Counseling Association.

Anderson, C. E. (2000). Dealing constructively with managed care: Suggestions from an insider. *Journal of Mental Health Counseling, 22,* 343–353.

Anderson, D., & Swanson, C. D. (1994). *Legal issues in licensure.* Alexandria, VA: American Counseling Association.

Anderson, S. K., & Kitchener, K. S. (1996). Nonromantic, nonsexual post-therapy relationships between psychologists and former clients: An exploratory study of critical incidents. *Professional Psychology: Research and Practice, 27,* 59–66.

Aponte, J. F., & Wohl, J. (2000). *Psychological intervention and cultural diversity.* Boston: Allyn & Bacon.

Appelbaum, P. S., Lidz, C. W., & Meisel, A. (1987). *Informed consent: Legal theory and clinical practice.* New York: Oxford University Press.

Applebaum, P. (1993). Legal liability and managed care. *American Psychologist, 48,* 251–257.

Application of Striegel, 92 Misc2d 113, 399 N.Y.S.2d 584 (1977).

Arias, I., Samios, M., & O'Leary, K. D. (1987). Prevalence and correlates of physical aggression during courtship. *Journal of Interpersonal Violence, 2,* 82–90.

Arredondo, P., Toporek, R., Brown, S. P., Jones, J., Locke, D., Sanchez, J., et al. (1996). Operationalization of the multicultural counseling competencies. *Journal of Multicultural Counseling and Development, 24,* 42–78.

Arthur, G. L., Jr., & Swanson, C. D. (1993). *Confidentiality and privileged communication.* Alexandria, VA: American Counseling Association.

Association for Counselor Education and Supervision. (1977). Standards for the preparation of counselors and other personnel service specialists. *Personnel and Guidance Journal, 55,* 596–601.

Association for Counselor Education and Supervision. (1990). Standards for counseling supervisors. *Journal of Counseling and Development, 69,* 30–32.

Association for Counselor Education and Supervision. (1993). *Ethical guidelines for counseling supervisors.* Retrieved on October 4, 2003, from http://www.acesonline.net/ethicalguidelines.htm

Association for Counselor Education and Supervision. (1999a). *ACES guidelines for online instruction in counselor education.* Retrieved on October 4, 2003, from http://www.acesonline.net/onlineguidelines.htm

Association for Counselor Education and Supervision. (1999b). *Technical competencies for counselor education students: Recommended guidelines for program development.* Retrieved on October 4, 2003, from http://www.acesonline.net/competencies.htm

Association for Specialists in Group Work. (1989). *Ethical guidelines for group counselors.* Alexandria, VA: Author.

Association for Specialists in Group Work. (1992). *Professional standards for the training of group workers.* Alexandria, VA: Author.

Association for Specialists in Group Work. (1998a). ASGW best practice guidelines. *Journal for Specialists in Group Work, 23,* 237–244.

Association for Specialists in Group Work. (1998b). *Principles for diversity-competent group workers.* Alexandria, VA: Author.

Atkinson, D. R., Thompson, C. E., & Grant, S. K. (1993). A three-dimensional model for counseling racial/ethnic minorities. *The Counseling Psychologist, 21,* 257–277.

Austin, K. M., Moline, M. E., & Williams, G. T. (1990). *Confronting malpractice: Legal and ethical dilemmas in psychotherapy.* Newbury Park, CA: Sage.

Axelson, J. A. (1993). *Counseling and development in a multicultural society* (2nd ed.). Pacific Grove, CA: Brooks/Cole.

Baird, K. A., & Rupert, P. A. (1987). Clinical management of confidentiality: A survey of psychologists in seven states. *Professional Psychology: Research and Practice, 18,* 347–352.

Bakke v. Regents of the University of California, 438 U.S. 265 (1978).

Barrett, K. A., & McWhirter, B. T. (2002). Counselor trainees' perceptions of clients based on client sexual orientation. *Counselor Education and Supervision, 41,* 219–232.

Bartell, P. A., & Rubin, L. J. (1990). Dangerous liaisons: Sexual intimacies in supervision. *Professional Psychology: Research and Practice, 21,* 442–450.

Beamish, P. M., Navin, S. L., & Davidson, P. (1994). Ethical dilemmas in marriage and family therapy: Implications for training. *Journal of Mental Health Counseling, 16,* 129–142.

Beauchamp, T. L., & Childress, J. F. (1994). *Principles of biomedical ethics* (3rd ed.). New York: Oxford University Press.

Beck, E. S. (1999). Mental health counseling: A stakeholder's manifesto. *Journal of Mental Health Counseling, 21,* 203–214.

Becker, R. F. (1997). *Scientific evidence and expert testimony handbook: A guide for lawyers, criminal investigators and forensic specialists.* Springfield, II: Charles C Thomas.

Behling, J., Curtis, C., & Foster, S. A. (1988). Impact of sex-role combinations on student performance in field instruction. *Clinical Supervisor, 6*(3), 161–168.

Belton, R., & Avery, D. (1999). *Employment discrimination law* (6th ed.). St. Paul, MN: West.

Bennett, A. G., & Werth, J. L. (2006). Working with clients who may harm themselves. In B. Herlihy & G. Corey, *ACA Ethical Standards Casebook* (6th ed., pp. 223–228).

Beren, P., & Bunnin, B. (1983). *Author law and strategies.* Berkeley, CA: Nolo Press.

Berg, J. (2001). Grave secrets: Legal and ethical analysis of postmortem confidentiality. *Connecticut Law Review, 34,* 81. Retrieved October 11, 2003, from http://seg802.ocs.lsu.edu: 2077/universe/document?_m=30d0e889893b7d842d26b9c0f863f2c6&_docnum=1&wchp=dGLbVzz-zSkVb&_md5=47 efdc4b305d91a1f8b6e8c52ec351f0

Berge, Z. L. (1994). Electronic discussion groups. *Communication education, 43,* 102–111.

Berlin, I. N. (1987). Suicide among American Indian adolescents: An overview. *Suicide & Life-Threatening Behavior, 17,* 218–232.

Berman, A. L., & Cohen-Sandler, R. (1982). Suicide and the standard of care: Optimal v. acceptable. *Suicide and Life-Threatening Behavior, 12,* 114–122.

Bernard, J. M., & Goodyear, R. K. (2004). *Fundamentals of clinical supervision* (3rd ed.). Boston: Allyn & Bacon.

Berner, M. (1998). Informed consent. In L. E. Lifson, & R. I. Simon (Eds.), *The mental health practitioner and the law* (pp. 23–43). Cambridge, MA: Harvard University Press.

Bernsen, A., Tabachnick, B. G., & Pope, K. S. (1994). National survey of social workers' sexual attraction to their clients: Results, implications, and comparison to psychologists. *Ethics & Behavior, 4,* 369–388.

Bernstein, B. E., & Hartsell, T. L., Jr. (1998). *The portable lawyer for mental health professionals.* New York: Wiley.

Bersoff, D. N. (1996). The virtue of principle ethics. *Counseling Psychologist, 24,* 86–91.

Biaggio, M., Paget, T. L., & Chenoweth, M. S. (1997). A model for ethical management of faculty-student dual relationships. *Professional Psychology: Research and Practice, 28,* 184–189.

Biele, N., & Barnhill, E. (1995). The art of advocacy. In J. C. Gonsiorek (Ed.), *Breach of trust: Sexual exploitation by health care professionals and clergy* (pp. 317–332). Thousand Oaks, CA: Sage.

Black, H. C. (1990). *Black's law dictionary* (6th ed.). St. Paul, MN: West.

Blevins-Knabe, B. (1992). The ethics of dual relationships in higher education. *Ethics and Behavior, 2,* 151–163.

Blocher, D. H. (1987). *The professional counselor.* New York: Macmillan.

Bograd, M. (1993, January/February). The duel over dual relationships. *The California Therapist,* 7–16.

Bogust v. Iverson. 10 Wisc.2d 129, 102 N.W.2d 228 (1960).

Bok, S. (1983). *Secrets: On the ethics of concealment and revelation.* New York: Vintage Books.

Boling v. Superior Court. 105 Cal. App.3d 430, 164 Cal. Rptr. 432 (App. 1980).

Borders, L. D. (1991). A systematic approach to peer group supervision. *Journal of Counseling and Development, 69,* 248–252.

Borders, L. D., Cashwell, C. S., & Rotter, J. C. (1995). Supervision of counselor licensure applicants: A comparative study. *Counselor Education and Supervision, 35,* 54–69.

Borders, L. D., & Leddick, G. R. (1987). *Handbook of counseling supervision.* Alexandria, VA: Association for Counselor Education and Supervision.

Borys, D. S. (1988). *Dual relationships between therapist and client: A national survey of clinicians' attitudes and practices.* Unpublished doctoral dissertation, University of California, Los Angeles.

Borys, D. S., & Pope, K. S. (1989). Dual relationships between therapist and client: A national study of psychologists, psychiatrists and social workers. *Professional Psychology: Research and Practice, 20,* 283–293.

Boughner, S. R., & Logan, J. P. (1999). Robert H. Woody: Legal issues in couple and family counseling. *The Family Journal, 7,* 302–310.

Bouhoutsos, J., Holroyd, J., Lerman, H., Forer, B., & Greenberg, M. (1983). Sexual intimacy between psychologists and patients. *Professional Psychology, 14,* 185–196.

Bowman, V. E., Hatley, L. D., & Bowman, R. L. (1995). Faculty–student relationships: The dual role controversy. *Counselor Education and Supervision, 34,* 232–242.

Braaten, E. E., Otto, S., & Handelsman, M. M. (1993). What do people want to know about psychotherapy? *Psychotherapy, 30,* 565–570.

Bradley, L. & Lewis, J. (2000). Introduction. In J. Lewis & L. Bradley (Eds.), *Advocacy in counseling: Counselors, clients & community* (pp. 3–4). Greensboro, NC: ERIC Clearinghouse on Counseling and Student Services.

Bradley, R. W., & Cox, J. A. (2001). Counseling: Evolution of the profession. In D. C. Locke, J. E. Myers, & E. L Herr (Eds.), *The handbook of counseling* (pp. 27–41). Thousand Oaks, CA: Sage.

Bray, J. H., Shepherd, J. N., & Hays, J. R. (1985). Legal and ethical issues in informed consent to psychotherapy. *American Journal of Family Therapy, 13,* 50–60.

Breaux, W. (2006). An inadvertent breach of confidentiality. In B. Herlihy & G. Corey, *ACA Ethical standards casebook* (6th ed., pp. 176–178). Alexandria, VA: American Counseling Association.

Brendel, J. M., & Nelson, K. W. (1999). The stream of family secrets: Navigating the islands of confidentiality and triangulation involving family therapists. *The Family Journal, 7,* 112–117.

Brinson, J., & Kottler, J. (1993). Cross-cultural mentoring in counselor education. *Counselor Education & Supervision, 32,* 241–254.

Brott, P. E., & Myers, J. E. (1999). Development of professional school counselor identity: A grounded theory. *Professional School Counseling, 2,* 339–348.

Broverman, I. K., Broverman, D., Clarkson, F. E., Rosencrantz, P., & Vogel, S. (1970). Sex role stereotypes and clinical judgments of mental health. *Journal of Consulting and Clinical Psychology, 34,* 1–7.

Brown, D. (1993). Training consultants: A call to action. *Journal of Counseling and Development, 72,* 139–143.

Brown v. Board of Education, 347 U.S. 483 (1954).

Brown, M. T., & Landrum-Brown, J. (1995). Counselor supervision: Cross-cultural perspectives. In J. C. Ponterotto, J. M. Casas, L. A. Suzuki, & C. M. Alexander (Eds), *Handbook of multicultural counseling* (pp. 263–286). Thousand Oaks, CA: Sage.

Burkemper, E. M. (2002). Family therapists' ethical decision-making processes in two duty-to-warn situations. *Journal of Martial and Family Therapy, 28,* 203–211.

Burn, D. (1992). Ethical implications in cross-cultural counseling and training. *Journal of Counseling and Developmemt. 70,* 578–583.

Bursztajn, H., Gutheil, T. G., Hamm, R. M., & Brodsky, A. (1983). Subjective data and suicide assessment in the light of recent legal developments. Part II: Clinical uses of legal standards in the interpretation of subjective data. *International Journal of Law and Psychiatry, 6,* 331–350.

Butler, S. F. (1998). *Assessment preparation and practices reported by mental health and related professionals.* Unpublished doctoral dissertation, University of New Orleans.

Calamari, J. D., Perillo, J. M., & Bender, H. H. (1989). *Cases and problems on contracts* (2nd ed.). St. Paul, MN: West.

Campbell, J. M. (2000). *Becoming an effective supervisor: A workbook for counselors and psychotherapists.* Philadelphia: Accelerated Development.

Canterbury v. Spence, 464 F.2d 772 (D.C. Cir 1972).

Cantor, P. (1976). Personality characteristics found among youthful female suicide attempters. *Journal of Abnormal Psychology, 85,* 324–329.

Caplow, T. (1966). The sequence of professionalization. In H. M. Vollmer & D. L. Mills (Eds.), *Professionalization* (pp.19–21). Upper Saddle River, NJ: Prentice-Hall.

Capuzzi, D. (1994). *Suicide prevention in the schools: Guidelines for middle and high school settings.* Alexandria, VA: American Counseling Association.

Capuzzi, D. (2002). Legal and ethical challenges in counseling suicidal students. *Professional School Counseling, 6,* 36–45.

Capuzzi, D., & Golden, L. (Eds.). (1988). *Preventing adolescent suicide.* Muncie, IN: Accelerated Development, Inc.

Carabillo, J. A. (1986). Liability for treatment decisions: How far does it extend? In C. M. Combe (Ed.), *Managed health care: Legal and operational issues facing providers, insurers, and employers* (pp. 341–407). New York: Practising Law Institute.

Carlson, J., Sperry, L., & Lewis, J. A. (1997). *Family therapy: Ensuring treatment efficacy.* Pacific Grove, CA: Brooks/Cole.

Carroll, T. (1994). [Online] Available at http://www.usq.edu.au/faculty/arts/journ/copyus.htm

Cashwell, C. C., Shcherbakova, J., & Cashwell, T. H. (2003). Effect of client and counselor ethnicity on preference for counselor self-disclosure. *Journal of Counseling & Development, 81,* 196–201.

Cavanagh, M. E. (1982). *The counseling experience.* Monterey, CA: Brooks/Cole.

Center for Credentialing and Education. (2003). *The ACS credential.* Retrieved October 4, 2003, from http://www.cce-global.org/acs.htm

Chafee, Z. (1943). Privileged communications: Is justice served or obstructed by closing the doctor's mouth on the witness stand? *Yale Law Journal, 52,* 607–612.

Chamallas, M. (1988). Consent, equality and the legal control of sexual conduct. *Southern California Law Review, 61,* 777–862.

Chauvin, J. C., & Remley, T. P., Jr. (1996). Responding to allegations of unethical conduct. *Journal of Counseling and Development, 74,* 563–568.

Christensen, L. L., & Miller, R. B. (2001). Marriage and family therapists evaluate managed mental health care: A qualitative inquiry. *Journal of Marital and Family Therapy, 27,* 509–514.

Christie, G. C., Meeks, J. E., Pryor, E. S., & Sanders, J. (1997). *Cases and materials on the law of torts* (3rd ed.). St. Paul, MN: West.

Chung, R. C., & Bemak, F. (2002). The relationship of culture and empathy in crosscultural counseling. *Journal of Counseling & Development, 80,* 154–159.

Claim of Gerkin, 106 Misc.2d 643,434 N.Y.S.2d 607 (1980).

Clausen v. Clausen, 675 P.2d 562 (Utah, 1983).

Clawson, T. W., & Henderson, D. A. (Eds., 2002). *Counselor preparation 2002-2003: Programs, faculty, trends* (11th ed.). Greensboro, NC: National Board of Certified Counselors.

Cleary, E. (Ed.). (1984). *McCormick's handbook on the law of evidence* (3rd ed.). St. Paul. MN: West.

Cohen, E. D. (1997). Ethical standards in counseling sexually active clients with HIV. In *Ethics in therapy* (pp. 211–233). New York: Hatherleigh.

Cohen, R. J. (1979). *Malpractice: A guide for mental health professionals.* New York: The Free Press.

Cohen, R. J., & Mariano, W. E. (1982). *Legal guidebook in mental health.* New York: The Free Press.

Coleman, P., & Shellow, R. A. (1992). Suicide: Unpredictable and unavoidable—Proposed guidelines provide rational test for physician's liability. *Nebraska Law Review, 71,* 643–693.

Collison, B. B. (2001). Professional associations, standards, and credentials in counseling. In D. C. Locke, J. E. Myers, & E. L Herr (Eds.), *The handbook of counseling* (pp. 55–68). Thousand Oaks, CA: Sage.

Commission on Rehabilitation Counselor Certification. (2003). *About CRCC.* Retrieved September 3, 2003, from http://www.nbcc.org/cert/checklist.htm *Commonwealth ex rel. Platt v. Platt,* 404 A.2d 410 (Pa. Super. 1979).

Comprehensive Alcohol Abuse and Alcoholism Prevention. Treatment and Rehabilitation Act of 1972, 42 U.S.C.A. §290dd-2 (West, 1997).

Comstock, G. D. (1991). *Violence against lesbians and gay men.* New York: Columbia University Press.

Connelly v. University of Vermont, 244 F.Supp. 156 (D.Vt. 1965).

Constantine, M. G. (2001a). Addressing racial, ethnic, gender, and social class issues in counselor training and practice. In D. B. Pope-Davis & H. L. K. Coleman (Eds.), *The intersection of race, class and gender in multicultural counseling* (pp. 341–350). Thousand Oaks, CA: Sage.

Constantine, M. G. (2001b). Perspectives on multicultural supervision. *Journal of Multicultural Counseling and Development, 29,* 98–101.

Constantine, M. G. (2002). The intersection of race, ethnicity, gender, and social class in counseling: Examining selves in cultural contexts. *Journal for Multicultural Counseling and Development, 30,* 210–215.

Conyne, R. K., & Horne, A. M. (2001). The current status of groups being used for prevention. *The Journal for Specialists in Group Work, 3,* 289–292.

Cook, D. A., & Helms, J. E. (1988). Visible racial/ethnic group supervisees' satisfaction with cross-cultural counseling as predicted by relationship characteristics. *Journal of Counseling Psychology, 35,* 268–274.

Cooper, C. C., & Gottlieb, M. C. (2000). Ethical issues with managed care: Challenges facing counseling psychology. *The Counseling Psychologist, 28,* 179–236.

Corcoran, M. E. (1989). Managing the risks in managed care. In M. E. Corcoran (Ed.), *Managed health care 1989* (pp. 7–70). New York: Practising Law Institute.

Corey, G. (2000). *Theory and practice of group counseling* (6th ed.). Pacific Grove, CA: Brooks/Cole.

Corey, G., Corey, M., & Callanan, P. (2007). *Issues and ethics in the helping professions* (7th ed.). Pacific Grove, CA: Brooks/Cole.

Costa, L., & Altekruse, M. (1994). Duty-to-warn guidelines for mental health counselors. *Journal of Counseling and Development, 72,* 346–350.

Cottle, M. (1956). Witnesses—Privilege-communications to psychotherapists. *University of Kansas Law Review, 4,* 597–599.

Cottone, R. R. (1985). The need for counselor licensure: A rehabilitation counseling perspective. *Journal of Counseling and Development, 63,* 625–629.

Cottone, R. R. (1992). *Theories and paradigms of counseling and psychotherapy.* Needham Heights, MA: Allyn & Bacon.

Cottone, R. R. (2001). A social constructivism model of ethical decision making in counseling. *Journal of Counseling & Development, 79,* 39–45.

Cottone, R. R. (2005). Detrimental therapist-client relationships – Beyond thinking of "dual" or "multiple" roles: Reflections on the 2001 *AAMFT Code of Ethics. American Journal of Family Therapy, 33,* 1–17.

Cottone, R. R., & Claus, R. E. (2000). Ethical decision-making models: A review of the literature. *Journal of Counseling & Development, 78,* 275–283.

Cottone, R. R., & Tarvydas, V. M. (2003). *Ethical and professional issues in counseling* (2nd ed.). Upper Saddle River, NJ: Merrill/Prentice Hall.

Council for Accreditation of Counseling and Related Educational Programs. (2001). *CACREP accreditation standards and procedures manual*. Alexandria. VA: Author.

Council for Accreditation of Counseling and Related Educational Programs. (2005). *Directory of CACREP accredited programs*. Retrieved November 3, 2005, from http://www.cacrep.org/directory.html

Cramton, R. C. (1981). Incompetence: The North American experience. In L. E. Trakman & D. Watters (Eds.), *Professional competence and the law* (pp. 158–163). Halifax, Nova Scotia, Canada: Dalhousie University.

Crane, D. R., & Law, D. D. (2002). Conducting medical offset research in a health maintenance organization: Challenges, opportunities, and insights. *Journal of Marital and Family Therapy, 28*, 15–19.

Crawford, R. L. (1994). *Avoiding counselor malpractice*. Alexandria, VA: American Counseling Association.

Crawford, R. (1999). Counseling a client whose family member is planning a suicide. *The Family Journal, 7*, 165–169.

Croteau, J. M., Talbot, D. M., Lance, T. S., & Evans, N. J. (2002). A qualitative study of the interplay between privilege and oppression. *Journal for Multicultural Counseling and Development, 30*, 239–258.

Curd, T. (1938). Privileged communications between the doctor and his patient—An anomaly of the law. *West Virginia Law Review, 44*, 165–174.

Curran, D. F. (1987). *Adolescent suicidal behavior*. Washington, DC: Hemisphere Publishing.

Cynthia B. v. New Rochelle Hospital, 86 A.D.2d 256, 449 N.Y.S.2d 755 (App. Div. 1982).

D'Andrea, M., & Arredondo, P. (2002, September). Multicultural competence: A national campaign. *Counseling Today, 33*, 36, 41.

Daniels, J. A. (2001). Managed care, ethics, and counseling. *Journal of Counseling & Development, 79*, 119–122.

Daniels, J. A. (2002). Assessing threats of school violence: Implications for counselors. *Journal of Counseling & Development, 80*, 215–218.

Daniluk, J. C., & Haverkamp, B. E. (1993). Ethical issues in counseling adult survivors of incest. *Journal of Counseling & Development, 72*, 16–22.

Danzinger, P. R., & Welfel, E. R. (2000). Age, gender, and health bias in counselors: An empirical analysis. *Journal of Mental Health Counseling, 22*, 135–149.

Danzinger, P. R., & Welfel, E. R. (2001). The impact of managed care on mental health counselors: A survey of perceptions, practices, and compliance with ethical standards. *Journal of Mental Health Counseling, 23*, 137–150.

Davidson, V. (1977) Psychiatry's problem with no name: Therapist–patient sex. *American Journal of Psychoanalysis, 37*, 43–50.

Davis, P. A. (1983). *Suicidal adolescents*. Springfield, IL: Charles C. Thomas.

Davis, J. L., & Mickelson, D. J. (1994). School counselors: Are you aware of ethical and legal aspects of counseling? *The School Counselor, 42*, 5–13.

Dean, L. A., & Meadows, M. E. (1995). College counseling: Union and intersection. *Journal of Counseling and Development, 74*, 139–142.

DeChiara, P. (1988). The need for universities to have rules on consensual sexual relationships between faculty members and students. *Columbia Journal of Law and Social Problems, 21*, 137–162.

Dedden, L., & James, S. (1998, Summer). A comprehensive guide to free career counseling resources on the Internet. *The ASCA Counselor, 17*, 19.

DeFunis v. Odegaard, 507 P.2d 1169 (Wash. 1973), dismissed as moot, 416 U.S. 312 (1973), on remand, 529 P.2d 438 (Wash. 1974).

DeRonde v. Regents of the University of California, 625 P.2d 220 (Cal. 1981).

Deutsch, C. J. (1985). A survey of therapists' personal problems and treatment. *Professional Psychology: Research and Practice, 16*, 305–315.

Dinkmeyer, D., Jr., Carlson, J., & Dinkmeyer, D. (1994). *Consultation: School mental health professionals as consultants*. Muncie, IN: Accelerated Development.

Donigian, J. (1991). Dual relationships: An ethical issue. *Together, 19*(2), 6–7.

Dorken, H., & Webb, J. T. (1980). 1976 third-party reimbursement experience: An interstate comparison by insurance carrier. *American Psychologist, 35*, 355–363.

Dougherty, A. M. (1995). *Consultation: Practice and perspectives in school and community settings* (2nd ed.). Pacific Grove, CA: Brooks/Cole.

Dougherty, A. M. (2000). *Psychological consultation and collaboration* (3rd ed.). Pacific Grove, CA: Brooks/Cole.

Driscoll, J. M. (1992). Keeping covenants and confidence sacred: One point of view. *Journal of Counseling and Development, 70*, 704–708.

Drukteinis, A. M. (1985). Psychiatric perspectives on civil liability for suicide. *Bulletin of American Academy of Psychiatry Law, 13*, 71–83.

Duan, C., & Roehlke, H. (2001). A descriptive "snapshot" of cross-racial supervision in university counseling center internships. *Journal of Multicultural Counseling and Development, 29*, 131–146.

Dugan, W. E. (1965). Preface. In J. W. Loughary, R. O. Stripling, & P. W. Fitzgerald (Eds.), *Counseling, a growing profession* (pp. i–iii). Alexandria, VA: American Counseling Association.

Durodoye, B. A. (2006). Ethical issues in multicultural counseling. In C. C. Lee (Ed.)., *Multicultural issues in counseling: New approaches to diversity* (3rd ed.)., pp. 357–368). Alexandria, VA: American Counseling Association.

Eisel v. Board of Education of Montgomery County, 597 A.2d 447 (Md. 1991).

Ellis v. Ellis, 472 S.W.2d 741 (Tenn. App. 1971).

Emener, W. G., & Cottone, R. R. (1989). Professionalization, deprofessionalization, and reprofessionalization of rehabilitation counseling according to criteria of professions. *Journal of Counseling and Development, 67,* 576–581.

Emerson, S., & Markos, P. A. (1996). Signs and symptoms of the impaired counselor. *Journal of Humanistic Education and Development, 34,* 108–117.

Engels, D. W., Minor, C. W., Sampson, J. P., Jr., & Splete, H. H. (1995). Career counseling specialty: History, development, and prospect. *Journal of Counseling and Development, 74,* 134–138.

Enns, C. Z. (2004). Counseling girls and women: Attitudes, knowledge, and skills. In D. R. Atkinson & G. Hackett (Eds.), *Counseling diverse populations* (pp. 285–307). Boston: McGraw-Hill.

Enzer, N. B. (1985). Ethics in child psychiatry—An overview. In D. H. Schetky & E. P. Benedek (Eds.), *Emerging issues in child psychiatry and the law* (pp. 3–21). New York: Brunner/Mazel.

Epperson, D. L., & Lewis, K. N. (1987). Issues of informed entry into counseling: Perceptions and preferences resulting from different types and amounts of pretherapy information. *Journal of Counseling Psychology, 34,* 266–275.

Erickson, S. (1993). Ethics and confidentiality in AIDS counseling: A professional dilemma. *Journal of Mental Health Counseling, 15,* 118–131.

Erickson, S. H. (2001). Multiple relationships in rural counseling. *The Family Journal, 9,* 302–304.

Espelage, D. L., Bosworth, K., & Simon, T. R. (2000). Examining the social context of bullying behaviors in early adolescence. *Journal of Counseling & Development, 78,* 326–333.

Etzioni, A. (1969). *The semi-professions and their organization.* New York: The Free Press.

Fall, K. A., Levitov, J. E., Jennings, M., & Eberts, S. (2000). The public perception of mental health professions: An empirical examination. *Journal of Mental Health Counseling, 22,* 122–134.

Family Educational Rights and Privacy Act of 1974, 20 U.S.C.A. §1232g (West, 1997).

Farber, B. A., & Heifetz, L. J. (1982). The process and dimensions of burnout in psychotherapists. *Professional Psychology, 13,* 293–301.

Fay v. South Colonie Cent. School Dist., C.A.2 (N.Y.) 1986, 802 F.2d 21.

Fazio, J. R., III (1997). Wrongful termination law in Florida. [Online] Available at http://www.cafelaw.com/wrongfultermination

Finn, S. E., & Tonsager, M. E. (1992). Therapeutic effects of providing MMPI-2 test feedback to college students awaiting therapy. *Psychological Assessment, 4,* 278–287.

Fisher, R. M. (1964). The psychotherapeutic professions and the law of privileged communications. *Wayne Law Review, 10,* 609–654.

Fong, M. L., & Silien, K. A. (1999). Assessment and diagnosis of *DSM-IV* anxiety disorders. *Journal of Counseling & Development, 77,* 209–217.

Fontes, L. A. (2002). Child discipline in immigrant Latino families: Reducing violence and misunderstandings. *Journal of Counseling & Development, 80,* 31–40.

Ford, D. Y., Harris, J. J., & Schuerger, J. M. (1993). Racial identity development among gifted black students. *Journal of Counseling and Development, 71,* 409–417.

Forester-Miller, H. (1997). Dual relationships in training group workers. In B. Herlihy & G. Corey, *Boundary issues in counseling* (pp. 87–89). Alexandria, VA: American Counseling Association.

Forester-Miller, H., & Davis, T. E. (1995). *A practitioner's guide to ethical decision making.* Alexandria, VA: American Counseling Association.

Foster, V. A., & McAdams, C. R., III (1999). The impact of client suicide in counselor training: Implications for counselor education and supervision. *Counselor Education and Supervison, 39,* 22–33

Fox, R. E. (1994). Training professional psychologists for the twenty-first century. *American Psychologist, 49,* 200–206.

Frame, M. W. (2000). Spiritual and religious issues in counseling: Ethical considerations. *The Family Journal, 8,* 72–74.

Frame, M. S., & Stevens-Smith, P. (1995). Out of harm's way: Enhancing monitoring and dismissal processes in counselor education programs. *Counselor Education & Supervision, 35,* 118–129.

Freeman, B., & McHenry, S. (1996). Clinical supervision of counselors-in-training: A nationwide survey of ideal delivery, goals, and theoretical influences. *Counselor Education & Supervision, 36,* 144–158.

Freeman, S. J. (2000). *Ethics: An introduction to philosophy and practice.* Belmont, CA: Wadsworth.

Friedman, J., & Boumil, M. M. (1995). *Betrayal of trust: Sex and power in professional relationships.* Westport, CT: Praeger.

Friedson, E. (1983). The theory of professions: State-of-the-art. In R. Dingwall & P. Lewis (Eds.), *The sociology of the professions.* New York: St. Martin's Press.

Furr, S. R., & Barret, B. (2000). Teaching group counseling skills: Problems and solutions. *Counselor Education & Supervision, 40,* 94–105.

Gabbard, G. O. (1995, April). What are boundaries in psychotherapy? *The Menninger Letter, 3*(4), 1–2.

Gale, A. U., & Austin, B. D. (2003). Professionalism's challenges to professional counselors' collective identity. *Journal of Counseling & Development, 81,* 3–10.

Garcia, J., Glosoff, H. L., & Smith, J. L. (1994). Report of the ACA Ethics Committee: 1993–1994. *Journal of Counseling and Development, 73,* 253–256.

Garcia, J., Salo, M., & Hamilton, W. M. (1995). Report of the ACA Ethics Committee: 1994–1995. *Journal of Counseling and Development, 72,* 221–224.

Garcia, J. G., Cartwright, B., Winston, S. M., & Borzuchowska, B. (2003). A transcultural integrative model for ethical decision making in counseling. *Journal of Counseling & Development, 81,* 268–277.

Gartrell, N., Herman, J., Olarte, S., Feldstein, M., & Localio, R. (1987). Reporting practices of psychologists who knew of sexual misconduct by colleagues. *American Journal of Orthopsychiatry, 57*(2), 287–295.

Gatmon, D., Jackson, D., Koshkarian, L., Martos-Perry, N., Molina, A., Patel, N., et al. (2001). Exploring ethnic, gender, and sexual orientation variables in supervision: Do they really matter? *Journal of Multicultural Counseling and Development, 29,* 102–113.

Gaubatz, M. D., & Vera, E. M. (2002). Do formalized gatekeeping procedures increase programs' follow-up with deficient trainees? *Counselor Education and Supervision, 41,* 294–305.

Gelso, C. J., & Carter, J. A. (1985). The relationship in counseling and psychotherapy: Components, consequences, and theoretical antecedents. *The Counseling Psychologist, 13,* 155–243.

General Revision of the Copyright Law, 17 U.S.C. 101 *et seq.* (1999).

Gibson, R. L., & Mitchell, M. H. (2003). *Introduction to counseling and guidance* (6th ed.). Upper Saddle River, NJ: Merrill/Prentice Hall.

Gibson, W. T., & Pope, K. S. (1993). The ethics of counseling: A national survey of certified counselors. *Journal of Counseling and Development, 71,* 330–336.

Gilbert, L. A., & Rossman, K. M. (1992). Gender and the mentoring process for women: Implications for professional development. *Professional Psychology: Research and Practice, 23,* 233–238.

Gilbert, L. A., & Scher, M. (1987). The power of an unconscious belief: Male entitlement and sexual intimacy with clients. *Professional Practice of Psychology, 8,* 94–108.

Gilbert, M. L. (2002). "Time-out" for student threats?: Imposing a duty to protect on school officials. *UCLA Law Review, 49,* 917. Retrieved October 11, 2003, from http://seg802.ocs.lsu.edu:2077/universe/document?_m=33cb640e0440b9b9625daa76fc5fd67f&_docnum=5&wchp=dGLbVzz-zSkVb&_md5=c9c 99088e02c6d70d01304ca4fe6d7e0

Gilbert, S. P. (1992). Ethical issues in the treatment of severe psychopathology in university and college counseling centers. *Journal of Counseling & Development, 71,* 330–336.

Ginter, E. J. (1999). David K. Brooks' contribution to the developmentally based lifeskills approach. *Journal of Mental Health Counseling, 21,* 191–202.

Ginter, E. J. (2001). Private practice: The professional counselor. In D. C. Locke, J. E. Myers, & E. L. Herr (Eds.), *The handbook of counseling* (pp. 355–372). Thousand Oaks, CA: Sage.

Gladding, S. T. (1995). *Group work: A counseling specialty* (3rd ed.). Upper Saddle River, NJ: Merrill/Prentice Hall.

Gladding, S. T. (1998). *Family therapy: History, theory, and practice* (2nd ed.). Upper Saddle River, NJ: Merrill/Prentice Hall.

Gladding, S. T. (2000). *Counseling: A comprehensive profession* (4th ed.). Upper Saddle River, NJ: Merrill/Prentice Hall.

Gladding, S. T., Remley, T. P., Jr., & Huber, C. H. (2001). *Ethical, legal, and professional issues in the practice of marriage and family therapy* (3rd ed.). Upple Saddle River, NJ: Merrill/Prentice Hall.

Glaser, R. D., & Thorpe, J. S. (1986). Unethical intimacy: A survey of sexual contact and advances between psychology educators and female graduate students. *American Psychologist, 41,* 43–51.

Glickhauf-Hughes, C., & Mehlman, E. (1996). Narcissistic issues in therapists: Diagnostic and treatment considerations. *Psychotherapy, 32,* 213–221.

Glosoff, H. L. (1997). Multiple relationships in private practice. In B. Herlihy & G. Corey, *Boundary issues in counseling* (pp. 114–120). Alexandria, VA: American Counseling Association.

Glosoff, H. L. (1998). Managed care: A critical ethical issue for counselors. *Counseling and Human Development, 31*(2), 1–16.

Glosoff, H. L. (2001). Ethical issues related to interprofessional communication. In E. R. Welfel & R. E. Ingersoll (Eds.), *Mental health desk reference* (pp. 419–426). New York: Wiley.

Glosoff, H. L, Corey, G., & Herlihy, B. (2006). Avoiding detrimental multiple relationships. In B. Herlihy & G. Corey, *ACA Ethical Standards Casebook* (6th ed., pp. 209–215). Alexandria, VA: American Counseling Association.

Glosoff, H. L., Garcia, J., Herlihy, B., & Remley, T. P., Jr. (1999). Managed care: Ethical considerations for counselors. *Counseling and Values, 44,* 8–16.

Glosoff, H. L., & Herlihy, B. (1995, Winter). Teaching, training, and supervision standards in the 1995 ACA Code of Ethics: What's new, what's different? *ACES Spectrum, 10*–13.

Glosoff, H. L., Herlihy, S., Herlihy, B., & Spence, B. (1997). Privileged communication in the psychologist-client relationship. *Professional Psychology: Research and Practice, 28,* 573–581.

Glosoff, H. L. Herlihy, B., & Spence, B. (2000). Privileged communication in the counselor–client relationship. *Journal of Counseling and Development, 78,* 454–462.

Glosoff, H. L., & Pate, R. H. (2002). Privacy and confidentiality in school counseling. *Professional School Counseling, 6,* 20–28.

Glosoff, H. L., Watson, Z. E., & Herlihy, B. (2002). *Cultural issues in the career paths of counselor educators.* Paper presented at Association for Counselor Education and Supervision National Conference, Park City, UT.

Golden, L. (1990, March 1). In Schafer, C. Ethics: Dual relationships come under scrutiny. *Guidepost,* pp. 1, 3, 16.

Goldenberg, H., & Goldenberg, I. (1998). *Counseling today's families* (3rd ed.). Pacific Grove, CA: Brooks/Cole.

Goldenberg, I., & Goldenberg, H. (1996). *Family therapy: An overview* (4th ed.). Pacific Grove, CA: Brooks/Cole.

Goldman, S., & Beardslee, W. R. (1999). Suicide in children and adolescents. In D. G. Jacobs (Ed.), *Guide to suicide assessment and intervention* (pp. 417–442). San Francisco: Jossey-Bass.

Goodyear, R. K. (2000). An unwarranted escalation of counselor-counseling psychologist professional conflict: Comments on

Weinrach, Lustig, Chan, and Thomas (1998). *Journal of Counseling & Development, 78,* 103–106.

Goodyear, R. K., Arcinue, F., & Getzelman, M. (2001). Counseling supervision: Essential concepts and practices. In E. R. Welfel & R. E. Ingersoll (Eds.), *Mental health desk reference* (pp. 490–496). New York: Wiley.

Gostin, L. O. (1995). Informed consent, cultural sensitivity, and respect for persons [Editorial]. *Journal of the American Medical Association, 274,* 844–845.

Gould, D. (1998a). Listen to your lawyer. In L. E. Lifson & R. I. Simon (Eds.), *The mental health practitioner and the law* (pp. 344–356). Cambridge, MA: Harvard University Press.

Gould, J. W. (1998b). *Conducting scientifically crafted child custody evaluations.* Thousand Oaks, CA: Sage.

Grabois, E. W. (1997/1998). The liability of psychotherapists for breach of confidentiality. *Journal of Law and Health, 12,* 39. Retrieved October 11, 2003, from http://seg802. ocs.lsu.edu:2077/universe/document?_m=582c9eaa0908 3fd41b92e849a2f4baf8&_docnum=9&wchp=dGLbVzz-zSkVb&_md5=db8 f2cb26af0c898d724e65ca80ee62b

Granello, P. F., & Hanna, F. J. (2003). Incarcerated and court-involved adolescents: Counseling an at-risk population. *Journal of Counseling & Development, 81,* 11–18.

Gray, L., & Harding, A. (1988). Confidentiality limits with clients who have the AIDS virus. *Journal of Counseling and Development, 65,* 219–226.

Greenburg, S. L., Lewis, G. J., & Johnson, J. (1985). Peer consultation groups for private practitioners. *Professional Psychology: Research and Practice, 16,* 437–447.

Grosch, W. N., & Olsen, D. C. (1994). *When helping starts to hurt.* New York: Norton.

Guest, C. L., Jr., & Dooley, K. (1999). Supervisor malpractice: Liability to the supervisee in clinical supervision. *Counselor Education and Supervision, 38,* 269–279.

Gumper, L. L. (1984). *Legal issues in the practice of ministry.* Minneapolis, MN: Ministers Life Resources.

Gutheil, T. G. (1989). Borderline personality disorder, boundary violations, and patient–therapist sex: Medicolegal pitfalls. *American Journal of Psychiatry, 146,* 597–602.

Gutheil, T. G. (1999). Liability issues and liability prevention in suicide. In D. G. Jacobs (Ed.), *The Harvard Medical School guide to suicide assessment and intervention* (pp. 561–578). San Francisco: Jossey-Bass.

Gutheil, T. G., & Gabbard, G. O. (1993). The concept of boundaries in clinical practice: Theoretical and risk-management dimensions. *American Journal of Psychiatry, 150,* 188–196.

Guterman, M. (1991). Working couples: Finding a balance between family and career. In J. M. Kummerow (Ed.), *New directions in career planning and the workplace* (pp. 167–193). Palo Alto, CA: Consulting Psychologists Press.

Guttmacher, M., & Weihofen, H. (1952). Privileged communications between psychiatrist and patient. *Indiana Law Journal, 28,* 32–44.

Guy, J. D. (1987). *The personal life of the psychotherapist.* New York: Wiley.

Haas, L. J., & Alexander, J. R. (1981). *Ethical and legal issues in family therapy.* Paper presented at the meeting of the American Psychological Association, Los Angeles.

Haas, L. J., & Cummings, N. A. (1991). Managed outpatient mental health plans: Clinical, ethical, and practical guidelines for participation. *Professional Psychology: Research and Practice, 22,* 45–51.

Haas, L. J., & Malouf, J. L. (1995). *Keeping up the good work: A practitioner's guide to mental health ethics* (2nd ed.). Sarasota, FL: Professional Resource Exchange.

Haddock, S. A. (2002). Training family therapists to assess for and intervene in partner abuse: A curriculum for graduate courses, professional workshops, and self-study. *Journal of Marital and Family Therapy, 28,* 193–202.

Hafen, B. Q., & Frandsen, K. J. (1986). *Youth suicide: Depression and loneliness.* Provo, UT: Behavioral Health Associates.

Hagan, M. A. (1997). *Whores of the court: The fraud of psychiatric testimony and the rape of American justice.* New York: Regan Books.

Haley, J. (1976). *Problem solving therapy.* San Francisco: Jossey-Bass.

Hamilton, R. W. (1990). *Cases and materials on corporations including partnerships and limited partnerships* (4th ed.). St. Paul, MN: West.

Handelsman, M. M. (2001). Accurate and effective informed consent. In E. R. Welfel & R. E. Engersoll (Eds.), *The mental health desk reference* (pp. 453–458). New York: Wiley.

Handler, J. F. (1990). *Law and the search for community.* Philadelphia: University of Pennsylvania Press.

Harding, A., Gray, L., & Neal, M. (1993). Confidentiality limits with clients who have HIV: A review of ethical and legal guidelines and professional policies. *Journal of Counseling and Development, 71,* 297–305.

Hare-Mustin, R. T. (1980). Family therapy may be dangerous to your health. *Professional Psychology, 11,* 935–938.

Haring-Hidore, M., & Paludi, M. A. (1989). Sexuality and sex in mentoring and tutoring: Implications for women's opportunities and achievement. *Peabody Journal of Education, 64,* 164–172.

Harley, D. A., Jolivette, K., McCormick, K., & Tice, K. (2002). Race, class, and gender: A constellation of positionalities with implications for counseling. *Journal of Multicultural Counseling and Development, 30,* 216–238.

Harrar, W. R., VandeCreek, L., & Knapp, S. (1990). Ethical and legal aspects of clinical supervision. *Professional Psychology: Research and Practice, 21,* 37–41.

Harris, A. D. (1997). *Licensing requirements* (2nd ed.). Alexandria, VA: American Counseling Association.

Haug, I. E. (1999). Boundaries and the use and misuse of power and authority: Ethical complexities for clergy psychotherapists. *Journal of Counseling & Development, 77,* 411–417.

Hayman, P., & Covert, J. (1986). Ethical dilemmas in college counseling centers. *Journal of Counseling and Development, 64,* 315–317.

Haynes, R., Corey, G., & Moulton, P. (2003). *Clinical supervision in the helping professions: A practical guide.* Pacific Grove, CA: Brooks/Cole.

Haynsworth, H. J. (1986). *Organizing a small business entity.* Philadelphia: American Law Institute-American Bar Association Committee on Continuing Professional Education.

Hazler, R. J. (2001). Bullying: Counseling perpetrators and victims. In D. C. Locke, J. E. Myers, & E. L. Herr (Eds.), *Handbook of multicultural counseling* (pp. 191–198). Thousand Oaks, CA: Sage.

Hedges, L. E. (1993, July/August). In praise of dual relationships. Part II: Essential dual relatedness in developmental psychotherapy. *The California Therapist, 42–46.*

Hedlund v. Superior Court of Orange County, 34 Cal. 3d 695, 669 P.2d 41, 194 Cal. Rptr. 805 (1983).

Heller, M. S. (1957). Some comments to lawyers on the practice of psychiatry. *Temple Law Quarterly, 30,* 401–407.

Helms, J. E., & Cook, D. A. (1999). *Using race and culture in counseling and psychotherapy: Theory and practice.* Boston: Allyn & Bacon.

Hendrick, S. S. (1988). Counselor self-disclosure. *Journal of Counseling and Development, 66,* 419–424.

Hendrix, D. H. (1991). Ethics and intrafamily confidentiality in counseling with children. *Journal of Mental Health Counseling, 13,* 323–333.

Henn, H. G. (1991). *Henn on copyright law: A practitioner's guide.* New York: Practising Law Institute.

Hensley, L. G., Smith, S. L., & Thompson, R. W. (2003). Assessing competencies of counselors in training: Complexities in evaluating personal and professional development. *Counselor Education & Supervision, 42,* 219–230.

Herlihy, B., & Corey, G. (2006). *ACA ethical standards casebook* (6th ed.). Alexandria. VA: American Counseling Association.

Herlihy, B., & Corey, G. (1997). Codes of ethics as catalysts for improving practice. In *Ethics in therapy* (pp. 37–56). New York: Hatherleigh.

Herlihy, B., Gray, N., & McCollum, V. (2002). Legal and ethical issues in school counselor supervision. *Professional School Counseling, 6,* 55–60.

Herlihy, B., & Remley, T. P. (1995). Unified ethical standards: A challenge for professionalism. *Journal of Counseling and Development, 74,* 130–133.

Herlihy, B., & Remley, T. P., Jr. (2001). Legal and ethical challenges in counseling. In D. C. Locke, J. E. Myers, & E. L. Herr (Eds.), *The handbook of counseling* (pp. 69–89). Thousand Oaks, CA: Sage.

Herlihy, B., & Sheeley, V. L. (1988). Counselor liability and the duty to warn: Selected cases, statutory trends, and implications for practice. *Counselor Education and Supervision, 27,* 203–215.

Herlihy, B., & Watson, Z. E. (2003). Ethical issues and multicultural competence in counseling. In F. D. Harper & J. McFadden (Eds.), *Culture and counseling: New approaches* (pp. 363–378). Boston: Allyn & Bacon.

Herlihy, B. R., & Watson, Z. E. (2004). Ethical issues in assisted suicide. In D. Capuzzi (Ed.), *Suicide across the life span.* Alexandria, VA: American Counseling Association.

Herlihy, B., & Watson, Z. E. (2006). Social justice and counseling ethics. In C. C. Lee (Ed.), Counseling for social justice. Alexandria, VA: American Counseling Association.

Hermann (2001). *Legal issues in counseling: Incident preparation and consultation.* Unpublished doctoral dissertation, University of New Orleans, Louisiana.

Hermann, M. A., & Finn, A. (2002). An ethical and legal perspective on the role of school counselors in preventing violence in schools. *Professional School Counseling, 6,* 46–54.

Hermann, M. A., & Herlihy, B. (In press). Legal and ethical implications of refusing to counsel homosexual clients. *Journal of Counseling and Development.*

Hermann, M. A., & Remley, T. P., Jr. (2000). Guns, violence, and schools: The results of school violence—Litigation against educators and students—Shedding more constitutional rights at the school house gate. *Loyola Law Review, 46,* 389–439.

Hermanson, G. L. (1997). Boundaries and boundary management in counselling: The never-ending story. *British Journal of Guidance and Counselling, 25*(2), 133–146.

Hermon, D. A., & Hazler, R. J. (1999). Adherence to a wellness model and perceptions of psychological well-being. *Journal of Counseling & Development, 77,* 339–343.

Hershenson, D. B., & Berger, G. P. (2001). The state of community counseling: A survey of directors of CACREP-accredited programs. *Journal of Counseling & Development, 79,* 188–193.

Hershenson, D. B., Power, P. W., & Waldo, M. (1996). *Community counseling: Contemporary theory and practice.* Boston: Allyn & Bacon.

Hill, M. (1990). On creating a theory of feminist therapy. *Women and Therapy, 91,* 53–65.

Hill, M., Glaser, K., & Harden, J. (1995). A feminist model for ethical decision making. In E. J. Rave & C. C. Larsen (Eds.), *Ethical decision making in therapy: Feminist perspectives* (pp. 18–37). New York: Guilford Press.

Hilliard, J. (1998). Termination of treatment with troublesome patients. In L. E. Lifson, & R. I. Simon (Eds.), *The mental health practitioner and the law* (pp. 216–221). Cambridge, MA: Harvard University Press.

Hines, P. L., & Fields, T. H. (2002). Pregroup screening issues for school counselors. *Journal for Specialists in Group Work, 27,* 358–376.

Hird, J. S., Cavalieri, C. E., Dulko, J. P., Felice, A. A. D., & Ho, T. A. (2001). Visions and realities: Supervisee perspectives of multicultural supervision. *Journal of Multicultural Counseling and Development, 29,* 114–130.

Hogan, D. B. (1979). *The regulation of psychotherapists.* Cambridge, MA: Ballinger Publishing.

Hohenshil. T. H. (1996). Editorial: Role of assessment and diagnosis in counseling. *Journal of Counseling & Development, 75,* 64–67.

Hohenshil, T. H. (2000). High tech counseling. *Journal of Counseling & Development, 78,* 365–368.

Holcomb-McCoy, C., & Bradley, C. (2003). Recruitment and retention of ethnic minority counselor educators: An exploratory study of CACREP-accredited counseling programs. *Counselor Education & Supervision, 42,* 231–243.

Holcomb-McCoy, C. C., & Myers, J. E. (1999). Multicultural competence and counselor training: A national survey. *Journal of Counseling & Development, 77,* 294–302.

Holroyd, J. C., & Brodsky, A. M. (1977). Psychologists' attitudes and practices regarding erotic and nonerotic physical contact with patients. *American Psychologist, 32,* 843–849.

Hopewell v. Adebimpe, 130 Pitt. L. J. 107 (1982).

Hopkins, W. E. (1997). *Ethical dimensions of diversity.* Thousand Oaks, CA: Sage.

Horowitz v. Board of Curators of the University of Missouri, 435 U.S. 78 (1978).

Hosie, T. W., & Glosoff, H. L. (2001). Counselor education. In D. C. Locke, J. E. Myers, & E. L. Herr (Eds.), *Handbook of counseling* (pp. 393–415). Thousand Oaks, CA: Sage.

Houskamp, B. (1994). Assessing and treating battered women: A clinical review of issues and approaches. *New Directions for Mental Health Services, 64,* 79–89.

Howe, G. E. (1999, April 19). Safety net critical for health care of working poor. [Online] Available at http://www. amcity.com/milwaukee/starts/1999/04/19/editoria14.html

Howell, J. A. (1988). Civil liability for suicide: An analysis of the causation issue. *Arizona State Law Journal,* 573–615.

Hoyt, M. F. (1995). *Brief therapy and managed care: Readings for contemporary practice.*

Huber, C. H. (1994). *Ethical, legal, and professional issues in the practice of marriage and family therapy* (2nd ed.). Upper Saddle River, NJ: Merrill/Prentice Hall.

Huber, C. H., & Baruth, L. G. (1987). *Ethical, legal and professional issues in the practice of marriage and family therapy.* Upper Saddle River, NJ: Merrill/Prentice Hall.

Huey, W. C. (1996). Counseling minor clients. In B. Herlihy & G. Corey (Eds.), *ACA ethical standards casebook* (5th ed., pp. 241–245). Alexandria, VA: American Counseling Association.

Hughes, E. C. (1965). Professions. In K. S. Lynn (Ed.), *The professions in America* (pp. 1–14). Boston: Houghton Mifflin.

Hussain, S. A., & Vandiver, K. T. (1984). *Suicide in children and adolescents.* New York: SP Medical and Scientific Books.

Ideal Publishing Corp. v. Creative Features, 59 A.2d 862, 399 N.Y.S.2d 118 (1977).

In re marriage of Kovash, 858 P.2d 351 (Mont. 1993).

Irish, D. P. (1993). Multiculturalism and the majority population. In D. P. Irish, K. F. Lundquist, & V. J. Nelson (Eds.), *Ethnic variations in dying, death, and grief: Diversity in universality* (pp. 1–12). Washington, DC: Taylor & Francis.

Isaacs, M. L., & Stone, C. (1999). School counselors and confidentiality: Factors affecting professional choices. *Professional School Counseling, 2,* 258–266.

Isaacs, M. L., & Stone, C. (2001). Confidentiality with minors: Mental health counselors' attitudes toward breaching or preserving confidentiality. *Journal of Mental Health Counseling, 23,* 342–356.

Ivey, A. E., & Ivey, M. B. (1998). Reframing *DSM-IV:* Positive strategies from developmental counseling and therapy. *Journal of Counseling & Development, 76,* 334–350.

Ivey, A. E., & Ivey, M. B. (1999). Toward a developmental diagnostic and statistical manual: The vitality of a contextual framework. *Journal of Counseling & Development, 77,* 484–490.

Jablonski v. United States, 712 F.2d 391 (9th Cir. 1983).

Jacobs, D. G., Brewer, M., & Klein-Benheim, M. (1999). Suicide assessment: An overview and recommended protocal. In D. G. Jacobs (Ed.), *The Harvard Medical School guide to suicide assessment and intervention* (pp. 3–39). San Francisco: Jossey-Bass.

Jacobs, E. E., Harvill, R. L., & Masson, R. L. (1994). *Group counseling: Strategies and skills* (2nd ed.). Pacific Grove, CA: Brooks/Cole.

Jacobs, E. E., Masson, R. L., & Harvill, R. L. (1998). *Group counseling: Strategies and skills* (3rd ed.). Pacific Grove, CA: Brooks/Cole.

Jaffee v. Redmond et al., 1996 WL 314841 (U.S. June 13 1996).

Jagers, J. L. (1998). Record keeping. *The Examiner, 11*(2), 6–7.

Jago, J. D. (1984). To protect the public: Professionalism vs. competence in dentistry. *Social Science and Medicine. 19,* 117–122.

James, J. (1996, May 11). University to adopt rules that put limits on dating. *Register-Guard,* Eugene, OR, pp. 1, 6A.

Jamison, S. (1998). Legalized physician-assisted suicide would improve treatment of the terminally ill. In *Assisted suicide: Current controversies* (pp. 115–121). San Francisco: Jossey-Bass.

Janson, G. R., & Steigerwald, F. J. (2002). Family counseling and ethical challenges with gay, lesbian, bisexual, and transgendered (GLBT) clients: More questions than answers. *The Family Journal, 10,* 415–418.

Jencius, M. (2003). Applications of technological advances for multicultural counseling professionals. In F. D. Harper & J. McFadden (Eds.), *Culture and counseling: New approaches* (pp. 350–362). Boston: Pearson.

Jencius, M., & Sager, D. E. (2001). The practice of marriage and family counseling in cyberspace. *The Family Journal, 9,* 295–301.

Jencius, M., & West, J. (2003). Traditional counseling theories and cross-cultural implications. In F. D. Harper & J. McFadden (Eds.), *Culture and counseling: New approaches* (pp. 339–349). Boston: Pearson.

Jilek-Aall, L. (1988). Suicidal behavior among youth: A cross-cultural comparison. *Transcultural Psychiatry Research Review, 25,* 86–105.

John R. v. Oakland Unified School District, 48 Ca.3d 438, 256 Cal.Rptr. 766, 769 P.2d 948 (1989).

Johnson, S. J. (2000). Promoting professional identity in an era of educational reform. *Professional School Counseling, 4,* 31–40.

Johnson, S. W., & Maile, L. J. (1987). *Suicide and the schools: A handbook for prevention, intervention, and rehabilitation.* Springfield, IL: Charles C Thomas.

Johnson, W. B., Ralph, J., & Johnson, S. J. (2005). Managing multiple roles in embedded environments: The case of aircraft carrier psychology. *Professional Psychology: Research and Practice, 36,* 73–81.

Johnson, W. K., & Roark, D. B. (1996). *A copyright sampler.* Chicago: American Library Association.

Jones, P. A. (1996). Interstate testimony by child protective agency workers in the child custody context. *Vermont Law Review, 21,* 633–675.

Jordan, K. (2001a). Monitoring our own: Suggested additions to the IAMFC Code of Ethics. *The Family Journal, 9,* 43–46.

Jordan, K. (2001b). Teaching ethics to graduate students: A course model. *Family Journal, 9,* 178–184.

Jordan, A. E., & Meara, N. M. (1990). Ethics and the professional practice of psychologists. *Professional Psychology: Research and Practice, 21,* 107–114.

Jordan, K., & Stevens, P. (2001). Teaching ethics to graduate students: A course model. *The Family Journal, 9,* 178–184.

Jorgenson, L. M. (1995). Sexual contact in fiduciary relationships. In J. C. Gonsiorek (Ed.), *Breach of trust: Sexual exploitation by health care professionals and clergy* (pp. 237–283). Thousand Oaks, CA: Sage.

Kain, C. (Ed.). (1989). *No longer immune: A counselor's guide to AIDS.* Alexandria, VA: American Counseling Association.

Kain, C. D. (1997). Coloring outside the lines: Multiple relationships in working with people living with HIV. In B. Herlihy & G. Corey (Eds.), *Boundary issues in counseling* (pp. 131–134). Alexandria, VA: American Counseling Association.

Kane, A. W. (1995). The effects of criminalization of sexual misconduct by therapists. In J. C. Gonsiorek (Ed.), *Breach of trust: Sexual exploitation by health care professionals and clergy* (pp. 317–332). Thousand Oaks, CA: Sage.

Kaplin, W. A., & Lee, B. A. (1995). *The law of higher education* (3rd ed.). San Francisco: Jossey-Bass.

Katherine, A. (1991). *Boundaries: Where you end and I begin.* New York: Simon & Schuster.

Katz, J. (1977). Informed consent—A fairy tale? Law's vision. *University of Pittsburgh Law Review, 39,* 137–174.

Kearney, M. (1984). Confidentiality in group psychotherapy. *Psychotherapy in Private Practice, 2*(2), 19–20.

Keith-Spiegel, P. (1994). Teaching psychologists and the new APA ethics code: Do we fit in? *Professional Psychology: Research and Practice, 25,* 362–368.

Keith-Spiegel, P., & Koocher, G. P. (1985). *Ethics in psychology: Professional standards and cases.* New York: Random House.

Keller, E. (1988). Consensual amorous relationships between faculty and students: The Constitutional right to privacy. *Journal of College and University Law, 15,* 21–42.

Kelly, K. R. (2001). Introduction to the revised AMHCA Code of Ethics. *Journal of Mental Health Counseling, 23,* 1–21.

Kemp, A. (1998). *Abuse in the family: An introduction.* Pacific Grove, CA: Brooks/Cole.

Kenyon, P. (1999). *What would you do? An ethical case workbook for human service professionals.* Pacific Grove, CA: Brooks/Cole.

Kerl, S. B., Garcia, J. L., McCullough, S., & Maxwell, M. E. (2002). Systematic evaluation of professional performance: Legally suppported procedure and process. *Counselor Education and Supervision, 41,* 321–334.

Kett, J. F. (1968). *The formation of the American medical profession: The role of institutions, 1780–1860.* New Haven, CT: Yale University Press.

King, K. A., Tribble, J. L., & Price, J. H. (1999). School counselors' perceptions of nonconsensual sexual activity among high school students. *Professional School Counseling, 2,* 286–290.

Kiselica, M. S. (1999a). Confronting my own ethnocentrism and racism: A process of pain and growth. *Journal of Counseling and Development, 77,* 14–17.

Kiselica, M. S. (Ed.). (1999b). *Confronting prejudice and racism during multicultural training.* Alexandria, VA: American Counseling Association.

Kiselica, M. S., & Ramsey, M. L. (2001). Multicultural counselor education: Historical perspectives and future dimensions. In D. C. Locke, J. E. Myers, & E. L. Herr (Eds.), *Handbook of counseling* (pp. 443–451). Thousand Oaks, CA: Sage.

Kiselica, M. S., & Robinson, M. (2001). Bringing advocacy counseling to life: The history, issues, and human dramas of social justice work in counseling. *Journal of Counseling & Development, 79,* 387–397.

Kitchener, K. S. (1984). Intuition, critical evaluation and ethical principles: The foundation for ethical decisions in counseling psychology. *Counseling Psychologist, 12,* 43–55.

Kitchener, K. S. (1988). Dual role relationships: What makes them so problematic? *Journal of Counseling and Development, 67,* 217–221.

Kitchener, K. S. (1992). Posttherapy relationships: Ever or never? In B. Herlihy & G. Corey (Eds.), *Dual relationships in counseling* (pp. 145–148). Alexandria, VA: American Association for Counseling and Development.

Kitchener, K. S., & Harding, S. S. (1990). Dual role relationships. In B. Herlihy & L. Golden (Eds.), *Ethical standards casebook* (4th ed., pp. 145–148). Alexandria, VA: American Association for Counseling and Development.

Kitzrow, M. A. (2002). Survey of CACREP-accredited programs: Training counselors to provide treatment for sexual abuse. *Counselor Education and Supervision, 42,* 107–118.

Knapp, S., & VandeCreek, L. (1987). *Privileged communications in the mental health professions.* New York: Van Nostrand Reinhold.

Knuth, M. O. (1979). Civil liability for causing or failing to prevent suicide. *Loyola of Los Angeles Law Review, 12,* 965–991.

Kolbert, J. B., Morgan, B., Brendel, B., & Johnston, M. B. (2002). Faculty and student perceptions of dual relationships within counselor education: A qualitative analysis. *Counselor Education and Supervision, 41,* 193–206.

Korman, M. (1974). National conference on levels and patterns of professional training in psychology: Major themes. *American Psychologist, 13,* 615–624.

Kottler, J. (1993). *On being a therapist.* San Francisco, CA: Jossey-Bass.

Kottler, J. A., & Schofield, M. (2001). When therapists face stress and crisis: Selfinitiated coping strategies. In E. R. Welfel &

R. E. Ingersoll (Eds.), *The mental health desk reference* (pp. 426–432). New York: Wiley.

Kramer, D. T. (1994). *Legal rights of children* (2nd ed.). New York: McGraw-Hill.

Kulic, K. R., Dagley, J. C., & Horne, A. M. (2001). Prevention groups with children and adolescents. *The Journal for Specialists in Group Work, 26,* 211–218.

Kurasaki, K. S., Sue, S., Chun, C., & Gee, K. (2000). Ethnic minority intervention and treatment research. In J. E. Aponte & J. Wohl (Eds.), *Psychological intervention and cultural diversity* (pp. 234–249). Needham Heights, MA: Allyn & Bacon.

Kutchins, H., & Kirk, S. (1987, May). *DSM-IIIR* and social work malpractice. *Social Work,* 205–211.

La. Rev. Stat. Ann. § 37:1101–1115 (West, 1999).

Ladany, N., & Friedlander, M. L. (1995). The relationship between the supervisory working alliance and trainees' experience of role conflict and role ambiguity. *Counselor Education and Supervision, 34,* 220–231.

LaFleur, N. K., Rowe, W., & Leach, M. M. (2002). Reconceptualizing White racial consciousness. *Journal of Multicultural Counseling and Development, 30,* 148–152.

LaFountain, R. M., & Baer, E. C. (2001). Increasing CACREP's name recognition: The effect of written correspondence on site supervisors' awareness level. *Journal of Counseling & Development, 79,* 194–199.

Lake, P., & Tribbensee, N. (2002). The emerging crisis of college student suicide: Law and policy responses to serious forms of self-inflicted injury. *Stetson Law Review, 32,* 125. Retrieved October 11, 2003, from http://seg802.ocs.lsu. edu:2077/ universe/document?_m=7db3c69cd06df1980a9838e79cf1b8 e0&_docnum=3&wchp=dGLbVzz-zSkVb&_md5=52e3fdd ac 81fc559f5e59a15e2dc7d63

Lakin, M. (1994). Morality in group and family therapies: Multiperson therapies and the 1992 ethics code. *Professional Psychology: Research and Practice, 25,* 344–348.

Lamadue, C. A., & Duffey, T. H. (1999). The role of graduate programs as gatekeepers: A model for evaluating student counselor competence. *Counselor Education & Supervision, 39,* 101–109.

Lambert, M. J., & Cattani-Thompson, K. (1996). Current findings regarding the effectiveness of counseling: Implications for practice. *Journal of Counseling and Development, 74,* 601–608.

Langer, E. J., & Abelson, R. P. (1974). A patient by any other name...: Clinician group differences and labeling bias. *Journal of Consulting and Clinical Psychology, 42,* 4–9.

Laux, J. M. (2002). A primer on suicidology: Implications for counselors. *Journal of Counseling & Development, 80,* 380–383.

Lawless, L. L., Ginter, E. J., & Kelly, K. R. (1999). Managed care: What mental health counselors need to know. *Journal of Mental Health Counseling, 21,* 50–65.

Lawrence, G., & Robinson Kurpius, S. E. (2000). Legal and ethical issues involved when counseling minors in nonschool settings. *Journal of Counseling & Development, 78,* 130–137.

Lawson, D. M. (2001). The development of abusive personality: A trauma response. *Journal of Counseling & Development, 79,* 505–509.

Lawson, D. M. (2003). Incidence, explanations, and treatment of partner violence. *Journal of Counseling & Development, 81,* 19–32.

Lazarus, A. A., & Zur, O. (Eds.). (2002). *Dual relationships and psychotherapy.* New York: Springer.

Leaffer, M. A. (1989). *Understanding copyright law.* New York: Matthew Bender.

Leahy, M. J., & Szymanski, E. M. (1995). Rehabilitation counseling: Evolution and current status. *Journal of Counseling and Development, 74,* 163–166.

Leatherman, C. (1993). In the debate over faculty-student dating, the talk turns to ethics, sex, even love. *Chronicle of Higher Education, 24*(37), A15–A17.

Lee, C. C. (2001). Defining and responding to racial and ethnic diversity. In D. C. Locke, J. E. Myers, & E. L. Herr (Eds.), *Handbook of multicultural counseling* (pp. 581–588). Thousand Oaks, CA: Sage.

Lee, C. C. (Ed.). (2003a). *Multicultural issues in counseling: New approaches to diversity* (3rd ed.). Alexandria, VA: American Counseling Association.

Lee, C. C. (2003b). Counseling in a changing world. *Chi Sigma Iota Exemplar, 18(3),* 1–3, 6–7.

Lee, C. C. (2006). Ethical issues in multicultural counseling. In B. Herlihy & G. Corey, *ACA Ethical standards casebook* (6th ed.; pp. 159–162). Alexandria, VA: American Counseling Association.

Lee, C. C. (Ed.) (2006). *Counseling for social justice.* Alexandria, VA: American Counseling Association.

Lee, C. C., & Kurilla, V. (1997). Ethics and multiculturalism: The challenge of diversity. In *Hatherleigh guide to ethics in therapy* (pp. 235–248). New York: Hatherleigh Press.

Leong, F. T. L., & Wagner, N. S. (1994). Cross-cultural counseling supervision: What do we want to know? *Counselor Education and Supervision, 34,* 117–131.

Lerman, H., & Porter, N. (1990). The contribution of feminism to ethics in psychotherapy. In H. Lerman & N. Porter (Eds.), *Feminist ethics in psychotherapy* (pp. 5–13). New York: Springer.

Levitov, J. E., Fall, K. A., & Jennings, M. C. (1999). Counselor clinical training with client-actors. *Counselor Education and Supervision, 1999,* 249–259.

Levy, C. S. (1972). The context of social work ethics. *Social Work, 17,* 95–101.

Lewis, H. D. (2001). Third parties beware: The Texas Supreme Court Strengthens psychotherapist–client confidentiality in *Thapar v. Zezulka. Houston Journal of Health Law and Policy, 1,* 263. Retrieved October 11, 2003, from http://seg802. ocs.lsu.edu:2077/universe/document?_m=8cf15c8c117d06a 95c48c26a17a2efac&_docnum=1&wchp=dGLbVzz-zSkVb&_md5=58f1a18d7317a44f9119a3036f6645a8

Lidz, C. W., Meisel, A., Zerubavel, M. C., Sestak, R. M., & Roth, L. H. (1984). *Informed consent: A study of decision making in psychiatry.* New York: Guilford Press.

Lipari v. Sears, Roebuck & Co., 836 F.2d 209 (1987).

Lisa M. v. Henry Mayo Newhall Memorial Hosp., 12 Cal.4th 291, 48 Cal.Rptr.2d 510, 907 P.2d 358 (1995).

Lloyd, A. P. (1992). Dual relationship problems in counselor education. In B. Herlihy & G. Corey (Eds.), *Dual relationships in counseling* (pp. 59–64). Alexandria, VA: American Association for Counseling and Development.

Logan v. District of Columbia, D.C.D.C. 1978, 447 F.Supp. 1328.

Lonner, W. J., & Ibrahim, F. A. (1996). Appraisal and assessment in cross-cultural counseling. In P. B. Pedersen, J. G. Draguns, W. J. Lonner, & J. E. Trimble (Eds.), *Counseling across cultures* (4th ed., pp. 293–322). Thousand Oaks, CA: Sage.

Louisell, D. W., & Sinclair, K. Jr. (1971). The Supreme Court of California, 1969–70–Forward: Reflections on the law of privileged communications—The psychotherapist–patient privilege in perspective. *California Law Review, 59,* 30–55.

Louisiana Licensed Mental Health Counselor Act, La. Rev. Stat. Ann. §37. (West, 1999).

Ludes, F. J., & Gilbert, H. J. (1998). Fiduciary. *Corpus Juris Secundum, 36A,* 381–389.

Lynch, G. (2002). *Pastoral care and counselling.* London: Sage.

Mabe, A. R., & Rollin, S. A. (1986). The role of a code of ethical standards in counseling. *Journal of Counseling and Development, 64,* 294–297.

Macbeth, J. E., Wheeler, A. M., Sither, J. W., & Onek, J. N. (1994). *Legal and risk management issues in the practice of psychiatry.* Washington, DC: Psychiatrists Purchasing Group.

MacCluskie, K. C. (2001). Responsible documentation. In E. R. Welfel & R. E. Ingersoll (Eds.), *The mental health desk reference* (pp. 459–465). New York: Wiley.

MacNair, R. R. (1992). Ethical dilemmas of child abuse reporting: Implications for mental health counselors. *Journal of Mental Health Counseling, 14,* 127–136.

Madden, R. G. (1998). *Legal issues in social work, counseling, and mental health.* Thousand Oaks, CA: Sage.

Magnuson, S., Norem, K., & Haberstroh, S. (2001). New assistant professors of counselor education: Their preparation and their induction. *Counselor Education and Supervision, 41,* 220–229.

Magnuson, S., Norem, K., & Wilcoxon, A. (2000). Clinical supervision of prelicensed counselors: Recommendations for consideration and practice. *Journal of Mental Health Counseling, 22,* 176–188.

Manderscheid, R., & Barrett, S. (Eds.). (1991). *Mental health in the United States, 1987* (National Institute of Mental Health, DHHS Publication No. ADM-87-1518). Washington, DC: U.S. Government Printing Office.

Maloney, D. M. (1984). *Protection of human research subjects.* New York: Plenum.

Manno v. McIntosh, 519 NW2d 815 (Iowa App. 1994).

Mappes, D. C., Robb, G. P., & Engels, D. W. (1985). Conflicts between ethics and law in counseling and psychotherapy. *Journal of Counseling and Development, 64,* 246–252.

Marczyk, G. R., & Wertheimer, E. (2001). The bitter pill of empiricism: Health maintenance organizations, informed consent and the reasonable psychotherapist standard of care. *Villanova Law Review, 46,* 33. Retrieved October 11, 2003, from http://seg802. ocs.lsu.edu:2077/universe/document?_m=195e04421e4f907ab 553bdcf3a1fa713&_docnum=7&wchp=dGLbVzz-zSkVb&_ md5=37660fdd2980a347aef6ea3e3153e475

Margolin, G. (1982). Ethical and legal considerations in marital and family therapy. *American Psychologist, 37,* 788–801.

Marotta, S. A. (2000). Best practices for counselors who treat posttraumatic stress disorder. *Journal of Counseling & Development, 78,* 492–493.

Maslow, A. (1968). *Toward a psychology of being* (Rev. ed.). New York: Van Nostrand Reinhold.

Massachusetts Board of Retirement v. Murgia, 427 U.S. 307 (1976).

Matarazzo, J. D. (1986). Computerized clinical psychological test interpretations: Unvalidated plus all mean and no sigma. *American Psychologist, 41,* 14–24.

Mathews, L. L., & Gerrity, D. A. (2002). Therapists' use of boundaries in sexual abuse groups: An exploratory study. *Journal for Specialists in Group Work, 27,* 78–91.

Mattie T. v. Johnson, D.C. Miss. 74 F.R.D. 498 (1976).

Mayfield, A. C. (1996). *Receptivity of counselors to insurance fraud in mental health.* Unpublished doctoral dissertation, University of New Orleans, Louisiana.

McAdams, C. R., III, & Foster, V. A. (2000). Client suicides: Its frequency and impact on counselors. *Journal of Mental Health Counseling, 22,* 107–121.

McAuliffe, G. J., & Eriksen, K. P. (1999). Toward a constructivist and developmental identity for the counseling profession: The context-phase-stage-style model. *Journal of Counseling & Development, 77,* 267–280.

McCarthy, C. J., & Mejía, O. L. (2001). Using groups to promote preventive coping: A case example with college students from migrant farm-working families. *The Journal for Specialists in Group Work, 26,* 267–275.

McCarthy, P., Sugden, S., Koker, M., Lamendola, F., Maurer, S., & Renninger, S. (1995). A practical guide to informed consent in clinical supervision. *Counselor Education and Supervision, 35,* 130–138.

McClarren, G. M. (1987). The psychiatric duty to warn: Walking a tightrope of uncertainty. *University of Cincinnati Law Review, 56,* 269–293.

McConnell, W. A., & Kerbs, J. J. (1993). Providing feedback in research with human subjects. *Professional Psychology: Research and Practice, 24,* 266–270.

McDonald v. Hogness, 598 P.2d 707 (Wash. 1979).

McFarland, W. P., & Dupuis, M. (2001). The legal duty to protect gay and lesbian students from violence in school. *Professional School Counseling, 4,* 171–179.

McGuire, J. M., Toal, P., & Blau, B. (1985). The adult client's conception of confidentiality in the therapeutic relationship. *Professional Psychology: Research and Practice, 16,* 375–384.

McIntosh, P. (1998). White privilege, color, and crime: A personal account. In C. R. Mann & M. S. Zatz (Eds.), *Images of color, images of crime* (pp. 207–216). Los Angeles: Roxbury.

McRoy, R. G., Freeman, E. M., Logan, S. L., & Blackmon, B. (1986). Cross cultural field supervision: Implications for social work education. *Journal of Social Work Education, 22,* 50–56.

Meara, N. M., Schmidt, L. D., & Day, J. D. (1996). Principles and virtues: A foundation for ethical decisions, policies, and character. *Counseling Psychologist, 24,* 4–77.

Megargee, E. (1979). *Classifying criminal offenders: A new system based on the MMPI.* Beverly Hills, CA: Sage.

Meloy, J. R. (1987). Unrequited love and the wish to kill: Diagnosis and treatment of borderline erotomania. *Bulletin of the Menniger Clinic, 53,* 477–492.

Melton, G. B. (1991). Ethical judgments amid uncertainty: Dilemmas in the AIDS epidemic. *Counseling Psychology, 19,* 561–565.

Meneese, W. B., & Yutrzenka, B. A. (1990). Correlates of suicidal ideation among rural adolescents. *Suicide and Life-Threatening Behavior, 20,* 206–212.

Merluzzi, T. V., & Brischetto, C. S. (1983). Breach of confidentiality and perceived trustworthiness of counselors. *Journal of Counseling Psychology, 30,* 245–251.

Merta, R. J., Wolfgang, L., & McNeil, K. (1993). Five models for using the experiential group in the preparation of group counselors. *Journal for Specialists in Group Work, 18,* 143–150.

Messina, J. J. (1999). What's next for the profession of mental health counseling? *Journal of Mental Health Counseling, 21,* 285–294.

Mihaly, P. H. (1991). Health care utilization review: Potential exposures to negligence liability. *Ohio State Law Journal, 52*(4), 1289–1308.

Miller, D. J., & Hersen, M. (1992). *Research fraud in the behavioral and biomedical sciences.* New York: Wiley.

Miller, D. J., & Thelan, M. H. (1986). Knowledge and beliefs about confidentiality in psychotherapy. *Professional Psychology: Research and Practice, 17,* 15–19.

Miller, G. M., & Larrabee, M. J. (1995). Sexual intimacy in counselor education and supervision: A national survey. *Counselor Education and Supervision, 34,* 332–343.

Miller, G. M., & Wooten, H. R., Jr. (1995). Sports counseling: A new counseling specialty area. *Journal of Counseling and Development, 74,* 172–173.

Miller, I. J. (1996). Managed care is harmful to outpatient mental health services. A call for accountability. *Professional Psychology: Research and Practice, 22,* 349–363.

Millner, V. S., & Hanks, R. B. (2002). Induced abortion: An ethical conundrum for counselors. *Journal of Counseling & Development, 80,* 57–63.

Millner, V. S., & Kiser, J. D. (2002). Sexual information and Internet resources. *The Family Journal, 10,* 234–239.

Milsome, A. S. (2002). Students with disabilities: School counselor involvement and preparation. *Professional School Counseling, 5,* 331–338.

Mitchell, C. W., Disque, J. G., & Robertson, P. (2002). When parents want to know: Responding to parental demands for confidential information. *Professional School Counseling, 6,* 156–161.

Mitchell, C. W., & Rogers, R. E. (2003). Rape, statutory rape, and child abuse: Legal distinctions and cousnelor duties. *Professional School Counseling, 6,* 332–338.

Mitchell, R. W. (1991). *Documentation of counseling records.* Alexandria, VA: American Counseling Association.

Mnookin, R. H., & Weisberg, D. K. (1995). *Child, family and state: Problems and materials on children and the law.* Boston: Little, Brown and Company.

Monahan, J. (1995). Violence prediction: The past twenty and the next twenty years. *Criminal Justice and Behavior, 23,* 107–134.

Moore, E. M. (1997). *The relationship between clinical graduate students' experiences with their educators and their views on therapist-client dual role relationships.* Unpublished dissertation, University of Windsor.

Morgan, E. (1943). Suggested remedy for obstructions to expert testimony by rules of evidence. *University of Chicago Law Review, 10,* 285–298.

Morris, W. O. (1984). *Revocation of professional licenses by governmental agencies.* Charlottesville, VA: Michie.

Muehleman, T., Pickens, B. K., & Robinson, F. (1985). Informing clients about the limits to confidentiality, risks, and their rights: Is self-disclosure inhibited? *Professional Psychology: Research and Practice, 16,* 385–397.

Mulvey, E., & Lidz, C. (1995). Conditional prediction: A model for research on dangerousness to others in a new era. *International Journal of Law and Psychiatry, 18,* 129–143.

Muratori, M. C. (2001). Examining supervisor impairment from the counselor trainee's perspective. *Counselor Education and Supervision, 41,* 41–56.

Murray, K. A. (2002). Religion and divorce: Implications and strategies for counseling. *The Family Journal, 10,* 190–194.

Murphy, E. J., Speidel, R. E., & Ayres, I. (1997). *Contract law* (5th ed.). Westbury, NY: The Foundation Press.

Myer, R. A. (2001). *Assessment for crisis intervention: A triage assessment model.* Belmont, CA: Brooks/Cole.

Myers, J. E. (1995a). From "forgotten and ignored" to standards and certification: Gerontological counseling comes of age. *Journal of Counseling and Development, 74,* 143–149.

Myers, J. E. (1995b). Specialties in counseling: Rich heritage or force for fragmentation? *Journal of Counseling and Development, 74,* 115–116.

Myers, J. E., Mobley, A. K., & Booth, C. S. (2003). Wellness of counseling students: Practicing what we preach. *Counselor Education and Supervision, 42,* 264–274.

Myers, J. E., & Sweeney, T. J. (2001). Specialties in counseling. In D. C. Locke, J. E. Myers, & E. L. Herr (Eds.), *The handbook of counseling* (pp. 43–54). Thousand Oaks, CA: Sage.

Myers, J. E., Sweeney, T. J., & Witmer, J. M. (2000). The wheel of wellness counseling for wellness: A holistic model for treatment planning. *Journal of Counseling & Development, 78,* 251–266.

Nagle v. Hooks, 295 Md. 133, 460 A.2d 49 (1983).

Nagpal, S., & Ritchie, M. H. (2002). Selection interviews of students for master's programs in counseling: An exploratory study. *Counselor Education and Supervision, 41,* 207–218.

Napoli, D. S. (1981). *Architects of adjustment: The history of the psychological profession in the United States.* Port Washington, NY: Kennikat Press.

National Association for Social Workers. (1997). *Social work speaks: NASW policy statements* (4th ed., pp. 156–163). Washington, DC: Author.

National Board for Certified Counselors. (2003b). *Eligibility checklist for prospective NCC applicants.* Retrieved August 31, 2003, from http://www.nbcc.org/cert/checklist.htm

National Board for Certified Counselors. (2005). *Statistics.* Retrieved November 3, 2005, from http://www.nbcc.org/stats

National Center on Elder Abuse. (2000). *A response to the abuse of vulnerable adults: The 2000 survey of state adult protective services.* Retrieved on September 20, 2003, from http://www.elderabusecenter.org/pdf/research/apsreport030703.pdf

National Center on Elder Abuse at the American Public Human Services Association. (1998). *The national elder abuse incidence study: Final report.* [Online]. Retrieved July 6, 2003, from http://www.aoa.dhhs.gov/abuse/report/default.htm

National Fair Access Coalition on Testing, The. (2003). *Model testing practices.* Retrieved on September 25, 2003, from http://www.fairaccess.org/code_of_ethics.htm

National Research Act of 1974 Regulations, 45 Code of Federal Regulations 46.

National Research Act of 1974, 42 U.S.C. 218 *et seq.* (Public Law 93-348).

Navin, S., Beamish, P., & Johanson, G. (1995). Ethical practices of field-based mental health counselor supervisors. *Journal of Mental Health Counseling, 17,* 243–253.

Nelson, M. L., & Holloway, E. L. (1990). Relation of gender to power and involvement in supervision. *Journal of Counseling Psychology, 37,* 473–481.

Neufeld, P. J. (2002). School violence—Family responsibility. *The Family Journal, 10,* 207–209.

Neukrug, E. S., Healy, M., & Herlihy, B. (1992). Ethical practices of licensed professional counselors: An updated survey of state licensing boards. *Counselor Education and Supervision, 32,* 130–141.

Neukrug, E., Milliken, T., & Walden, S. (2001). Ethical complaints made against credentialed counselors: An updated survey of state licensing boards. *Counselor Education and Supervision, 41,* 57–70.

Neville, H. A., Heppner, M. J., Louie, C. E., Thompson, C. E., Brooks, L., & Baker, C. E. (1996). The impact of multicultural training on White racial identity attitudes and therapy competencies. *Professional Psychology: Research and Practice, 27,* 83–89.

New York State Task Force on Life and the Law. (1994). *When death is sought: Assisted suicide and euthanasia in the medical context.* Albany, NY: Author.

Newman, J. L. (1993). Ethical issues in consultation. *Journal of Counseling and Development, 72,* 148–156.

Nixon, J. A. (1993). Gender considerations in the case of "The Jealous Husband": Strategic therapy in review. *The Family Journal, 1,* 161–163.

Nock, M. K., & Marzuk, P. M. (1999). Murder-Suicide. In D. G. Jacobs (Ed.), *Guide to suicide assessment and intervention* (pp. 188–209). San Francisco: Jossey-Bass.

Nugent, F. (1981). *Professional counseling: An overview.* Pacific Grove, CA: Brooks/Cole.

O'Laughlin, M. J. (2001). Dr. Strangelove: Therapist–client dual relationship bans and freedom of association, or how I learned to stop worrying and love my clients. *University of Missouri at Kansas City Law Review, 69,* 697. Retrieved October 11, 2003, from http://seg802.ocs.lsu.edu:2077/universe/document?_m=8c474616004d5113b0ca5247039cf77a&_do-cnum=9&wchp=dGLbVzz-zSkVb&_md5=70db125a27fda92d37199def2c5f1532

Orton, G. L. (1997). *Strategies for counseling with children and their parents.* Pacific Grove, CA: Brooks/Cole.

Ottavi, T. M., Pope-Davis, D. B., & Dings, J. G. (1994). Relationship between White racial identity attitudes and self-reported multicultural counseling competencies. *Journal of Counseling Psychology, 41,* 149–154.

Owen, D. W., Jr., & Weikel, W. J. (1999). Computer utilization by school counselors. *Professional School Counseling, 2,* 179–182.

Owens, P. C., & Kulic, K. R. (2001). What's needed now: Using groups for prevention. *The Journal for Specialists in Group Work, 26,* 205–210.

Packman, W. L., & Harris, E. A. (1998). Legal issues and risk management in suicidal patients. In B. Bongar, A. I. Berman, R. W. Maris, M. M. Silverman, E. A. Harris, & W. L. Packman (Eds.), *Risk management with suicidal patients* (pp. 150–186). New York: Guilford Press.

Page, R. C., & Bailey, J. B. (1995). Addictions counseling certification: An emerging counseling specialty. *Journal of Counseling and Development, 74,* 167–171.

Page v. Rotterdam-Mohanasen Central School Dist., 441 N.Y.S.2d 323, 109 Misc.2d 1049 (1981).

Paisley, P. O. (1997). Personalizing our history: Profiles of theorists, researchers, practitioners, and issues. *Journal of Counseling & Development, 76,* 4–5.

Paisley, P. O., & Borders, L. D. (1995). School counseling: An evolving specialty. *Journal of Counseling and Development, 74,* 150–153.

Palmo, A. J. (1999). The MHC child reaches maturity: Does the child seem short for its age? *Journal of Mental Health Counseling, 21,* 215–228.

Parham, T. A. (1997). An African-centered view of dual relationships. In B. Herlihy & G. Corey (Eds.), *Boundary issues in counseling* (pp. 109–111). Alexandria, VA: American Counseling Association.

Patry, W. F. (1986). *Latman's the copyright law* (6th ed.). Washington, DC: The Bureau of National Affairs.

Paulson, B. L., & Worth, M. (2002). Counseling for suicide: Client perspectives. *Journal of Counseling & Development, 80,* 86–93.

Pavkov, T. W., Lewis, D. A., & Lyons, J. S. (1989). Psychiatric diagnois and racial bias: An empirical investigation. *Professional Psychology: Research and Practice, 20,* 364–368.

Peck v. Counseling Service of Addison County, Inc., 146 Vt. 61, 499 A.2d 422 (1985).

Pedersen, P. B. (1991). Multiculturalism as a generic approach to counseling. *Journal of Counseling and Development, 70,* 6–12.

Pedersen, P. B. (1994). *A handbook for developing multicultural awareness* (2nd ed.). Alexandria, VA: American Counseling Association.

Pedersen, P. B., Draguns, J. G., Lonner, W. J., & Trimble, J. E. (2002). *Counseling across cultures* (5th ed.). Thousand Oaks, CA: Sage.

Pedersen, P. B., & Ivey, A. (1987). The ethical crisis for cross-cultural counseling and therapy. *Professional Psychology, 13,* 492–500.

People v. Cohen, 98 Misc.2d 874, 414 N.Y.S.2d 642 (1979).

People v. Lobaito, 133 Mich. App. 547, 351 N.W.2d 233 (App. 1984).

People v. Taylor, 618 P.2d 1127 (Colo. 1980).

Perr, I. N. (1985). Suicide litigation and risk management: A review of 32 cases. *The Bulletin of the American Academy of Psychiatry and the Law, 13,* 209–219.

Perritt, H. H., Jr. (1998). *Employee dismissal law and practice* (Vol. 1, 4th ed.). New York: Wiley.

Perry, S. (1989). Warning third parties at risk of AIDS: American Psychiatric Association's policy is a barrier to treatment. *Hospital and Community Psychiatry, 40*(2), 158–161.

Petersen v. State, 100 Wash. 2d 421, 671 P.2d 230 (1983) (en banc).

Peterson, C. (1996). Common problem areas and their causes resulting in disciplinary action. In L. J. Bass, S. T. De-Mers, J. R. Ogloff, C. Peterson, J. L. Pettifor, R. P. Reaves, et al. (Eds.), *Professional conduct and discipline in psychology* (pp. 71–89). Washington, DC: American Psychological Association.

Petrashek v. Petrashek, 232 Neb. 212, 440 N.W.2d 220 (1989).

Phillips, B. N. (1982). Regulation and control in psychology. *American Psychologist, 37,* 919–926.

Phillips-Green, M. J. (2002). Sibling incest. *The Family Journal, 10,* 195–202.

Piazza, N. J., & Baruth, N. E. (1990). Client record guidelines. *Journal of Counseling and Development, 68,* 313–316.

Pierce, K. A., & Baldwin, C. (1990). Participation versus privacy in the training of group counselors. *Journal for Specialists in Group Work, 15,* 149–158.

Pilkington, N. W., & D'Augelli, A. R. (1995). Victimization of lesbian, gay, and bisexual youth in community settings. *Journal of Community Psychology, 23,* 34–56.

Pillemer, K., & Finklehor, D. (1988). Causes of elder abuse: Caregiver stress versus problem relatives. *American Journal of Orthopsychiatry, 59,* 179–187.

Pine, A. M., & Aronson, E. (1988). *Career burnout: Causes and cures.* New York: The Free Press.

Pistole, M. C. (1999). Caregiving in attachment relationships: A perspectrive for counselors. *Journal of Counseling & Development, 77,* 437–446.

Ponterotto, J. G. (1997). Multicultural counseling training: A competency model and national survey. In D. B. Pope-Davis & H. L. K. Coleman (Eds.), *Multicultural counseling competencies: Assessment, education, training, and supervision* (pp. 111–130). Thousand Oaks, CA: Sage.

Pope, K. S. (1986). Research and laws regarding therapist-patient sexual involvement: Implications for therapists. *American Journal of Psychotherapy, 40,* 564–571.

Pope, K. S. (1988). How clients are harmed by sexual contact with mental health professionals: The syndrome and its prevalence. *Journal of Counseling and Development, 67,* 222–226.

Pope, K. S. (1994). *Sexual involvement with therapists: Patient assessment, subsequent therapy, forensics.* Washington, DC: American Psychological Association.

Pope, K. S., & Bouhoutsos, J. C. (1986). *Sexual intimacy between therapists and patients.* New York: Praeger Press.

Pope, K. S., Butcher, J. N., & Sheelen, J. (1993). The MMPI, MMPI-2, and MMPI-A in court: A practical guide for expert witnesses and attorneys. Washington, DC: American Psychological Association.

Pope, K. S., Keith-Spiegel, P., & Tabachnick, B. G. (1986). Sexual attraction to clients: The human therapist and the (sometimes) inhuman training system. *American Psychologist, 41,* 147–158.

Pope, K. S., Levinson, H., & Schover, L. R. (1979). Sexual intimacy in psychology training: Results and implications of a national survey. *American Psychologist, 34,* 682–689.

Pope, K. S., Sonne, J. L., & Holroyd, J. (1993). *Sexual feelings in psychotherapy: Explorations for therapists and therapists-in-training.* Washington, DC: American Psychological Association.

Pope, K. S., Tabachnick, B. G., & Keith-Spiegel, P. (1987a). Ethics of practice: The beliefs and behaviors of psychologists as therapists. *American Psychologist, 42,* 993–1006.

Pope, K. S., Tabachnick, B. G., & Keith-Spiegel, P. (1987b). Good and poor practices in psychotherapy: National survey of beliefs of psychologists. *Professional Psychology: Research and Practice, 19,* 547–552.

Pope, K. S., & Vasquez, M. J. T. (1998). *Ethics in psychotherapy and counseling: A practical guide for psychologists* (2nd ed.). San Francisco: Jossey-Bass.

Pope, K. S., & Vetter, V. A. (1991). Prior counselor-patient sexual involvement among patients seen by psychologists. *Psychocounseling, 28,* 429–438.

Pope, K. S., & Vetter, V. A. (1992). Ethical dilemmas encountered by members of the American Psychological Association: A national survey. *American Psychologist, 47,* 397–411.

Prochaska, J., & Norcross, J. (1983). Psychotherapists' perspectives on treating themselves and their clients for psychic distress. *Professional Psychology: Research and Practice, 14,* 642–655.

Prosser, W. (1971). *The law of torts,* St. Paul, MN: West.

Prosser, W. L., Wade, J. W., & Schwartz, V. E. (1988). *Cases and materials on torts* (8th ed.). Westbury, NY: The Foundation Press.

Purrington, W. (1906). An abused privilege. *Columbia Law Review, 6,* 388–422.

Quinn, M. J., & Tomita, S. K. (1997). *Elder abuse and neglect: Causes, diagnosis, and intervention strategies* (2nd ed.). New York: Springer.

Randall, V. R. (1994a). Impact of managed care organizations on ethnic Americans and underserved populations. *Journal of Health Care for the Poor and Underserved, 5*(3), 224.

Randall, V. R. (1994b). Utilization review and financial risk-shifting: Compensating patients for cost containment injuries. *University of Puget Sound Law Review, 17*(1), 1–100.

Rave, E. J., & Larsen, C. C. (1995). *Ethical decision making in therapy: Feminist perspectives.* New York: Guilford Press.

Regents of the University of Michigan v. Ewing, 474 U.S. 214 (1985).

Remley, T. P., Jr. (1991). *Preparing for court appearances.* Alexandria, VA: American Counseling Association.

Remley, T. P., Jr. (1993). Consultation contracts. *Journal of Counseling and Development, 72,* 157–158.

Remley, T. P., Jr. (1995). A proposed alternative to the licensing of specialties in counseling. *Journal of Counseling and Development, 74,* 126–129.

Remley, T. P., Jr., Benshoff, J. M., & Mowbray, C. A. (1987). A proposed model for peer supervision. *Counselor Education and Supervision, 27,* 53–60.

Remley, T. P., Jr., & Fry, L. J. (1993). Reporting suspected child abuse: Conflicting roles for the counselor. *The School Counselor, 40,* 253–259.

Remley, T. P., Jr., Herlihy, B., & Herlihy, S. (1997). The U.S. Supreme Court decision in *Jaffee v. Redmond:* Implications for counselors. *Journal of Counseling and Development, 75,* 213–218.

Remley, T. P., Jr., Hermann, M. A., & Huey, W. C. (Eds.). (2003). *Ethical and legal issues in school counseling* (2nd ed.). Alexandria, VA: American School Counselor Association.

Remley, T. P., Jr., & Huey, W. C. (2002). An ethics quiz for school counselors. *Professional School Counseling, 6,* 3–11.

Remley, T. P., Jr., Hulse-Killacky, D., Ashton, L., Keene, K., Kippers, S., Lazzari, S., et al. (1998, October). *Advanced students supervising other students.* Paper presented at Louisiana Counseling Association conference, Lafayette, LA; and Southern Association for Counselor Education and Supervision conference, Montgomery, AL.

Renshaw, D. C. (2001). Bullies. *The Family Journal, 9,* 341–342.

Reppucci, N. D., Weithorn, L. A., Mulvey, E. P., & Monahan, J. (1984). *Children, mental health, and the law.* Beverly Hills, CA: Sage.

Rice, P. R. (1993). *Attorney-client privilege in the United States.* Rochester, NY: Lawyers Cooperative Publishing.

Ridley, C. R. (1989). *Overcoming unintentional racism in counseling and therapy.* Thousand Oaks, CA: Sage.

Ridley, C. R. (1995). *Overcoming unintentional racism in counseling and therapy: A practitioner's guide to intentional interventions.* Thousand Oaks, CA: Sage.

Ridley, C. R., Espelage, D. L., & Rubinstein, K. J. (1997). Course development in multicultural counseling. In D. B. Pope-Davis & H. L. K. Coleman (Eds.), *Multicultural counseling competencies: Assessment, education, training, and supervision* (pp. 131–158). Thousand Oaks, CA: Sage.

Ridley, C. R., Liddle, M. C., Hill, C. L., & Li, L. C. (2001). Ethical decision making in multicultural counseling. In J. G. Ponterotto, J. M. Casas, L. A. Suzuki, & C. M. Alexander (Eds.), *Handbook of multicultural counseling* (pp. 165–188). Newbury Park, CA: Sage.

Ridley, C. R., & Lingle, D. W. (1996). Cultural empathy in multicultural counseling: A multidimensional process model. In P. B. Pedersen, J. C. Draguns, W. J. Lonner, & J. E. Trimble (Eds.), *Counseling across cultures* (4th ed., pp. 21–46). Thousand Oaks, CA: Sage.

Riemer-Reiss, M. L. (2000). Utilizing distance technology for mental health counseling. *Journal of Mental Health Counseling, 22,* 189–203.

Rigaxio-Digilio, S. A., Anderson, S. A., & Kunkler, K. P. (1995). Gender-aware supervision in marriage and family counseling and therapy: How far have we actually come? *Journal of Counseling Psychology, 34,* 344–355.

Rios v. Read, D.C.N.Y. 73 F.R.D. 589 (1977).

Ritchie, M. H., & Huss, S. N. (2000). Recruitment and screening of minors for group counseling. *Journal for Specialists in Group Work, 25,* 146–156.

Roberts v. Superior Court, 9 Cal.3d 330, 107 Cal. Rptr. 309, 508 P.2d 309 (1973).

Roberts, W. B., & Morotti, A. A. (2000). The bully as victim: Understanding bully behaviors to increase the effectiveness of interventions in the bully-victim dyad. *Professional School Counseling, 4,* 148–155.

Roberts-Henry, M. (1995). Criminalization of therapist sexual misconduct in Colorado. In J. C. Gonsiorek (Ed.), *Breach of trust: Sexual exploitation by health care professionals and clergy* (pp. 388–347). Thousand Oaks, CA: Sage.

Robertson, D. W., Powers, W., Jr., & Anderson, D. A. (1989). *Cases and materials on torts.* St. Paul, MN: West.

Robinson, T. L., & Watt, S. K. (2001). "Where no one goes begging": Converging gender, sexuality, and religious diversity in counseling. In D. C. Locke, J. E. Myers, & E. L. Herr (Eds.), *Handbook of multicultural counseling* (pp. 589–599). Thousand Oaks, CA: Sage.

Roeske, N. C. A. (1986). Risk factors: Predictable hazards of a health care career. In C. D. Scott & J. Hawk (Eds.), *Heal thyself: The health of health care professionals* (pp. 56–70). New York: Brunner/Mazel.

Rogers, C. R. (1961). *On becoming a person.* Boston: Houghton Mifflin.

Rogers, J. R. (2001). Suicide risk assessment. In E. R. Welfel & R. E. Ingersoll (Eds.), *The mental health desk reference* (pp. 259–264). New York: Wiley.

Rogers, J. R., Gueulette, C. M., Abbey-Hines, J., Carney, J. V., & Werth, J. L., Jr. (2001). Rational suicide: An empirical investigation of counselor attitudes. *Journal of Counseling & Development, 79,* 365–372.

Rogers, J. R., Lewis, M. M., & Subich, L. M. (2002). Validity of the Suicide Assessment Checklist in an emergency crisis center. *Journal of Counseling & Development, 80,* 493–502.

Rosenbach, W. E. (1993). Mentoring: Empowering followers to become leaders. In W. E. Rosenbach & R. L. Taylor (Eds.), *Contemporary issues in leadership* (3rd ed., pp. 141–151). Boulder, CO: Westview Press.

Rosenhan, D. L. (1973). On being sane in insane places. *Science, 179,* 250–258.

Rosenstock v. Board of Governors of the University of North Carolina, 423 F.Supp. 1321, 1326–27 (M.D.N.C. 1976).

Rosenthal, R. (1994). Science and ethics in conducting, analyzing, and reporting psychological research. *Psychological Science, 5,* 127–133.

Rottenberg, S. (Ed.). (1980). *Occupational licensure and regulation.* Washington, DC: American Enterprise Institute for Public Policy Research.

Rowe, W., Behrens, J. T., & Leach, M. M. (1995). White racial identity attitude development: A psychometric examination of two instruments. *Journal of Counseling Psychology, 46,* 70–79.

Rowe, W., Bennett, S. K., & Atkinson, D. R. (1994). White racial identity models: A critique and alternative proposal. *The Counseling Psychologist, 22,* 129–146.

Rowley, W. J., & MacDonald, D. (2001). Counseling and the law: A cross-cultural perspective. *Journal of Counseling and Development, 79,* 423–429.

Roysircar, G., Sandhu, D. S., & Bibbins, V. E. Sr., (Eds.). (2003). *AMCD multicultural competencies: A guidebook of practices.* Alexandria, VA: American Counseling Association.

Salgo v. Leland Stanford Jr. Univ. Bd. of Trustees, 317 P.2d 170 (Cal. Ct. App. 1957).

Salisbury, W. A., & Kinnier, R. T. (1996). Posttermination friendship between counselors and clients. *Journal of Counseling and Development, 74,* 495–500.

Salo, M. (2006). Counseling minor clients. In B. Herlihy & G. Corey, *ACA Ethical standards casebook* (6th ed., pp. 201–203).

Salzman, M., & D'Andrea, M. (2001). Assessing the impact of a prejudice prevention project. *Journal of Counseling & Development, 79,* 341–346.

Sampson, J. P., Jr. (1996). A computer-aided violation of confidentiality. In B. Herlihy & G. Corey (Eds.), *ACA ethical standards casebook* (5th ed., pp. 213–215). Alexandria, VA: American Counseling Association.

Sampson, J. P., Jr. (2000). Using the Internet to enhance testing in counseling. *Journal of Counseling & Development, 78,* 348–356.

Sampson, J. P., Jr., & Bloom, J. W. (2001). The potential for success and failure of computer applications in counseling and guidance. In D. C. Locke, J. E. Myers, & E. L. Herr (Eds.), *The handbook of counseling* (pp. 613–627). Thousand Oaks, CA: Sage.

Sampson, J. P., Jr., Kolodinsky, R. W., & Greeno, B. P. (1997). Counseling on the information highway: Future possibilities and potential problems. *Journal of Counseling and Development, 75,* 203–212.

Sandhu, D. S. (2000). Special issue: School violence and counselors. *Professional School Counseling, 4,* iv–v.

Sapia, J. L. (2001). Using groups for the prevention of eating disorders among college women. *The Journal for Specialists in Group Work, 26,* 256–266.

Schaffer, S. J. (1997). Don't be aloof about record-keeping; it may be your best liability coverage. *The National Psychologist, 6*(1), 21.

Schank, J. A., & Skovholt, T. M. (1997). Dual-relationship dilemmas of rural and small-community psychologists. *Professional Psychology: Research and Practice, 28,* 44–49.

Schmid, D., Applebaum, P., Roth, L. H., & Lidz, C. (1983). Confidentiality in psychiatry. A study of the patient's view. *Hospital and Community, Psychiatry, 34,* 353–356.

Schmidt, J. J., & Osborne, W. L. (1981). Counseling and consulting: Separate processes or the same? *Personnel and Guidance Journal, 59,* 168–171.

Schoener, G., & Gonsiorek, J. (1988). Assessment and development of rehabilitation plans for counselors who have sexually exploited their clients. *Journal of Counseling and Development, 67,* 227–232.

Schoener, G. R. (1989). Self-help and consumer groups. In G. R. Schoener, J. H. Milgrom, J. C. Gonsiorek, E. T. Luepker, & R. M. Conroe (Eds.). *Psychotherapists' sexual involvement with clients: Intervention and prevention* (pp. 375–399). Minneapolis, MN: Walk-In Counseling Center.

Schutz, B. M. (1990). *Legal liability in psychotherapy.* San Francisco: Jossey-Bass.

Schwab, R., & Neukrug, E. (1994). A survey of counselor educators' ethical concerns. *Counseling and Values, 39,* 42–45.

Schwartz, R. C. (2000). Suicidality in schizophrenia: Implications for the counseling profession. *Journal of Counseling & Development, 78,* 496–499.

Schwartz, R. C., & Cohen, B. N. (2001). Risk factors for suicidality among clients with schizophrenia. *Journal of Counseling & Development, 79,* 314–319.

Schwiebert, V. L., Myers, J. E., & Dice, C. (2000). Ethical guidelines for counselors working with older adults. *Journal of Counseling & Development, 78,* 123–129.

Sciarra, D. T. (1999). *Multiculturalism in counseling.* Itasca, IL: F. E. Peacock.

Scott, W. R. (1969). Professional employees in a bureaucratic structure: Social work. In A. Etzioni (Ed.), *The semi-professions and their organization* (pp. 102–156). New York: The Free Press.

Section 504 of the Rehabilitation Act of 1973 (29 U.S.C. §794).

Sekaran, U. (1986). *Dual career families.* San Francisco: Jossey-Bass.

Seligman, L. (1986). *Diagnosis and treatment planning in counseling.* New York: Human Sciences Press.

Seligman, L. (1999). Twenty years of diagnosis and the DSM. *Journal of Mental Health Counseling, 21,* 229–239.

Sexton, T. L. (2001). Evidence-based counseling intervention programs: Practicing "best practices." In D. C. Locke, J. E. Myers, & E. L. Herr (Eds.), *The handbook of counseling* (pp. 499–512). Thousand Oaks, CA: Sage.

Sheeley, V. L. (2002). American Counseling Association: The 50th year celebration of excellence. *Journal of Counseling & Development, 80,* 387–393.

Shepard, D. S. (2002). Using screenwriting techniques to create realistic and ethical role plays. *Counselor Education and Supervision, 42,* 145–158.

Shuman, D. W., & Weiner, M. F. (1987). *The psychotherapist-patient privilege: A critical examination.* Springfield, IL: Charles C Thomas.

Sieber, J. E. (1992). *Planning ethically responsible research—Methods series.* Newbury Park, CA: Sage.

Simon, R. I. (1987). *Clinical psychiatry and the law.* Washington, DC: American Psychiatric Press.

Simon, R. I. (1989). Sexual exploitation of patients: How it begins before it happens. *Psychiatric Annals, 19,* 104–112.

Simon, R. I. (1991). Psychological injury caused by boundary violations: Precursors to therapist–patient sex. *Psychiatry Annals, 19,* 104–112.

Simon, R. I. (1992). Treatment boundary violations: Clinical, ethical, and legal considerations. *Bulletin of the American Academy of Psychiatry and the Law, 20,* 269–288.

Simon, R. I. (1998). Boundary violations in psychotherapy. In L. E. Lifson & R. I. Simon (Eds.), *The mental health practitioner and the law* (pp. 195–215). Cambridge, MA: Harvard University Press.

Sims v. State, 251 Ga. 877, 311 S.E.2d 161 (1984).

Singley, S. J. (1998). Failure to report suspected child abuse: Civil liability of mandated reporters. *Journal of Juvenile Law, 19,* 236. Retrieved October 11, 2003, from http://seg802.ocs.lsu.edu:2077/universe/document?_m=886 8c24f3aca250391ddeb-692e4f286a&_docnum=12&wc hp=dGLbVzz-zSkVb&_md5=875a5ad9f921317af340d2 25e56a7b93

Slaby, A. E. (1999). Outpatient management of suicidal patients. In B. Bongar, A. L. Berman, R. W. Maris, M. M. Silverman, E. A. Harris, & W. L. Packman (Eds.), *Risk management with suicidal patients* (pp. 34–64). New York: Guilford Press.

Slater v. Baker & Stapleton, 95 Eng. Rep. 860 (K.B. 1767).

Sleek, P. (1996, April). Ensuring accuracy in clinical decisions. *APA Monitor, 26,* 30.

Slimp, P. A., & Burian, B. K. (1994). Multiple role relationships during internship: Consequences and recommendations. *Professional Psychology: Research and Practice, 25,* 39–45.

Slovenko, R. (1960). Psychiatry and a second look at the medical privilege. *Wayne Law Review, 6,* 174–203.

Slovenko, R. (1966). *Psychotherapy, confidentiality, and privileged communication.* Springfield, IL: Charles C Thomas.

Slovenko, R., & Usdin, G. (1961). The psychiatrist and privileged communication. *Archives of General Psychiatry, 4,* 431–444.

Slovic, P., & Monahan, J. (1995). Probability, danger, and coercion: A study of risk perception and decision making in mental health law. *Law and Human Behavior, 19,* 49–73.

Smart, D. W., & Smart, J. F. (1997). *DSM-IV* and culturally sensitive diagnosis: Some observations for counselors. *Journal of Counseling & Development, 75,* 392–398.

Smith, D., & Fitzpatrick, M. (1995). Patient-therapist boundary issues: An integrative review of theory and research. *Professional Psychology: Research and Practice, 26,* 499–506.

Smith, H. B. (2001). Counseling: Professional identity for counselors. In D. C. Locke, J. E. Myers, & E. L. Herr (Eds.), *The handbook of counseling* (pp. 569–579). Thousand Oaks, CA: Sage.

Smith, H. B., & Robinson, G. P. (1995). Mental health counseling: Past, present, and future. *Journal of Counseling and Development, 75,* 158–162.

Smith, J. A., & Smith, A. H. (2001). Dual relationships and professional integrity: An ethical dilemma case of a family counselor as clergy. *The Family Journal, 9,* 438–443.

Smith, J. M., & Mallen, R. E. (1989). *Preventing legal malpractice.* St. Paul, MN: West.

Smith, R. L., Carlson, J., Stevens-Smith, P., & Dennison, M. (1995). Marriage and family counseling. *Journal of Counseling and Development, 74,* 154–157.

Snider, P. D. (1985). The duty to warn: A potential issue of litigation for the counseling supervisor. *Counselor Education and Supervision, 25,* 66–73.

Snider, P. D. (1987). Client records: Inexpensive liability protection for mental health counselors. *Journal of Mental Health Counseling, 9,* 134–141.

Sommers-Flanagan, R., Sommers-Flanagan, J., & Lynch, K L. (2001). Counseling interventions with suicidal clients. In E. R. Welfel & R. E. Ingersoll (Eds.), *The mental health desk reference* (pp. 264–270). New York: Wiley.

Sonne, J. L. (1994). Multiple relationships: Does the new ethics code answer the right questions? *Professional Psychology: Research and Practice, 25,* 336–443.

Squyres, E. (1986). An alternative view of the spouse of the therapist. *Journal of Contemporary Psychology, 16,* 97–106.

St. Germaine, J. (1993). Dual relationships: What's wrong with them? *American Counselor, 2,* 25–30.

Stadler, H., Willing, K., Eberhage, M., & Ward, W. (1988). Impairment: Implications for the counseling profession. *Journal of Counseling and Development, 66,* 258–260.

Stadler, H. A. (1986). Making hard choices: Clarifying controversial ethical issues. *Counseling and Human Development, 19,* 1–10.

Stadler, H. A. (1990a). Confidentiality. In B. Herlihy & L. Golden (Eds.), *Ethical standards casebook* (4th ed., pp. 102–110). Alexandria, VA: American Association for Counseling and Development.

Stadler, H. A. (1990b). Counselor impairment. In B. Herlihy & L. Golden (Eds.), *Ethical standards casebook* (4th ed., pp. 177–187). Alexandria, VA: American Association for Counseling and Development.

Stadler, H. A. (2001). Impairment in the mental health professions. In E. R. Welfel & R. E. Ingersoll (Eds.), *The mental health desk reference* (pp. 413–418). New York: Wiley.

Stanard, R. P. (2000). Assessment and treatment of adolescent depression and suicidality. *Journal of Mental Health Counseling, 22,* 204–217.

State of Louisiana through the Louisiana State Board of Examiners of Psychologists of the Department of Health and Human Services v. Atterberry. 664 So.2d 1216, La. App. 1 Cir., 1995.

State v. Andring, 342 N.W.2d 128 (Minn. 1984).

State v. Brown, 376 N.W.2d 451, review denied (Minn. App. 1985).

State v. Hungerford, 84 Wisc.2d 236, 267 N.W.2d 258 (1978).

State v. Kupchun, 117 N.H. 417, 373 A.2d 1325 (1977).

State v. Magnuson, 682 P.2d 1365, 210 Mont. 401 (Mont. 1984).

Stokes, L. S., & Remley, T. P., Jr. (2001). Counselors as expert witnesses. In E. R. Welfel & R. E. Ingersoll (Eds.), *The mental health desk reference* (pp. 404–410). New York: Wiley.

Stone, C. (2002). Negligence in academic advising and abortion counseling: Courts rulings and implications. *Professional School Counseling, 6,* 28–35.

Stone, C. B. (2000). Advocacy for sexual harassment victims: Legal support and ethical aspects. *Professional School Counseling, 4,* 23–30.

Stone, C. B., & Hanson, C. (2002). Selection of school counselor candidates: Future directions at two universities. *Counselor Education and Supervision, 41,* 175–192.

Stone, L. A. (1985). National Board for Certified Counselors: History, relationships, and projections. *Journal of Counseling and Development, 63,* 605–606.

Storm, C. L., Todd, T. C., Sprenkle, D. H., & Morgan, M. M. (2001). Gaps between MFT supervision assumptions and common practice: Suggested best practices. *Journal of Marital and Family Therapy, 27,* 227–239.

Strasburger, L. H. (1998). Suggestions for expert witnesses. In L. E. Lifson & R. I. Simon (Eds.), *The mental health practitioner and the law* (pp. 281–298). Cambridge, MA: Harvard University Press.

Straus, M. A. (1999). The controversy over domestic violence by women: A methodological, theoretical, and sociology of science analysis. In X. B. Arriaga & S. Oskamp (Eds.), *Violence in intimate relationships* (pp. 17–44). Thousand Oaks, CA: Sage.

Straus, M. A., & Gelles, R. J. (1992). *Physical violence in American families.* New Brunswick, NJ: Transaction.

Sudak, H., Ford, A., & Rushforth, N. (1984). Adolescent suicide: An overview. *American Journal of Psychotherapy, 38,* 350–369.

Sue, D. W. (1996). Ethical issues in multicultural counseling. In B. Herlihy & G. Corey (Eds.), *ACA ethical standards casebook* (5th ed., pp. 193–197). Alexandria, VA: American Counseling Association.

Sue, D. W. (1997). Multicultural perspectives on multiple relationships. In B. Herlihy & G. Corey (Eds.), *Boundary issues in counseling* (pp. 106–109). Alexandria, VA: American Counseling Association.

Sue, D. W., & Sue, D. (1999). *Counseling the culturally different: Theory and practice* (3rd ed.). New York: Wiley.

Sue, D. W., & Zane, N. (1987). The role of culture and cultural techniques in psychotherapy: A critique and reformulation. *American Psychologist, 42,* 37–45.

Sue, S., Fujino, D., Takeuchi, D., Hu, L-T., & Zane, N. (1991). Community mental health services for ethnic minority groups: A test of the cultural responsiveness hypothesis. *Journal of Consulting and Clinical Psychology, 59,* 533–540.

Sullivan, T., Martin, W. L., & Handelsman, M. M. (1993). Practical benefits of an informed consent procedure: An empirical investigation. *Professional Psychology: Research and Practice, 24,* 160–163.

Sullivan v. O'Connor, 363 Mass. 579 (1973).

Sumerel, M. B., & Borders, L. D. (1996). Addressing personal issues in supervision: Impact of counselors' experience level on various aspects of the supervisory relationship. *Counselor Education and Supervision, 35,* 268–285.

Summers, N. (2001). *Fundamentals of case management practice: Exercises and readings.* Belmont, CA: Brooks/Cole.

Suzuki, L. A., Meller, P. J., & Ponterotto, J. G. (1996). *Handbook of multicultural assessment.* San Francisco: Jossey-Bass.

Sweeney, T. (1995). Accreditation, credentialing, professionalization: The role of specialties. *Journal of Counseling and Development, 74,* 117–125.

Sweeney, T. J. (2001). Counseling: Historical origins and philosophical roots. In D. C. Locke, J. E. Myers, & E. L. Herr (Eds.), *The handbook of counseling* (pp. 3–26). Thousand Oaks, CA: Sage.

Swenson, L. C. (1997). *Psychology and the law for the helping professions* (2nd ed.). Pacific Grove, CA: Brooks/Cole.

Syme, G. (2003). *Dual relationships in counseling and psychotherapy.* London: Sage.

Szymanski, E. M., & Parker, R. M. (2001). Epistemological and methodological issues in counseling. In D. C. Locke, J. E. Myers, & E. L. Herr (Eds.), *Handbook of counseling* (pp. 455–466). Thousand Oaks, CA: Sage.

Tarasoff v. Regents of University of California, 529 P.2d 553, 118 Cal. Rptr. 129 (1974), vacated, 17 Cal. 3d 425, 551 P.2d 334, 131 Cal. Rptr. 14 (1976).

Tarka v. Franklin, C.A.5 (Tex.) 891 F.2d 102, certiori denied 110 S.Ct. 1809, 494 U.S. 1080, 108 (1989).

Tarvydas, V. M. (1998). Ethical decision-making processes. In R. R. Cottone & V. M. Tarvydas (Eds.), *Ethical and professional issues in counseling* (pp. 144–154). Upper Saddle River, NJ: Prentice Hall.

Tatara, T. (1996). *Elder abuse: Questions and answers.* Washington, DC: National Center on Elder Abuse.

Taube, D. O., & Elwork, A. (1990). Researching the effects of confidentiality law on patients' self-disclosures. *Professional Psychology: Research and Practice, 21,* 72–75.

Taylor, K. (1995). *The ethics of caring.* Santa Cruz, CA: Hanford Mead.

Tayyari v. New Mexico State University, 495 F.Supp. 1365 (D.N.M. 1980).

Thapar v. Zezulka, 994 S.W.2d 635 (Tex. 1999).

Thomas, E. (July 7, 2003). The war over gay marriages. *Newsweek.* Retrieved September 9, 2003, from http://stacks. msnbc.com/news/932621.asp?cp1=1

Thompson, T. L. (1999). Managed care: Views, practices, and burnout of psychologists. *Dissertation Abstracts International, 60* (1318B) 449. (UMI No. 91-14).

Thoreson, R., Nathan, P., Skorina, J., & Kilberg, R. (1983). The alcoholic psychologist: Issues, problems, and implications for the profession. *Professional Psychology: Research and Practice, 14,* 670–684.

Thoreson, R. W., Morrow, K. A., Frazier, P. A., & Kerstner, P. L. (1990, March). *Needs and concerns of women in AACD: Preliminary results.* Paper presented at the annual convention of the American Association for Counseling and Development, Cincinnati, OH.

Thoreson, R. W., Shaughnessy, P., & Frazier, P. A. (1995). Sexual contact during and after professional relationships: Practices and attitudes of female counselors. *Journal of Counseling and Development, 74,* 84–88.

Thoreson, R. W., Shaughnessy, P., Heppner, P. P., & Cook, S. W. (1993). Sexual contact during and after the professional relationship: Attitudes and practices of male counselors. *Journal of Counseling and Development, 71,* 429–434.

Title I of the Americans with Disabilities Act of 1990, 42 U.S.C. §1211 *et seq.*

Title VI of the Civil Rights Act of 1964, 42 U.S.C. §2000e *et seq.*

Title VII of the Civil Rights Act of 1964, 42 U.S.C. §2000f *et seq.*

Title IX of the Education Amendments of 1972, 20 U.S.C. §12101 *et seq.*

Tomm, K. (1993, January/February). The ethics of dual relationships. *The California Therapist,* 7–19.

Toren, N. (1969). Semi-professionalism and social work: A theoretical perspective. In A. Etzioni (Eds.), *The semi-professions and their organization* (pp. 12–63). New York: The Free Press.

Tracey, T. J. (1991). Counseling research as an applied science. In C. E. Watkins, Jr., & L. J. Schneider (Eds.), *Research in counseling* (pp. 3–31). Hillsdale, NJ: Lawrence Erlbaum Associates.

Truax v. Raich, 239 U.S. 33, 36 S.Ct. 7, 60 L.Ed. 131 (1915).

Trudeau, L. S., Russell, D. W., de la Mora, A., & Schmitz, M. F. (2001). Comparisons of marriage and family therapists, psychologists, psychiatrists, and social workers on job-related measures and reactions to managed care in Iowa. *Journal of Marital and Family Therapy, 27,* 501–507.

Truscott, D., & Evans, J. (2001). Responding to dangerous clients. In E. R. Welfel & R. E. Ingersoll (Eds.), *The mental health desk reference* (pp. 271–276). New York: Wiley.

Truscott, D., Evans, J., & Mansell, S. (1995). Outpatient psychotherapy with dangerous clients: A model for clinical decision making. *Professional Psychology: Research and Practice, 26,* 484–490.

Tyler, J. M., & Tyler, C. (1994). Ethics in supervision: Managing supervisee rights and supervisor responsibilities. *Directions in Mental Health Counseling, 4*(11), 4–25.

Tylitzki v. Triple X Service, Inc., 126 Ill. App.2d 144, 261 N.E.2d 533 (1970).

U.S. CONST. amend. XIV.

United States Department of Commerce. (2002). Falling through the net. Retrieved June 24, 2003, from http://www.ntia.doc. gov/ntiahome/fttn00/contents00.htm

United States Department of Health and Human Services. (2003). Summary of the HIPAA privacy rule. Retrived September 16, 2003, from http://www.hhs.gov/ocr/privacysummary.pdf

Usher, C. H., & Borders, L. D. (1993). Practicing counselors' preferences for supervisory style and supervisory emphasis. *Counselor Education and Supervision, 33,* 66–79.

Vacc, N. A., Juhnke, G. A., & Nilsen, K. A. (2001). Community mental health service providers' codes of ethics and the *Standards for Educational and Psychological Testing. Journal of Counseling & Development, 79,* 217–224.

Van Hoose, W. H., & Kottler, J. (1985). *Ethical and legal issues in counseling and psychotherapy* (2nd ed.). San Francisco, CA: Jossey-Bass.

Van Hoose, W. H., & Paradise, L. V. (1979). *Ethics in counseling and psychotherapy: Perspectives in issues and decision-making.* Cranston, RI: Carroll.

Van Zandt, C. E. (1990). Professionalism: A matter of personal initiative. *Journal of Counseling and Development, 68,* 243–245.

VandeCreek, L., Miars, R. D., & Herzog, C. E. (1987). Client anticipations and preferences for confidentiality of records. *Journal of Counseling Psychology, 34,* 62–67.

VanderKolk, C. (1974). The relationship of personality, values, and race to anticipation of the supervisory relationship. *Rehabilitation Counseling Bulletin, 18,* 41–46.

Vasquez, L. A. (1996). A systemic multicultural curriculum model: The pedagogical process. In D. B. Pope-Davis & H. L. K. Coleman (Eds.), *Multicultural counseling competencies: Assessment, education, training, and supervision* (pp. 159–179). Thousand Oaks, CA: Sage.

Vasquez, M. J. T. (1988). Counselor-client sexual contact: Implications for ethics training. *Journal of Counseling and Development, 67,* 238–241.

Vasquez, M. J. T. (1991). Sexual intimacies with clients after termination: Should a prohibition be explicit? *Ethics and Behavior, 1,* 45–61.

Vasquez, M. J. T. (1996). Will virtue ethics improve ethical conduct in multicultural settings and interactions? *Counseling Psychologist, 24,* 98–104.

Vidmar, N. (1995). *Medical malpractice and the American jury: Confronting the myths about jury incompetence, deep pockets, and outrageous damage awards.* Ann Arbor, MI: University of Michigan Press.

Vinson, T., & Neimeyer, G. J. (2000). The relationship between racial identity development and multicultural counseling competency. *Journal of Multicultural Counseling and Development, 28,* 177–192.

Vinson, T., & Neimeyer, G. J. (2003). The relationship between racial identity development and multicultural counseling competency: A second look. *Journal of Multicultural Counseling and Development, 31,* 262–263.

Virginia court ruling stirs concern about confidentiality protections in group therapy (1979). *Hospital and Community Psychiatry, 30,* 428.

Vontress, C. E. (2002). Introduction: Multicultural awareness as a generic competence for counseling. In B. P. Petersen, J. G. Draguns, W. J. Lonner, & J. E. Trimble (Eds.)., *Counseling across cultures* (5th ed., pp. xiii–xix). Thousand Oaks, CA: Sage.

Walden, S. L. (2006). Inclusion of the client perspective in ethical practice. In B. Herlihy & G. Corey (Eds.), *Boundary issues in counseling* (2nd ed., pp. 40–47). Alexandria, VA: American Counseling Association.

Walden, S. L., Herlihy, B., & Ashton, L. (2003). The evolution of ethics: Personal perspectives of ACA Ethics Committee chairs. *Journal of Counseling & Development, 81,* 106–110.

Walsh, W. B., & Betz, N. E. (1995). *Tests and assessment* (3rd ed.). Upper Saddle River, NJ: Prentice Hall.

Warnke, M. A. (2001). In E. R. Welfel & R. E. Ingersoll (Eds.), *The mental health desk reference* (pp. 379–383). New York: Wiley.

Watson, Z. E., Herlihy, B. R., & Pierce, L. A. (2006). Forging the link between multicultural competence and ethical practice: A historical perspective. *Counseling & Values, 50,* 99–108.

Webb v. Quincy City Lines, Inc., 73 Ill. App.2d 405, 219 N.E.2d 165 (1966).

Wehrly, B. (1991). Preparing multicultural counselors. *Counseling and Human Development, 24*(3), 1–24.

Weil, R. I. (1983). Are professional corporations dead? *The North Carolina State Bar Quarterly, 30*(1), 8–9.

Weinapple, M., & Perr, I. (1979). The rights of minors to confidentiality: An aftermath of *Bartley v. Kremens. Bulletin of the American Academy of Psychiatry and the Law, 9,* 247–254.

Weinrach, S. G. (1989). Guidelines for clients of private practitioners: Committing the structure to print. *Journal of Counseling and Development, 67,* 299–300.

Weinrach, S. G., Lustig, D., Chan, F., & Thomas, K. R. (1998). Publication patterns of *The Personnel and Guidance Journal/Journal of Counseling & Development*: 1978–1993. *Journal of Counseling & Development, 76,* 427–435.

Weinrach, S. G., & Thomas, K. R. (1996). The counseling profession's commitment to diversity-sensitive counseling: A critical reassessment. *Journal of Counseling and Development, 74,* 472–477.

Weinrach, S. G., Thomas, K. R., & Chan, F. (2001). The professional identity of contributors to the *Journal of Counseling & Development*: Does it matter? *Journal of Counseling & Development, 79,* 166–170.

Welfel, E. R. (2001). Responsible interactions with managed care organizations. In E. R. Welfel & R. E. Ingersoll (Eds.), *The mental health desk reference* (pp. 496–502). New York: Wiley.

Welfel, E. R. (2006). *Ethics in counseling and psychotherapy: Standards, research, and emerging issues* (3rd ed.). Pacific Grove, CA: Brooks/Cole.

Welfel, E. R., Danzinger, P. R., & Santoro, S. (2000). Mandated reporting of abuse/maltreatment of older adults: A primer for counselors. *Journal of Counseling & Development, 78,* 284–293.

Welfel, E. R., & Heinlen, K. T. (2001). The responsible use of technology in mental health practice. In E. R. Welfel & R. E. Ingersoll (Eds.), *The mental health desk reference* (pp. 484–490). New York: Wiley.

Wendorf, D. J., & Wendorf, R. J. (1992). A systemic view of family therapy ethics. In R. L. Smith & P. Stevens-Smith (Eds.), *Family counseling and therapy* (pp. 304–320). Ann Arbor, MI: ERIC/CAPS.

Werth, J. L., & Gordon, J. R. (2002). Amicus curiae brief for the United States Supreme Court on mental health issues associated with "physician-assisted suicide." *Journal of Counseling & Development, 80,* 160–163.

Wheeler, S. (2000). What makes a good counselor? An analysis of ways in which counselor trainers construe good and bad counseling trainees. *Counseling Psychology Quarterly, 13,* 65–83.

Whitley, B. E. (1997). Gender differences in computer-related attitudes and behavior: A meta-analysis. *Computers in Human Behavior, 13*(1), 1–22.

Whittinghill, D. (2002). Ethical considerations for the use of family therapy in substance abuse treatment. *The Family Journal, 10,* 75–78.

Wichansky v. Wichansky, 126 N.J. Super. 156, 313 A.2d 222 (1973).

Wickline v. California, 192 Cal.App.3d 1630 (1986); 239 Cal. Rptr. 810 (Ct. App. 1986).

Wiger, D. E. (1999a). *The clinical documentation sourcebook* (2nd ed.). New York: Wiley.

Wiger, D. E. (1999b). *The psychotherapy documentation primer.* New York: Wiley.

Wigmore, J. H. (1961). *Evidence in trials at common law* (Vol. 8, McNaughton Rev.). Boston: Little, Brown.

Wilcoxin, A., & Fennel, D. (1983). Engaging non-attending spouse in marital therapy through the use of therapist-initiated written communication. *Journal of Marital and Family Therapy, 9,* 199–203.

Wilcoxon, S. A., & Magnuson, S. (1999). Considerations for school counselors serving noncustodial parents: Premises and suggestions. *Professional School Counseling, 2,* 275–279.

Wilkinson, W. K., & McNeil, K. (1996). *Research for the helping professions.* Pacific Grove, CA: Brooks/Cole.

Williams, C. B. (2001). Ethics complaints: Procedures for filing and responding. In E. R. Welfel & R. E. Ingersoll (Eds.), *The mental health desk reference* (pp. 441–447). New York: Wiley.

Williams, S., & Halgin, R. P. (1995). Issues in psychotherapy supervision between the white supervisor and the black supervisee. *The Clinical Supervisor, 13,* 39–61.

Wilson, F. R., Jencius, M., & Duncan, D. (1997). Introduction to the Internet: Opportunities and dilemmas. *Counseling and Human Development, 29*(6), 1–16.

Wilson, F. R., & Owens, P. C. (2001). Group-based prevention programs for at-risk adolescents and adults. *The Journal for Specialists in Group Work, 26,* 246–255.

Wilson v. Blue Cross, 271 Cal.Rptr. 876 (Ct. App. 1990).

Wineburgh, M. (1998). Ethics, managed care and outpatient psychotherapy. *Clinical Social Work Journal, 26,* 433–443.

Winston, M. E. (1991). AIDS, confidentiality, and the right to know. In T. A. Mappes & J. S. Zembaty (Eds.), *Biomedical ethics* (3rd ed., pp. 173–180). New York: McGraw-Hill.

Witmer, J. M., & Young, M. E. (1996). Preventing counselor impairment: A wellness approach. *Journal of Humanistic Education and Development, 34,* 141–155.

Wohlberg, J. W. (1999). Treatment subsequent to abuse by a mental health professional: The victim's perspective of what works and what doesn't. *Journal of Sex Education & Counseling, 24,* 252–261.

Woody, R. H. (1988a). *Fifty ways to avoid malpractice.* Sarasota, FL: Professional Resource Exchange.

Woody, R. H. (1988b). *Protecting your mental health practice: How to minimize legal and financial risk.* San Francisco: Jossey-Bass.

Wrenn, G. (1962). *The counselor in a changing world.* Washington, DC: American Personnel and Guidance Association.

Wyatt, T., & Daniels, M. H. (2000). Noncompetition agreements and the counseling profession: An unrecognized reality for private practitioners. *Journal of Counseling & Development, 78,* 14–20.

Wylie, M. S. (1995, May/June). The power of DSM-IV: Diagnosing for dollars. *Networker,* 22–32.

Yalom, I. D. (1995). *The theory and practice of group psychotherapy* (4th ed.). New York: Basic Books.

Yamamoto, J., & Chang, C. (1987, August). *Empathy for the family and individual in the racial context.* Paper presented at the Interactive Forum on Transference and Empathy in Psychotherapy with Asian Americans. Boston, MA.

Yaron v. Yaron, 83 Misc.2d 276, 372 N.Y.S.2d 518 (Sup. 1975).

Yeh, C. J. (2001). An exploratory study of school counselors' experiences with and perceptions of Asian-American students. *Professional School Counseling, 4,* 349–356.

Ziskin, J. (1995). *Coping with psychiatric and psychological testimony* (Vols. I–III, 5th ed.). Los Angeles, CA: Law and Psychology Press.

Author Index

Subject Index